REAL EGG COFFEE

and Other Favorite Recipes

from

Family and Friends

Good Luck and Best Wishes!

Ruth Petersen Harbour

Ruth Petersen Harbour

Happy 50th Anniversary, Carol and Mike!

REAL EGG COFFEE was the fragrant beverage and symbol of hospitality served whenever groups of early Midwestern settlers came together on occasions of work, celebration or remembrance. *(Recipe on p. 374)*

ISBN: 1-58597-221-5

Library of Congress Control Number: 2003113395

LEATHERS
PUBLISHING

A division of Squire Publishers, Inc.
4500 College Blvd.
Leawood, KS 66211
1/888/888-7696
www.leatherspublishing.com

To my grandmothers, Christena Olesen Paulsen
and Martha Jansen Petersen —
two early settlers who epitomized
the character, devotion and commitment
that forged the Heartland spirit —
I dedicate this book.
You will always be remembered and loved.

Acknowledgments

This collection of recipes features Midwestern cooking — nutritious, affordable, and appetizing. It extends over the years 1882 to 2002, and includes recipes from my grandparents and from my grandchildren, who enjoy both cooking and sampling. To them and to the countless other family members, neighbors, teachers, and friends who have shared recipes after dinner or morning coffee, at potlucks, picnics, and all the other occasions where we mingled and lingered to socialize — thank you!

Thank you to the mentors who encouraged my early interest in preparing foods: Grandma Paulsen, who had endless patience when a little girl stood on a kitchen chair to help make peppernuts; Eva Larsen, home economics teacher who taught the importance of accuracy with measuring spoons, cups, and timer, and who by example encouraged her class to keep a neat kitchen with a place for everything; the 4-H leaders who made baking bread such fun; my dad, who appreciated every successful baking and tactfully overlooked the others; and my mother, who gave me encouragement to try new methods and recipes and to continue our heritage of Danish and German cookery.

For their encouragement and persistent nudging me to compile our family's and friends' favorite recipes, I thank my four daughters — Anne, Janet, Laurel and Lea Harbour. To Jason, Christina, and Alexis, who are carrying on the family tradition of enjoying the cooking and sampling — thanks, and *bon appétit* from Grandma Ruth!

For her editorial and design assistance, I thank my daughter, Anne Harbour. Her experience in publishing and her interest in the Midwest, its history and culture, made her an ideal partner in this project. We have been a good team.

Table of Contents

Preface ix

Introduction xv

Bread, Rolls, Quick Breads 1
  ♣ *Vignette: Visit to the Village*
  ♣ *Bread-Making Suggestions*

Cookies 47
  ♣ *Vignette: Preparing the School*

Cakes, Frostings and Candies 81
  ♣ *Vignette: Barn Dance*

Desserts and Pies 131
  ♣ *Vignette: Old Settlers Reunion*

Main Dishes 181
  ♣ *Vignette: Threshing*

Vegetables 251
  ♣ *Vignette: Gardens and County Fair*

Salads 289
  ♣ *Vignette: Moving Day*

Soups and Sandwiches 339
  ♣ *Vignette: Country School Program and Box Social*

Beverages and Appetizers 369
  ♣ *Vignette: Church Potluck Dinner*

Index 393

Preface

This book is dedicated to the early settlers who came to the heartland, following their dreams to make it their hearts' home. My grandmothers were two of those settlers.

Martha Jansen left her native Schleswig-Holstein in northern Germany in 1882. With her mother, Mary, and brother, Andrew, she sailed in steerage. They traveled by train to Jones County, Iowa, and farmed. There she met and married Barnhard (Ben) Petersen. They moved to western Iowa, where they settled to farm and rear their family of two daughters and five sons. They were real partners in field, dairy, and livestock. All their children followed this tradition and were expert farmers and stockmen. The family shared their parents' strong work ethic, religious faith and belief in America.

Martha Jansen Petersen was a woman of strong character, a devoted daughter who nursed her aged mother, and a loving mother who guided her children's education and religious training. She and her husband worked together to overcome the challenges of a harsh climate, crop failures, war, and depression. Their faith and loyalty helped them survive, strong examples for their descendants.

Christena Olesen met her future husband when both were students in the Danish Folk School near their homes. Jens Paulsen served in the Danish army before immigrating to America in 1891. Christena completed her studies in home management and was employed in that field until 1894, when she sailed to join her fiancé. She traveled in steerage with her heavy trunk full of linens and provisions for their future home as well as carefully stowed packages of food for the voyage. She passed through immigration at Ellis Island in November 1894. Her name is listed there as "Jensena K. Olesen" on the wall memorializing immigrants.

Christena married Jens in January 1895. The same day they rode in a farm wagon to their first home south of Ida Grove, Iowa. In 1905 they moved their family and worldly goods fourteen miles west to their 240-acre homestead, Elm Front Farm. There they reared two sons and five daughters.

The Paulsens were hard-working, thrifty and community oriented. Their education and experience in Denmark had prepared them for leadership roles. They planted hundreds of trees. He built the farmstead to be efficient and the house to be as modern as possible. She raised poultry and made dairy products that were sold in the town nearest the farm. Both worked side by side chopping out sunflowers and cockleburs, plant pests that overran the clay hills of their farm. They carried water to the windbreaks and new orchards during droughts and replanted when the seedlings shriveled in scorching winds. During harvest, both piled the bundles of grain into shocks; in fall, they worked as a team shocking corn or unloading wagons. Both encouraged their children to get a good education. All five daughters completed high school or teacher's training, and three became teachers. The sons entered fields related to farming.

Throughout her life, Grandma Paulsen was kind and patient, ministering to the sick and unfortunate, sharing food and warm clothing. She was an expert homemaker, seamstress, and cook. Her baking was a bond that she shared with grandchildren; she loved to teach the secrets of baking bread, shaping cookies, and making Danish pastries. She understood how food warms the heart, long before the expression "comfort food" came into being. She was truly a modern woman of spirit and an island of security.

The vignettes are based on my recollections of times my family refer to fondly as "the olden days." These word pictures of life in rural Iowa include memories shared with me by my grandparents about their arrival in America in the 1880s and 1890s; my parents' recollections, 1900-1940s; and my own experiences, 1920 to the present. Invariably, the recollections include the meals that brought people together. Some meals were associated with the work of grain harvesting, corn picking or other cooperative tasks. Others were celebrations. Whatever the occasion, the feeling of community was enhanced. Food shared drew settlers together and built bonds that made the Midwest their new homeland.

Wherever folks gathered to share food, the fragrance that welcomed them was unforgettable — "Real Egg Coffee"! Steaming hot coffee was the beverage of the Midwestern settlers. On farms and ranches, the coffee pot was always ready for the workers' rest breaks. It welcomed the infrequent passing visitor who brought news, and it drew the family together at mealtimes. A generous cup of coffee was the symbol of Midwestern hospitality in the "olden days," and sharing generously with others is a Midwest tradition today.

My German-American grandparents, Ben and Martha Petersen, with family friend Mrs. Strackbein (far left), 1940. It was Grandpa Ben's birthday.

Four generations of Midwestern Danish ancestry: Anna Petersen, daughter (back left); Ruth Harbour, granddaughter (back right); Ruth Anne Harbour, great-granddaughter (front left); and Christena Paulsen, grandmother (front right).

Wading in a creek after a picnic lunch.

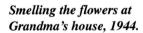

(Left) Anne sits in the old swing at Grandma's.

Smelling the flowers at Grandma's house, 1944.

Alexis Lanyce Harbour Crowley, age 11 in November 2003, carries on the family tradition. Born in London, Alexis loves making breads and here demonstrates kneading wheat bread.

Introduction

A map of the United States has at its heart a broad, deep area colored green, intersected from north to south and east to west by a powerful river system, the Missouri-Mississippi Rivers. Like a giant oval platter, the green, fertile land holds one of the world's most productive agricultural areas, the American Midwest.

The settlers came in waves often determined by circumstances beyond their control: famine, outbreaks of contagious disease, military conscription and political boundary changes. In addition, primogeniture limited the prospects for younger family members, who immigrated to expand their economic opportunities. On the European continent, those living in small countries whose borders faced the sea or mountains found little land available for farming and little opportunity for ownership. In the close-packed cities, survival came first. The education of children, recognition of their needs and talents, and the development of individual potential had low priority.

But there were people who wanted a different life and who had the spark of determination and grit that would propel them to act. Call it ambition or drive. Whatever their place of birth, this was a force that motivated and united them — a common goal: a new beginning in a region where there was space to expand, to find tolerance and peace among others of similar mind, and to participate in a community where each person was valued and encouraged to contribute. The Middle West met the requirements. There was an abundance of cheap land for farmers; small developing villages that welcomed tradespeople; the beginnings of education, churches, and local government needing volunteers; and opportunity to achieve one's ambitions.

For thousands of immigrants this was their goal for a new beginning. It pushed them to cross an ocean in cramped, miserable ship steerage and to go on by wagon, train and boat to face unknown hardships on the American frontier. Uncles, brothers and neighbors who had preceded them welcomed them as they reached Wisconsin, Minnesota, Illinois or Iowa. Some stopped and settled there; others pushed on to the Dakotas, Nebraska or Kansas. There they found others of Scandinavian, Dutch, German and Middle European origin. The Irish, Scots and English had arrived earlier, and the French had settlements along the Mississippi. They were united by their love of the land and by their strong determination to make this place their own.

Appreciation of family values was not unique to these settlers. Most had come from well-populated areas where neighbors were nearby and distances between homes, villages and cities were short. Several generations often shared the home. In contrast, settlers in the Middle West often had no other homestead or village in sight, and communication was not well developed. Farms did not cluster on the outskirts of towns, as they usually did in Europe. Settling close to relatives established in a neighborhood helped newcomers adjust to customs, language differences, and the loneliness of life in sparsely populated areas. It helped the settlers to put down roots.

Their emphasis on orderly patterns of establishing the new family homestead is shown in the windbreaks they planted to shelter homes and farm buildings from the extreme cold and winds of the region. They planned for permanence — planting orchards; starting garden plots with perennials such as berries, asparagus and rhubarb; building fences and windmills; and considering sanitation when locating feed yards for livestock.

Many settlers came out of a culture where religious observance was a decision made by the state. Not many came as protesters. Their upbringing in their homelands encouraged participation. Here where there was more choice, settlers might participate in formally organized churches or be part of a congregation that was a "community" church.

When sizable numbers originating from one country lived near one another, a "brotherhood" that might offer insurance death benefits or, later, casualty insurance, often met, built a hall, and extended their mutual interests on social occasions — the potluck dinner, holiday observances, marriage celebrations and occasions of mourning. These associations helped the newcomer integrate into the community and strengthened his ties both to his heritage and to the new land. He became committed to his new heartland, while retaining respect for the old.

A dominant element of American life has always been its recognition of the value of education and its contributions to a culture founded on democratic principles. The rural one-room schoolhouses that once dotted the Midwestern countryside were symbols of the early settlers' determination to provide education for their children that would give them the tools to achieve a good life. Located at intersections where two roads cross, the schoolhouse was a lonely sentinel that drew pupils from the families living within an area of 16 square miles. The pupils ranged from four to twenty years of age. They walked, rode ponies or were accompanied by a parent driving a horse and buggy when weather was bad. A school might number as few as five or as many as 30 pupils, ranging from beginners learning their numbers and ABC's to strapping stubble-faced boys who attended only when not needed at home for fieldwork.

Although schools in older areas of the United States had made education a priority soon after the country was settled, free public education was not a given. Midwestern settlers embraced the concept that education should be available to all. The one-room country school might be imperfect, but it represented recognition of the need, and it evolved through the efforts of elected representatives. Often the teacher had attended high school or had taken normal training courses before taking tests to become certified to teach in a rural one-room school.

The school was the responsibility of an elected director, unpaid, who saw that the building was clean and ready for the fall term, that fuel was provided for the greedy black stove, and that supplies used for instruction were secured. He attended to weed-cutting, made repairs, and hired the teacher for the term. It was sometimes the duty of the director's household to provide room and board for the teacher.

With such a system, it was a wonder that pupils received an education, but most picked up as much as they could absorb. Eager learners grew curious and began a lifelong search for learning. Teachers, too, grew and learned the satisfaction that comes from guiding *pupils* toward becoming *scholars*. So the early settlers' dreams for education for their children were nurtured, and the one-room rural schools did their part.

Besides the civic responsibilities of being a school director, an early settler might be elected to a local position such as township trustee, who would oversee the roads in his township and suggest improvements; justice of the peace, who heard disputes such as fence boundaries and liability; and county juror. A man's good judgment and integrity were his qualifications for being chosen.

These threads — strong family values and the desire for roots and permanence, respect for others' religious beliefs and encouragement of religious expression, the recognition of a need for accessible free education, and participation in government at various levels — linked the early settlers of diverse backgrounds and united them in dreams and aspirations.

The early settlers found satisfaction in hard work and the rewards it brought. They had good times with neighbors and friends. Churches and meetinghouses sprang up. Lodges, the grange and brotherhoods provided social life. Barn dances, picnics and potluck dinners were occasions when women brought their best cooking and enjoyed applause. This continues today, as families recall the special way mothers and aunts fixed foods.

This great Midwestern area of the United States with its vast rolling prairies and rich productive land has been called America's bread basket, but it is more than that. The Midwest is a symbol for the steadfast heart of all the pioneers who left their birthplaces and struck out to establish a new homeland for themselves and their descendants. This is where they found their heart's home, the heartland of their dreams.

♣   ♣   ♣

This collection of recipes from the Midwest represents over 100 years of cooking that is tried and true. It ranges from the simple basic foods we call "home cooking" to recipes acquired from travel and from other cooks who cherish the recipes their grandmas prepared long after they came to America. They have been our family's favorites for over 100 years. Many are foods teenagers can prepare for family meals. Preparing foods together is a bonding experience when the child is really participating. Stirring counts. The three- or four-year-old stirs a pudding and proudly reports, "I helped Mommy make the dinner!" Of such first efforts, enthusiastic chefs are born. The satisfaction provides genuine motivation to do more.

Nine vignettes, one at the beginning of each section of the book, focus on aspects of life in the Midwest during the early years of the twentieth century. We get glimpses of the settlers as they work together, support community activities and celebrate successes. A common thread linking the vignettes is the part that food and cooking play in forging bonds of cooperation and fellowship that nurture community spirit.

We are inheritors of the spirit of the Heartland of America! Many recipes recall methods and old customs the early settlers followed as they raised and prepared food for their families. The recipes recall happy memories of a time and place our grandchildren call "the olden days" as they join us in the kitchen to cook. Cooking together is a recipe for family bonding — have fun!

— *Ruth Petersen Harbour*
July 2003

Breads

Yeast Breads ♣ *Rolls*
♣ *Quick Breads* ♣ *Muffins*
Pancakes ♣ *Waffles*

<u>Visit to the Village</u>

Who can forget the fragrance that drifted through the house after school the days Mom was baking bread? It hung over the kitchen as she cut generous slices and spread them with margarine or butter. The warm, melting slices became even more delectable with a sprinkle of brown sugar. Few foods are as satisfying. The texture and flavor of bread appeal to all ages.

Bread has been basic in man's diet since first he gathered stalks of wild grains. When the grain was pounded and baked on hot stones, the delicious aroma and taste pleased him. Grain was precious because it was seasonal. So from early times man stored it in skins or clay storage vessels. Museums have clay pots holding grain that is thousands of years old.

Old Settlers brought seed grain and treasured family recipes to use in their new homes in the Middle West. They preferred rye, a crop that matured in the short summers of northern Europe. It produced a firm, dense, chewy bread that kept well. Several rye bread recipes in this collection remind us of the expensive "artisan" breads popular today. The homemaker was the bread baker well into the twentieth century. Her skills were learned from her mother, along with other cookery and household skills.

In her role as cook, baker, and gardener in her rural home in the Midwest, the young housewife had to make do with a primitive stove and unregulated oven, contend with the kitchen's extremes of heat and cold that might cause dough to rise too fast or to sit heavy and lumpish, and find substitutes for unavailable ingredients. Most women needed to bake bread every day; it was essential, truly the staff of life. Using a homemade "starter" comprised of a piece of raw dough saved from the last baking, warm water, and flour, the housewife kept the cycle of bread-making continuous. She baked variations of rye and whole wheat breads. Combined with home-made cheeses, butter and patés, garden produce, milk, and eggs produced on the farm, her breads and baked goods helped make the household self-sufficient.

The settlers were isolated from villages and towns in the early years. There was an inadequate patchwork of roads. Most were narrow lanes with room for one vehicle. They were often level with the adjacent fields, without drainage; heavy rains sent rivulets racing down the rutted tracks. When these miry trails were put to grade and the ruts and potholes leveled with heavy drags loaded with stones, rural people were able to use horse and buggy to reach the village or town half an hour's drive away. They could take produce to sell and explore what they might buy.

On a mild fall day, early settlers and immigrants only a few years ago but now experienced Midwesterners, a farm couple drove their team and neat buggy to the village. They rolled along the dirt road, raising some dust, and noted the changes of color in the sumac that grew on either side, the purple and white of tall asters, the bright orange of butterfly weed, and the constant flutter of birds starting up at their passing. When they reached the village, the husband drove to the Tie Barn, a large barn where teams could be tied by their owners for a small fee. The farmer tied his horses and slipped nosebags of oats over their heads. Then he and his wife sauntered along the main street toward the harness shop, where he had business.

The farmwife passed other wood-fronted buildings with signs designating the kind of business located there: "Justice of the

Peace," "Farms for Sale," "Printer," "Shoe and Boot Shop"—all kinds of businesses. At last she spied her goal, "Dry Goods and Notions." She entered and looked around. She had noted the display of bolts of cloth in the window. There were pale flannels for infants, chambrays for boys' shirts, heavy denim and corduroy for pants, and fancy poplin, percales, and calico for shirtwaists, skirts, or aprons. She examined the cloth thoughtfully; she was a competent plain seamstress and sewed most of her family's clothing on the new machine they had bought with the egg and cream money. She bought spools of thread.

Leaving the dry goods store, she came next to the bakery. This interested her. She smiled; this was *her* business! The glassed front held several kinds of fancy pies, not apple or prune; cookies, dough-nuts with frosting, many light buns made with white flour, and squares of gingerbread. She resolved to bake gingerbread as she went inside. The same array of baked goods was displayed in a glass-sided counter. Behind the counter, open shelves held dozens of fat loaves of bread: German rye with caraway; long, plump loaves of Danish rye; long, pale brown loaves of Swedish *limpa*—she had baked them all in her mother's kitchen. Flat, dark, round loaves of black bread, clusters of light rolls, shiny rounds of egg-washed sweet breads sprinkled with poppy seeds. She pondered. She wanted to buy one of these breads. She pointed shyly at a large square of gingerbread. The woman behind the counter wrapped it in a square of paper and took her coins. Thirty-five cents. She carried her pur-chases and walked to the brick-fronted post office.

The post office was partitioned into two areas: one where the post office workers did their work behind a long wall, the other for people there to get mail, buy stamps, or use their boxes. The boxes were built into the wall. The wood-framed, glass-fronted pigeon-holes had numbers and knobs so the renters could open their box to get their mail. On the other side, postal workers slid mail into the open back of the box. It was a fine invention. People who didn't rent a box ($2.00 a year) waited in line and asked if they had any mail. There was a line of people buying penny postcards or stamps, and the farm wife stepped to the end of it.

As she tucked away the postcards she had bought, the farm wife thought about the postal service and the neat boxes and counter. When she continued walking, she paused briefly in front of the butcher shop. Half a dozen fowl, plucked and rather skinny and pale, hung in a row. In front were large platters holding meats: a beef roast, sausages, pork chops, a large liver, and a slab of fat side meat. A length of mosquito netting was draped over the meat. She saw her husband, who had hitched the team to the buggy, and quickened her step. He helped her up into the buggy, and they started home.

The team moved along smartly. The couple discussed their purchases and the way times had changed over ten years. They reached the crossroads where their tin mailbox clustered with ten others. These sat on a crosspiece of heavy timber fastened at each end to a stout post. When the weather and roads permitted, the mailman drove from the village on his route in an odd buggy with a box built on top. He put the mail into the boxes. The farmer leaned over to take out his weekly market paper, mailed from Chicago. In another ten minutes they turned into the familiar lane, the little house a welcome sight.

The wife remembered the gingerbread squares in the bakery and touched the paper-wrapped package. How happy the children would be! Again she resolved to bake gingerbread herself soon.

Elm Front Farm, settled in 1905 by Danish immigrants, was planned in the Danish style, an open square with farm buildings on four sides. A four-room house was moved here in 1903. Additions gave this house nine rooms by 1925. The home had a furnace, water, and a Delco lighting system.

Jens and Christena Paulsen brought their family by farm wagon to the new home called Elm Front Farm in 1905. They were dressed in their best to have this picture taken in 1925. Mrs. Paulsen came through Ellis Island in 1894 to join her husband-to-be.

Scattered homesteads had few trees; windmills supplied water. The settlers soon built buildings to shelter livestock and store grain and hay. They enlarged houses and planted windbreaks.

The early settlers often had large families who helped with the fieldwork and barnyard chores. This young girl is taking care of her nephew and niece on a crisp fall day in 1920 (left). Her niece stays close by her loyal dog (right).

Woodbury and Ida Counties had large Danish settlements that met for social occasions, such as dances, religious services, or this 1918 picnic to welcome home the young man in uniform, who had been serving in WWI. Some of this group had come to America in the 1890s.

Recipes

Homemade bread is delectable at room temperature, buttered, just after baking. Next best, cut half an inch thick and toast it. Cut thick, it makes excellent "natural" sandwiches with tomatoes, sprouts, lettuce, and avocado.

My White Bread

2 pkg dry yeast	2 T. melted shortening
1 qt. lukewarm water	11 to 12 c. sifted flour
2 T. sugar	2 T. salt

Dissolve yeast and sugar in lukewarm water. Add shortening. Add flour, 2 c. at a time, beating with each addition, until 6 c. have been added. Beat until smooth. Then add salt and 5 c. more flour. Mix until very smooth, adding more flour if dough is sticky. Turn out dough onto lightly floured board and knead until smooth and elastic, 10-12 min.

Place dough into a well-greased bowl and turn so it is greased lightly all over. Set aside in a warm place (82F) to rise until light, about 1-1/2 hr. Punch down. Divide into three parts. Cover and let rest 15 min.-

Form each part into a loaf; place in greased 5 x 9 x 2 in. loaf pans. Cover to rise 1 hr. or until double in bulk. Bake in preheated 375F oven for 10 min. Reduce heat to 350F and bake another 40-50 min. The loaf will be well browned and sound hollow when tapped.

Cool loaves 10 min., then turn out on racks. Brush tops lightly with melted butter. Yield: 3 large loaves.

♣ *When your kitchen seems too cool for the bread dough to rise, cover the dough with a clean towel and put it in the cold oven with a pan of hot water on the bottom shelf.*

No-Knead White Bread

1-1/4 c. warm water	2 t. salt
1 pkg dry yeast	2 T. sugar
2 T. soft shortening	3 c. sifted flour

In large mixing bowl, dissolve yeast in water. Add shortening, salt, sugar, and half the flour. Beat in mixer 2 min. at medium speed or for 5 min. by hand. Scrape dough to the center often. Add remaining flour and blend in with spoon until smooth. Cover with cloth, let rise in warm place 30 min. Beat batter about 30 strokes with spoon. Spread evenly in a greased loaf pan, 9 x 5 in. Smooth top. Let rise 40 min. or until batter is within 1 in. of top of pan.

Preheat oven to 375F. Bake 45 min., until brown. Remove from pan to cooling rack. Brush top with melted shortening. Cover with clean towel and cool.

Dorothy's Oatmeal Bread   Dorothy Biwer Smith

1-1/2 c. boiling water	1/2 c. warm water
1 c. oatmeal (quick cooking)	1 pkg yeast
1/2 c. brown sugar	1 t. salt
1 T. salt	2 c. flour
1/3 c. shortening	2 beaten eggs

Add boiling water to oatmeal, brown sugar, salt and shortening; cool mixture. Mix warm water, yeast, salt; set aside. Add flour and eggs to oatmeal mixture. Then add yeast mixture and, gradually, flour to make a stiff dough. Turn onto floured board and knead until smooth. Grease bowl and turn dough. Let double in bulk. Divide into two loaves and put in well-greased 8-1/2 x 4-1/2 in. bread pans. Let rise again. Bake 40 min. in 375F oven. Grease with butter and cool. Yield: 2 loaves.

Raisin Bread   Aunt Martha Sterrett

2 pkg quick yeast	1 c. sugar, divided
1/2 c. lukewarm water	2 T. melted shortening or lard
2 c. warm water	1-1/2 t. salt
2 c. flour	1 c. washed raisins
4 c. additional flour	2 t. cinnamon

Dissolve yeast in 1/2 c. lukewarm water. Stir in 2 c. warm water and flour. Beat 8-10 min. until bubbly. Add 1/2 c. sugar, shortening, salt, and raisins. Stir well, adding flour to make a soft dough. Knead. Return to greased bowl. Let rise until double in bulk. Roll out 1 in. thick. Sprinkle with mixture of 1/2 c. sugar and cinnamon. Roll as for jelly roll. Seal seam and ends. Place in 9 x 14 in. greased pan or divide into 2 smaller loaves using 5 x 9 in. pans. Let rise until double. Bake at 350F for 15 min., then at 300F for 45 min. until loaf sounds hollow. Cool on rack.

Grandma Paulsen made raisin bread often and passed this recipe on to her five daughters. She used about 2 T. cinnamon, which resulted in a dark spicy swirl in this bread. Her bread pans measured 9 x 14 in. and held three standard size loaves. This is one of our best Danish breads, usually served buttered, with coffee, for afternoon refreshments.

Rye Bread

1-1/4 c. warm water	2-1/2 c. sifted flour
1 pkg active dry yeast	2 t. salt
2 T. brown sugar or light molasses	1 T. caraway seeds, if desired
1 c. sifted rye flour	2 T. soft shortening

Dissolve yeast in water. Add brown sugar, half the flours, salt, caraway seeds, and shortening. Beat 2 min. at medium mixer speed or 300 vigorous strokes by hand. Scrape sides and bottom of bowl frequently. Add remaining flour and blend in with spoon until smooth, 1 to 1-1/2 min. Scrape batter from sides of bowl, cover with cloth, let rise in warm place (85F) about 30 min. Beat batter about 25 strokes and spread evenly in greased loaf pan, 9 x 5 x 3 in. Batter will be sticky. Smooth top and pat into shape with floured hand.

Let rise again until batter reaches 1 in. from top of pan, about 30 min. Preheat oven to 375F. Bake 45-50 min. or until brown. Remove from pan, cool on rack. Brush top with melted butter. Before cutting, cool, but not in direct draft.

♣ *Stir whole wheat and rye flours rather than sift them; the coarser flours will clog the sifter.*

Charlotte's Rye Bread   Charlotte Petersen

2 pkg yeast	1/4 c. margarine
1 t. sugar	1 t. salt
1 c. very warm water	2 c. white flour
2 c. milk	1/4 c. wheat germ
1/3 c. honey or light molasses	2 c. rye flour

Dissolve yeast with sugar in warm water. Combine milk, honey, margarine, and salt. Cool. Add white flour; beat; add yeast mixture, wheat germ, rye flour; beat. Add white flour as needed; knead 5-10 min. Let rise until double in bulk. Shape into 2 large loaves. Let rise until double in bulk. Bake at 400F for 15 min. and then at 350F for 30 min.

Grandma's Rye Bread   Martha Jansen Petersen

1-1/2 c. boiling water	1/2 c. lukewarm water
1/2 c. molasses	1 pkg dry yeast
1/3 c. shortening	2-1/2 c. rye flour
1 t. salt	4 c. white flour
1 t. sugar	

Soak yeast and sugar in 1/2 c. water. Combine molasses, shortening, salt and boiling water in a large bowl. Cool to lukewarm. Add yeast mixture and mix well. Add rye flour and beat smooth. Add white flour. Knead 5 min.; place in greased bowl. Let rise until double in bulk. Punch down. Turn onto floured board and divide into two parts. Let rest 10 min.

Roll into a rectangle the length of the pan and then, beginning at narrow end, roll up as if for jelly roll. Seal. Place in greased 5 x 9 in. bread pans. Let rise until double in bulk. Bake at 350F for about 50 minutes. Cool on rack. Butter tops. Yield: 2 loaves.

Grandma Petersen always served brick cheese, a pale creamy cheese with a mild flavor, with this firm-textured rye bread. She had immigrated with her mother, Mary Jansen, and brother Andrew to Jones County, Iowa, in the 1880s. She took pride in her neat kitchen garden.

Norwegian Rye Bread

2 c. boiling water	2 pkg dry yeast
3 T. molasses	1 c. lukewarm water
1 c. rolled oats (not quick cooking)	4 c. white flour
1/2 c. brown sugar	2 c. rye flour
2 T. shortening (may be lard)	1 T. salt

Pour boiling water over molasses, rolled oats, brown sugar, and shortening. Mix well and let stand until lukewarm. Dissolve yeast in 1 c. lukewarm water. Mix together with first ingredients. Gradually add white flour, rye flour, and salt. Knead 8-10 min. Form into a ball; turn into greased bowl. Let rise in warm place until double. Punch down. Form into two loaves and place in greased loaf pans. Let rise to double in size. Bake in preheated 350F oven for 45 min. Remove from pans after 5-10 min., butter tops, and cover with clean cloth to cool.

♣ *If a recipe calls for lard and you have none available, substitute vegetable shortening in a ratio of 1 part lard to 1 1/4 parts shortening.*

Rye Cardamom Bread   Anna M. Petersen

1 pkg yeast	1/3 c. sugar
1 c. hot mashed potatoes	1/2 c. molasses
1 c. water drained from potatoes	1 t. salt
1 c. lukewarm water	3 c. rye flour
3/4 c. softened lard or Crisco	7 c. white flour
1 t. cardamom	

Start bread in the morning, making stiff dough at once. Cover and let rise until double in bulk. (Rye bread is slower than white.) Be sure to use rye flour — not rye graham. Make into 3 loaves, let rise until bread is above edges of pan. Bake at 375F 10 min., then reduce heat to 350F for 45 min. Lay a piece of brown paper over the loaves to keep from browning too much. Grease tops of bread and cool, covered with a thin towel. Yield:
3 loaves.

This was Mother's favorite rye bread recipe. It is moist and flavorful.

♣ *When bread is removed from the oven, brush the top with melted butter for a soft, tender crust.*

Raisin Rye Bread

1-1/2 c. boiling water	1/2 brown sugar
1 c. raisins	1/2 c. Green Label molasses
2 pkg dry yeast	2 t. salt
1/2 c. warm water	2 c. boiling water
1/3 c. shortening	4-1/2 c. white flour
2 c. rye flour	

Pour 1-1/2 c. boiling water over raisins. Dissolve yeast in warm water. In a large bowl, combine shortening, brown sugar, molasses, salt, and 2 c. boiling water. Let cool somewhat, then beat in 2-1/2 c. flour until dough is smooth, about 10 min. Add yeast mixture, stir thoroughly. Use a spoon to stir in the raisins, well drained, 2 c. rye flour, and about 2 c. white flour. Knead on floured board (adding flour if dough is sticky) until smooth and elastic. Shape into a ball, turn into greased bowl. Cover and let rise until doubled. Punch dough down. Divide in half. Shape into loaves in greased 8 x 4 x 2 in. pans. Let double. Bake 45 min. at 350F. Brush with butter.

♣ *An investment in a set of steel or aluminum graduated measuring cups and spoons will help you to measure accurately and save time.*

Brown Wheat Bread

1-1/2 c. hot water	1 pkg yeast
3 T. oil	1/4 c. warm water
3 T. brown sugar	3 c. whole wheat flour
3 T. honey or Karo syrup	2 c. white flour
1-1/2 t. salt	

Combine first five ingredients; set aside to cool. Mix yeast in warm water. Add whole wheat flour to first cooled mixture. Stir in yeast mixture. Add white flour.

Knead 10-15 min. Place in greased bowl, cover, and let rise 1-1/2 hr. Punch down. Divide in two and let rest 10 min. Form into loaves. Let rise in loaf pans 1-1/4 hr. Bake at 375F for 40-45 min. Grease tops. Turn onto cooling rack. Cover with clean towel.

♣ *Whole wheat flour should be stored in a tightly closed plastic bag in the refrigerator or freezer to protect flavor and shelf life.*

Whole Wheat Bread

2 pkg dry yeast	1/3 c. shortening
1/4 c. lukewarm water	1/3 c. mild molasses
1 t. sugar	1 c. cold water
1 c. milk	2 c. whole wheat flour
3 T. sugar	3-1/2 to 4-1/2 c. white flour
1 t. salt	

Dissolve yeast in lukewarm water and 1 t. sugar; let stand. Scald milk and pour into large bowl; blend in 3 T. sugar, salt, shortening, molasses, and cold water. Add the yeast mixture. Stir in 2 c. whole wheat flour; beat hard. Add half the white flour at a time, mixing well.

Turn onto floured board. Knead to a soft dough. Grease top lightly. Place in greased bowl and let rise to double. Punch down and shape into 2 large loaves. Let rise until nearly double. Place in two 5 x 3 x 9 in. bread pans, greased well. Bake in preheated 375F oven 5 min. Turn oven back to 350F and bake 40-50 min. more. Let loaves cool in pans 5-10 min., grease tops, and turn out on cooling rack. Yield:

2 large loaves.

Batter Bread   Linda Marple

3 c. whole wheat flour	1/3 c. butter
2 pkg active dry yeast	1-1/2 c. regular rolled oats
2-1/2 c. buttermilk	2 eggs
1/4 c. molasses	2-1/2 to 3 c. flour
1/4 c. honey	2 T. butter
1 T. salt	

Preheat oven to 375F. Grease two 1-1/2 qt. round x 2-1/2 in. deep casseroles. Combine whole wheat flour and yeast. Heat buttermilk, molasses, honey, salt, and butter until warm (105-115F). Pour into 3-qt. mixer bowl. Add oats, whole wheat yeast mixture, and eggs. Blend at low speed until moistened. Beat 3 min. at high speed. Stir in enough flour to make a stiff dough. Brush with melted butter. Cover;

let rise in warm place until doubled, about 1 hr. Punch down; shape into 2 round loaves. Place in casseroles; cover. Let rise until double, about 45 min. Bake at 375F for 25-35 min., or until loaf sounds hollow when tapped. Yield: 2 round loaves.

An expert baker, Linda often shares these loaves with friends. She bakes wonderful sweet coffee breads too.

Dilly Bread

1 pkg dry yeast	2 t. dill seed
1/4 c. warm water	1 t. salt
1 c. warm creamed cottage cheese	1/4 t. soda
2 T. sugar	1 unbeaten egg
1 T. instant minced onion	2-1/4 to 2-1/2 c. flour
1 T. melted butter	

Soften yeast in warm water. Combine in large mixing bowl all ingredients except flour. Add flour gradually to form a soft dough, beating well after each addition. Cover and let rise in warm place (80-90F) until doubled, about 50-60 min.

Stir down dough and turn into a well-greased 8-in. round casserole. Let rise 30-40 min. Bake at 350F for 35-40 min. Brush loaf with butter and sprinkle lightly with salt. Remove from casserole to a cooling rack.

Butter Flake Brioche

1 pkg dry yeast	2 eggs
1/4 c. lukewarm water	1/2 c. melted butter
1 c. scalded milk	5 to 5-1/2 c. sifted flour
1/3 c. sugar	1 egg yolk
1 t. salt	1 T. cream

Soften yeast in lukewarm water. Combine scalded milk, sugar, and salt in large mixing bowl. Cool to lukewarm. Blend in 2 well-beaten eggs and melted butter. Gradually add flour to form a stiff dough. Knead on floured board for 2 min. Place in greased bowl, turn, and cover. Let rise in warm place (85-90F) about 2 hr. or until double in bulk.

Take one third of dough and set aside, covered. Shape remainder of dough into 24 2-in. balls. Place in well-greased muffin pans. Shape remaining dough into 24 3/4-

in. balls, tapering one side to a point. Press deep indentation in large balls, moisten hole, and insert pointed side of small balls firmly. Let rise in warm place until double in bulk, about 45-60 min.

If desired, brush with egg glaze made by beating 1 egg yolk with 1 T. cream. Bake in moderate oven (350F) 20-25 min. Remove from pan. Serve warm with butter. Yield: 2 dozen.

♣ *A minute timer is valuable for baking and stovetop timing. A timer would be a wonderful shower gift for a new bride.*

Butterhorns

1/2 c. warm water	1 c. (2 sticks) butter or margarine,
1/2 c. sugar, divided	divided
1 (1/4 oz.) pkg active dry yeast	1/2 c. instant potato flakes
1 c. milk	4-1/2 c. all-purpose flour
3 large eggs	

Pour warm water into 1-c. measure. Sprinkle 1 t. sugar and yeast over the water and set aside 5 min. When yeast bubbles to top of the cup, it is ready. Meanwhile, heat milk and 1/2 c. butter over medium-high heat until butter melts into milk. Do not boil.

In large bowl, mix remaining sugar, eggs, and potato flakes. Pour in warm milk mixture and blend well. Pour in yeast and mix well. Beat in flour, 1 c. at a time, until you have a sticky dough. Cover bowl with tea towel and set aside to rise in warm place until doubled in bulk, about 1 hr.

Grease 2 baking sheets and set aside. Divide dough into thirds. Turn each portion of dough onto a floured surface and roll out to 12-in. circle. Melt remaining 1/2 c. butter. Brush about 2 T. melted butter over dough. Cut dough into 12 pie-shaped wedges. Starting at the wide end of each wedge, roll into a crescent shape and place on prepared baking sheet about 1 in. apart. Repeat with remaining 2 portions dough. Cover with tea towel. Let rise until doubled in bulk, about 1 hr.

Preheat oven to 350F. Bake 12-15 min., or until the rolls are risen and browned. Remove the rolls to wire racks to cool. Yield: 3 dozen.

Butterscotch Pecan Rolls

1 pkg dry or fresh yeast	1 egg, beaten
1/4 c. warm water	Extra butter, melted
1 c. milk (scalded and cooled)	1/2 c. sugar
1/4 c. shortening	2 t. cinnamon
1/4 c. sugar	1 c. brown sugar
1 t. salt	1/2 c. oleo or butter
3-1/4 to 3-1/2 c. flour	2 T. corn syrup
3/4 c. pecans or English walnuts	

Soften yeast in warm water. Combine scalded milk, shortening, 1/4 c. sugar, and salt. Add 1 c. flour and beat well; then beat in yeast and egg. Gradually add rest of flour, beating well. Round dough into ball, brush top with soft shortening. Cover and let rise until double. Punch down, turn out on surface, and divide in half. Roll each half into an 8 x 12 in. rectangle; brush with 2 T. melted butter. Mix 1/2 c. sugar and cinnamon; sprinkle half on each rectangle. Roll each up to make a 12-in. roll. Seal. Cut each roll into 10 slices.

In a 9 x 13 greased pan, melt brown sugar, 1/2 c. butter, corn syrup. Heat slowly until mixture is blended. Sprinkle with pecans or walnuts, chopped or whole. Place slices in pan and cover. Let rise until double. Bake for 30-40 min. at 375F. Turn out onto cooling rack. (You may prefer to bake these in two pans. Round 10-in. layer cake pans or 8 x 8 in. pans work well.) Yield: 20 rolls.

Gerry's Rohliky-Crescent Rolls   Gerry Vrbicek

1 pkg dry yeast	1/2 c. sugar
1/4 c. warm water	4-1/2 to 4-3/4 c. flour
3/4 c. scalded milk	1 t. salt
1/2 c. margarine	3 beaten eggs

Soften yeast in warm water with 1 tsp. sugar. Combine hot milk, margarine, sugar, and salt; cool. Add 1 c. flour. Add yeast mixture and eggs and beat well. Stir in remaining flour. Turn out on floured board and knead 5 to 8 times *only*.

Put dough in greased bowl, turn to coat top. Cover and let rise until double (1 to 2 hr.). Divide into thirds. Roll each to a 9-in. circle. Cut into 12 wedges. Brush with soft butter. Roll each wedge to center to form crescents. Put on greased cookie sheet. Brush each roll lightly with melted butter. Let rise 30-45 min. Bake at 400F for 10 min. Remove and brush with butter. Yield: 36 crescent rolls.

Variation: For sweet rolls, roll half the dough into an oblong about 8 x 14 in. Sprinkle with a mixture made of 1 t. cinnamon, 1/2 c. brown sugar, 1/2 c. chopped nuts, and 2 T. soft butter. Roll as for jelly roll. Cut into slices about 1 in. thick.

Bake at 375F about 25 min. in 3 round 9-in. pans. Drizzle with frosting made of 2 c. powdered sugar, hot milk, and vanilla.

Danish Rolls

1 pkg yeast	2 eggs, beaten
1 T. sugar	2-3 c. flour
3/4 c. warm water	3 sticks softened margarine

In a large bowl, stir sugar into warm water. Add yeast; let dissolve. Stir in eggs and flour to make a soft dough. Roll dough out into a rectangle about 1/2 in. thick. Spread with first stick of margarine. Fold dough into thirds; refrigerate at least 15 min. Roll dough out, spread with second stick of margarine. Fold again; refrigerate another 15 min. Repeat process with third stick of margarine.

After the third refrigeration, roll dough into a thin rectangle, 8 x 14 in. Roll up jelly roll fashion. Cut dough into slices about 1 in. thick. Place on ungreased pan, cut side up. Cover and let rise 1 hr. Bake at 350F for 7 min. or until lightly browned. Frost if desired.

Dinner Rolls

2 pkg dry yeast	1/4 c. butter, soft
1/2 c. warm (105F) water	5 to 5-1/2 c. flour
1/3 c. sugar	2 eggs
3/4 c. warm milk	Melted butter
1 t. salt	

Sprinkle yeast over water in large bowl of electric mixer. Add 1 T. of sugar. Let stand until yeast is soft. Add remaining sugar, milk, salt, and butter. Mix in 2-1/2 c. flour; beat on medium-low speed about 5 min. Beat in eggs one at a time. Stir in about 2 c. more flour to make a soft dough.

Turn dough onto floured board. Knead 8-10 min. until dough is smooth and satiny. Put dough into greased bowl and turn so all sides are greased. Cover with Saran Wrap. Let rise until double, about 1 hr. (or refrigerate 6-8 hr.). Punch dough down. Knead into smooth ball, cover, and let rest 10 min. Flour work surface and shape dough into desired shapes. Cover shaped rolls with plastic wrap and towel. Let rise in warm place until almost doubled in bulk (30-45 min.; 1 hr. if dough was refrigerated).

Preheat oven to 400F. Brush rolls with melted butter. Bake until golden brown (12-15 min.). Cool on wire racks. Yield: 2 dozen.

♣ *Bread stays fresh longer at room temperature or frozen. Do not store in refrigerator.*

Dutch Buns

Anna M. Petersen

1 c. white bread dough	1/2 c. sugar
1 c. warm water	Flour
1 T. lard or shortening	

Save one cupful of white bread dough when ready to mold it into loaves. Put it in a cool place, covered with Saran wrap or a tea towel. At about 4 p.m., cut the dough into small pieces and add 1 c. warm water, using a medium-sized mixing bowl. Add lard or shortening, sugar, and enough flour to make it easy to handle. Knead until elastic and smooth. Cover with a tea towel and place in a warm place (80F).

At 8:30 or 9:00 p.m., roll the dough out to 1-in. thickness. Cut with a 2- or 3-in. biscuit cutter and place on lightly greased baking sheet. Cover with a towel and put in draft-free place to rise overnight. About 7 or 8 a.m., bake buns in a hot oven (400F) for 15 min. until nicely browned. Cool on rack. Yield: 24-30 buns.

These buns are a delicious light bread for breakfast served with strawberry jam or honey. The recipe employs the homemade starter used by the early settlers, who could not purchase the active dry yeast and refrigerated yeasts available today.

Hot Cross Buns

1 c. scalded milk	1/4 c. butter
1 T. sugar	1 T. shortening
1 pkg yeast	1/4 c. sugar
1 c. flour	1 t. grated lemon rind
Additional flour	1/2 c. chopped raisins
2/3 t. salt	1 egg yolk, beaten

Mix 1 T. sugar, milk, and when cool, yeast. Cover and let stand 20 min. Add 1 c. flour and salt. Beat. Cover and let rise until light. Cream butter, shortening; add sugar and lemon rind. Combine mixtures. Add flour to make a stiff batter — about 1 1/2 c. Cover, let rise again. Add raisins and more flour if needed to make a soft dough. Shape into balls 2 in. in diameter. Place on greased sheet 1 in. apart. Cover, let rise. Brush with yolk of egg blended with 1 t. cold water. Bake in hot oven 400F for 25 min. Cool. Pipe a cross of icing on top of each bun. Yield: 2 dozen.

Czech Town Kolaches

1 c. warm milk	1/2 t. salt
1/3 c. butter, room temperature	1 pkg or cake yeast
1 t. lemon rind, grated	2 egg yolks
1/2 t. mace	3 c. flour
1 T. sugar for yeast	1/3 c. sugar

Crumble yeast in warm milk with 1 T. sugar; set aside to rise. Put butter into large bowl of electric mixer and cream with sugar and salt. Add egg yolks, lemon rind, and mace. Add milk with yeast. Mix, then add flour slowly, mixing with a wooden spoon. Beat until smooth. Cover with waxed paper, with a tea towel over waxed paper. Set in refrigerator overnight.

Put dough on slightly floured board. Form into balls the size of walnuts and place an inch apart on greased cookie sheet. Brush with melted butter. Cover. Let rise until double in bulk. Press down the center of each with your fingers and fill with your choice of filling — prune, apricot, cottage cheese, poppy seed; you will find a variety in grocery baking aisles.

Let rise again 20 min. Bake in 425F oven 8-10 min. or until nicely brown. Brush with butter, remove to rack to cool. Yield: 32 kolaches.

There were old-time bakeries along the Main Street known as "Czech Town," and the fragrance of their baked breads and pastries drew buyers from every part of Cedar Rapids. As newcomers, my family joined the crowd every Saturday morning especially to select kolaches, a sweet Czechoslovakian bun filled with prune, apricot, cherry, or cheese in "open" style. The "closed" kind had the tempting fillings tucked in with a crimped seal. What a delicious choice it was! An experienced kolache baker used this recipe. I can vouch that a first-timer can produce perfect kolaches. Luckily, one can still find kolaches at the historic bakeries in Czech Town today.

Sharon's Kolaches   Sharon Schultz

2 pkg dry yeast	1 stick butter
2 t. sugar	3 eggs
1/2 c. warm milk	1 t. salt
1-1/2 c. warm milk	6 c. flour
1/2 c. sugar	

Dissolve yeast and 2 t. sugar in 1/2 c. warm milk; let them dissolve and bubble. Add rest of milk. Cream 1/2 c. sugar with butter. Add 3 whole eggs, one at a time, and salt. Add milk and sugar mixture to yeast mixture. Gradually add 6 c. flour (more or less), stirring well. Beat until dough blisters. Set in warm place covered with a towel. Let rise until double in bulk. Shape dough into 2-in. balls and space an inch apart on greased cookie sheets. Let rise 15 min. Prepare sweetened prune, apricot, or cherry filling. Make an indentation in each ball and place 1 t. desired filling in dented place. Let rise until doubled in bulk. Bake at 375F for 12-15 min. or until nicely browned.

Sharon headed the school lunchroom staff at Pierce School in Cedar Rapids, Iowa. This is just one of the wonderful baked treats they made every day for 400 pupils.

Light Rolls — Bake and Brown*

1-1/2 scalded milk	1/3 c. very warm water
2 T. sugar	1 egg, well beaten
1-1/2 t. salt	4-1/2 to 5 c. all-purpose flour
1/3 c. shortening	Melted margarine
2 pkg dry yeast	

Combine milk, sugar, salt, and shortening; let stand until lukewarm. Dissolve yeast in very warm water; add to milk mixture. Stir in egg. Gradually add enough flour to make a soft dough that leaves sides of bowl.

Cover with a towel, and let rise in a warm place until doubled in bulk. Punch dough down and turn out on a lightly floured board or pastry cloth; knead lightly. Shape as desired. Brush with melted margarine. Let rise until doubled in bulk (about 45 min.). Bake at 425F 10-15 min. Yield: 3 dozen.

*To freeze rolls and brown later: Bake rolls at 250F about 25 min. Do not brown. Cool; wrap in moisture-proof wrapping, and freeze. To serve, remove from freezer, and let stand about 10 min. Bake at 425F until brown (5-10 min.).

These are excellent, and it is so convenient to have fresh, light rolls ready to serve in 25 min.

No-Knead Refrigerator Rolls

2 c. warm (not hot) water	2 t. salt
1 pkg dry yeast	1 egg
6-1/2 to 7 c. sifted white flour	1/4 c. soft shortening
1/2 c. sugar	

In large electric mixer bowl, dissolve yeast in water. Add sugar, salt, and half the flour. Beat at medium speed 2 min. Add egg and shortening. Beat rest of flour in gradually by hand until smooth. Cover with damp cloth, place in refrigerator. Punch down occasionally.

About 2 hr. before baking, cut off amount needed and return rest of dough to refrigerator. Shape while cold into desired type of rolls and place on greased baking sheet. Brush tops with melted butter. Let rise until light, 1-1/2 to 2 hr. Heat oven to 400F. Bake 12-15 min. Yield: 4 dozen medium rolls.

To Shape Yeast Rolls:

Traditional Pan Rolls. Form balls 1-1/2 to 2 in. in diameter, and place in greased 9-in. square or 9-in. round cake tin about 1/2 in. apart.

Parker House Rolls. Named for the famous hotel in Boston, where they are still served. Roll dough 1/4 in. thick. Cut 2 1/2-in. circles with biscuit cutter. Make a crease across middle of circle and fold so top half slightly overlaps. Press edges together at crease. Place rolls close together on greased baking sheet.

Cloverleaf Rolls. Grease muffin tins and place three 1-in. balls in each muffin pan. Brush baked rolls with melted butter.

Crescent Rolls. Roll a piece of dough into a 12-in. circle 1/4 in. thick. Spread thinly with soft butter. Cut into 12 pie-shaped pieces. Beginning at outer edge, roll each piece to form crescent. Bake on greased cookie sheet.

Fan-Tans. Roll dough into a 6 x 8 in. rectangle 1/2 in. thick. Cut into eight 6 x 1 in. strips. Cut each 6-in. strip into four pieces, 1-1/2 in. long. Stack three pieces upright in each greased muffin cup. Spread tops to a fan shape.

4-H Basic Sweet Rolls   Iowa Extension Service

2 pkg dry yeast	1-1/2 t. salt
1 c. warm water	1/4 c. butter or Crisco
1/2 c. milk	2 beaten eggs
1/2 c. sugar	5 c. sifted flour

Soften yeast in warm water. Scald milk; add sugar, salt, and butter. Cool. Add yeast mixture and beaten eggs. Gradually add flour, about 2 c. at a time.

Mix thoroughly. Let dough rest 10 min. Knead 10 min. on floured board. Grease bowl and turn dough. Let rise until double or dough holds thumbprint. Punch dough down and let rest 10 min. Shape into cloverleaf, fan-tan, or butterhorns and let double. Bake at 400F for 12-15 min. or until golden brown. For best results, add only enough flour to make a soft batter.

Bernice's Rolls
Bernice Peterson

2 cakes dry yeast
1 T. sugar
1 c. lukewarm water
1 c. milk
6 T. shortening

1/2 c. sugar
1 t. salt
7 c. flour
3 eggs, beaten

Dissolve yeast and 1 T. sugar in water. Scald milk; add shortening, sugar, and salt. Cool. Add 2 c. flour, yeast, eggs; beat well. Add flour, knead. Let rise 2 hr. When light, punch down and shape. Let rise 45 min. Bake 20 min. at 375F or lower.

Bernice, an Iowa State College grad, excelled in all cookery, but these rolls were her masterpiece. She developed many original recipes that earned recognition.

♣ *Canned evaporated milk diluted with an equal amount of hot water may be substituted for scalded milk in yeast bread recipes.*

Cinnamon Rolls
Mrs. A. E. Thompson

1 pkg yeast
1/4 c. warm water
2 T. sugar
1-1/2 c. milk
3 T. sugar
1/3 c. butter

1 egg
Flour
1/2 c. soft butter
1-1/3 c. brown sugar
3 T. cinnamon

Dissolve yeast and 2 T. sugar in warm water. Scald and cool milk; set aside. Cream together 3 T. sugar and 1/3 c. butter. Add egg and mix into milk. Combine with yeast mixture. Add flour to make soft dough. Knead well and let rise until double in bulk. Punch down. Roll out and spread with 1/2 c. soft butter. Sprinkle with mixture of brown sugar and cinnamon. Roll up and cut in 1-in. slices. Cover and let double again. Bake at 350F.

When light brown, spread with topping (mix 1/2 c. cream, 1 c. brown sugar, and 1 t. vanilla). Return to oven and finish baking 10 min.

Sweet French Buns

1 pkg dry yeast
1/4 c. lukewarm water
1 T. sugar
1 c. milk
4 c. flour

1/4 c. sugar
3 T. butter
1 egg, beaten
1/2 t. lemon extract
1 t. salt

Dissolve yeast and 1 T. sugar in warm water. Scald and cool milk. Add
1 1/2 c. flour to make sponge. Beat smooth. Let rise 50 min. Add 1/4 c. sugar
creamed with 3 T. butter, beaten egg, lemon extract, and salt; mix well. Slowly add
2-1/2 c. sifted flour, blending in. Knead about 5 min. until smooth and elastic.
Place in greased bowl to rise 1 hr. Cover. Turn out on lightly floured board and
shape into rolls or fancy twist. Let rise until light, 50 min. or more. Bake at 375F
15 min. Yield: 30 buns or rolls.

A fragrant, tasty bread. Very good as toast.

Sally Lunn

1 lb. (3 c.) flour	2 oz. fat
2 t. salt	4 oz. milk
1/2 oz. fresh yeast	2 beaten eggs
1/2 t. sugar	

If fresh yeast is not available, substitute 1 pkg dry yeast. Sift flour and salt; add
yeast creamed with the sugar, fat melted in warm milk, and one beaten egg. Mix to
a smooth dough. Let rise to double in size. Punch the dough back and shape to fit
greased round baking rings about 6 in. wide; let rise until rings are full. Bake in
hot oven (425F, 220C) 15-20 min. Brush with beaten egg halfway through baking.
Serve hot, sprinkled with crushed sugar.

*This recipe was given to me at the original Sally Lunn shop in Bath, England, by
the shop owner in 1977. The original owner of the bakeshop was Sally Lunn, who
baked this light bread about A.D. 1600. A basement fireplace oven is still intact.*

Steamed Boston Brown Bread

1 c. cornmeal	1/2 t. salt
3/4 c. molasses	2 c. graham or whole wheat flour
2 c. buttermilk	1 egg
1-1/2 t. soda	1 c. raisins

Mix all ingredients well. Pour into three well-greased #2-1/2 cans, about 2/3 full.
Tie foil over tops of cans. Steam 3 hr. Cool. Cut into 1/2-in. slices and serve warm
with butter. Yield: 24 slices.

Steamed Boston Brown Bread — 1920s
Anna M. Petersen

1 c. sour milk	1 c. raisins
1 c. sweet milk	1/2 t. soda
1/2 c. sugar	3/4 t. salt
1/2 c. Brer Rabbit molasses	Graham flour

Combine ingredients, adding enough graham flour to make a stiff batter. Steam 2-1/2 hrs. in 1-lb. greased cans. Cool and serve warm with butter. Yield: about 16 slices.

My mother prepared this recipe in the 1920s. It is a dense moist bread, and the combination of molasses and raisins is very flavorful. This recipe has remained popular with our family and friends.

Banana Nut Bread
Hazel Galvin

1 c. sugar	1-1/2 t. baking powder
1/2 c. shortening	1/2 t. soda
2 eggs, beaten	1/4 t. salt
2 c. mashed ripe bananas	1-1/2 T. sour milk
2 c. flour	1/2 c. chopped nuts

Cream sugar and shortening. Add beaten eggs and bananas. Sift together flour, baking powder, soda, and salt. Add and blend. Do not overstir. Add sour milk and nuts. Bake in 5 x 9 x 3 in. greased pan at 350F for 50 min. Test with toothpick after 40 min. Yield: 12-16 slices.

♣ *It is important not to overstir any quick bread. Mix ingredients just enough to moisten them.*

Edna's Cranberry Orange Bread
Edna Kenney

2 c. all purpose flour	1/2 c. orange juice
1-1/2 t. baking powder	Grated rind of one orange
1 t. baking soda	2 T. melted butter or oleo
1/2 t. salt	2 T. hot water
1 c. sugar	1 c. raw whole cranberries
1 egg, beaten	1 c. coarsely chopped walnuts

Sift flour, baking powder, soda, salt, and sugar into large bowl; set aside. Mix beaten egg with orange juice, rind, butter, and hot water. Fold flour mixture into egg mixture until blended. Do not beat! Gently fold in cranberries and walnuts. Spoon into greased 9 x 5 x 3 in. pan or smaller pans of choice. Bake at 325F for 60-70 min. Test in center with wooden pick. Cool on rack for 15 min. before removing from pan.

Nut Bread

2 well-beaten eggs
2 c. brown sugar
2 c. sour milk
4 c. flour
1/2 t. salt

2 t. soda
1 t. baking powder
1 c. chopped nuts
1/2 c. shortening

Beat shortening and sugar; add eggs. Add flour sifted with salt, soda, and baking powder. Stir in nuts. Bake 1 hr. at 350F. Will make three loaves in 5-1/2 x 10-1/2 in. pans. Texture and flavor improve after 12 hr.

Betty's Nut Bread   Betty Burum

3 c. flour
1/2 t. soda
3/4 c. sugar
2 scant t. baking powder

1 level t. soda
1 c. buttermilk
1 T. melted shortening
1 c. chopped nuts

Sift flour, 1/2 t. soda, sugar, and baking powder. Dissolve 1 t. soda in buttermilk, add shortening; stir in flour mixture. Add nuts. Bake 1 hr.
at 350F in a greased 9 x 5 in. loaf pan.

Brazil Nut Apricot Loaf   Lucile O'Neill

1/2 c. dried apricots
1/2 c. water
1 egg
1 c. sugar
2 T. melted butter
2 c. flour
3 t. baking powder

1/4 t. soda
1/2 t. salt
1/2 c. orange juice
1/4 c. sour milk
Grated rind of orange
1 c. chopped Brazil nuts

Soak apricots in water 30 min. Drain and grind. Beat egg with sugar. Stir in melted butter. Sift flour, baking powder, soda, and salt. Add alternately with orange juice, sour milk, and grated orange rind. Add Brazil nuts and ground apricots, and mix well. Pour into greased 5 x 9 bread loaf pan and bake 1 hr. at 350F. Let cool in pan 7-8 min.; then turn out on rack.

This is great sliced thin and spread with cream cheese. It is better after freezing or being refrigerated overnight. Our family enjoys this festive bread for Thanksgiving and Christmas.

♣ *To make shelling brazil nuts easier, pour boiling water over the whole nut—and let stand for about 10 min. Shelling nuts saves money and allows older children to help prepare holiday treats.*

Date Nut Bread   Mrs. Wilbert Walter

1/2 lb. pitted dates	1 c. chopped walnuts
1-1/2 c. boiling water	2-3/4 c. flour
1 c. brown sugar	2 t. soda
3 T. shortening	1/2 t. baking powder
1 egg	1/8 t. salt
1 t. vanilla	

Cut up dates. Pour boiling water over dates and let mixture cool. Cream brown sugar and shortening. Add egg, vanilla, and walnuts; beat well. Add date mixture; mix well. Sift together flour, soda, baking powder, and salt. Add to batter in two parts, mixing gently. Pour into greased 5 x 9 x 3 in. bread pan and bake 50 min. at 350F. If the bread is getting too brown, cover with foil. For a darker loaf, substitute coffee for the water.

Date Nut Whole Wheat Bread

1 c. buttermilk	1 t. baking powder
1/4 c. honey or molasses	1 t. salt
1 egg	1 c. coarsely ground nuts
1/4 c. melted fat	1/2 c. coarsely ground dates
1-1/2 c. whole wheat flour	or raisins
3/4 t. baking soda	

Mix by the muffin method just enough to dampen the dry ingredients. Bake in buttered bread pan 1 hr — for the first 15 min. in a hot oven (400F - 450F), remainder of time in a moderate oven (350F). Cool on rack 10 min.

Best Gingerbread

1/2 c. shortening	1 t. ginger
1/2 c. sugar	1/2 t. cloves
1 egg	1 t. cinnamon
1 c. light molasses	1/4 t. salt
2-1/2 c. flour	1 c. boiling water
1-1/2 t. soda	

Cream shortening, sugar, and egg. Add and mix in molasses. Sift together flour, soda, spices, and salt. Add to creamed mixture and mix. Add boiling water and stir in. Beat well. Bake in 9 x 12 in. pan at 350F about 40 min. Serve with whipped cream or lemon sauce, or eat plain.

Laura's Gingerbread   Laura Ingalls Wilder

1 c. brown sugar	1 t. cinnamon
1/2 c. shortening	1 t. allspice
1 c. molasses	1 t. nutmeg
2 t. baking soda	1 t. cloves
1 c. boiling water	1/2 t. salt
3 c. flour	2 eggs
1 t. ginger	Raisins or candied fruit (optional)

Blend brown sugar with shortening (Laura used lard). Add molasses and mix well. Dissolve baking soda in boiling water and add to mixture (make sure cup is full of water after foam is run off into cake mixture). Mix all well. Add spices and salt to flour and sift into cake mixture; mix well. Lastly, beat and add eggs. Mixture will be quite thin. Pour into greased, floured 9 x 13 in. pan. Bake in moderate (350F) oven for 30-40 min. Laura suggested that raisins and or candied fruit could be added and that chocolate frosting adds to the goodness.

"Mother's Gingerbread"   Mrs. A. E. Thompson

1/2 c. butter and lard mixed	1 t ginger
1/2 c. brown sugar	1 t. soda
1/2 c. sorghum or light molasses	1/2 c. boiling water
1 egg, well beaten	1-1/2 c. flour

Dissolve soda in boiling water. Cream shortening and brown sugar. Add sorghum or molasses and egg; beat well. Add sifted ginger and flour and water; mix well. Bake in 8-in. square pan at 350F for 25-30 min.

Hot Sauce for Gingerbread

1 c. brown sugar	2 T. grated orange rind
1/2 c. water	1 t. vanilla
1 T. butter	

Combine ingredients and cook until the consistency of Karo syrup, about 12 min. Serve on gingerbread, plain cake, or applesauce or raisin cake.

Irish Soda Bread

3 c. flour
1/2 c. sugar
1 t. baking soda
1/2 t. baking powder

Pinch of salt
1 c. raisins
1-3/4 c. buttermilk

Thoroughly mix all ingredients except buttermilk. Then make a well, pour buttermilk into it, and mix. Pour into a greased and floured 5 x 9 in. bread pan. Bake 45 min. at 350F. When done, let stand in pan 5 min., turn out onto cooling rack. Brush top with butter.

Orange-Date Loaf

Juice of one large orange
Grated rind of orange
Hot water
1 t. soda
1 c. chopped dates
1 egg, beaten

2 T. shortening
1 c. sugar
1 t. vanilla
2 c. flour
1 t. baking powder
1/4 t. salt

Grate orange rind. Squeeze orange, and add hot water to juice to make 1 cup; add soda. Pour hot liquid over dates and orange rind. Add egg, shortening, sugar, and vanilla. Beat well. Sift flour, baking powder, and salt; blend into date mixture. Do not overbeat. Bake in 5 x 9 x 3 in. greased loaf pan about 1 hr. Let cool 5-10 min. in pan, and turn onto cake rack to finish cooling.

Pecan Breakfast Loaf

2 cans Pillsbury crescent
   dinner rolls
2 T. butter, softened
1/2 c. sugar
1-2 t. cinnamon

1-1/4 c. powdered sugar
1 T. soft butter
1 t. vanilla
1/4 c. chopped pecans
1/4 c. pecan halves

Unroll crescent dough and separate into 16 triangles. Spread each with softened butter. Combine 1/2 c. sugar, cinnamon, and chopped pecans and sprinkle over triangles. Roll up each triangle, starting at wide end. Place rolls, point side down, in greased 9 x 5 in. loaf bread pan, forming two layers of 8 rolls each. Bake at 375F for 35-40 min. or until center is done.

Remove from pan at once, place right side up, and top with frosting (cream together 1 c. powdered sugar, 1 T. butter, and 1/2 t. vanilla) and whole pecans.

Kim's Pumpkin Bread   Kim Rudisel

4 c. sugar
6 eggs
1 c. Crisco
1 c. water
1 large can pumpkin (or
  3 small cans)
4-1/2 c. flour

3/4 t. baking powder
3 t. baking soda
2-1/4 t. salt
2 t. cinnamon
1 t. ground cloves
32 oz. chopped English walnuts

Cream shortening and sugar; beat in eggs. Add pumpkin, water, and spices; mix well. Add flour 1 cup at a time. Add nuts. Pour into three greased and floured bread loaf pans. Bake 1 hr. at 350F.

This is a large recipe that may also be baked in 5 or 6 small loaf pans. Kim wraps the cooled loaves in foil to give as gifts or to freeze. This will win you compliments!

Pumpkin Bread

3-1/3 c. flour
2 t. soda
1 t. salt
3 t. cinnamon
3 t. nutmeg
1/2 t. ginger

3 c. sugar
1 c. salad oil
4 eggs
2/3 c. water
2 c. canned pumpkin

Sift together dry ingredients, including sugar, into bowl. Add remaining ingredients and mix until smooth. Pour batter into three greased 9 x 5 x 3 in. loaf pans. Bake at 350F for 1 hr. Cool in pans 10 min., then turn onto cooling rack. When cool, you may wrap in foil and freeze. Nuts may be added if desired.

Zucchini Bread

3 eggs
1 c. oil
2 c. sugar
2 c. raw grated zucchini squash
3 t. vanilla

3 c. flour
1 t. salt
1/2 t. soda
3 t. cinnamon
1/4 t. baking powder

Combine all ingredients in order listed. Pour into two well-greased 9 x 5 x 3 in. bread pans. Bake at 325F for 1 hr. Test with toothpick. Let stand in pan 5 min. before turning out on rack. This will make 5 or 6 small pans, 3 x 5 in. Freezes well.

Raisin Pecan Coffee Bread

1/2 c. milk	1/2 c. warm water
1/2 c. sugar	2 eggs
1/2 t. salt	3-3/4 c. flour
1/2 c. margarine	1 c. raisins
2 pkg dry yeast	1/2 c. chopped pecans
Confectioners' sugar frosting	

Place raisins in pan with 2 c. cold water. Cook until water boils 1 min. Drain, chop.

Scald milk, stir in sugar, salt, and margarine. Cool to lukewarm. Dissolve yeast in warm water. Add lukewarm milk mixture, eggs, and 2-1/4 c. flour. Beat smooth. Take 1 c. batter, add raisins and pecans. Beat 1-1/2 c. flour into rest of batter. Let both mixtures rise about 1 hr.

Roll larger portion to 10 x 16 in. oblong. Spread with fruit-nut batter. Roll to 16 in. Place in greased tube pan. Let rise until double. Bake at 350F for 35 min. Cool. Frost.

Blueberry Coffee Cake

2 c. enriched flour	2 eggs, beaten
1 c. sugar	1 c. milk
3 t. baking powder	1-1/2 c. blueberries
1/4 t. salt	1-1/3 c. coconut
1/2 c. shortening	

Mix and sift flour, sugar, baking powder, and salt. Cut in shortening with two knives or pastry blender. Combine eggs and milk; stir into dry ingredients. Fold in blueberries. Divide batter between two greased 9-in. cake pans. Sprinkle coconut over tops. Bake at 375F for 25 min.

Marie's Heath Brickle Coffee Cake   Marie Harbour Fisher

1/4 lb. butter	1 t. soda
2 c. flour	1 egg
1 c. brown sugar	1 t. vanilla
1/2 c. white sugar	1 c. Heath brickle chips
1 c. buttermilk	1/4 c. pecans or almonds

Blend flour, butter, and sugars. Take out 1/2 c. of the mixture. To the rest, add buttermilk, soda, egg, vanilla, and 1/2 c. Heath brickle chips. Blend well. Pour into a greased and floured 14 x 10 x 2 in. pan. For topping, mix 1/2 c. chips, nuts, and 1/2 c. mixture of flour, butter, and sugars. Sprinkle over the top of the batter and bake in 350F oven for 50 min.

Marie has been my dear friend and sister-in-law for nearly 62 years. The youngest of her family, she celebrated her ninety-second birthday in March 2002 in New Sharon, Iowa.

My Quick Streusel Coffee Cake

1-1/2 c. flour	1 t. vanilla
3 t. baking powder	1/2 c. brown sugar
1/2 t. salt	2 T. flour
1/4 c. shortening	2 t. soft butter
3/4 c. sugar	2 t. cinnamon
1 egg	1/2 c. nut meats, chopped
1/2 c. milk	

Sift flour, baking powder, and salt. Cream shortening and sugar. Blend in egg, milk, and vanilla. Add sifted dry ingredients. Stir only enough to blend. Pour half of batter into greased 6 x 10 in. pan. Sprinkle half of streusel mixture over batter, add remainder of batter and streusel. Bake 30 min. at 375F.

Streusel Mixture: Cut brown sugar, 2 T. flour, butter, and cinnamon with pastry blender; stir in nut meats.

Aunt Luella's Filled Coffee Cake   Mrs. Jens Petersen

1-1/2 c. brown sugar	3 c. sifted flour
2 t. cinnamon	3 t. baking powder
1 c. chopped walnuts	1/2 t. salt
1 c. sugar	1 c. milk
1 c. shortening	1 t. vanilla
2 eggs	1/2 c. melted butter

Mix brown sugar, cinnamon, and walnuts well for filling. Set aside. Cream sugar and shortening. Add eggs and beat. Add sifted flour, baking powder, and salt alternately with milk. Mix well. Spread half of batter into a 9 x 13 in. greased pan. Sprinkle with half the filling. Spread on remaining batter and top with rest of filling. Pour melted butter over top. Bake 20-30 min. at 375F.

Spicy Breakfast Puffs

1/3 c. soft shortening	1/2 t. salt
1/2 c. sugar	1/4 t. nutmeg
1 egg	1/2 c. milk
1-1/2 c. sifted flour	1/3 c. butter, melted
1-1/2 t. baking power	1 t. cinnamon

Mix shortening, sugar, and egg thoroughly. Sift flour, baking powder, salt, and nutmeg; add alternately with milk. Fill 12 greased muffin cups 2/3 full. Bake 20-25 min. at 350F until golden brown. Immediately roll muffins in melted butter, then in a bowl of mixed sugar and cinnamon. Serve hot.

Peanut Bubble Ring

1 loaf packaged frozen bread dough	1/2 c. chopped peanuts
	3/4 c. brown sugar
1 pkg (3 3/4 oz.) regular butterscotch pudding mix	1 t. cinnamon
	4 T. melted margarine or butter

Thaw bread dough in refrigerator overnight. Quarter loaf lengthwise. Cut each quarter into 8 cubes.

Combine dry pudding, brown sugar, peanuts, and cinnamon in a small bowl. Dip each dough cube in melted butter, then roll in the pudding mixture. Place in greased bundt (or tube) pan, making three layers. Drizzle with remaining butter; sprinkle with remaining dry mixture. Cover and let rise until doubled in bulk, about 1 hr. Bake at 350F for 25 min. Yield: 6-8 servings.

Blueberry Muffins

1 c. fresh or canned and drained blueberries	3 t. baking powder
	4 T. sugar
3 t. sugar	1/2 t. salt
1 t. flour	2 eggs, beaten
2 c. flour	4 T. butter, melted

Sprinkle blueberries with 3 t. sugar and 1 t. flour. In a large bowl, mix dry ingredients with eggs, milk, and butter. Beat about 25 strokes or until flour disappears. Fold in berries. Fill 12 greased muffin tins about 2/3 full. Bake 30 min. at 375F. Yield: 12 large or 18 small muffins.

Kansas Blueberry Muffins

2/3 c. shortening	1/2 t. salt
1 c. sugar	1 c. milk
3 eggs	2 c. fresh or frozen
3 c. flour	Kansas blueberries
2-1/2 t. baking powder	

Cream sugar and shortening. Add eggs one at a time. Sift dry ingredients and add alternately with milk. Stir in blueberries. Fill greased muffin tins 2/3 full. Bake at 375F for 20-25 min. Yield: 2 dozen.

Big fresh berries picked at our favorite berry farm make these muffins pop with goodness.

Blueberry Streusel Muffins

1 c. sugar	1 c. milk
1/2 c. shortening	1 c. fresh blueberries
2 eggs, beaten	3/4 c. flour
2-3/4 c. flour	1/2 c. brown sugar
2 t. baking powder	2 T. soft butter
3/4 t. salt	1 t. cinnamon

Prepare streusel by cutting 3/4 c. flour, brown sugar, butter, and cinnamon with pastry blender. Set aside.

Cream sugar and shortening until light. Add beaten eggs. Sift dry ingredients and add alternately with milk. Do not overbeat. Fold in blueberries. Spoon batter into greased muffin pans, filling 2/3 full. Top each muffin with 1/2 t. streusel. Bake at 375F for 20-25 min. Let set in pans 5 min. before turning onto rack. Yield: 24 muffins.

Bran Muffins

1/2 c. bran	1 t. soda
1-1/2 c. graham flour	2 eggs
1/2 c. sugar	Pinch of salt
1 c. sour milk	1/2 c. cut dates or raisins
2 T. molasses	1/2 c. nuts

Mix following muffin method. Bake in well-greased muffin tins at 375F for 20-25 min.

Alexis's Bran Muffins   Alexis Harbour Crowley

1 c. bran (100% plain bran)   2-1/2 t. soda
1 c. boiling water   1/2 t. salt
1-3/4 c. sugar   1-3/4 c. buttermilk
1/2 c. butter or margarine   2 c. All Bran
2 eggs   1 c. raisins, blueberries, cut-up prunes,
2-1/2 c. flour   or coconut (optional)

Pour boiling water over 100% bran, which is available at a health food store; set aside to cool. In a large bowl, cream sugar and butter. Beat in eggs, one at a time. Sift together flour, soda, and salt. Add to creamed mixture alternately with buttermilk, stirring well after each addition. Fold in All Bran lightly. Last, stir in bran-water mixture. If desired, raisins or other fruit can be added at this point. Cover bowl and let batter sit in refrigerator overnight if possible. This batter keeps in the refrigerator for 6 weeks, allowing for muffins every weekend.

Spoon batter into well-greased muffin tin. Bake at 400F for 20 min. Yield: 2 to 2-1/2 dozen muffins.

This recipe was one of the first that Alexis learned to make at age seven or eight (with help handling the stove and oven). Making muffins for breakfast or brunch on Sunday is a great way for the family to start a special day together.

Bran Flakes Muffins

2 eggs   1-1/2 c. sifted flour
1/2 c. sugar   1 t. salt
1/4 c. molasses   1-1/2 t. baking soda
1-1/2 c. sour milk or buttermilk   2-1/2 c. bran cereal (flakes)
2-1/2 T. melted shortening   1/2 c. chopped raisins

Beat eggs; add sugar, molasses, sour milk, and shortening. Sift flour with salt and baking soda. Add bran, raisins, and flour to the liquid mixture, mixing only enough to moisten. Fill greased muffin pans 2/3 full. Bake in hot oven (400F) for 20-25 min. Yield: 18 muffins.

Cranberry Muffins

1/4 c. shortening   1/2 t. salt
1/4 c. sugar   1 c. milk
1 egg, beaten   1 c. finely chopped raw cranberries
2 c. sifted flour   1 t. grated orange rind
3 t. baking powder

Cream shortening, sugar, and egg. Add sifted dry ingredients alternately with milk, with just enough strokes of the spoon to mix. Fold in cranberries and orange rind. Fill greased muffin tins 2/3 full. Bake at 400F for 25 min. or until light brown. Yield: 12 muffins.

♣ *Buy fresh cranberries in season when they are plentiful. Put the bags directly into the freezer. When ready to use, remove amount needed and close/tie the bag. Wash berries before using. I watch for specials and put 10-20 bags of cranberries into the freezer each fall.*

Early Riser Muffins

1 1/2 c. flour	1 large egg
1/4 c. sugar	1/2 c. milk
2 t. baking powder	3 T. vegetable oil (canola preferred)
1/2 t. salt	

In the evening, sift together flour, sugar, baking powder, and salt into a mixing bowl. Lightly grease 12 muffin cups. Set aside.

Rise and shine, early bird! Stir egg, milk, and oil together in a mixing cup. Make a well in dry ingredients, pour in liquids, and stir only to moisten. Spoon batter into muffin cups, to 2/3 full. Bake in 400F oven 18-20 min. Turn out of pans at once. Yield: 12 muffins.

Minute Muffins

2 c. flour	1 c. buttermilk
1 T. baking powder	1/4 c. mayonnaise
1 t. salt	

In large mixing bowl, combine all ingredients; blend until smooth. Fill greased muffin cups 2/3 full. Bake at 375F for 18-20 min. or until light golden brown. Yield: 12 muffins

You may vary the recipe by adding 1/2 c. chopped dates.

Morning Glory Muffins

1/2 c. raisins, plumped	2 c. flour
1 c. sugar	2 t. soda
2 t. cinnamon	1/2 t. salt
2 c. grated carrots	1 large tart apple, grated
1/2 c. sliced almonds	1/2 shredded coconut
3 eggs	2/3 c. oil
2 t. vanilla	

Combine dry ingredients. Add raisins, carrots, apple, almonds, and coconut.
Combine eggs, oil, and vanilla. Add to dry mixture. Pour into greased muffin cups.
Bake 20-25 min. at 350F. Cool 5 min., remove from pan.

Aunt Amy's Surprise Muffins   Amy Ruth Thrall

2 c. flour	1 c. milk
3 t. baking powder	2 eggs
1 T. sugar	2 T. shortening, melted
1/2 t. salt	Fruit jam, prunes, or dates

Sift flour, baking powder, sugar, and salt. Add milk, well-beaten eggs, and melted
shortening; mix well. Put a tablespoonful of batter into twelve greased muffin tins.
Drop pieces of prune or date or a teaspoonful of fruit jam in center of each; top
with more batter. Bake in 400F oven for 20 min. Yield: 12 muffins.

Baking Powder Biscuits

2 c. flour	1/4 t. salt
3 t. baking powder	1/2 c. shortening
2 t. sugar	2/3 c. milk
1/2 t. cream of tartar	

Sift together dry ingredients. Cut in shortening. Add milk all at once. Stir just until
dough clings together. Knead 10-20 strokes on floured surface. Pat to 1/2-in.
thickness. Cut with 2 1/2-in. round cutter. Bake on ungreased baking sheet 10-12
min. at 450F. Yield: 10-12 biscuits.

Aunt Millie's Corn Bread   Mrs. R. W. Manning

1-1/4 c. flour	1/2 t. salt
1 c. yellow cornmeal	1 c. milk
4 T. sugar	1 egg, beaten
2 T. baking powder	2 T. butter, melted

Mix together dry ingredients. Combine milk, egg, and butter. Add liquid mixture slowly to dry, then beat hard until batter is smooth. Bake in 9-in. square greased tin about 20 min. at 375F. Yield: 9 squares.

Southern Spoon Bread

1 c. yellow cornmeal	2 eggs, well beaten
2 c. water	1/4 t. salt
1 c. milk	2 T. butter

Bring water and salt to a boil. Add cornmeal very slowly, stirring continually. Cook until thick. Remove from heat, add milk. Add butter and eggs, stir smooth. Pour into a buttered casserole. Bake 25 min. in hot oven (425F). Cool slightly and serve. Yield: 6-8 servings.

Dumplings

1-1/2 c. all-purpose flour	3 T. vegetable oil or shortening
2 t. baking powder	1/4 c. milk
3/4 t. salt	

Stir together flour, baking powder, and salt in mixing bowl. Cut in oil or shortening with a pastry blender or two knives until mixture resembles coarse crumbs. Stir in milk. Drop mixture by spoonfuls onto hot meat or vegetables in a boiling stew or soup. (Do not drop directly into liquid.) Cook, uncovered, 10 min. Cover and cook 10 min. longer or until dumplings are fluffy. Yield: about 6 servings.

Tama Fried Bread

1 pkg dry yeast	3-1/2 c. flour (*or* 2-1/2 c. flour
1 c. warm water	and 1 c. cornmeal)
1 T. olive or vegetable oil	1 t. salt

Soften yeast in water. Beat in 1-1/2 c. flour. Mix in olive oil and salt. Blend in remaining flour. Knead 10-12 min. Dough will be firm. Place in lightly oiled bowl, turn over. Cover and let rise in a warm place until more than doubled (2 hr.).

Punch down. Take pieces about 1-1/2 in. in diameter and stretch to about 5 in. diameter. Deep fry. (Slow frying will make them crisp. Fast frying will make them softer.) Remove from fat and drain on paper towels or brown paper. Serve hot.

The Mesquakies have lived near Tama, Iowa, for nearly a hundred years. Their annual tribal powwow features traditional games, contests, and dances. This recipe for fried bread is prepared for sale at this gathering.

Scones

2 c. all-purpose flour	1/2 c. shortening
1/2 c. sugar	3/4 c. dried currants or raisins
2 t. cream of tartar	2 eggs, slightly beaten
1 t. baking soda	1/4 c. milk
1/2 t. salt	

Sift dry ingredients together. Cut in shortening until mixture is fine crumbs. Add eggs with milk and mix with fork. Divide into two parts and turn one on floured board. Do not handle. Use rolling pin to flatten dough into an 8-in. circle about 1/2 in. thick. Cut into 8 triangles and put on greased and floured cookie sheet. Repeat with second part of dough.

Bake in preheated hot oven (400F) for 15 min. or until golden. Watch carefully to avoid overbrowning the bottom. Serve with a teaspoonful of strawberry or raspberry jam and a teaspoonful of dairy sour cream or clotted cream. Yield: 16 scones.

Festive Scones

2 c. self-rising flour	1/3 c. fresh orange juice
1/2 c. sugar	1/2 c. buttermilk
2 t. orange rind, grated	1/2 t. nutmeg
1/3 c. butter	2/3 c. pecans, finely chopped

Lightly grease bottoms of two 10-in. round cake pans. Set aside. Preheat oven to 425F.

Combine flour, sugar, and grated orange rind. With pastry blender, cut in butter until crumbly. Add orange juice, buttermilk, nutmeg, and pecans together; stir only until dry ingredients are moistened. Turn dough onto floured board, and knead about 5 strokes.

Divide dough into two parts. Form each into an 8-in. circle. Place each into the prepared cake pan and cut each into eight equal, pie-shaped pieces.

Bake at 425F for 14-15 min. or until light golden color. Cool in pan 5 min.; then remove with a narrow spatula to a rack to finish cooling. Yield: 16 scones.

Grandma's Plain Griddle Cakes   Christena Paulsen

1 c. flour
2 t. baking powder
1/4 t. salt
1 t. sugar

1 c. milk
1 egg, beaten
1 t. melted butter

Sift the dry ingredients. Combine beaten egg and melted butter, and stir into dry ingredients gradually. Then beat briskly to make a smooth batter. Drop or pour about 1/4 c. on hot oiled griddle to make pancakes, or 1 T. for dollar-size cakes. This recipe serves 4 with 12 cakes; double recipe for 8 people.

These were a special breakfast treat for grandchildren staying overnight, and the boys could eat the entire recipe. Serve with applesauce.

♣ *A preheated griddle will brown pancakes evenly. Test the heat by sprinkling a few drops of water on the surface. The drops will sputter and leap about if temperature is hot enough.*

Griddle Cakes and Variations

1-1/2 c. flour
3 t. baking powder
1/2 t. salt
3 T. sugar

1 egg
2 c. milk
2 T. butter, melted

Sift flour and measure. Sift dry ingredients with flour. Beat egg well. Add milk and melted butter. Combine wet and dry ingredients and beat enough to be smooth. Pour or spoon 1/4 c. batter for each cake on preheated oiled griddle. Cook on first side until tiny bubbles form. Turn and cook 2-3 min. Serve with maple or fruit syrup.

Corn Cakes: Add 1 c. cream style corn with wet ingredients.

Blueberry Cakes: Add 1 c. fresh blueberries to batter.

Swedish Pancakes   Hazel Maddison

2 eggs   1-1/2 t. sugar
1 c. milk   1/4 t. salt
1/2 c. flour, sifted

Combine and beat all ingredients. Let stand 2 hr. to thicken. Stir before baking on a hot greased griddle. Use 2 T. batter for each cake. Turn when bubbles form in batter. Serve hot with strawberry jam.

Blueberry Topping for Pancakes

2 pt. fresh blueberries, rinsed   2 c. water
1/2 c. sugar

Mash 1 c. blueberries. Then combine all the blueberries with sugar and water and bring to a boil, stirring as needed. Cook at low heat 5 min. Cool and store in refrigerator. To serve, warm 1 min. Serve with butter on hot pancakes.

Honey Butter

2 c. honey   1/4 t. vanilla
1 stick butter or margarine

Have ingredients at room temperature. Whip honey, soft butter, and vanilla together with mixer. Beat until quite stiff. Store in covered refrigerator container.

A great-tasting spread for hot biscuits, corn bread, or pancakes.

Norwegian Pancakes (Lefse)   Edna Aschom

6 medium potatoes, halved   1 T. sugar
1/4 c. butter   1/8 t. pepper
1/4 c. milk   2-1/2 to 3 c. sifted flour
1-1/2 t. salt

Cook potatoes until tender. Drain. Mash potatoes, whip in butter and milk until potatoes are fluffy; add salt, sugar, and pepper. Chill potatoes in refrigerator.

Remove potatoes; add half the flour and beat until smooth. Beat in enough remaining flour to make a soft dough.

Take part of the dough and roll about 1/8 in. thick. Cut into 6-in. rounds. Place *lefse* on heated ungreased griddle, cook until slightly browned. Turn and lightly brown other side. Then, turning often, continue cooking until *lefse* are light brown and dry. Remove to a clean dry towel. Cool *lefse* completely. Spread with softened butter. Sprinkle with sugar and roll loosely. Serve as a meal or snack. Yield: 2 dozen *lefse*.

Belgian Waffles

3 eggs
1-1/2 c. milk
1/2 c. butter or margarine,
   melted
1 T. vanilla

2 c. flour
1/2 t. salt
1 T. baking powder
2 t. sugar

Beat eggs in bowl until thick. Add milk, butter, and vanilla and beat for 2 min. Combine dry ingredients and sift them into the egg mixture; beat well. Batter should be thick but pourable; add milk if necessary. Oil Belgian waffle iron, heat according to indicator, and pour 3/4 c. onto the hot iron. Serve with topping of slices of fresh fruit or berries, or sprinkle lightly with cinnamon sugar and a little butter. Yield: 8 waffles.

♣   *A Belgian waffle iron makes attractive waffles, but if you do not have one, use the regular iron, in which waffles will cook quicker.*

Jean's Waffles   Jean Petersen

2 c. flour
4 t. baking powder
1/2 t. salt
2 egg yolks

1-3/4 c. milk
4 T. melted shortening or oil
2 egg whites, stiffly beaten

Mix egg yolks and milk. Add to dry ingredients with melted shortening. Mix well. Add stiffly beaten egg whites and fold in lightly. Bake in preheated waffle iron. Very good with maple syrup and butter or with fruit-flavored syrups.

Wesson Waffles

2 c. sifted cake flour
3 t. baking powder
1 t. salt
1 T. sugar

2 egg yolks
1-1/4 c. milk
1/2 c. Wesson oil
2 egg whites, stiffly beaten

42

Mix milk into well-beaten egg yolks. Stir in oil. Sift together dry ingredients and combine with first mixture. Beat until smooth. Fold in beaten egg whites. Bake on hot waffle iron. Serve hot with maple syrup.

The cake flour is the secret!

Herb Bread

Whole French or Italian loaf	1/2 t. oregano
1/2 c. butter	1/2 t. dill seed
1 t. parsley flakes	Garlic salt

Use bread knife to cut thick slices. Mix other ingredients, adding garlic salt to taste. Spread over one side of each slice. Top loaf with butter; sprinkle with Parmesan cheese. Wrap in aluminum foil leaving top open. Bake in 375F oven for 12 to 15 min. or until heated through. Serve with grilled steak, lasagna, or spaghetti. Serves 8-10.

Bread-Making Suggestions

Making bread is a creative process with a satisfying product. Enjoy!

All ingredients should be at room temperature as you start bread making. Measure accurately with standard measuring spoons and cups. If a recipe states "sifted flour," sift, then measure (you may sift into the cup), and level off cup with a straight edge (such as a narrow spatula). If a recipe states "1 c. flour, sifted," measure first, then sift the flour.

1. Check the expiration date on packages of yeast and discard any past the "use by" date. When you buy packages, check the date and avoid those that aren't fresh.

2. Temperature: Most recipes call for dissolving the dry yeast and a small amount of sugar in a small amount of warm, not hot, water. Pour the dry yeast (and sugar) into the cup holding the warm water and stir gently. Fresh "active" yeast will foam and form a bubbly mixture in 3-5 min. Stale yeast is slow to do this and probably will not allow dough to rise fully. Better to check the date and discard old or stale yeast than to have a ruined batch of half-risen bread.

"Warm" water is about 98F. Very hot water, too hot to one's hand, kills the yeast action. (Hot air temperature while dough is rising can also kill yeast action; see sections 8(e), 8(h), and 8(j) below).

3. Bread requires salt for good flavor. Follow the recipe for the amount of salt.

4. If directions require "scalding" milk, heat milk over low heat until a skin forms. Remove from heat and cool. Discard skin. For accurate measure, scald a slightly larger amount, cool, then measure the amount needed in a glass measuring cup.

5. The above suggestions apply to all bread making.

6. You do not need to sift any whole-wheat, rye, or other coarser flours, or cornmeal, grits, etc. unless directed to do so. Measure them with cups of varying sizes — from 1/4 cup to 1 quart (4 c.) rather than estimate.

7. To measure with spoons accurately, dip the measuring spoon for a rounded amount; then use the straight edge of a knife or small spatula drawn across the top of the spoon to make the level teaspoonful. A tablespoonful equals 3 level teaspoonfuls.

8. The usual steps for making bread are:

   (a) Mix yeast and warm liquid to foaming stage.

   (b) Combine yeast, other required liquid, and part or all the flour (plus salt, sugar, soft fat, as directed).

   (c) Stir around to "combine."

   (d) "Beat" with a heavy wooden or metal spoon in an under-and-over vigorous motion to thoroughly "blend" so all ingredients make a smooth "batter."

   (e) Some recipes stop to let batter rise at this point. "Cover batter/dough" with a clean thin dishtowel. Let stand in warm (80-85F) place free from drafts.

   (f) Some recipes require adding more flour at this point. Add the required amount one cup at a time, "beating" one or two minutes to "blend." Continue until dough does not absorb more flour. At this point, put dough onto a floured surface — large board, marble, tile or other hard surface — and "knead" for 8-10 min.

(g) *Kneading:* Use the back part (heel) of your palms, and press down, giving dough a quarter turn. Repeat this rhythmically, pushing and turning. If dough seems sticky, sprinkle a tablespoonful of flour over the surface. Try not to over-flour the surface, but use enough to keep dough from sticking. Well-kneaded dough will "blister," developing very thin surface layers.

(h) *Rising:* When the dough is smooth and elastic, grease the bread bowl well, put dough in and pressing down, turn and rotate dough to grease top and sides. Cover with towel, let rise in a warm (80-85F) place until dough is double in bulk, about 50-60 min.

(i) "Punch dough down" by turning it onto board, kneading 3-5 strokes, and dividing into loaves. Cover and let rest 10-15 min. Set oven at required temperature.

(j) Grease pans well. "Shape" dough into loaves. Place in greased pans. Cover and let rise until dough rises to top of bread pan.

(k) Bake in preheated oven for suggested time. Put one pan in center. For two or more, arrange pans with two inches or more between. Many ovens have "hot spots" at the rear corners. Pull the pans nearer front and center.

(l) Bread will have risen several inches and be light or medium brown when done; if tapped, it should sound hollow. If it browns too fast, cover lightly with foil.

(m) Put pans on cooling racks for 10 min. With pastry brush or paper towel, brush soft butter or margarine thinly on top of crusts. Turn pans over to release loaves. Rest loaves on bottom or side on racks and cool completely.

(n) When cooled, wrap bread in foil to freeze or place in plastic bag and store in cool place.

Cookies

Bars ♣ *Cookies* ♣
Christmas and Other Special
Cookies ♣ *Doughnuts* ♣
Unbaked Cookies

<u>Preparing for School</u>

Newcomers to the Midwest soon learned that a farmer needed to be a jack of all trades. With his team of horses pulling the plow, he walked behind guiding the plow and keeping it steady to turn a straight furrow across the field. He lifted and set the plowshare again after making the turn at the end. When the corn had sprouted rows of tender green, the farmer hitched his team to a cultivator that loosened the soil between rows and uprooted weeds that would compete with the new corn. Each step in farming required different skills.

The ability to perform the multiple tasks of farming made the hard-working farmer a valuable member of his community. Among the jobs citizens were elected to perform, being director of a rural school district required common sense and the ability to work with others. After being elected director and accepting because he and his wife had two children who would be pupils in the school, the new director had a talk with his wife. They knew that last term's teacher, a young man who rode horseback to and from his home each day, would return for the fall term. The immediate need was to clean the schoolhouse, order supplies, put in loads of fuel, and tackle the tall weeds that had sprung up over the schoolyard. They agreed to work at the school the next day. They would make a list of the supplies to buy at the drugstore in the county seat, which was authorized to sell the recommended supplies, as well as the new and used textbooks pupils were required to buy.

The next morning after finishing milking and other chores, the couple loaded cleaning supplies into the buggy. They didn't know if the school had usable brooms or cloths, so they took brooms, scrub brushes, pails, mops, homemade lye soap, cleaning rags and big covered pails full of hot water. There were containers of water to drink, a basket of lunch and coffee. The youngest child was spending the day with an aunt, but the older children promised to help. The new director tied a scythe to the buggy for the tall weeds.

When the supplies were unloaded, the director drove his team to the shade of trees nearby, tied their halters to a post, and went to inspect the coalhouse. It was a small, gabled building about 16 feet square, partitioned to provide space in the middle half for coal, chunks of split wood and corncobs for the big base-burner standing in the center of the schoolroom. On either side of the fuel space, partitions rising to the roof created small primitive outhouses, one for girls and, on the opposite side of the fuel room, the other for boys. With a good scrubbing, these would be ready.

Inside the schoolhouse, the farmer's wife had tied a big cloth over the broom and swept the walls. Her husband took the broom and volunteered to brush the ceiling, so she dusted out the desks and began scrubbing the tops. There were dozens of initials carved into the desktops. The largest desks would be occupied by the older teenagers. Some of the boys did not attend school regularly. They worked at home during corn-picking season and again when fieldwork started in March, and their spasmodic attendance and lack of interest contributed to their failure to meet scholastic standards. When they turned 16, they could choose to drop out but a few continued to attend until they were 18 or 20. Beginners aged five and six would occupy the row of small desks attached to a long, movable double runner.

After scrubbing all the desktops with lye soap, the woman wiped them with clear hot water and then rinsed again until they gleamed. She decided to wait a few days and then apply a coat of varnish that would make them easier to keep clean. Then she turned to the windows, four high, narrow ones on each of the two long walls. She took down thin, dirty curtains and swept dead flies into a dustpan. She noticed a five-gallon ironstone crockery jar with a spigot near the bottom. The jar was empty and clean; she would scrub it to fill with drinking water when school started.

When she finished polishing the windows, she saw the sun high overhead and called her family to lunch. The children munched on bread filled with cold sliced meat or soft cheese and nibbled at hard-boiled eggs sprinkled with salt and parsley. They happily ate fresh raisin cookies with applesauce and mugs of milk. Their father reminded them that they would be carrying their lunch to school, and their mother assured them she had two tin pails they could use.

The couple's last job was cleaning and scrubbing the floor. It had been laid at least 50 years earlier and bore signs of scraping by hob-nailed work shoes and the scuffing of restless feet. The director sprinkled cleaning compound that absorbed the dust, and he swept vigorously. His wife brought hot, soapy water, and they scrubbed until the wood looked clean, then rinsed. As they surveyed their work, they listed tasks to complete on the next trip. She would wash and hang the curtains; they would use stove blacking on the big base-burner and polish the shiny, curlicued top, clean and fill the water cooler, varnish the desks, bring the supplies bought in the county seat, and put fuel into the coal shed.

There was so much left to do! Being director was an unpaid job, but they agreed there was lots of satisfaction. They packed cleaning supplies, lunch basket and coffeepot into the buggy, and with their sleepy children between them, headed home to do the farm chores.

His first tasks as school director accomplished, the farmer smiled appreciatively at his wife. Soon their children would walk to this rural school, and teacher and pupils would start the fall term. The new director looked back at the school, rather small on the newly scythed playground. He thought the school needed a bell, a good bell to call the children to school to learn. He would look into getting the school a bell.

Recipes

Apricot Bars
Aunt Elta Petersen

1 c. brown sugar
1-1/2 c. sifted flour
1-1/2 c. quick oatmeal
1 t. baking powder

3/4 c. soft butter
1 #2 can apricots (soft)
1 c. sugar

Sift flour and baking powder; stir in brown sugar and oatmeal; and cut in soft butter as for piecrust. Line a 7 x 10 in. buttered pan on bottom and sides with 2/3 of the mixture. Spread with cooled apricot filling. Sprinkle remainder of crumb mixture on top of filling. Bake in very slow oven (275-300F) about 35 min. Cool and cut into bars about 2 x 4 in.

Filling: Drain apricots (mushy type is best). Beat in 1 c. sugar; whip together. Cook over medium heat, stirring occasionally, until mixture comes to boil. Cool.

Variation: Add 1 c. chopped dates to apricots before cooking.

Delicious as dessert with whipped cream — this is similar to a torte.

Bohemian Cherry Bars

1 c. margarine
1 3/4 c. sugar
4 eggs
3 c. flour
1-1/2 t. baking powder
1 t. vanilla

1/2 t. salt
1 large can Wilderness cherry
  pie filling
1 c. sifted powdered sugar
2 T. hot milk
1 t. almond flavoring

Cream margarine and sugar well. Add eggs one at a time, beating well after each egg. Add vanilla; beat well. Sift flour, baking powder, and salt; add to creamed mixture and blend. Spread in greased jelly roll pan, about 11 x 17 in., reserving 1-1/2 c. batter.

Spread cherry pie filling evenly over batter. Drop the remaining batter by tea-spoonfuls over cherries. Smooth to cover. Bake at 350F about 40 min. Cool 5 min. Drizzle with glaze of powdered sugar, hot milk, and almond flavoring. Cut into bars 3 x 2 in. Yield: 32 bars.

Best Brownies

4 sq. Baker's	1 t. vanilla
unsweetened chocolate	1 c. chopped nuts
1 c. butter or oleo	1 c. sifted flour
2 c. sugar	1/4 t. salt
3 eggs, beaten	

Melt butter and chocolate in top of double boiler. Take off heat, and add sugar, eggs, and vanilla, mixing well. Mix in nuts. Combine salt and flour. Add gradually to chocolate mixture; blend well. Pour into a greased and floured 9-in. square pan. Bake at 350F for 25 min. Do not overbake. Cool completely. Frost if desired. Yield: 24 bars.

Blond Brownies

1/3 c. melted butter	1/2 t. salt
1 c. brown sugar	1 6-oz. pkg chocolate chips
1 egg	1/2 c. nuts, chopped
1 c. flour	1/2 t. vanilla
1/2 t. baking powder	

Cream butter and sugar; add egg and beat. Sift flour, baking powder, and salt. Add egg mixture and blend. Mix in chocolate chips, nuts, and vanilla. Pour into greased 9 x 9 in. pan. Bake at 350F for 25 min. Do not overbake. Cut into bars 3 x 1-1/2 in. Yield: 18 bars.

Fudge Brownies

2 sq. unsweetened chocolate	1/2 c. flour
1/2 c. butter	1/4 t. salt
1 c. sugar	1 t. vanilla
2 eggs	1/2 c. chopped nuts

Grease and flour 13 x 9 in. pan. Melt chocolate and butter in double boiler. Add sugar and eggs; beat well. Sift flour with salt and stir into mixture. Add vanilla and nuts; beat well. Bake at 350F about 20-25 min.

Helen's Brownies
Helen Petersen

1/2 c. margarine or butter	1/2 t. baking powder
3-1/2 sq. baking chocolate	Dash of salt
2 c. sugar	2 t. vanilla
4 eggs	Nut meats (optional)
1 c. flour	

Melt butter and chocolate in top of double boiler; set aside to cool. Combine sugar and eggs. Beat well and add chocolate mixture and flour sifted with baking powder and salt. Add vanilla and beat well. Stir in nuts. Bake in well-greased jelly roll pan 11 x 15-1/2 in. at 325F for 35 min. Do not overbake.

Frosting: Using same pan as for chocolate mixture, combine 2 T. butter, 2 T. cocoa, and 2 T. milk. Heat and add powdered sugar while hot until frosting is right consistency for spreading over brownies.

Rocky Road Fudge Brownies

1 large pkg brownie mix	1/3 c. milk
1 c. chopped pecans	1/2 c. butter
3 c. miniature marshmallows	1 lb. pkg powdered sugar
2 oz. unsweetened chocolate	1/2 t. vanilla

Prepare brownie mix according to directions. Stir in pecans and spoon into greased 9 x 13 in. pan. Bake at 350F for 25 min. Remove from oven and sprinkle miniature marshmallows over hot brownies.

Frosting: Combine chocolate, milk, and butter in heavy saucepan. Cook over low heat until chocolate and butter melt, stirring often. Remove from heat and transfer to mixing bowl. Add sifted powdered sugar and vanilla; beat at low speed until smooth. If frosting is too stiff to spread, add milk 1 T. at a time, stirring until smooth. Spread over brownies. Cool on wire rack, and cut into bars 1-1/2 x 3 in. Yield: 18 brownies.

F.J.'s Brownies
Florence Jean Dearborn

2 c. sugar	1 c. flour
3/4 c. margarine	1/4 t. salt
4 eggs	1/2 c. cocoa
1 t. vanilla	

Cream butter and sugar; beat and add eggs, one at a time. Add vanilla. Sift dry ingredients. Mix with spoon until moistened. Pour into greased and floured 9 x 13 in. pan. Bake at 350F for 25-30 min.

Southern Brownies

1 stick butter	1/2 t. baking powder
1 c. sugar	Pinch of salt
4 T. cocoa	1/2 t. vanilla
2 eggs	1/2 c. chopped nuts
1 c. flour	

Melt butter in medium saucepan. Remove from heat. Add sugar and cocoa. Mix thoroughly. Add eggs and beat. Sift flour, baking powder, and salt; add to mixture and stir well. Add vanilla and nuts. Pour batter evenly into greased and floured 9 x 9 in. pan. Bake at 350F for 25-30 min. Cool. Cut while slightly warm.

May's Chocolate Tops   **May Marshall**

1 c. butter (or 1/2 c. oleo with 1/2 c. butter)	1 t. vanilla
	1 egg
Dash of salt	1 c. sifted flour
1/2 c. brown sugar, packed	1 c. oats
1/2 c. sugar	Chocolate chips

Cream butter and sugars. Beat in vanilla and egg. Add flour and oats; mix well. Spread in greased pan. Bake at 350F for 25 min. Turn oven off. Sprinkle chocolate chips over top and return to oven for a few minutes. Spread chocolate evenly over surface. Chill in refrigerator. Store in refrigerator. (I use a 6 x 10 in. pan.)

Orange Coconut Bars

1/2 c. soft butter	1 c. chopped walnuts
1 c. sifted flour	1/2 c. coconut
1-1/2 c. brown sugar	1-1/2 c. sifted powdered sugar
2 T. flour	2 T. melted butter
1/4 t. baking powder	2 T. frozen orange concentrate
1/2 t. salt	2 T. lemon juice
2 eggs	Orange food coloring

First layer: Cut 1/2 c. butter into 1 c. flour with pastry blender. Press firmly into 9 x 9 in. pan. Bake at 350F for 15 min.

Second layer: Slightly beat eggs. Add brown sugar, 2 T. flour, baking powder, salt, walnuts, and coconut. Mix well. Pour on baked crust. Bake at 350F for 25 min. Cool.

Orange Frosting: Combine powdered sugar with melted butter, orange concentrate, lemon juice, and a few drops of orange food coloring. Blend and spread over coconut layer. Cut into 3 x 1-1/2 in. bars. Store in tightly covered container. Yield: 18 bars.

Date Bars   Hazel Galvin

1/2 c. flour	1 c. chopped nuts
1/2 t. salt	40 dates, chopped
1/2 t. soda	1 c. water
1 c. brown sugar	2/3 c. sugar
1-1/2 c. rolled oats	1/2 t. vanilla
1 c. melted butter	

Sift 1/2 c. flour with salt and soda. Add brown sugar and rolled oats. Add melted butter and chopped nuts. Mix well. Put half crumb mixture in greased 9 x 9 in. pan. Put date filling on top, and pat remaining crumb mixture on date filling. Bake at 350F about 30 min. Cool and cut in squares.

Date Filling: Cook dates, water, and sugar together until thick. Remove from heat. Add vanilla. Cool partially before putting on crumb crust.

Makes a delicious dessert with whipped cream.

Date and Apricot Bars   Mildred M. Thompson

1/2 lb. (1 c.) dates	1 c. brown sugar
1 #2-1/2 can apricots	1 t. vanilla
1/2 c. brown sugar	2 c. flour
2 T. water	1 t. soda
3/4 c. melted butter	2 c. quick cooking oatmeal

Chop dates. Combine with 1/2 c. brown sugar, apricots, and water. Cook over medium heat, stirring continuously, until thickened (3 min.). Cool.

Blend melted butter, 1 c. brown sugar, and vanilla. Sift flour and soda; add to creamed mixture. Mix in oatmeal. Blend thoroughly. Press half of this mixture on bottom of a well-greased baking pan. Spread date-apricot mixture over it. Put rest of crumb mixture on top and bake at 350F for 30 min. Cool. Cut into bars or into 4 x 4 in. dessert squares. Top dessert with whipped cream.

Chewy Date Bars   Cora Long

2 c. sugar
1-1/2 c. sifted flour
2 t. baking powder
1/2 t. salt

2 c. chopped dates
1 c. chopped nuts
4 eggs
Powdered sugar

Sift together sugar, flour, baking powder, and salt. Stir in dates and nuts. Add well-beaten eggs and mix well. Spread on large greased 9 x 13 in. pan. Bake at 375F for 20 min. Cut while warm and roll in powdered sugar. Store in tight container.

This bar has a chewy texture that is different — really great!

Crispy Date Bars   Dorothy Jansen

1 c. flour
1/2 c. brown sugar, packed
1/2 c. margarine or butter
1 c. chopped dates
1/2 c. sugar
1/2 c. margarine or butter
1 egg, well beaten

2 c. Kellogg's Rice Krispies
1 c. chopped nuts (optional)
1 t. vanilla
2 c. powdered sugar
1/2 t. vanilla
2 to 3 t. milk
3 oz. cream cheese

Combine flour, brown sugar, and 1/2 c. butter. Press into 11 x 7 in. or 8 x 8 in. pan. Bake at 375F for 10-12 min.

Combine dates, sugar, and 1/2 c. butter in saucepan. Simmer 3 min. Combine with egg. Let bubble. Stir in Rice Krispies. Spread over baked crust. Cool and top with frosting.

Frosting: Sift powdered sugar. Stir in vanilla, milk, and cream cheese.

Dream Bars   Hattie Paulsen, Roberta Petersen

1/2 c. butter or margarine
1/2 t. salt
1/2 c. brown sugar
1 c. sifted flour
1 c. coconut
1 c. chopped walnuts

1 c. brown sugar
2 eggs, beaten
1 t. vanilla
2 T. flour
1/2 t. salt

Cut 1/2 c. butter into salt, brown sugar, and sifted flour. Pat into bottom of 9 x 13 in. pan. Bake at 350F for 15 min. Remove from oven and sprinkle with coconut

56

and chopped walnuts. Combine remaining ingredients and pour over above layers. Bake at 350F for 20 min. Do not overbake. Cut into bars.

A great tasting blend: coconut and butterscotch.

Seven Layer Bars   Aunt Elta Petersen

1 stick margarine
1 c. graham cracker crumbs
1 c. coconut
1 c. pecan pieces

1 6-oz. pkg butterscotch pieces
1 6-oz. pkg chocolate chips
1 can Eagle Brand milk

Melt margarine in a 9 x 13 in. pan. Then layer other ingredients in order: graham cracker crumbs, coconut, pecans, butterscotch, chocolate, and condensed milk. Bake in preheated 300F oven for 30 min. Cut in 2 x 2 in. squares when cool. Yield: 24 bars.

Lemon Love Notes   Corinne Tucker

1/2 c. butter
1 c. flour
1/2 c. powdered sugar
2 T. lemon juice
Grated rind of 1 lemon

2 eggs, beaten
1 c. sugar
2 T. flour
1/2 t. baking powder
1/2 t. salt

Mix butter, 1 c. flour, and powdered sugar. Pat into 9 x 9 in. pan and bake at 325F for 15-20 min. Cool.

Stir together in this order: lemon juice and grated rind, eggs, sugar, 2 T. flour sifted with baking powder and salt. Mix well and pour over first crust. Bake at 325-350F for 25 min. Cool.

Frost with mixture of 3/4 c. powdered sugar, 1 T. soft butter, 1/2 t. vanilla, and 1-1/2 t. milk, well blended.

A piquant tart-sweet combination — very attractive.

Salted Peanut Bars   Meta Hinkhouse

4 eggs
2 c. sugar
1 c. cold water
1-1/2 c. salted peanuts

1 t. baking powder
2 c. flour
1 t. vanilla

Beat eggs 5 min. with electric mixer. Add sugar slowly while beating. Stir in water and vanilla. Sift in flour and baking powder, stirring just until mixed — don't beat. Pour into greased and floured 9 x 15 in. pan. Sprinkle with the salted peanuts. Bake at 350F for about 18 to 20 min. Yield: 24 bars.

Pecan Pie Bars

2 c. flour	1 c. light corn syrup
1/2 c. sugar	1/2 c. butter or margarine
1/8 t. salt	4 eggs
3/4 c. butter or margarine	2-1/2 c. chopped pecans
1 c. brown sugar, packed	1 t. vanilla extract

Sift together flour, sugar, and salt; cut in 3/4 c. butter with pastry blender to get fine crumbs. Press into greased 9 x 13 in. pan. Bake at 350F for 17 to 20 min. until lightly browned.

Combine brown sugar, corn syrup, and 1/2 c. butter in saucepan. Bring to boil, stirring gently. Remove from heat. Lightly beat eggs; gradually stir 1/4 of hot mixture into eggs. Add this mixture to remaining hot mixture. Stir in pecans and vanilla. Pour filling over crust. Bake at 350F for 35 min. or until set. Cool completely on rack. Cut into bars. Yield: 16 large bars.

Pecan Tassies   Bernice Peterson

2 sticks margarine	1-1/2 c. light brown sugar
2 3-oz. pkg cream cheese	2 T. melted butter
2 c. sifted flour	1/4 t. salt
1 c. pecans, coarsely cut	1 t. vanilla
2 eggs	

Cut margarine and cream cheese into flour. Press into miniature muffin tins to make shells. Sprinkle half the pecans into the shells.

Beat eggs slightly; add sugar and blend. Add salt, melted butter, and vanilla; blend. Pour over nuts in shells. Sprinkle rest of nuts over top. Bake at 350F for 15 min., then at 250F for 10 min. Remove from pan and cool on cake rack.

My Prayer Bars

1/2 c. butter or margarine
4 T. cocoa
1/2 c. powdered sugar
1 egg
2 t. vanilla
1/2 c. walnuts
1 c. flake coconut
2 c. crushed graham crackers

1/4 c. butter
3 T. cream (or half and half)
2 t. dry vanilla pudding mix
 (not instant pudding)
3 c. sifted powdered sugar
1 t. vanilla
1 9-3/4-oz. chocolate bar

First layer: Melt 1/2 c. butter and cocoa in top of double boiler. Add
1/2 c. powdered sugar, slightly beaten egg, and 1 t. vanilla and stir well. Set aside.
Mix walnuts, coconut, and graham crackers. Add to first mixture and mix well.
Press into bottom of a 9 x 12 in. pan. Chill.

Second layer: Combine 1/4 c. butter, cream, pudding mix, and 1 t. vanilla in
saucepan. Cook 1 min., stirring constantly. Remove from heat and add 3 c.
powdered sugar. Blend well and spread over first layer.

Third layer: Melt chocolate bar over low heat. Spread over second layer. Chill
thoroughly. Bring to room temperature to cut into 2 x 1 in. bars. Store in refrigerator with waxed paper between layers of bars. Yield:
44 bars.

These are a nice addition to a dessert plate or to a gift of Christmas candy.

Pumpkin Bars   **Anne Harbour**

1 c. butter
1-1/2 c. sugar
4 eggs
1 15-oz. can pumpkin
2 c. flour
2 t. baking powder
1/2 c. chopped walnuts

1 t. soda
1/2 t. salt
2 t. cinnamon
1/2 t. ginger
1/2 t. cloves
1/2 t. nutmeg

Cream butter and sugar. Beat eggs and add to mixture. Sift flour, soda, salt, and
spices into mixture and beat well. Pour into greased and floured 12 x 18 in. pan.
Sprinkle with walnuts. Bake at 350F for 25 to 30 min. Cut into 1-1/2 x 3 in. bars.
Yield: 48 bars.

Variation: Omit walnuts and frost with 2 3-oz. pkg cream cheese beaten with 3/4
stick butter and 1 T. milk until soft. Add 1 t. vanilla. Sift in 4 c. powdered sugar
until consistency to spread.

These bars are delicious served with coffee for a large group, but the recipe can be halved for smaller groups. Pumpkin bars freeze well.

Frosted Raisin Squares
Anna M. Petersen

1-1/2 c. sugar	1/2 t. cloves
1-1/2 c. water	1 scant t. salt
1 c. raisins	3 c. flour
1/2 c. lard (or Crisco)	1 t. baking powder
2 t. cinnamon	1-1/2 t. soda

Combine sugar, water, raisins, lard, cinnamon, cloves, and salt in a saucepan and boil 5 min. Cool in large bowl. Sift flour with baking powder and soda into water mixture and stir well. Add more water if needed to make medium batter. Bake in greased 10 x 15 in. jelly roll pan at 350F for 20-30 min. Cool. Frost with powdered sugar frosting. Cut into bars or squares.

This makes a lot of moist, nutritious bars.

Ammonia Cookies — White
Aunt Laura Albers

1 c. shortening (1/2 c. butter,	2-1/2 c. flour
1/2 c. lard or Crisco)	1 t. baking ammonia
2 c. sugar	1 c. Angel Flake coconut

Baking ammonia can be purchased at a pharmacy. Cream shortening and sugar until well blended. Sift in flour and ammonia, and mix well. Mix in coconut. Drop tablespoonfuls onto greased cookie sheet and flatten. Bake at 325F for 20 min. Cool on rack.

This is a traditional German Christmas cookie. I remember Grandma serving white ammonia cookies on Sunday afternoons with milk or clear, strong coffee to drink. Crisp and good!

Ammonia Cookies — Yellow

1 c. butter	Pinch of salt
2 c. sugar	1 T. baking ammonia
3 egg yolks	3 c. flour
1/2 t. vanilla	

Cream butter and sugar. Beat in egg yolks and vanilla. Sift salt and ammonia with flour and blend with first mixture. Roll 1/4 in. thick, and cut with 2-in. cutter. Bake on greased cookie sheet in 300F oven until lightly browned. Yield: 6 dozen.

These yellow cookies are crisp and keep well. Store in tightly covered tins.

Sugar Cookies   Evelyn Henrichson

1-1/2 c. sugar	1 t. cream of tartar
1 c. shortening	2 c. flour
3 egg yolks	1 t. vanilla
1 t. soda	Dash of salt

Combine sugar and shortening; cream well. Beat in egg yolks and vanilla. Sift dry ingredients and blend with first mixture. Chill 1 hr. Shape into balls the size of a walnut. Press with sugared bottom of a glass. Bake on greased cookie sheet at 350F for 10-12 min.

♣ *To loosen cookies left on the pan too long, return to the oven about 2 min.; then use a spatula to remove them at once.*

My Crisp Sugar Cookies

1 c. butter	1/2 t. cream of tartar
1 c. vegetable oil	1 level t. soda
1 c. powdered sugar	2 eggs
1 c. sugar	3/4 c. chocolate chips or
1/2 t. salt	coconut (optional)
1 t. vanilla	1/2 c. chopped nuts (optional)
4 c. flour	

Combine butter and oil at medium speed of mixer. Add sugars, salt, and vanilla; continue beating until creamy. Add eggs one at a time, beating well. Add half the flour sifted with cream of tartar and soda. Beat on lower speed until smooth. Add rest of dry ingredients and mix by hand. For plain sugar cookies, cover dough with wrap and chill 2 hr. To vary, stir in chocolate chips or coconut and nuts by hand; then chill. Form tablespoonful of dough into a ball, roll in sugar, flatten with a fork. Bake on greased cookie sheet at 350F for 12 min. Yield: 6 dozen.

These keep well.

Aunt Luella's Sugar Cookies   Luella Petersen

1 c. sugar	1/4 t. salt
1/2 c. butter	1/2 t. cream of tartar
1/2 c. vegetable shortening	1 t. vanilla
1 egg	1/4 t. lemon extract
1 t. soda	2 c. sifted flour

Cream sugar and shortenings. Add slightly beaten egg, and blend vanilla and lemon extract. Sift flour, soda, salt, and cream of tartar; add half to creamed mixture and blend well. Add the rest of flour and mix in. Roll dough into small balls and place on lightly greased cookie sheet. Press each ball with fork to form a checkerboard pattern. Bake at 350F for 10-12 min. until slightly brown.

♣ *Combine brown and white sugars to produce a cookie with a moderately crisp texture. All white sugar produces a crisper cookie.*

Meta's Rolled Sugar Cookies   Meta Hinkhouse

1 c. sugar	2 eggs
1 c. margarine	3 c. flour
1 c. syrup (1/2 sorghum	1 t. soda
and 1/2 white corn syrup)	

Combine ingredients and chill 1 hr. Roll with extra flour — or roll in sugar to make thin and crisp. Cut in decorative shapes. Bake on greased cookie sheet at 400F about 8-10 min.

Meta used star and rooster shapes, among others. She may have rolled the dough with sugar or simply with great skill, but her sugar cookies were exceptionally thin and crisp, melting on the tongue.

Tea Cookies

1 c. butter	1/4 t. salt
1 c. sugar	1 t. baking powder
2 eggs	4 c. flour
1 T. water	1/2 t. nutmeg
1 t. vanilla	

Cream butter and sugar. Beat in eggs one at a time. Stir in water and vanilla. Sift flour, salt, baking powder, and nutmeg into creamed mixture, stirring well. Cover and chill 1 hr. Roll out dough to 1/4 in. thick. Use

2-in. cookie cutter or a glass. Place on ungreased cookie sheet and bake at 350F for 12-15 min. Yield: 6 dozen.

White Butter Cookies   Madge Petersen

1-1/2 c. sugar	1 t. soda
1 c. butter	Pinch of salt
3 egg yolks	1 t. cream of tartar
2 c. sifted flour	1 t. vanilla

Cream sugar and butter together. Add egg yolks and mix well. Stir in vanilla. Sift flour, soda, salt, and cream of tartar into creamed mixture and mix well. Form into balls as large as a walnut. Bake on greased cookie sheet at 350F for 10 min.

Butterscotch Cookies   Marjorie Jansen

2 c. brown sugar	1 t. soda
1 c. shortening (part butter)	1 t. cream of tartar
2 eggs	1/2 c. chopped nutmeats
3-1/2 c. flour	1 t. vanilla

Cream brown sugar and shortening. Add eggs and blend. Sift flour, soda, and cream of tartar into first mixture, stirring well. Add nutmeats — black walnuts are especially good — and vanilla. Blend. Form dough into two rolls about 2 x 3 in. Wrap in waxed paper and refrigerate overnight. Slice and bake in 300F oven for 10-12 min. Yield: 4 dozen.

My Butterscotch Refrigerator Wafers

2 c. brown sugar	4 c. sifted flour
1 c. shortening (1/2 butter)	1/4 t. salt
2 eggs, well beaten	2/3 t. cream of tartar
1 1/4 t. soda	1 t. vanilla
2 T. hot water	1 c. chopped black walnuts

Cream sugar and butter. Blend in eggs. Mix hot water with soda and add to creamed egg mixture. Sift flour, salt, and cream of tartar and add gradually. Stir in vanilla and walnuts; mix well. Form into two or three bar-shaped rolls, wrap in Saran Wrap, and refrigerate 4-6 hr. Slice about 1/4 in. thick for wafers. Put on lightly greased cookie sheets and bake at 325F for 12 min. May freeze dough to bake later.

Delicious Chocolate Chip Cookies   Lea C. Harbour

1 c. butter	2 1/4 c. flour
3/4 c. sugar	1 t. soda
3/4 c. brown sugar, packed	1 t. salt
2 eggs	1 12-oz. pkg chocolate chips
1 t. vanilla	1 c. chopped nuts (optional)

Cream butter and sugars. Beat in eggs and vanilla. Sift flour, soda, and salt into mixture and beat well. Blend in chocolate chips and nuts. Drop teaspoonfuls onto lightly greased cookie sheet. Bake at 325F for 8-10 min. Let cool briefly on rack, then remove with spatula and cool on brown paper. Yield: 6 dozen.

♣ *For tender, softer chocolate chip cookies, use cake flour instead of all-purpose flour.*

Iced Chocolate Cookies   Wally Harmon

1 c. shortening	1 c. milk
2 c. brown sugar	4 T. cocoa
2 eggs	1 t. salt
3 c. flour	1 t. vanilla
1 t. soda	

Mix all ingredients. Drop by spoonful on well-greased cookie sheet. Bake at 350F for 12-15 min. Do not overbake. Ice with chocolate frosting. Top with half a walnut. Yield: 3 dozen large cookies.

Real chocolate taste!

Chocolate Top Hats

1 c. brown sugar	1/4 t. salt
1/2 c. shortening	2 oz. melted chocolate
1 egg	1 t. vanilla
1/2 c. milk	1/2 c. Angel Flake coconut
1/2 t. soda	1/2 c. chopped pecans *plus*
1-1/2 c. sifted flour	1 c. pecan halves

Cream shortening. Add sugar and egg; beat well. Sift flour, soda, and salt; add alternately with milk. Blend in melted chocolate and vanilla. Fold in 1/2 c. chopped pecans and coconut. Drop by teaspoonfuls on greased cookie sheet. Bake at 350F for 10-12 min. Frost with chocolate frosting when cool and top with a pecan half. Yield: 30 cookies.

These delicious cookies can be made slightly larger for children's parties or slightly smaller for elegant tea parties or for gift boxes of Christmas cookies.

Cherry Coconut Cookies   Anna M. Petersen

1 c. sugar	1/2 t. salt
1/2 c. shortening	1-1/2 t. lemon extract
3 eggs	2 t. grated orange rind
4 scant c. flour	1/2 c. maraschino cherries,
1 t. baking powder	cut up
1/2 t. soda	1 c. flake coconut

Cream shortening and sugar. Add eggs one at a time and beat. Sift flour with baking powder, soda, and salt; add to creamed mixture. Stir in lemon extract, grated orange rind, cherries, and coconut. Place by half-teaspoonfuls on greased cookie sheet. Bake at 350F for 10-15 min.

♣ *Experienced cookie bakers often modify recipes to use half butter and half shortening, to produce cookies with a buttery taste along with less spreading in the oven.*

Coconut Crispies

1/2 c. butter or margarine	1/4 t. baking powder
1/2 c. brown sugar, packed	1/4 t. salt
1/4 c. sugar	1 c. regular oatmeal
1 egg	1 c. Rice Krispies
1 c. flour	1/2 c. flaked coconut
1/2 t. soda	1/2 c. chopped pecans

Cream shortening and sugars. Beat in egg. Sift in flour, soda, baking powder, and salt, mixing well. Stir in oats, Rice Krispies, coconut, and pecans. Drop by teaspoonfuls onto lightly greased cookie sheet. Bake at 350F for 10 min. Yield: 4 dozen.

Coconut-Oatmeal Crispy Cookies

1 c. sugar	2 c. quick-cooking oatmeal
1 c. brown sugar	2-1/2 c. flour
1 c. soft shortening	1 t. soda
1 t. vanilla	1 t. salt
2 eggs	1 t. baking powder
2 c. coconut	

Cream shortening and sugars. Add vanilla and eggs; blend well. Add coconut and oatmeal. Blend. Sift together and add flour, soda, salt, and baking powder. Stir to blend. Drop by teaspoonful on lightly greased cookie sheet. Bake at 350F for 10-15 min. Yield: 6 dozen.

Chocolate Macaroons   Bernice Peterson

3 oz. chocolate	2 t. vanilla
1/2 c. Wesson oil	2 c. flour
2 c. sugar	2 t. baking powder
4 eggs	Powdered sugar

Melt together chocolate and oil. Beat in sugar, then beat in eggs one at a time. Add vanilla. Sift together and add flour and baking powder. Mix well. Cover with Saran Wrap and chill 2 hr. or longer. Roll in balls the size of a walnut and roll in sifted powdered sugar before baking. Do not press down. Macaroons will have a crackled top. Bake at 375F for 12 min. Remove from sheet at once.

My mother often baked these cookies, which were a great favorite with her grandchildren.

My Filled Date or Raisin Cookies

1 c. white sugar	2 eggs
1/2 c. brown sugar	1 t. soda
1 c. shortening	1/2 t. salt
1 c. butter	3/4 c. sour milk
6 c. quick cooking oatmeal	1 t. vanilla
2 c. flour	

Cream sugars and shortening well. Beat in eggs. Add 3 c. oatmeal and blend. Sift flour, soda, and salt and add alternately with sour milk. Blend in vanilla and add remainder of oatmeal. Chill dough for 1 hr. Roll 1/3 of dough at a time. Cut with 2-in. cutter and place cookies on lightly greased cookie sheet 1 in. apart. Drop a teaspoonful of filling on center of each cookie. Moisten edge and top with a second cookie. Use fork to press down outer edge all the way around. Bake at 350F for about 15 min. or until light brown. Remove with wide spatula to cooling racks or heavy brown paper. Cool. Store in tightly covered container.

Filling: Combine 2 c. ground dates or raisins, 1/2 c. sugar, 1/2 c. water, 1/2 c. chopped walnuts, and 1 T. flour in small saucepan and cook until thick, stirring often. Cool.

This makes an excellent cookie for lunchboxes or picnics. Use your family's favorite fruit for filling: apricots, dates, figs, raisins, or a combination. Nutritious and tender, these also make a great after-school snack with a glass of milk.

Date-Orange Softies   **Elizabeth Brandt**

1 8-oz. pkg dates	1 1/4 c. flour
1 c. brown sugar, packed	1 t. salt
1/2 c. butter	1/4 t. baking soda
1/2 c. orange juice	1 pkg butterscotch morsels
1 t. grated orange rind	1 c. chopped nuts
2 eggs	

Chop dates. Combine with brown sugar, butter, orange juice, and grated orange rind in saucepan. Cook over low heat until thickened. Cool. Beat in eggs. Sift together flour, salt, and baking soda. Blend into date mixture. Add butterscotch morsels and nuts. Drop by large teaspoonfuls 2 in. apart on ungreased cookie sheet. Bake at 375F for 8-10 min. Remove at once to rack. Yield: 3 dozen.

♣ *Always use a shiny cookie sheet to avoid over-browning cookie bottoms.*

Ginger Cookies (Pecan Top)   **Anna M. Petersen**

1 c. sugar	1 t. ginger
1 c. molasses	2 t. cinnamon
1 c. lard or Crisco	1 t. soda
1 egg	2 t. baking powder
4 c. flour	1/3 c. milk
1 t. salt	Pecan halves

Cream sugar and lard. Add egg and molasses; beat well. Sift in flour, salt, soda, baking powder, and spices. Add milk to moisten. Roll in balls the size of a walnut. Flatten with glass dipped in sugar. Place pecan half on each cookie. Bake at 375F for about 12 min. Watch carefully; these will burn easily. Yield: 80 cookies.

My favorite cookie. My mother included these ginger cookies in Christmas assortments, but they were a great favorite with her grandchildren all year round.

Crackly Ginger Snaps   **Arlys Walters**

3/4 c. soft shortening	1-1/2 t. soda
1 c. brown sugar, packed	1 t. cinnamon
1/4 c. dark molasses	1 t. ginger
1 egg	1/4 t. salt
2 1/4 c. sifted flour	1/2 t. cloves

Cream shortening and brown sugar. Add molasses and egg and beat well. Sift together and add flour, soda, salt, and spices. Mix well. Chill 1 hr. or overnight. Roll in 1-1/2 in. balls. Dip in sugar and press down with fork, or press down with fork and sprinkle with 2 or 3 drops of water. Bake at 350F for 10-12 min.

Soft Ginger Cookies   Maude Maddison

1 c. sugar   3 c. flour
1 c. shortening   1 t. soda
2 eggs   1 t. ginger
1 c. sour cream   1 t. cinnamon
1 c. dark molasses

Cream together sugar and shortening. Beat in eggs. Add sour cream and molasses; mix well. Sift together flour, soda, and spices; add and mix well. Roll 1/4 in. thick on lightly floured board. Cut into desired shapes. Bake at 375F for 10-12 min.

Nice topped with thin powdered sugar frosting.

Rolled Ginger Cookies   Pauline Pitkin

1 1/4 c. shortening, part butter   2 t. ginger
1/2 c. brown sugar   1-1/2 t. cinnamon
1-1/2 c. light molasses   1-1/2 t. allspice
1 egg   1/2 t. salt
5 c. sifted flour   1/2 c. boiling water

Cream shortening and brown sugar. Add molasses and egg; beat well. Sift spices and 2 c. of flour into creamed mixture. Add boiling water and 1 c. flour. Stir well. Refrigerate for 30 min. Now sift remaining 2 c. flour three times with soda and salt. Add to batter and blend. Refrigerate 1 hr. or longer.

Roll out 2-c. portions at a time about 1/4 in. thick on a lightly floured board. Cut with a 2-in round cutter, or with a gingerbread boy cutter. Place on lightly greased cookie sheet about an inch apart. Bake at 350F for 10-12 min. Cool on racks.

If desired, frost with 2 c. sifted powdered sugar, 3-4 T. top milk, and 1/2 t. vanilla. Add raisin eyes, nose, and buttons for gingerbread boy.

These cookies are tender and keep well, layered with waxed paper in a tin or plastic container. Children especially enjoy helping to make gingerbread boys.

M & M Cookies

1 c. shortening
1 c. brown sugar, packed
1/2 c. granulated sugar
2 t. vanilla
2 eggs

2 1/4 c. flour
1 t. soda
1/2 t. salt
1-1/2 c. M & M candies

Cream shortening with sugars. Beat in eggs and vanilla. Sift dry ingredients and add, mixing well. Stir in 1/2 c. of M & M's. Drop by teaspoonfuls onto ungreased cookie sheet. Press 3 or 4 M & M's into each cookie. Bake at 350F for 10-12 min. Cool on brown paper. Yield: 6 dozen.

Mexican Wedding Cakes

1 c. butter
1/2 c. powdered sugar
1/2 t. vanilla

1 3/4 c. sifted flour
1/4 t. salt
1/2 c. walnuts, finely chopped

Sift and measure powdered sugar. Cream with butter; add vanilla. Sift in flour and salt; blend well. Add walnuts. Blend. Shape into 1-in. balls and bake until very lightly brown. When cool, roll in sifted powdered sugar. Yield: 5 dozen.

Sometimes called Russian teacakes, these are traditional cookies for Christmas. They make an attractive addition to gift boxes.

My Mincemeat Surprise Cookies

1 c. shortening
1 t. salt
1 t. vanilla
1 c. brown sugar
2 eggs

1 2/3 c. flour
3/4 t. soda
2 c. quick-cooking rolled oats
1 jar mincemeat
    (or cooked raisin filling)

Beat shortening, salt, and vanilla well. Add brown sugar and well-beaten eggs. Sift together flour and soda; blend with creamed mixture and add oats. Chill 1 hr. Roll dough 1/8 in. thick. Cut with 2-1/2-in. cutter. Place teaspoonful of mincemeat (or cooked raisin filling) on a cookie and top with another. Press edges together with a fork. Bake at 350F for 10-12 min. Yield: 4 dozen filled cookies.

Molasses Cookies

Anne Harbour

3/4 c. softened shortening
3/4 c. molasses
2 eggs
2 1/4 c. sifted flour
1/2 t. salt

3/4 t. soda
2 t. cinnamon
1/2 c. milk
1 c. seedless raisins
  (optional)

Gradually beat molasses into shortening. Add eggs; beat well. Sift together dry ingredients and add alternately with milk. Stir in raisins. Drop by rounded teaspoonfuls 2 in. apart on greased cookie sheet. Bake at 425F for 6-8 min. or until done. Remove from pan at once and cool on brown paper. Yield: 5 dozen.

Scottish Oat Cakes

2 c. flour
3/4 c. sugar
3/4 t. salt
3/5 t. baking soda

3/4 t. ground nutmeg
2 c. quick-cooking rolled oats
1 c. shortening or lard
1/3 c. cold water

Sift flour, sugar, salt, soda, and nutmeg into a large bowl. Mix in rolled oats. Cut in shortening and blend in cold water to make a stiff dough. Roll out on a floured board 1/4 in. thick. Cut into 1-1/2-in. squares or use a 1-1/2-in. cookie cutter to make rounds. Bake at 375F for 15 min. or until just brown.

Serve with cheese. These cakes are a favorite in Scotland, where they can also be found on the breakfast table.

Spicy Oatmeal Cookies

1/2 c. shortening
1-1/2 c. sugar
1/2 c. molasses
2 eggs
1 3/4 c. flour
1 t. soda

1 t. salt
1 t. cinnamon
2 c. rolled oats
1-1/2 c. golden raisins
3/4 c. chopped pecans (optional)

Cream shortening and sugar. Stir in molasses and eggs; beat well. Sift together flour, soda, salt, and cinnamon; add to creamed mixture and beat well. Stir in oats, raisins, and pecans. Drop teaspoonfuls onto lightly greased cookie sheets. Bake at 350F for 10 min. or until golden brown. Yield: 7 dozen.

Unusual Oatmeal Raisin Cookies   May Marshall

2 c. raisins
1/2 c. water
1 t. soda
1 c. shortening (at least 1/4
  should be bacon drippings)
1 c. brown sugar
1 c. granulated sugar
1 c. oatmeal

2 eggs, well beaten
1 t. vanilla
1/2 t. salt
2 c. flour
1 t. cream of tartar
1/2 t. nutmeg
1/2 t. cinnamon

Cook raisins in 1/2 c. water 10 min. until 5 or 6 T. of liquid remains. Cream shortening, bacon drippings, sugars, and salt; beat in eggs. Add vanilla. Mix well and sift in flour, cream of tartar, nutmeg, and cinnamon. Drain hot raisins and add soda to juice. Stir raisins into batter while raisins are still hot. Then add soda and juice mixture. Drop by teaspoonfuls onto greased cookie sheet. Bake at 275F for 12-15 min. Yield: 60 cookies.

These cookies will spread to 3 in. wide. They will remain soft but not crumbly. The bacon drippings give them a uniquely tasty flavor.

Peanut Butter Cookies   Anna M. Petersen

1/2 c. granulated sugar
1/2 c. brown sugar, packed
1/2 c. shortening
1 egg
1/2 c. crunchy peanut butter

1 t. vanilla
1-1/2 c. flour
1 t. soda
1/2 t. salt

Cream sugars and shortening. Add egg, peanut butter, and vanilla. Sift in flour, soda, and salt. Mix well. Make into small balls. Place on lightly greased cookie sheet and crease with floured fork, then crease again crosshatching first crease. Bake at 350F for 12-15 min. Yield: 3 dozen.

This recipe can be doubled. Shortening can be a mix of half corn oil, half oleo.

Peanut Blossoms

1-1/2 c. flour
1 t. baking soda
1/2 t. salt
1/2 c. sugar
2 T. milk
1/2 c. brown sugar

1/2 c. butter
1/2 c. smooth peanut butter
1 egg
1 t. vanilla
48 Hershey's chocolate kisses
Sugar

71

Combine all ingredients except kisses in a large mixing bowl. Mix on low speed (about No. 3) until dough is formed. Shape dough, using about a rounded teaspoonful, into balls. Roll balls in sugar. Place on ungreased cookie sheets. Bake at 375F for 10-12 min. After removing from oven, top each cookie with a chocolate kiss; press down firmly to give the edge a crackled look. Yield: 4 dozen.

Salted Peanut Nuggets

1 c. brown sugar	2 c. sifted flour
1 c. granulated sugar	1 t. baking powder
1 c. shortening	1 t. soda
2 eggs	1 c. crushed cornflakes
1 t. vanilla	1 c. salted peanuts

Cream sugars and shortening. Beat in eggs and vanilla. Sift flour, baking powder, and soda together. Combine mixtures. Stir in cornflakes and peanuts. Roll into balls the size of walnuts. Dip tops into granulated sugar. Bake on greased cookie sheet at 375F for 10-12 min. Cool on wire racks.

Peter Pan Cookies

1 c. shortening	2 eggs, well beaten
1/2 t. salt	1 T. milk
1 c. smooth peanut butter	2 c. sifted flour
1 c. granulated sugar	1 t. soda
1 c. brown sugar	Chocolate kisses (optional)

Blend well shortening, salt, and peanut butter. Gradually add sugars. Cream well. Add eggs and milk; blend well. Sift together and add flour and soda. Blend. Drop by teaspoonful on greased baking sheet. Press lightly with fork to make ridged tops. Bake at 325F for 15-20 min.

For a fancier cookie, press an unwrapped chocolate kiss into the partially baked cookie after 10 min.

Pecan Ice Box Cookies

2 c. brown sugar	1 scant t. baking powder
1 c. shortening	Pinch salt
2 eggs, slightly beaten	1 t. vanilla extract
1 heaping t. baking soda	4 c. flour
1 heaping t. cream of tartar	1 c. chopped pecans or black walnuts

Cream brown sugar and shortening. Add eggs, soda, cream of tartar, baking powder, salt, and vanilla. Gradually mix in flour. Fold in nuts. Form into a roll about 2 in. wide and 2-1/2 in. long. Wrap in plastic or waxed paper and chill. Slice 1/4 in. thick and bake on ungreased cookie sheet at 425F about 8 min. or until golden brown. Yield: 7 or 8 dozen.

Pefferneuse / Peppernuts   Aunt Luella Petersen

1/2 c. molasses	1/2 t. salt
2 c. sugar	1 t. cinnamon
1/2 c. dark Karo syrup	2 t. soda
1-1/2 c. soft butter and	1 t. cloves
shortening (half each)	2 T. anise seed, finely crumbed
1 c. sweet cream	7 or 8 c. flour

Mix molasses, sugar, Karo syrup, and butter in saucepan. Bring to boil on slow fire (300F). Remove from heat and cool. Then add cream and sifted dry ingredients part at a time and mixed in well. Let dough chill for several hours.

Shape dough into long rolls about 1/2 in. in diameter. Keep chilled. Preheat oven to 375F. Slice rolls about 1/4 in. thick and place on very lightly greased cookie sheets. Bake at 375F about 10 min. or until very light brown. Cool.

Store peppernuts in tightly covered metal containers. These ripen and keep for weeks, a favorite Christmas nibbler and a family tradition. Aunt Luella made several two-gallon tins full in early December, which were empty by early January.

Potato Chip Cookies   Gladys Casford

1 c. margarine	1/2 c. crushed potato chips
1/2 c. sugar	1/2 c. chopped pecans
1 t. vanilla	2 c. sifted flour

Cream margarine with sugar and vanilla. Add potato chips, pecans, and flour. Form into small balls. Place on ungreased cookie sheet. Press flat. Bake at 350F for 20 min. Yield: 2 dozen.

Raisin Apple Drop Cookies   Anna M. Petersen

1 stick margarine
1 c. granulated sugar
1 c. brown sugar
1 c. raisins
2 c. coarsely chopped apple
1/2 c. chopped nutmeats
2 eggs

1 t. salt
1 t. soda
2 t. baking powder
2 t. vanilla
1/2 c. sour cream
3 c. flour

Cream margine with sugars. Beat eggs and mix well. Sift together salt, soda, baking powder, and flour and add with sour cream and vanilla. Add apple and raisins last. Drop by teaspoonfuls onto greased cookie sheet. Bake at 375F for 12 min.

Ranger Cookies

1 c. granulated sugar
1 c. brown sugar
1 c. butter
1 c. vegetable oil
1 egg
3 c. flour
1 t. cream of tartar
1 t. baking soda

1 t. salt
1 t. vanilla
1 c. quick-cooking oatmeal
1 c. crushed Rice Krispies
1 c. flake coconut
1 c. chopped nuts
1 c. chocolate chips

Cream butter, oil, and sugar; add egg and blend. Add oatmeal, Rice Krispies, coconut, nuts, chocolate chips, and vanilla. Mix. Sift flour, cream of tartar, baking soda, and salt. Mix until blended. Drop by teaspoonfuls onto ungreased cookie sheet. Bake at 350F for 12-15 min. Cool on wire racks. Yield: 6 dozen.

Snickerdoodles

1 c. softened butter
2 1/4 c. sugar, divided
2 eggs
1/4 c. milk
1 t. vanilla

3 3/4 c. flour
1/2 t. baking soda
1/2 t. cream of tartar
1 t. cinnamon

With mixer, beat butter with 2 c. sugar until fluffy. Add eggs, milk, and vanilla and beat thoroughly. Add dry ingredients, sifted together, and thoroughly combine. Chill dough 30 min.

Form tablespoonfuls of dough into balls. Roll them in a mixture of cinnamon and 1/4 c. sugar. Place cookies on ungreased cookie sheet, allowing 1/2 in. between them. Bake at 375F for 8-10 min. or until they begin to look crinkly on top. Yield: 5 dozen.

Ranger cookies and Snickerdoodles are especially good with milk for children's after-school snacks. With coffee, they are a tasty midmorning break.

Walnut Rolled Cookies

2 c. flour
1/2 t. baking powder
1/2 t. salt
2/3 c. butter
2/3 c. sugar

1 egg
2/3 c. finely chopped walnuts
1-1/2 t. vanilla
1/2 t. almond extract
2 T. milk

Sift flour, baking powder, and salt. Cream butter; add sugar slowly and cream. Add egg; blend. Stir in walnuts, vanilla, almond flavoring, and milk; then flour mixture. Blend. Wrap dough in waxed paper. Chill 2 hr. Roll on lightly floured board to 1/8 in. thickness. Cut 1-1/2-in. rounds. Bake on ungreased cookie sheet at 400F for 8-10 min.

St. Nicholas Koekjes

2 c. brown sugar
1-1/2 c. butter
3-1/2 c. flour
1 t. cinnamon
1 egg, beaten

1/2 t. nutmeg
1/2 t. cloves
1 t. baking powder
1/2 t. salt

Cream butter and sugar; stir in remaining ingredients. Chill dough. Roll in 1-in. balls the size of a walnut and press down. Bake on ungreased cookie sheet at 350F for 8-10 min. Yield: 4 dozen.

This is a traditional Dutch spice cookie, nice to include in a Christmas basket.

Festive Christmas Thins

3/4 c. sugar
1 c. butter
2 eggs, separated
1/3 c. additional sugar
3 T. cream

2 c. flour
1 t. baking powder
Sliced almonds, coconut, or
    maraschino cherries

Cream 3/4 c. sugar and butter. Beat in egg yolks well. Sift flour with baking powder, and sift about half into the creamed mixture. Add the cream slowly, and mix well; then stir in rest of flour. Add more flour, a teaspoon at time, if needed for a firm dough. Chill dough for 1 hr.

Roll out half the dough on floured board. Cut in 1-1/2-in. squares. Beat the egg whites stiff and add 1/3 c. sugar. Spread the rolled dough with about half the beaten egg whites. Top with sliced almonds. Put on lightly greased cookie sheet and bake in slow oven (300-325F) until lightly brown, about 20 min. After 10 min., separate squares gently with spatula. Repeat with second half, topping egg whites with coconut or centering with a cherry.

These make a tasty and attractive holiday cookie.

Thumbprint Cookies   Minnie Grell

1/2 c. butter	1/4 t. salt
1/4 c. brown sugar	1 c. sifted flour
1 beaten egg yolk	1 slightly beaten egg white
1/2 t. vanilla	3/4 c. finely chopped walnuts

Cream butter and brown sugar; add egg yolk and vanilla. Beat thoroughly. Stir in flour and salt. Chill. Roll into 1-in. balls, dip in egg white, and then roll in nuts. Bake at 375F for 4 min. Remove and press thumb print. Bake another 8 min. Yield: 2 dozen.

Variations: Press whole maraschino cherry into thumbprint.

Thumbprint Jewels: Let thumbprint cookies cool. Then fill with scant teaspoon of colored powdered sugar icing. Let harden and store in covered container.

Chopped pecans can be substituted for walnuts. This is a very pretty and tasty cookie, nice for special occasions when combined with other party fare.

Dutch Letters

2 c. butter	1 lb. almond paste
4 c. flour	1 T. almond extract
1 c. ice water	Extra egg whites
3 eggs	Sugar

Cut butter into flour, and add ice water, mixing with fork as for pie dough. Refrigerate overnight. Beat together almond paste, sugar, eggs, and almond flavoring. Refrigerate overnight. Next morning, separate dough into four portions.

76

Roll each like piecrust 1/4 in. thick into a rectangle. Cut into 3/4 in. wide strips. Spread filling down the center of a strip. Use slightly beaten egg white on edges and press a second strip to cover filling, being sure to seal all around edges. Shape the filled strip into desired letter shape, and place on lightly greased cookie sheet. Brush top of each filled letter with egg white, sprinkle with a little sugar. Bake at 400F for 30 min. If they brown too fast, reduce heat to 350F and cover lightly with foil.

An unusual pastry found in bakeries in Pella, Iowa, which was settled in the nineteenth century by immigrants from The Netherlands. "Dutch letters" are fun to make and delectable to eat.

Scottish Shortbread / Petticoat Tails I

1 lb. butter, softened (do
   not substitute)
1 1/4 c. sugar

6 c. flour
2 t. almond extract (optional)

Cream butter and sugar in mixer until fluffy. Add flour 1 c. at a time, blending thoroughly. It may be better to use your hands to blend in the last cups. Press into two 9-in. ungreased round cake pans or two 9-in. square pans. Smooth tops flat. Bake at 325F for 40-50 min. While hot, cut as desired. Cut rounds like pie into 12 triangles. Cut squares into 1 x 2 in. pieces. Let cool in pans. Store in covered tins. Do not freeze. Yield: 24 to 32 pieces.

Scottish Shortbread / Petticoat Tails II

2 sticks butter
   (do not substitute)
1/3 c. powdered sugar

1/4 t. baking powder
2 c. flour
1/8 t. salt

Cream butter and sugar well. Sift flour, salt, and baking powder together. Blend with butter mixture into a firm, soft dough. Press by hand into pans. Use two ungreased round 8-in. cake pans to make traditional "Petticoat Tails." Prick dough all over with a table fork. Press down to cut evenly into 8 or 12 pie-shaped wedges — do not use a sawing motion. If you prefer, cut the dough into squares or diamond shapes in two 8-in. square pans. Bake at 325F for 45 min. to 1 hr. until golden brown. If the shortbread rises unevenly, take it out of the oven, and use the back of a wide spatula to press top down. Return to oven. Yield: 16 to 24 pieces.

Spritz Cookies   **Sarah Kossove**

1 c. butter
2/3 c. sugar
3 egg yolks

2-1/2 c. sifted cake flour
1 t. almond flavoring

Cream butter; add sugar and mix thoroughly. Add beaten egg yolks, flour, and flavoring. Chill dough 1 hr. Fill cookie press and press cookies in shapes as desired on ungreased cookie sheet. Bake in hot oven 375-400F for 8-10 min. Watch carefully; spritz should be very light brown. Store in covered tins.

For holidays, divide dough and tint with food coloring.

Cake Doughnuts

3 T. shortening	1 t. nutmeg
2/3 c. sugar	1 t. salt
1 egg, beaten	3 c. flour
2/3 c. milk	4 t. baking powder

Cream shortening. Add sugar and egg. Stir in milk and nutmeg. Add sifted flour, salt, and baking powder. Stir until all dry ingredients are mixed in. You may chill dough for 1 hr. at this point.

Roll out 1/3 of dough on a floured board, 1/2 in. thick. Cut with a 2-in. cutter. Let rest 15 min. Fry in hot lard or oil. Drain on brown paper. If you wish, frost or roll in sugar. Yield: 24 to 30 doughnuts.

♣ *After cutting doughnuts, let them rest 15 min. before frying. Test temperature of fat; a doughnut should rise at once if fat is hot enough.*

Favorite Doughnuts   Jean Petersen

4 egg yolks (or 2 eggs)	2 t. baking powder
1 c. sugar	1 t. soda
2 T. soft shortening	1/2 t. salt
3/4 c. buttermilk or sour milk	1/4 t. cinnamon
3-1/2 c. flour	1/2 t. nutmeg

Beat egg yolks; add sugar and shortening and blend. Stir in buttermilk. Sift in dry ingredients, beating smooth. Turn dough onto flour board and roll out 1/3 in. thick. Let rest 20 min. Cut and fry in hot fat (370-380F) until light brown, turning once. Drain on brown paper. Doughnuts may be frosted, sugared, or glazed.

Unbaked Butterscotch Cookies

2 pkg butterscotch chips   4 c. crushed cornflakes
1/2 c. peanut butter

Melt butterscotch chips over hot water. Add peanut butter and stir until soft. Stir in cornflakes. Drop by teaspoonful on waxed paper on cookie sheet. Do not bake.

Unbaked Chocolate Cookies

2 c. sugar   3 c. quick-cooking oatmeal
1/2 c. butter or margarine   1 c. coconut
1/2 c. milk   4 T. cocoa
1 t. vanilla   1/2 c. chopped nuts

Boil sugar, butter, and milk for 3 min. Add vanilla. Pour over mixture of oatmeal, coconut, cocoa, and nuts. Mix and drop by teaspoonfuls on waxed paper on cookie sheet. Chill to set.

Unbaked Date Cookies   Anna M. Petersen

1 c. pitted dates   2 T. butter
1 egg   2 c. Rice Krispies
1/8 t. salt   1 t. vanilla
1/2 c. sugar   1/2 c. chopped nutmeats
Angel Flake coconut

Place dates, egg, salt, and sugar in saucepan. Stir and add butter. Cook 3 min. Take from heat and add Rice Krispies, vanilla, and nuts. Form into small balls with teaspoon. Roll in coconut. Set on waxed paper. Yield:
18 or 20 cookies.

No-Bake Peanut Butter Cookies   Arlys Walters

2 c. sugar   1/2 c. peanut butter
1/2 c. milk   1 t. vanilla
1/4 c. butter   3 c. quick-cooking oatmeal
3 T. cocoa   Chopped nuts (optional)

Cook sugar, milk, butter, and cocoa for 1 min. Remove from heat. Add remaining ingredients; stir. Drop by spoonfuls onto waxed paper. Cool to harden.

Unbaked Ritz Cookies   **Wally Harmon**

Creamy peanut butter   1-1/2 lb. almond bark
Ritz crackers   12 oz. chocolate chips

Melt together almond bark and chocolate chips. Put 1/2 t. peanut butter between 2 Ritz crackers. Dip each "cookie" into melted mixture, covering each side (use two forks to handle this). Place on racks to dry.

These are nice with plain vanilla bark also. A sweet change for holidays.

Cakes, Frostings and Candies

Cakes ♣ Icings ♣ Fillings ♣ Candies

Barn Dance

Midwestern housewives have always have been long on practicality and common sense when it comes to meals. As they used to say, men don't want potato chips and olives when they come in from the fields, walk'n behind a harrow! But after a soak in the washtub, even a sun-burned, bone-weary farmer may feel frisky as a colt when the fiddle tunes up for a barn dance.

It was not often that everything came together just right. The corn had been laid by, cultivated for the third time and too big for a fourth; the oats were shocked ready for threshing; the weather was clear, and the barn loft was standing empty until the summer crop of hay was put in. The barn was the type common in the Midwest, built into a side hill so the ground level faced south. It was topped by a full loft that was entered from the north through a large hay door only a step up from the ground. All that was needed for a barn dance was to build a short ramp to the hay door opening, sweep and clean the loft, and put some planks on bales for seats.

The prospect of seeing their farm neighbors who worked together for threshing rings, corn shelling, wood sawing and fence building and old friends who would come from the villages and farther away met with hearty approval. The next Saturday night was chosen, only five days away, and the flurry of preparations began. Several men volunteered to ride to extend the invitations, since the mail service was undependable and most did not have the telephone. Another promised to see that a fiddler and an accordion player would play, along with other musicians they knew might come.

The owner of the barn supplied the planks for the short ramp and lumber for handrails. Before long, other men were at work brushing down cobwebs and old wasps' nests before sweeping the well-built loft flooring. They laid planks across hay bales for seating along three sides, leaving a space for the musicians. The owner and his wife agreed that a long worktable in the laundry lean-to could be used for refreshments. Before long, everything was ready.

Ladies all around the district set aside plain one-egg cake recipes and found their Lady Baltimore or Three-Layer Chocolate or Angel Food Supreme to carry to the ball. The acknowledged expert on making Real Egg Coffee set out her huge enamel coffee pot and strainer. And everyone else was finding her best jar of sweet pickles or calculating how many sandwiches to take. The occasion displayed one's culinary skills — a competition, but civilized, where everyone gets a prize.

The merrymakers arrive: families of parents with timid or brash teenagers who will dance with each other or with older relatives, very young parents with a baby in a basket, bachelors from 19 to 65, hoping to take a pretty girl "to supper," and unattached young men who have crashed the party but are welcome as extra partners. The cake ladies bear their triumph in domed containers to a chorus of awe and amazement. The coffee expert disappears into the farmhouse.

The fiddler tunes up, and his partners, banjo and accordion, pluck and finger their instruments. Suddenly a path opens up for the caller, a lively fellow who knows a hundred calls. The fiddler opens with "Turkey in the Straw," and the oldest couple steps out spryly to lead the dancers. Later they will dance the old-country schottische, and the crowd will polka, two-step and dance the romantic, graceful waltz.

By 11 p.m., folks are looking toward the corner where the serving table is set up. The selections are a dilemma: chocolate or angel food? spice or apple cake? egg salad or ham-and-cheese? The cake ladies smile complacently. The coffee expert smiles graciously. And the musicians and caller confer: a square dance, or a round dance where everyone changes partners?

Until 1 a.m., or even 1:15 a.m., the dance goes on. And the ladies who baked and cooked and made coffee smile at one another. This is the best dance. And the finest food! As tired parents gather their young, their shining eyes and happy smiles are proof that life on the farm is good. It's a family place. The night skies twinkle overhead, and constellations are clear in the Midwestern sky.

Recipes

Angel Food Cake

1 1/8 c. sifted cake flour
3/4 c. granulated sugar
1-1/2 c. egg whites at
  room temperature
1/2 t. salt

1-1/2 t. cream of tartar
1 c. sifted granulated sugar
1 t. vanilla
1 t. almond extract

Measure cake flour after sifting. Add 3/4 c. granulated sugar to flour and sift together five times. Put egg whites and salt in large bowl of electric mixer. Beat at high speed until foamy. Add cream of tartar. Continue beating on high speed until whites are stiff and stand in peaks. With mixer on medium speed, quickly sprinkle in 1 c. sifted granulated sugar. After sugar is dissolved, remove beaters. Using a wire whip, fold in vanilla and almond extract. Sprinkle in flour and sugar mixture quickly a third at a time, folding with the whip just until blended. Pour batter into an ungreased tube cake pan. Cut through the batter and around outer edge and tube edge to avoid air pockets.

Bake at 350F for 35-40 min. on the lowest oven rack. Let hang upside down until completely cooled. Run a serrated bread knife carefully around the outer edge and tube edge to loosen the cake.

This recipe makes a very fine-textured cake that remains moist. It freezes well. Angel food is especially recommended for heart-healthy diets.

♣ *Egg whites whip to greater volume at room temperature.*

Chocolate Angel Food   Caroline Etler

1 c. sifted flour
2 T. cocoa
1/2 c. sugar
1-1/2 c. egg whites
  at room temperature

1/2 t. salt
2 t. cream of tartar
1/2 c. sugar plus 2 T.
1/4 t. almond extract
1 t. vanilla

Sift together three to five times the flour, cocoa, and 1/2 c. sugar. Beat salt and egg whites until foamy, sprinkle in cream of tartar, and beat until whites hold up in soft peaks but are still moist and glossy.

Sift 1/2 c. plus 2 T. sugar three times. Using beater, gradually fold this sugar into egg whites. Next fold in flour and cocoa mixture. Fold in vanilla and almond extract. Bake on lowest oven rack at 350F for 45 min. Invert pan and cool completely before removing to plate. Frost with Brown Velvet Frosting.

Brown Velvet Frosting

1/2 c. sugar
1/2 c. evaporated milk *or*
  cream

1 c. semisweet chocolate pieces
  or chocolate chips

Mix sugar and milk together in saucepan. Cook over very low heat, stirring often. Bring to boiling point. Boil 1 min. Remove from heat. Stir in chocolate. Beat until smooth and spread on cake.

Gold Angel Cake

5 eggs, separated
1-1/2 c. sugar
1/2 c. ice cold water
1-1/2 c. cake flour
1/2 t. vanilla

1/2 t. lemon extract
1/2 t. baking powder
1/2 t. cream of tartar
1/2 t. salt

Beat egg yolks for 1 min. Add cold water and beat 1 min. Add sugar gradually; add flavorings. Sift flour, baking powder, and salt five times. Add to creamed mixture a third at a time, beating well after each addition. Beat egg whites with cream of tartar until stiff. Fold batter into egg whites. Turn into ungreased tube cake pan. Cut through the batter and around outer and tube edges.

Bake at 350F for 1 hr. or until cake pulls away from pan. Invert and let cool completely. Frost with preferred icing, or serve with berries and whipped cream. Serves 12.

♣ *Cream whips best at a cold temperature with a chilled beater.*

Apple Harvest Cake   Nancy Amerson

3 c. McIntosh apples
3 c. sifted flour
2 eggs
2 c. sugar
1-1/2 c. vegetable oil
1/2 t. salt

1 t. soda
1 t. cinnamon
1 t. vanilla
1 c. nuts, chopped
Powdered sugar

Peel and dice apples. Combine with nuts and mix with 1 c. sifted flour. Beat eggs and sugar well; add oil and vanilla. Sift in 2 c. flour, soda, and cinnamon. Beat well. Add apple-nut mixture, mixing thoroughly. Batter will be thick. Bake in buttered bundt pan or two loaf pans at 375F for 1 hr. Dust with powdered sugar while warm.

Nancy's Apple Cake

Nancy Amerson

4 large golden delicious apples	1 t. baking soda
1 c. walnuts, coarsely chopped	1 t. cinnamon
1 c. golden seedless raisins	1 t. salt
1 T. orange rind, grated	3 eggs
2 c. sugar	1 c. oil
3 c. flour	2 t. vanilla

Peel and chop apples. Combine in bowl with raisins, nuts, orange rind, and sugar. Mix well and let stand an hour. Sift dry ingredients. Beat eggs until thick; then beat in oil and vanilla. Stir in sifted dry ingredients. Add fruit with juice, and mix well. Spoon into a generously greased 9-in. tube pan, rapping pan on solid surface to eliminate bubbles. Bake at 350F for 1 hr. 15 min., or until a knife comes out clean. Cool on rack. Use a serrated bread knife around outer edge and tube edge to loosen cake; then unmold on rack.

♣ *Assemble all ingredients before starting to mix, and read the directions carefully. This saves time and avoids errors or omissions.*

Apple Pie Cake

Lynne Miller

1 c. sugar	1/2 c. chopped nuts
1/2 c. shortening	2 c. flour
2 eggs	2 t. soda
1 can apple pie filling	2 t. cinnamon
1 c. raisins	1/2 t. salt
2 t. vanilla	

Cream sugar and shortening; then beat in eggs. Stir in the apple pie filling, raisins, vanilla, and nuts. Sift together and add flour, soda, cinnamon, and salt. Bake in 9 x 13 in. pan at 350F for 45-50 min.

Applesauce Cake

1/2 c. margarine	1/2 t. soda
1-1/2 c. sugar	1 t. cinnamon
2 eggs, beaten	1/2 t. cloves
1 c. applesauce	1 c. pecans, chopped
2 c. flour	1 c. raisins
1/4 t. salt	Powdered sugar (optional)
1 t. baking powder	

In large mixing bowl cream margarine and sugar; add eggs and beat well. Add applesauce. Sift in all dry ingredients, and beat until smooth. Add chopped nuts and raisins. Bake in a well-greased bundt or tube pan at 350F for 50-60 min. Test with a toothpick near center of cake. Cool on a rack. Sift powdered sugar on top if desired. Yield: 12-14 servings.

♣ *Dark metal and glass pans absorb more heat than shiny ones, so lower oven temperatures 25F when using them.*

Banana Cake   Cathryn Reynolds

1-1/2 c. sugar	1/2 c. butter
2 eggs, separated	1/3 c. sour milk or buttermilk
1 t. soda	2 c. flour
1 t. baking powder	1 t. vanilla
2 large or 3 small very ripe bananas	

Cream sugar and butter. Add beaten egg yolks and vanilla. Dissolve soda in milk. Sift together flour and baking powder three times. Alternately add milk and flour, mixing well. Mash bananas and add. Lastly, beat egg whites stiff and fold into batter. Bake in two 9-in. layer pans at 350F for 20-22 min. Cool and frost with Harvest Moon Frosting.

Harvest Moon Frosting: Combine 2 egg whites slightly beaten, 1 c. brown sugar, dash of salt, and 1/4 c. water in top of double boiler. Beat with mixer or rotary beater, heating constantly, for 7 min. or until frosting stands in peaks. Remove from heat and beat until thick enough to spread. Add 3/4 c. blanched, chopped, and toasted almonds or sprinkle almonds on sides and top of frosting. Makes enough frosting to fill and frost tops and sides of two 9-in. layers.

♣ *Banana cake and banana bread both need very flavorful, ripe bananas. This is an ideal use for overripe bananas on sale at the grocery store.*

Aunt Anna's Banana Nut Cake   Mrs. Pete Petersen

2-1/2 c. sifted cake flour	2/3 c. soft butter
1 2/3 c. sugar	2/3 c. buttermilk, divided
1 1/4 t. baking powder	1 1/4 c. mashed bananas (3 large)
1 1/4 t. soda	2 large eggs
1 t. salt	2/3 c. chopped walnuts

Sift all dry ingredients into large mixer bowl. Add butter, 1/3 c. buttermilk, and mashed bananas. Beat 2 min. on medium speed. Add 1/3 c. buttermilk and unbeaten eggs. Beat 2 min. on medium. Fold in chopped nuts. Pour batter into two greased and floured 9-in. pans. Bake at 350F for 30-35 min. for a layer cake and 45 min. for a 9 x 13 in. cake. Good with cream cheese icing.

♣ *If you need to substitute flours, 1 c. cake flour equals 1 c. all-purpose flour minus 2 T.*

Burnt Sugar Cake   Carolyn Etler

1/2 scant c. butter	2 eggs, separated
1-1/2 c. sugar	2 c. cake flour
1 t. vanilla	2 t. baking powder
5 t. burnt sugar syrup	1 c. cold water

Cream butter, sugar, vanilla, and burnt sugar syrup until light and fluffy. Add egg yolks and cream again. Sift flour and baking powder. Add 1/4 c. of the flour to the creamed mixture and blend. Then alternately add water and rest of flour, mixing well. Last, stiffly beat egg whites and fold into batter. Pour into two greased and floured 9-in. cake pans or one 9 x 12 in. pan. Bake at 350F for 15 min. if layers; 30 min. if loaf pan.

Burnt Sugar Syrup: Put 1/2 c. sugar into small skillet or saucepan and heat on medium high until sugar melts to dark brown. Remove from heat and carefully add 1/2 c. hot water. Stir and boil until this becomes a thick syrup. Store in covered jar.

Frosting: Combine 1 c. brown sugar and 1/2 c. cream in saucepan. Boil to soft ball stage. Add 1 T. butter and cool. Add powdered sugar to spreading consistency. Flavor with vanilla.

Butternut Cake   Connie Woods

1/4 c. sugar	1 box instant vanilla pudding mix
1/4 c. nuts, chopped	3/4 c. water
1 t. cinnamon	3/4 c. corn oil
2 t. butternut flavoring	4 eggs
1 box yellow cake mix	

Blend together sugar, nuts, and cinnamon and set aside. Combine cake and pudding mixes, water, and oil; beat well. Add eggs one at a time. Beat at highest speed for 8 min. Add butternut flavoring toward end of beating.

Sprinkle a little nut mixture in bottom of well-greased bundt or angel food pan.

Alternate batter and nut mixture, ending with nut mixture. Bake at 350F for 35-40 min. Remove from oven. Let cool for 8 min., remove from pan, and add glaze.

Glaze: Mix 1 c. powdered sugar, 1/2 t. butternut flavoring, 1/2 t. vanilla, and 3 T. milk. Pour evenly over top of cake, letting it run down sides.

14-Carat Gold Cake

2 6-oz. jars baby food carrots	1-1/2 t. soda
1 8-oz. can crushed pineapple	2 t. baking powder
2 c. sugar	1 t. salt
1 c. oil	2 t. cinnamon
4 eggs	1/4 t. nutmeg
2 c. flour	1/2 c. nuts, chopped

Drain pineapple, mix with carrots in bowl, and set aside. Combine sugar and oil. Add eggs one at a time, beating well after each addition. Sift flour, soda, baking powder, and seasonings. Add to creamed mixture alternately with carrot mixture. Mix well. Stir in nuts. Pour batter into greased and floured 9 x 13 in. pan. Bake at 350F for 40-45 min. Cool on rack. Serves 16.

Cream Cheese Frosting: Cream together 1/2 c. softened butter, 8 oz. cream cheese, and 1 t. vanilla. Gradually add up to 1 lb. powdered sugar. Beat thoroughly. Add a teaspoonful or two of milk if frosting is too thick.

Carrot Cake

1 c. oil	1/2 t. salt
2 c. sugar	2 t. cinnamon
4 eggs	3 c. carrots, finely ground or
2 c. flour	grated
2 t. baking powder	1 c. nuts, chopped
2 t. soda	

Blend oil and sugar. Add eggs one at a time, beating well after each addition. Sift all dry ingredients and add. Mix well. Blend in carrots and nuts. Bake in greased and floured 9 x 13 in. pan at 300F for 1 hr. or until toothpick comes out clean.

Cream Cheese Frosting: Combine 4 oz. cream cheese, 1 stick soft margarine, 1 lb. sifted powdered sugar, and 2 t. vanilla. Add a teaspoonful of milk if needed to spread.

♣ *If there is a 7¢ difference between a dozen of one size egg and the next size, the larger size is the better buy. If there is more than 7¢ difference per dozen, the smaller size is a better buy.*

Maraschino Cherry Cake   Ilene Hamann

2 1/4 c. sifted cake flour
3 t. baking powder
1/2 t. salt
1/2 c. shortening
4 egg whites

1/2 c. milk
16 maraschino cherries, cut fine
1 1/3 c. sugar
1/4 c. cherry juice
1/2 c. nut meats, cut fine

Sift together the pre-sifted flour, baking powder, and salt; set aside. Combine in large mixer bowl the shortening, milk, cherries, sugar, and cherry juice; mix thoroughly. Mix in flour slowly, then beat 2 min. at medium speed. Add unbeaten egg whites and beat 2 min. longer. Turn off mixer and stir in nuts. Pour into two greased and floured layer pans. Bake at 350F about 30 min.

Frosting: Combine 1-1/2 c. Crisco, 2-1/2 c. powdered sugar, 2 T. finely cut maraschino cherries, and 1 T. cherry juice. Add a teaspoonful or two of milk if needed to reach spreading consistency.

Lemon Chiffon Cake

6 eggs, separated
2 c. sifted cake flour
2 c. sugar
1/2 t. cream of tartar
Pinch of salt
1/2 c. Mazola oil

1/2 c. cold water
2 T. lemon juice
1 T. lemon rind, grated
1/2 t. lemon flavoring
3 t. baking powder

Sift flour and sugar. Beat together oil, egg yolks, water, lemon rind and juice, and flavoring. Beat egg whites and cream of tartar until they hold stiff peaks. *Do not underbeat.* Fold flour and sugar into egg yolk mixture; blend thoroughly. Fold this batter lightly into stiff egg whites with a wire whip, blending thoroughly. Pour into ungreased angel food tube pan. Bake at 350F for 40 min. Invert pan to cool. Remove from pan when completely cool.

Frost with 7-Minute Frosting and decorate with a little grated lemon peel. Unfrosted, this cake is a delicious base for fresh fruits or berries.

♣ *Chiffon and angel food batters should be cut through and around tube and outer edge of pan with a silver knife before baking to eliminate air pockets.*

Orange Chiffon Cake

2 1/4 c. sifted cake flour	5 eggs, separated
1-1/2 c. sugar	3 extra egg whites
3 t. baking powder	3/4 c. cold water
1 t. salt	Grated peel of 2 oranges
1/2 c. vegetable oil	1/2 t. cream of tartar

Sift together into a large mixing bowl the pre-sifted flour, sugar, baking powder, and salt. Make a well in the center and add in order: oil, egg yolks, water, and grated orange peel. Beat until mixture is smooth. Beat 1 c. egg whites with cream of tartar until they form stiff peaks. Do not underbeat. Gradually fold egg yolk mixture into egg whites with rubber spatula until just blended. Pour batter into ungreased angel food tube pan. Bake at 325F for 55 min.; increase to 350F for another 10-15 min. Invert pan to cool. Remove from pan when completely cool.

Orange Frosting: Combine 3 oz. softened cream cheese, 2 1/4 c. sifted powdered sugar, grated peel of 2 oranges, and a few teaspoonfuls of orange juice if needed to get spreading consistency.

Golden Chiffon Cake

2 1/4 c. sifted cake flour	3 extra egg whites
1-1/2 c. sugar	3/4 c. water
3 t. baking powder	1 t. vanilla
1 t. salt	2 t. grated lemon peel
1/2 c. salad oil	1/2 t. cream of tartar
5 eggs, separated	

Sift together pre-sifted flour, sugar, baking powder, and salt. Make a well in the center and add in order: oil, egg yolks, water, vanilla, and grated lemon peel. Beat until satin smooth. Add cream of tartar to egg whites and beat *very stiff*. Add batter in thin stream over whites, folding it in gently. Pour into ungreased angel food tube pan. Bake at 325F for 1 hr. and 10 min. Invert pan to cool.

Frost with 7-Minute Frosting. May be sprinkled with coconut (Angel Flake).

Best Red Chocolate Cake   Aunt Alice Paulsen

1/2 c. shortening	1 c. cold water
1 c. sugar	1 t. vanilla
Dash of salt	3 egg whites
1/3 c. cocoa	3/4 c. sugar
1/3 c. cold water	1-1/2 t. soda
2-1/2 c. sifted cake flour	2 T. vinegar

Cream shortening, 1 c. sugar, and salt. Make paste of cocoa with 1/3 c. water; add to creamed mixture. Alternately add flour and 1 c. water to mixture; mix well and add vanilla. Beat egg whites to stiff peaks; fold in 3/4 c. sugar. Dissolve soda in 1 t. cold water; add vinegar. Blend into batter. Then gently fold in beaten egg whites. Pour into a 9 x 12 in. greased pan. Bake at 350F for 30-40 min. Frost with Caramel Frosting or other brown sugar icing.

♣ *Store chocolate in a moderately cool cupboard (60-75F is ideal), never in the refrigerator.*

Chocolate Joy Cake   Aunt Alice McDermott

3 oz. unsweetened chocolate	2 c flour
1/2 c. hot water	3 t. baking powder
1/2 c. shortening	1/4 t. soda
1 2/3 c. sugar	1/2 t. salt
3 eggs, beaten	1 c. sour milk or buttermilk

Combine chocolate and hot water in top of double boiler; cook to a paste over low heat. Cool. Cream shortening and sugar. Blend in beaten eggs and chocolate mixture. Sift together flour, baking powder, soda, and salt. Add alternately with sour milk to creamed mixture. Beat well. Pour into greased 8-in. layer pans dusted with cocoa or 9 x 12 in. pan. Bake at 325F for 35-40 min. Frost with Chocolate Frosting or with 7-Minute boiled frosting and Birthday Glaze.

Birthday Glaze: Melt 1 oz. unsweetened chocolate and 1 t. butter in double boiler. Add 2 T. boiling water and up to 1 c. powdered sugar. Beat until smooth. Drizzle over the edge of iced layer cake.

When my children were small, they could choose their preferred birthday cake. Favorites were an angel food and this two-layer chocolate cake, iced with 7-Minute Frosting dripping chocolate.

♣ *When baking a chocolate cake, dust buttered cake pans with cocoa instead of flour.*

Chocolate Cake   Anne Harbour

3 oz. unsweetened chocolate	2 1/4 c. sifted cake flour
1 c. butter	1 t. soda
1-1/2 c. sugar	1/2 t. salt
5 eggs	1 c. sour milk or buttermilk
2 t. vanilla	

Melt chocolate over low heat in top of double boiler. Cool. Cream butter and sugar. Stir in vanilla and melted chocolate. Add eggs one at a time, beating well after each. Sift together flour, soda, and salt. Add alternately with sour milk to creamed mixture. Beat well. Pour into greased 8-in. layer pans or 9 x 12 in. pan. Bake at 325F for 30-35 min. or until cake springs back when pressed gently. Cool on rack.

Frosting: Combine 1/2 c. softened butter, 1 lb. sifted powdered sugar, 1 t. vanilla, and 1 T. instant coffee. Add a teaspoonful or two of strong coffee to arrive at spreading consistency.

Sunbeam Chocolate Cake

2 c. sifted cake flour
1 t. soda
3/4 t. salt
1 1/3 c. sugar
1/2 c. soft shortening

1 t. vanilla
1 c. milk, divided
2 eggs
3 oz. unsweetened chocolate

Melt chocolate in top of double boiler; cool. Sift together into large mixer bowl the pre-sifted flour, soda, salt, and sugar. Add shortening, vanilla, and 3/4 c. milk. Beat at #2 speed for 2 min., scraping bowl while mixing. Stop mixer. Scrape beaters. Add eggs, melted chocolate, and 1/4 c. milk. Beat on #2 speed for 1 min., scraping bowl while beating. Pour into greased 9-in. layer pans. Bake at 350F for 30-40 min. Cool on rack. Ice as desired.

♣ *To measure a fraction of a cup of shortening easily, for example, 1/3 cup, put in 2/3 cup of water. The remainder, 1/3 cup, will be filled when you spoon in the shortening. Drain the cup, and you have 1/3 c. shortening to use.*

Abby's Fabulous Chocolate Cake   Abigail Van Buren

4 oz. unsweetened chocolate
1/2 c. butter or margarine
1 c. water
2 c. sifted cake flour
1 1/4 t. soda

1 t. salt
2 eggs
1 c. sour cream
2 c. sugar
1-1/2 t. vanilla

Combine chocolate, butter, and water in top of double boiler. Heat over simmering water until chocolate and butter melt. Remove from heat; cool. Sift flour, soda, and salt into large bowl. Beat eggs with sour cream until blended in smaller bowl. Beat in sugar and vanilla. Stir in melted chocolate mixture. Beat this into flour mixture, half at a time, just until smooth. Batter will be thin. Pour evenly into greased 8-in. round pans. Bake at 350F for 30 min. or until center springs back when lightly pressed with finger. Cool in pans on racks. Loosen edges with knife and turn out onto racks.

Fluffy White Frosting: Combine 2 egg whites, 3/4 c. sugar, 1/2 t. cream of tartar, dash of salt, and 2-1/2 t. cold water in top of large double boiler. Beat until blended. Place top over simmering water. Cook, beating constantly with electric or rotary beater, about 7 min., or until mixture stands in firm peaks. Remove from water. Stir in vanilla. Makes enough to fill and frost 8-in two-layer cake. Use one quarter of frosting between layers. Frost top and sides with remainder, making deep swirls with spatula.

Cocoa Fudge Cake

3/4 c. butter	2 1/4 c. sifted cake flour
1-1/2 c. sugar	1/2 c. cocoa
3 eggs, separated	3 t. baking powder
1-1/2 t. vanilla	1 c. cold water
1 t. red food coloring	

Cream butter and sugar. Add egg yolks one at a time, beating well after each addition. Stir in vanilla and food coloring. Sift together dry ingredients and add to creamed mixture alternately with cold water. Beat well. Beat egg whites until they form stiff peaks; fold into batter. Pour batter into two greased 9-in. layer pans. Bake at 350F for 25-30 min.

 Grease only the bottom of cake pans.

Prize Chocolate Cake

1/2 c. butter	1/4 t. salt
2 c. sugar	2 t. baking powder
4 oz. chocolate	1-1/2 c. milk
2 eggs	1 t. vanilla
2 c. sifted cake flour	

Melt chocolate over low heat in top of double boiler. Cool. Cream butter and sugar. Add melted chocolate and eggs; beat well. Add vanilla to milk. Sift flour, salt, and baking powder together and add alternately with milk and vanilla mixture; beat well after each addition. Pour into two greased 9-in. cake pans. Bake at 350F for 45 min.

Frosting: Melt together 1/2 c. butter and 2 oz. chocolate. Add pinch of salt, 1 t. lemon juice, and 1 t. vanilla. Then beat in 1-1/2 c. powdered sugar. Beat until thick enough to spread.

Creole Chocolate Cake

1/2 c. strong hot coffee	1/2 c. sour cream
1/2 c. cocoa	2 c. flour
1/2 c. butter	1/2 t. salt
2 c. brown sugar, packed	1 t. soda
1/2 t. vanilla	3 eggs, separated

Make paste of coffee and cocoa; set aside to cool. Cream butter and brown sugar. Beat egg yolks well, and add to creamed mixture. Stir in vanilla. Beat in chocolate and coffee, then sour cream. Sift flour, salt, and soda; add to mixture. Beat egg whites until they form stiff peaks. Gradually fold egg whites into batter. Pour into two greased 8-in. layer pans. Bake at 350F for 30-35 min. Cool on rack.

German Sweet Chocolate Cake   Ruby Phillips

1 pkg Baker's German sweet chocolate	4 eggs, separated
	1 t. vanilla
1/2 c. boiling water	2-1/2 c. sifted cake flour
1 c. butter	1/2 t. salt
2 c. sugar	1 t. soda
1 c. buttermilk	

Melt chocolate in boiling water. Cool. Cream butter and sugar. Add unbeaten egg yolks one at a time, beating after each addition. Add vanilla and melted chocolate. Beat well. Sift together flour, salt, and soda. Add flour alternately with buttermilk, beating until smooth after each addition. Beat egg whites until they form stiff peaks. Fold egg whites into batter. Pour into three 8- or 9-in. greased layer pans, lined with waxed paper. Bake at 350F for about 30 min. Cool on racks.

Coconut-Pecan Frosting: Combine 1 c. evaporated milk, 1 c. sugar, and 3 egg yolks. Cook over medium heat, stirring constantly, until thickened. Add 1 1/3 c. coconut and 1 c. chopped pecans. Beat until thick and spread on tops only of chocolate layers, allowing generous amount to show between layers.

Brazil Nut Sensation / Fruit Cake

3/4 c. sifted flour	1 lb. pitted dates, cut in half
3/4 c. granulated sugar	1 c. whole maraschino
1 t. baking powder	cherries, well drained
1/2 t. salt	3 eggs
3 c. whole shelled Brazil nuts	1 t. vanilla

Preheat oven to 300F. In a large bowl, place nuts, dates, and cherries. Sift flour, sugar, baking powder, and salt over these. Mix with hands until all are well coated. Beat eggs 5 min. until foamy. Add vanilla and stir into nut mixture. Pour batter into 9 x 5 x 3 in. pan lined with waxed paper. Bake at 350F for 1 hr. and 45 min. Cool in pan on wire rack for 10 min. Remove from pan, cool entirely, and double wrap in foil. Store in refrigerator.

The fruit cake should ripen several days. To serve, use a very sharp knife and cut in thin slices. Delicious served with coffee as a holiday treat.

♣ *If a recipe reads "flour, sifted" sift after measuring. If it reads "sifted flour" sift flour before measuring.*

Crystal Fruit Cake

1-1/2 c. sugar, divided
1/2 c. butter
1 egg
1 c. raisins or dates,
   chopped fine
Dash of salt

1 c. sour milk
1 t. soda
2 c. sifted flour
3 oranges
1 lemon

Cream 1 c. sugar with butter and salt. Add egg and blend. Mix in raisins or dates. Grate and juice oranges. Measure 1/2 c. orange juice and 1 t. grated orange rind and blend with batter. Mix sour milk with soda and add alternately with flour. Bake in a greased 9 x 13 in. Pyrex pan at 325F for 45-50 min. While cake is baking, combine remainder of orange juice, the juice of 1 lemon, and 1/2 c. sugar; mix well. Stir and pour over cake when it is done. Put cake back into oven for 2 min. at 325F to firm the topping.

Dark Sweet Fruit Cake   Mary Schrum

1 pkg Pillsbury date-nut
   bread mix
1 egg
1 c. water
1 c. pecans, coarsely chopped

1 T. flour
1 c. raisins, plumped
1 c. candied cherries, quartered
1/2 c. candied pineapple,
   cut in cubes

Add egg to water and beat slightly. Add to date-nut bread mix and mix lightly. Plump raisins by pouring a cup of boiling water over them; allow to sit 1/2 hr. Combine flour, fruits, and nuts; toss. Add the fruit-and-nut mixture to batter; mix well but do not beat. If using mini-muffin tins, grease tins well with Crisco or other hard shortening, or use foil muffin liners. Fill tins 2/3 full. Bake at 350F for 25-30 min. (If preferred, bake in 9 x 5 in. loaf pan at 350F for 60-70 min.) Cool 15 min. Glaze while warm with white corn syrup. Yield: 18-24 mini-muffins.

Deluxe Fruit Cake

1 c. cooking oil	1 c. pineapple or orange juice
1-1/2 c. brown sugar	1 c. flour
4 eggs	1 c. citron
2 c. sifted flour	1 c. candied pineapple
1 t. baking powder	1-1/2 c. whole candied cherries
2 t. salt	1 c. golden raisins
2 t. cinnamon	1 c. dried figs, chopped
2 t. allspice	3 c. nuts, chopped
1 t. ground cloves	

Mix oil and sugar. Add eggs and beat well. Sift together 2 c. flour, baking powder, and spices. Add to creamed mixture alternately with fruit juice. In separate bowl, sift 1 c. flour over fruits and nuts. Mix well with large wooden or slotted spoon. Then pour creamed mixture over fruit-and-nut mixture, folding with spoon until well blended. Pour into two well-greased 8 1/2 x 4-1/2 x 2-1/2 in. loaf pans lined with waxed paper. Bake at 275F for 2-1/2 to 3 hr. Let stand 15 min. before removing from pans.

♣ *Keeping a shopping list up to date and making additions when you read the week's grocery ads will save time and money.*

Holiday Fruit Cake
Anna M. Petersen

2 c. English walnut halves	1 t. salt
2 c. Brazil nuts, whole	4 eggs, separated
1 lb. whole pitted dates	1 c. sugar
1 jar whole red candied cherries	2 T. orange juice
1 c. flour	1 t. vanilla
1 t. baking powder	

Put nuts and fruits into a large mixing bowl. Sift together flour, baking powder, and salt; sift this over fruit and nuts and mix well. In small bowl, blend egg yolks, sugar, orange juice, and vanilla. Add to fruit-flour mixture and mix well. Beat egg whites very stiff but not dry. Fold them thoroughly into fruit batter.

Pour into two greased 9 x 5 in. loaf pans that have been lined with greased waxed paper. Bake at 325F for 1 hr. 10 min. Brush with orange juice, and remove to cooling rack to cool completely. Wrap in foil to age.

♣ *Set a pan of water on the lowest oven rack when baking fruit cakes to prevent the cake's becoming dry.*

Lee Corn's Fruit Cake   Lee Corn

1 c. shortening	1 lb. glacée cherries
1 c. sugar	1 lb. dried pineapple
5 eggs	1/4 lb. orange peel
2 c. flour	1 to 1-1/2 lb. nuts
1 t. salt	1 lb. white raisins
1-1/2 t. baking powder	1/4 lb. lemon peel
1/4 c. unsweetened pineapple juice	

Thoroughly cream shortening and sugar; add eggs one at a time, beating well after each addition. Reserve 1/2 c. flour for fruits. Sift remaining flour, salt, and baking powder; add to creamed mixture alternately with pineapple juice. Add floured fruit and nuts (whole or chopped nuts, as you prefer), stirring only until well blended. Pour into two greased 3-1/2 x 7 1/2 in. loaf pans lined with waxed paper. Bake in slow oven (275F) for 2-1/2 hr. If using one funnel pan, bake for 2 hr. Makes a 5-lb. cake.

♣ *Dried vacuum-packed fruit with no added sugar produces a moist cake containing less sugar.*

White Fruit Cake

2 c. butter	1 lb. (3 c.) pecan halves
2 c. sugar	2 c. white raisins
6 eggs	2 c. candied cherries
4 c. flour (1/4 c. reserved)	1 c. crushed pineapple,
1/4 t. salt	drained
1/2 t. baking powder	1/4 c. lemon juice

Cream butter and sugar. Beat in eggs, one at a time. Sift 3 3/4 c. flour, salt, and baking powder and add to creamed mixture, stirring to make a smooth batter. In a small bowl, combine pecans, raisins, and cherries; sift reserved 1/4 c. flour over, and mix gently. Add to first mixture and fold to blend. Add pineapple and lemon juice, mixing well.

Bake in greased and floured tube pan at 250F for 3 hr. Cool 10 min. Turn out onto rack and cool completely. Wrap with foil and refrigerate.

♣ *To keep raisins, nuts, and candied fruits from falling to the bottom of the cake, use 1 T. of the flour called for by the recipe and coat the fruit, etc., by sifting it with this flour. Add to the recipe when directed.*

Gold Cake

3 c. sifted cake flour	2 c. sugar
2 t. baking powder	1 t. vanilla
1/2 t. salt	1/2 t. lemon extract
10-12 egg yolks (left from angel food cake)	1 c. cold water

Arrange oven racks to bake cake on lowest level. Preheat to 350F. Sift flour before measuring. Then sift together three times the flour, baking powder, and salt. In large mixer bowl, beat egg yolks until thick and fluffy. Gradually add sugar, continuing to beat. Add vanilla, lemon extract, and cold water. Quickly sprinkle in flour; mix only enough to blend. Pour into ungreased tube cake pan. Bake at 350F about 1 hr. or until golden brown. Invert on cooling rack until cool. Loosen sides with serrated bread knife or slim spatula, then remove from pan.

Gold Cake uses egg yolks left over from angel food cake and other purposes. It is perfect with strawberries and whipped cream. Slices may be used as the basis for trifle. It is delicious when generously frosted with fluffy boiled white frosting or with chocolate-peanut butter frosting. It is also good with lemon sauce. This versatile cake is a real find!

Hummingbird Cake

3 c. flour	1-1/2 t. vanilla
1 t. soda	1 18-oz. can crushed pineapple, undrained
1/2 t. salt	
2 c. sugar	1 c. pecans, chopped
1 t. ground cinnamon	1 3/4 c. bananas, mashed
3 eggs	1/2 c. pecans, chopped
3/4 c. vegetable oil	

Sift flour, soda, salt, sugar, and cinnamon into large bowl. Make a hole in the center and add beaten eggs and oil, stirring until dry ingredients are moistened. Do not beat. Stir in vanilla, pineapple, 1 c. pecans, and bananas. Pour batter into three greased and floured 9-in. round cake pans. Bake at 350F for about 25 min. or a wooden pick inserted comes out clean. Cool in pans 10 min., invert on wire racks, and cool completely. Frost with Cream Cheese Frosting and sprinkle 1/2 c. pecans on top.

Cream Cheese Frosting: Combine 1/2 c. softened butter, 8 oz. softened cream cheese, 1 lb. sifted powdered sugar. Add 1 t. vanilla. A teaspoonful of milk may be added to reach spreading consistency. Frost between layers, on sides and top of Hummingbird Cake and sprinkle with chopped pecans.

Jiffy One-Egg Cupcakes   1930s Recipe

2 c. sifted flour
1/2 t. salt
2-1/2 t. baking powder
1 c. sugar

1/3 c. softened shortening
3/4 c. milk
1 t. vanilla
1 egg

Sift flour once before measuring. Sift into large mixer bowl the flour, salt, baking powder, and sugar. Add shortening, milk, and vanilla. Beat on #2 speed for 2 min., scraping bowl while beating. Stop mixer, scrape beaters. Add egg. Beat on #2 speed for 1 min., scraping bowl. Pour batter into 12 greased and floured cupcake pans. Bake at 325F for 25-30 min. This cake can also be baked in a 9-in. square pan.

This simple recipe can also be mixed by hand. Making and decorating cupcakes together is an activity that children enjoy on a rainy day or a gray wintry one.

Lady Baltimore Cake

1/2 c. plus 2 t. shortening
  (part butter)
1 1/4 c. sugar
6 egg yolks
2 1/4 c. sifted cake flour

2-1/2 t. baking powder
1/2 t. salt
3/4 c. milk
1 t. lemon extract
1/2 t. vanilla

Cream shortening and sugar. Beat egg yolks until thick and lemon colored; add to creamed mixture. Sift flour, baking powder, and salt together and add alternately with milk to which lemon extract and vanilla have been added. Pour into two 8-in. layer pans. Bake at 350F for 25 min. Cool. Fill with nut or fruit filling, and frost with 7-Minute Frosting. Or fill and frost with Lady Baltimore Cake Filling.

Lady Baltimore Cake Filling

3 c. sugar
1 c. water
3 egg whites
3 c. light corn syrup
2 c. seeded raisins,
  chopped fine

2 c. toasted pecans or walnuts,
  chopped fine
12 dried figs, chopped, *or*
  maraschino cherries, chopped
1/2 t. vanilla
1/2 t. almond extract

Mix sugar, water, and corn syrup in saucepan. Cook until it forms a firm ball in cold water. Beat egg whites in large mixer bowl until they form stiff peaks. Gradually pour cooked mixture over egg whites, beating constantly. When frosting begins to lose gloss, remove beaters and fold in raisins, pecans, figs or cherries, and flavorings. Spread between layers, on top and side of cake. Serves 12 to 18.

This cake is a rich, flavorful ending for a special dinner.

Lazy Daisy Oatmeal Cake

1-1/2 c. boiling water	2 eggs
1 c. uncooked oatmeal	1-1/2 c. flour
1/2 c. butter, softened	1 t. soda
1 c. sugar	1/2 t. salt
1 c. brown sugar	3/4 t. cinnamon
1 t. vanilla	1/4 t. nutmeg

Pour boiling water over oats; let stand 20 min. Beat butter until creamy. Gradually add sugar, beating until fluffy. Blend in vanilla and eggs. Add oat mixture, mix well. Sift flour, soda, and seasonings. Add to creamed mixture and mix well. Pour batter into greased and floured 9-in. square pan. Bake at 350F for 50-55 min. Do not remove from pan.

Frosting: Combine 1/4 c. melted butter, 1/2 c. brown sugar, 3 T. light cream, 1/2 c. chopped nuts, and 3/4 c. shredded coconut. Spread evenly over cake. Broil until frosting becomes bubbly. Serve warm or cold.

Lemon Bundt Cake

1 18-1/4-oz. pkg yellow cake mix	2/3 c. oil
3-1/2-oz. pkg instant lemon pudding mix	4 eggs
1/4 c. lemon juice, with water added to make 2/3 c. liquid	1 c. powdered sugar
	1/4 c. additional lemon juice

Combine cake mix, pudding mix, lemon juice and water, oil, and slightly beaten eggs. Pour into greased and floured 9-in. bundt pan. Bake at 350F for 50 min. or until done. Cool slightly.

While cake is still warm, remove from pan. Combine sifted powdered sugar and 1/4 c. lemon juice, beating until smooth. Punch holes in cake with fork and pour icing over. Serves 10-12.

Citrus Dream Cake

1 c. softened butter	1/2 t. soda
1/4 c. Crisco	1/2 t. salt
2 c. sugar	1 c. sour milk or buttermilk
5 eggs	1 t. vanilla
3 c. sifted flour	1/2 t. lemon extract
1 t. baking powder	

Cream butter, Crisco, and sugar. Add eggs one at a time, beating well after each addition. Sift together flour, baking powder, soda, and salt; add alternately with milk. Mix well. Stir in vanilla and lemon extract. Pour into three greased and floured 9-in. round pans. Bake at 350F for 25-30 min. or until done. Cool for 10 min. in pans; then remove to racks to cool.

Lemon-Orange Frosting: Combine 1/2 c. softened butter, 3 T. orange juice, 3 T. lemon juice, 2 T. grated orange peel, 2 T. grated lemon peel, 1 t. lemon extract, and up to 1-1/2 lb. sifted powdered sugar. Beat well. Add a little more orange juice if needed to reach spreading consistency. Frost between layers, on top and sides of cake. Serves 10-12.

Mocha Cake   Karen Pickett

5 eggs, separated   1 c. flour
1 c. sugar   1 t. baking powder
4 t. instant coffee

Beat egg yolks until thick; gradually add sugar and beat until thick. Mix coffee with water to fill a cup. Add 3 T. of coffee liquid to sugar and eggs and beat. Sift flour and baking powder, and beat into mixture. Beat egg whites until stiff and fold into batter. Pour into ungreased angel food pan and bake at 300F for 1 hr. Cool. Split in half crosswise and fill.

Filling: Whip 1/2 pt. cream and add sugar and coffee to taste. Spread on bottom layer of cake. Replace top layer and frost cake with butter cream frosting, substituting coffee mixture for milk and vanilla. Refrigerate 2 hr.

Delicate Nut Cake   Aunt Ella Goodman

2 c. sugar   2 t. baking powder
1 c. butter   6 egg whites
1 c. milk   1 t. vanilla
3 c. sifted cake flour

Cream butter and sugar. Sift together flour and baking powder. Add alternately with milk to creamed mixture. Stir in vanilla. Beat egg whites until they form stiff peaks. Fold them lightly into batter. Pour into two greased and floured 9-in. layer pans. Bake at 350F about 30 min. Cool and turn out on racks.

Filling: Combine 1 c. sugar, 3/4 c. sour cream, 1 c. chopped nuts, and 6 egg yolks in saucepan. Cook over low heat (325F), stirring constantly, until mixture thickens. Cool. Place one layer, top down, on cake plate. Cover with filling, being careful to have a generous amount on outer edges. Place second layer, top side up, carefully on filled layer.

Frosting: Boil 2 c. sugar in 3/4 c. water until it spins a strong thread. Beat 2 egg whites until they form stiff peaks. Beating rapidly with electric mixer or whisk, pour syrup gradually into egg whites. When thick and cool, spread on sides and top of cake, swirling decoratively.

This makes a large, elegant party cake that serves 12-14. This cake was one of Aunt Ella's specialties, eagerly anticipated by family and guests.

Lisa's Orange Cake

1 c. shortening	1 t. salt
2 c. sugar	1 t. vanilla
4 eggs	1/2 c. milk
3 c. flour	1/2 c. orange juice
4 t. baking powder	1/2 orange rind, grated

Cream shortening and sugar. Add eggs one at a time, beating well after each addition. Stir in vanilla. Sift together flour, baking powder, and salt and add to creamed mixture alternately with liquids. You may add 2 T. more liquid to make a smooth cake batter. Pour into two greased and floured 9-in. cake pans. Bake at 350F for 35 min. Test with a toothpick at 32 min. Fill with Orange Cake Filling, and top with 7-Minute Frosting.

Orange Cake Filling: In a saucepan, combine 1 c. fresh orange juice, grated rind of half an orange, 1 c. sugar, 1/2 c. flour, a pinch of salt, and 2 beaten egg yolks. Cook over medium heat, stirring constantly, until filling is thick and clear. Stir in 2 T. butter. Cool. Fill cake generously.

Orange Glaze Cake   Aunt Luella Petersen

3/4 c. butter	1/2 t. salt
1 c. sugar	1 c. buttermilk
2 eggs	Grated peel of 2 oranges
2-1/2 c. sifted cake flour	1 t. vanilla
1-1/2 t. baking powder	1 c. walnuts, chopped
1 t. soda	

Cream butter and sugar. Add eggs one at a time, beating well after each addition. Sift together flour, baking powder, soda, and salt. Add to creamed mixture alternately with buttermilk. Stir in vanilla, walnuts, and grated orange peel. Pour into greased 7 x 12 in. loaf pan. Bake at 300F for 35 min. Cool cake for 10 min. Then pour glaze over cake.

Orange Glaze: In saucepan, combine juice and pulp of 2 oranges with
1 c. sugar. Boil 3 min. to dissolve sugar. Pour over cake. Let stand several hours
before serving.

Orange-Raisin Cake

2 1/4 c. flour	2 eggs
1 t. soda	Peel of 1 large orange,
1/2 t. salt	chopped very fine
1/2 c. butter or margarine	1 c. raisins, chopped fine
1 c. sugar	1/2 c. walnuts, coarsely chopped
1 t. vanilla	1 c. buttermilk

Sift together cake flour, soda, and salt. In large bowl, cream butter, sugar, and
vanilla. Beat in eggs one at a time. Add the chopped orange peel (no white; grate
if easier), raisins, and walnuts. Alternately add in thirds the flour and buttermilk.
Stir well. Turn batter into a greased 9-in. square cake pan. Bake at 350F about 40
min. or until a toothpick comes out clean. Remove cake from oven and spread
glaze over top of hot cake. Return to 350F oven until glaze bubbles, 3-5 min.
Place cake on rack to cool. Serves 12.

Glaze: Combine 1 c. sugar and juice from 1 orange (about 1/3 c.).

Orange Surprise Cake

1 pkg yellow cake mix	1 pkg lemon Jell-O
4 eggs	1/2 c. orange juice
3/4 c. oil	2 c. powdered sugar
3/4 c. water	

Mix orange juice and powdered sugar well. Set aside. In electric mixer, blend cake
mix, Jell-O, eggs, oil, and water for 5 min. on medium speed. Pour into a greased
9 x 13 in. pan. Bake at 350F for 40 min. Cool 5 min. Using fork with long tines,
puncture cake top, spacing holes about 1 in. apart. Spread the orange juice mixture
evenly. Cool. Delicious with whipped cream. Serves 15.

Paprika Cake   Luella Petersen

1 c. shortening	1/2 t. salt
1 c. sugar	3 t. paprika
1/2 t. lemon extract	1 c. milk
1/2 t. orange peel, grated	1 c. crushed pineapple, drained
3 c. sifted cake flour	1 c. seedless raisins, ground *or*
5 t. baking powder	very finely chopped
4 eggs, separated	1 c. walnuts, chopped

Cream shortening and sugar well. Add lemon extract and orange peel. Add well-beaten egg yolks. Sift together three times the cake flour, baking powder, salt, and paprika. Add alternately with milk. Beat well. Stir in crushed pineapple, raisins, and walnuts. Beat egg whites until they form stiff peaks. Fold egg whites into batter. Pour into two greased and floured 10-in. layer pans or 9 x 13 in. pan. Bake at 350F for about 25 min. for layers or 50 min. for loaf. Cool on rack.

Frosting: Blend 3 t. butter with 2 c. powdered sugar sifted with 1 t. paprika, and 1/4 c. pineapple juice. Beat well and spread on cooled cake. Sprinkle with additional nuts if desired.

Petits Fours   Ruth Harbour

1 c. white sugar	1/2 t. vanilla
1/2 c. butter and shortening mixed	1/4 t. almond extract
	3/4 c. milk
2 c. sifted cake flour	6 egg whites
3 t. baking powder	4 T. sugar
1/4 t. salt	

Cream 1 c. sugar and butter-shortening mix until very light. Blend in vanilla and almond extracts. Sift flour, baking powder, and salt. Add alternately with milk, beating after each addition. Beat egg whites until foamy. Gradually add 4 T. sugar and beat until soft peaks form. Fold into batter. Pour into a greased 9 x 13 x 2 in. pan that has been lined with greased waxed paper. Bake at 350F about 35-40 min., or until a toothpick comes out clean.

Cool cake 5 min., then turn onto a cooling rack. Remove waxed paper. Let cool completely. With a sharp serrated knife, cut into 1-1/2-in. squares, or use a 1-1/2-in. round cutter to vary shapes. Place cakes on rack with waxed paper or cookie sheet underneath. Frost with icing, and if desired, spoon second coat over cakes to glaze. Pipe decorative trim if desired.

Petits Fours Icing and Glaze

2 c. white sugar	1 t. vanilla
1/4 t. cream of tartar	1-1/2 c. sifted powdered sugar
1 c. hot water	2 drops food coloring (optional)

Combine white sugar, cream of tartar, and hot water in 1-qt. saucepan. Cook to a thin syrup (about 212F) — about 5 min.; do not stir. Cool to lukewarm. Add vanilla. Stir in powdered sugar 1/2 c. at a time, blending well with each addition. Icing should be of pouring consistency; if too stiff, set it over hot water. Spoon icing over cakes evenly. (Use a small spatula to coat sides if needed.) If icing is too thick to pour, add 1/2 t. boiling water and blend.

If you wish to tint the icing, add coloring a drop at a time. Pastel pink, green, and yellow are attractive. Use a pastry tube to pipe a flower if desired. Let icing harden completely. Store cakes in a covered cake pan with space between cakes. Serve on a tiered stand or cake plate with bonbons or other fancy cakes. Yield: 48 1-1/2-in. square cakes.

♣ *Delicate white cake squares frosted with a creamy glaze make this a traditional party dessert. Tint the icing a delicate pastel to complement your color scheme for a bridal shower, graduation party, or birthday party.*

Poppy Seed Bundt Cake

1/2 c. butter or margarine	2 oz. poppy seeds
4 eggs, separated	1/2 c. sour cream *or*
1-1/2 c. sugar	half and half
2 c. flour	1 t. vanilla
1 t. soda	

Cream butter and sugar. Beat in egg yolks well. Sift flour and soda together and add to creamed mixture with poppy seeds, sour cream, and vanilla. Blend to a smooth batter. In a separate bowl, beat egg whites until they are very stiff. Fold egg whites into batter until it is just mixed. Pour into well-greased bundt pan or tube pan. Bake at 350F for 1 hr. Invert to cool. Remove from pan and sprinkle with powdered sugar.

This cake stays very moist.

Poppy Seed Cake I

1 pkg yellow cake mix	1/2 c. oil
1 pkg toasted coconut	1 c. hot water
pudding mix	1 T. poppy seeds
4 eggs	

Combine all ingredients in large mixer bowl, beating 3 min. on medium speed. Pour into greased tube pan. Bake in 350F oven 50-60 min. Cool before cutting. May be refrigerated. Serves 12-16.

Poppy Seed Cake II   Doris Dickson

6 eggs, separated
3 c. sugar
1 c. shortening
1 c. buttermilk or
  sour milk
1/4 t. soda

3-1/2 c. flour
1 T. butter flavoring
1+ T. poppy seeds
1/2 c. milk
1 t. almond flavoring
1 t. lemon flavoring

Soak poppy seeds in milk for 1 to 2 hr. Grease and flour bundt pan and a small loaf pan. In large bowl, combine sugar, shortening, and egg yolks. Beat until well mixed. Sift together flour and soda, and add alternately with buttermilk. Add flavorings, poppy seeds, and milk. Beat egg whites until stiff and fold in gently. Pour into pans. Bake at 350F for 1 hr. Rest 5 min. Turn out and glaze.

Glaze: Combine 1-1/2 c. powdered sugar, 1/2 c. orange juice, 1 t. butter flavoring, and 1 t. almond flavoring. Drizzle over warm cake.

Pound Cake I

3 c. sugar
1 c. soft butter
5 eggs
3 c. sifted cake flour

1/2 t. baking powder
1 c. milk
1 t. vanilla
1 t. almond or lemon extract

Cream butter and sugar. Beat in eggs one at a time until well blended. Sift flour and baking powder together, and add alternately with milk. Stir in flavorings. Pour into a greased and floured tube cake pan. Bake at 325F for 1 hr. 20 min. Remove from oven; let sit 10 min. before removing from pan.

This makes an excellent base for trifle or shortcake. Or slice and serve as afternoon tea cake.

Pound Cake II

2 sticks unsalted butter,
  softened
2 c. sugar
4 eggs
1 t. vanilla

3 c. sifted flour
3 t. baking powder
1 t. salt
1 c. milk

Cream butter and sugar. Add eggs one at a time, beating well after each addition. Stir in vanilla. Sift together flour, baking powder, and salt and gradually beat into creamed mixture. Stir in milk until smooth. Pour into a greased and floured bundt pan. Bake at 350F for 1 hr. 15 min.

Chocolate Pound Cake

2 sticks butter or margarine	3 c. sifted cake flour
1/2 c. solid shortening	1/2 c. cocoa
3 c. sugar	1 t. salt
5 eggs	1/2 t. baking powder
1 1/4 c. milk	1 T. vanilla

Cream butter and sugar. Beat in eggs one at a time. Sift flour, cocoa, salt, and baking powder together. Add to creamed mixture alternately with milk. Stir in vanilla and blend well. Pour into greased and floured tube pan. Bake at 325F for 1 hr. 45 min. Cool. Wrap in foil to keep.

Mrs. Kringel's Prune Cake   Amelia Kringel

1/2 c. shortening	1 c. sugar
3/4 t. salt	2 eggs
1 t. cinnamon	1 t. soda
1/4 t. allspice	2 c. flour
1/4 t. cloves	1 c. prune juice
1/4 t. nutmeg	1 c. cooked prunes, cut fine

Combine softened shortening with salt and spices. Add sugar and eggs and beat well. Sift flour and soda. Add alternately with prune juice. Fold in cooked prunes. Bake at 375F for 55 min.

Raisin Layer Cake

2/3 to 1 c. dark or golden raisins	2 1/4 c. sifted flour
2/3 c. soft shortening	2-1/2 t. baking powder
1-1/2 c. sugar, divided	1 t. salt
1-1/2 t. vanilla	1 t. cream of tartar
3 eggs, 2 separated	1 c. milk

Chop raisins coarsely. Cream shortening, 1 1/4 c. sugar, and vanilla until light and fluffy. Beat 1 egg and 2 egg yolks together well. Beat into creamed mixture. Beat 2 egg whites until they form soft peaks, then beat in remaining 1/4 c. sugar to make medium stiff meringue. Sift flour together twice with baking powder, salt, and cream of tartar. Add to creamed mixture alternately with milk, beginning and ending with flour. Stir in raisins. Gently fold in meringue. Spoon batter into two greased and floured 8- or 9-in. round cake pans. Bake at 350F for 30-35 min. or until done. Cool on wire racks.

Variations: For *Chocolate Raisin Cake*, use basic recipe, adding 1-1/2 oz. unsweetened chocolate, melted and cooled, to creamed mixture. Decrease flour to 2 c.

For *Raisin Spice Cake*, substitute 3/4 c. packed brown sugar plus 3/4 c. granulated sugar for the 1-1/2 c. sugar in basic recipe. Add 1 t. cinnamon, 1/2 t. nutmeg, and 1/4 t. ground cloves along with the vanilla.

Raisin Nuggets Cupcakes   Anna M. Petersen

3/4 c. butter (or half butter,   2 c. sifted flour
  half lard)   1/2 t. soda
1 c. sugar   2 t. baking powder
2 eggs   1 t. cinnamon
1 to 2 c. raisins (cooked) and   1/2 t. nutmeg
  2/3 c. raisin juice

Cover raisins with water in saucepan and cook until tender; drain, conserving juice. Cream butter. Beat in sugar. Add eggs, and beat well. Sift together flour, soda, baking powder, and spices. Add to creamed mixture, and beat. Add raisins and 2/3 c. raisin juice. Stir to combine. Spoon into well-greased muffin tins. Bake at 350F for 45 min. Yield: about 20 to 24 raisin cupcakes. Ice with butter cream or cream cheese frosting.

This simple 1920's recipe was one my mother made often. I liked her chocolate frosting. We children were delighted to find a raisin nugget in our school lunch pail. Mother was very resourceful; she prepared excellent meals with simple ingredients. I try to follow her example.

Southern Favorite Cake

3/4 c. butter   1 t. vanilla
1-1/2 c. sugar   1/2 t. maple flavoring
2 3/4 c. sifted cake flour   1/4 t. black walnut flavoring
3 t. baking powder   5 egg whites
1 c. strong cold coffee

Cream butter and sugar thoroughly. Sift flour and baking powder together and add alternately with coffee, beating well after each addition. Beat egg whites until they form stiff peaks. Fold in flavorings. Then fold egg whites into batter. Pour into two greased and floured 9-in. layer cake pans. Bake at 350F for about 30 min.

Frosting: In saucepan, combine 1/2 c. butter and 1 c. brown sugar. Boil for 2 min. Add 1/4 c. milk, and bring to boil. Remove from heat and beat in 2 c. powdered sugar and 1/2 t. maple flavoring.

Spice Cake

1/2 c. shortening	2 c. sifted flour
1-1/2 c. brown sugar	1 t. cinnamon
1 egg	1/4 t. cloves
1 c. raisins, chopped	1/4 t. nutmeg
1 c. sour milk	1/2 t. soda
Pinch of salt	1 t. baking powder

Cream shortening with brown sugar. Beat egg until light and then beat into creamed mixture. Add sour milk alternately with raisins and flour sifted together with other dry ingredients, ending with flour. Beat smooth. Pour into greased 9 x 12 in. pan. Bake at 350F for 50-60 min. Frost with caramel or cream cheese frosting.

This cake keeps well.

♣ *Arrange herbs and spices in alphabetical order for convenience.*

♣ *Use a plastic turntable to make small containers visible and quickly available in cupboards.*

Strawberry Cake   Anna M. Petersen

1 pkg white cake mix	1/2 c. water
1 pkg strawberry Jell-O	4 eggs
1/2 c. salad oil	1 box frozen strawberries

Combine Jell-O with cake mix. Add oil, water, and eggs. Beat on medium speed about 4 min. Fold in thawed strawberries. Pour into greased 9 x 13 in. pan. Bake at 350F for 40 min.

Serve warm sprinkled with powdered sugar or topped with whipped cream. This cake is the consistency of chiffon cake.

Sunshine Cake   Mrs. Hans Hamann

1 c. sugar	11 egg yolks
1-1/2 c. sifted cake flour	1/2 c. cold water
1/2 t. baking powder	1/2 t. salt
1/2 t. cream of tartar	1 t. vanilla

Sift flour, baking powder, and cream of tartar five times. Set aside. Put egg yolks, cold water, salt, and vanilla into small mixer bowl. Beat 15 min. or until mixture stands up in peaks. Beat in sugar gradually. Fold flour mixture lightly and care-fully into egg mixture. Pour into ungreased tube pan. Bake at 350F for about 1 hr. Invert pan until cake is completely cool.

Frost with butter cream frosting flavored with orange or lemon. This is a good way to use egg yolks when baking angel food.

♣ *Freeze leftover egg whites and store in freezer until you need them for meringues or other uses.*

Tea Cupcakes

1 c. sugar	1 t. baking powder
1/2 c. butter	2 eggs
1/2 c. milk	1 t. vanilla
1-1/2 c. flour	

Cream butter and sugar. Add eggs and beat hard. Sift flour with baking powder and add to creamed mixture alternately with milk. Pour into 16 greased muffin tins. Bake at 350F for 20 min.

These may be frosted with chocolate, caramel, or plain buttercream icing. Unfrosted, they are very good when served with a lemon or caramel sauce.

Texas Sheet Cake

1 stick margarine	2 c. sifted flour
1/2 c. Mazola or other oil	1/2 t. baking powder
1 c. water	1/4 t. salt
4 T. cocoa	1 t. vanilla
2 c. sugar	2 eggs

In a medium saucepan combine margarine, oil, water, and cocoa. Bring to a quick boil; remove from heat and stir in sugar, flour sifted with baking powder and salt, beaten eggs, and vanilla. Pour into greased and floured 9 x 15 in. pan. Bake at 400F for 20 min.

Frosting: In a saucepan, bring 1 stick margarine, 2 T. cocoa, and 1/3 c. milk to boil. Remove from heat and add 2 c. sifted powdered sguar, 1 t. vanilla, and 1 c. chopped nuts. Beat well and spread over warm cake. Serves 20-24.

White Layer Cake

2 1/4 c. sifted cake flour
1-1/2 c. sugar
3-1/2 t. baking powder
1 t. salt

1/2 c. shortening
1 c. milk, divided
1 t. vanilla
4 egg whites

Sift flour, sugar, baking powder, and salt into large mixer bowl. Add shortening, 2/3 c. milk, and vanilla and beat on medium speed for 2 min. Add remaining milk and egg whites. Beat 2 min., scraping sides of bowl often. Pour batter into two greased 9-in. round pans lined with waxed paper. Bake at 350F for 30-35 min. Cool on racks 10 min. Remove from pans and peel off waxed paper. Fill and frost cake as desired.

Lemon, nut, and pineapple fillings are good with this delicate cake. See recipes on pages 113 and 115.

Wine Cake
Dorothy Harbour

1 pkg yellow cake mix
1 pkg vanilla instant
 pudding mix
4 eggs

3/4 c. Mazola oil
3/4 c. cream sherry
1 t. nutmeg

Combine cake and pudding mixes in large mixer bowl. Add eggs, oil, sherry, and nutmeg. Beat well for 3 min. Pour into greased springform pan. Bake at 350F for 45 min. Cool and then turn out of pan. Sprinkle with powdered sugar.

Butter Frosting

1/2 c. soft butter
3 c. sifted powdered sugar
1 t. vanilla

1/8 t. salt
1 T. cream

Combine ingredients and beat with mixer until fluffy. Spread on cake.

Chocolate Icing

4 oz. semisweet chocolate
1 T. butter
1/2 c. milk
1 c. granulated sugar

1 t. vanilla
Dash of salt
Powdered sugar

Melt chocolate and butter over boiling water. Add milk and granulated sugar alternately, stirring after each addition. When mixture is smooth, transfer pan to direct heat and bring to boiling point. Boil until mixture will holds a soft ball when dropped into cold water. Remove from heat and cool slightly. Stir in vanilla and salt. Beat until mixture is of spreading consistency, adding a little powdered sugar if necessary to thicken it. Spread on cake.

Chocolate Frosting

1 c. brown sugar	1/4 c. cream
1 oz. unsweetened chocolate	3 T. butter
1/2 t. salt	1/2 t. vanilla

Melt chocolate over low heat. Stir in sugar, salt, cream, and butter. Bring to boil and boil 2 min. Add vanilla and beat until thickened. Spread on cake.

Caramel Frosting   Anna M. Petersen

1-1/2 c. brown sugar	1 t. vanilla
1/2 c. half and half	1 T. cornstarch
1 T. butter	1 t. baking powder

Mix sugar, half and half, butter, and cornstarch in saucepan. Cook to soft ball stage, stirring to prevent burning. Remove from heat and beat in vanilla and baking powder. Beat until thick and spread on cake.

This frosts a 9 x 13 in. cake. Use on yellow, chocolate, or spice cake.

Lemon Butter Cream

6 T. butter	Dash of salt
4 T. lemon juice	3 c. sifted powdered sugar
Grated rind of 1 lemon	

Cream butter and lemon rind. Add half the powdered sugar and mix thoroughly. Add salt. Then add remaining sugar alternately with lemon juice, using just enough juice to make frosting easy to spread. Enough for a large cake.

Lemon Filling for White Cake

3 large egg yolks	2 T. grated lemon rind
1 c. sugar	1/4 t. salt
1/2 c. lemon juice	

Beat egg yolks well. Add sugar, lemon juice and rind, and salt. Place mixture in top of double boiler and cook until thick. Let filling cool before spreading between two cake layers.

Lemon Sauce

2 c. sugar
1/3 c. cornstarch
1/3 c. lemon juice
1 T. grated lemon rind

1/4 t. salt
4 c. boiling water
1/4 c. butter

Mix sugar, cornstarch, and salt in saucepan. Add boiling water and boil until thick and clear. Stir in butter, lemon juice, and rind. Yield: 12 servings of 1/3 cup each.

Cool to lukewarm and serve about 1/3 c. over a plain cupcake, gingerbread, or square of yellow cake. Very good.

Mocha Frosting

1/2 c. butter, soft
1 egg
1 lb. sifted powdered sugar

1-1/2 T. cocoa
1/4 c. hot strong coffee
1 t. vanilla

Cream butter and egg. Sift powdered sugar and cocoa together. Add alternately with hot coffee. Beat until smooth. Stir in vanilla. If too thick, add a bit more hot coffee. Spread on cake.

Nutmeg Sauce

2 c. boiling water
1 c. sugar
1/2 t. salt
1 T. vinegar

1 t. nutmeg
1 T. flour
1 T. butter

Combine sugar, salt, nutmeg, and flour. Add to boiling water. Add butter and simmer 5 min. Remove from heat and add vinegar. Serve over spice cake.

Orange–Cream Cheese Frosting

1/2 c. low-fat cottage cheese
8 oz. softened cream cheese
2 t. vanilla

1 t. grated orange rind
1 c. sifted powdered sugar

Process cottage cheese in food processor until smooth. Add cream cheese, vanilla, and orange rind; process until just smooth. Add powdered sugar. Pulse 3 to 5 times or until smooth. Yield: 1-1/2 cups.

Orange Fluff Topping   Anna M. Petersen

3 egg yolks
1/2 c. sugar
Juice of 1 large orange
1 T. grated orange rind

1 c. heavy cream, whipped
1/2 c. grated coconut *or*
   1/2 c. toasted almonds, chopped

Mix egg yolks, sugar, and orange juice in top of double boiler. Cook over hot water until mixture thickens, about 15 min. Remove from heat. Stir in grated orange rind. Cool. Fold in whipped cream and almonds or coconut. Serve on angel cake wedges. Yield: about 3 cups.

My Peanut Butter Icing

1/3 c. cocoa
2 T. soft butter
2-1/2 to 3 c. powdered sugar
1/4 c. chopped peanuts (optional)

1 c. creamy peanut butter
3/4 c. hot strong coffee
1 t. vanilla

Sift cocoa and powdered sugar. Blend with butter, peanut butter, and coffee until smooth. Add vanilla, beat to spreading consistency. Ice cake and sprinkle with chopped peanuts if desired.

Penuche

1 c. brown sugar
1 c. granulated sugar
1 T. white Karo syrup
1/2 t. vanilla

4 T. butter
1/4 t. salt
1/2 c. top milk *or*
   half and half

In saucepan, combine ingredients and bring to boil. Boil 2-1/2 min until soft ball will form in cold water. Cool. Add vanilla. Beat until thickened, and spread on cake.

Pineapple Filling or Topping for White Cake

1 #2 can crushed pineapple,
   drained; save juice
1 egg
3/4 c. sugar

1 T. cornstarch
1 t. butter
1/2 t. vanilla
1/2 t. milk

Mix sugar and cornstarch; beat egg and pineapple juice. Combine with pineapple in saucepan and cook until thick, stirring often. Remove from heat and add butter and vanilla. Add milk if needed to spread.

Use between layers of a white or yellow cake, with a boiled white icing on top. This filling is equally good on top of a 9 x 12 in. cake; drizzle a powdered sugar glaze atop. Refrigerate.

Sea Foam

2 egg whites	1/3 c. water
1-1/2 c. brown sugar	1/2 t. cream of tartar

Mix all ingredients in top of double boiler. Beat with rotary beater 7 min. or until it stands in peaks. Remove from heat and beat until stiff enough to spread.

This is a delicious icing for a chocolate cake.

Seven-Minute Frosting I / Boiled Frosting

7/8 c. sugar	2 T. water
2 egg whites	Pinch of cream of tartar
1 T. white Karo syrup	Pinch of salt
1/2 t. vanilla	

Combine all ingredients except vanilla in top of double boiler. Beat constantly while cooking over boiling water for 7 min. Do not let water touch bottom of the upper boiler. Add vanilla and spread.

Seven-Minute Icing II

2 egg whites	1/4 t. cream of tartar
1-1/2 c. sugar	1 T. light corn syrup
5 T. cold water	1/2 t. vanilla

Place all ingredients except vanilla into top of double boiler and beat with rotary or electric mixer 1/2 min. Then place over rapidly boiling water — but not letting water touch bottom of the upper boiler. Beat steadily for 7 min. Remove from heat and add vanilla. Beat until frosting is of spreading consistency.

This icing is very good with chocolate or white cakes. One may add chopped nuts or sprinkle nuts or coconut on top. Frosts one 9 x 13 in. cake or fills and frosts a two-layer cake.

Anise Candy   Sharon Jepsen Albers

3 c. sugar
1 c. white Karo syrup
1/2 c. boiling water

1 t. red food coloring
1 t. anise oil

In a saucepan, combine sugar, syrup, and boiling water. Cook but don't stir until mixture thickens. Test in cold water: a drop should stand up in peaks. Add red food coloring and anise oil. Shake the candy to mix. Pour into a large buttered pan. When cooled, break into small pieces.

Anise oil can be purchased in a drug store.

Bourbon Balls

3 c. vanilla wafers in fine
  crumbs
1-1/2 c. nuts, finely chopped

5 T. bourbon
1 c. powdered sugar
3 T. white Karo syrup

Combine ingredients. Make small balls and then roll in sifted powdered sugar. Do not bake. Store in air-tight containers with foil between layers. Yield: 4 to 5 dozen 3/4-in. balls.

Buckeyes

1 c. butter, softened
2 c. crunchy peanut butter
3 to 4 c. powdered sugar

1/4 bar paraffin wax
1 12-oz. pkg real chocolate chips

Combine butter, peanut butter, and powdered sugar, blending well. Roll small balls (about 1 t.) and refrigerate 3-4 hr. Melt wax and chocolate chips in top of double boiler. Stick toothpick in peanut butter ball and dip, leaving half undipped. Place on waxed paper. May be frozen. Yield: about 100.

Cream Butterscotch Candy   Jackie Schneekloth

1 c. sugar
1 c. corn syrup
1/2 c. cream

1/4 c. butter
1/8 t. salt

Place all ingredients in saucepan. Heat slowly until sugar is dissolved, stirring constantly. Continue to stir constantly after mixture begins to thicken, lowering heat to prevent burning. Cook to firm ball stage. The process takes 45 min., stirring the whole time. Pour into buttered pan to 3/4 to 1 in. thickness. Mark into squares when cool and cut with sharp knife or scissors. Wrap pieces in cellophane.

This candy is similar to caramels.

Rice Krispies Treat / Children's Candy

1 c. sugar	1 c. peanut butter
1 c. white corn syrup	1 pkg chocolate chips
6 c. Kellogg's Rice Krispies	1 pkg butterscotch chips

Boil sugar and syrup to soft ball stage (236F). Remove from heat. Add peanut butter and stir until melted. Add cereal and mix well. Pour into 9 x 13 in. buttered pan and press down firmly. In double boiler, melt the chocolate and butterscotch chips. Pour over hardened Rice Krispies. Cut into 1 x 2 in. bars and cool. Yield: 4-1/2 dozen bars.

Children's Candy   Gertrude Davis

1/2 pkg cornflakes	1 c. light cream
1/2 pkg Rice Krispies	1 c. white corn syrup
1 c. flake coconut	1 c. sugar
1 c. peanuts or chopped walnuts	

Mix cereals, coconut, and nuts well and set aside. Combine cream, corn syrup, and sugar in saucepan. Cook until soft ball stage. Pour syrup over cereal mixture and mix well. Pour into lightly buttered 9 x 15 in. pan. When cool, cut into squares.

Choice Candy   Leila Fitchner

1 c. sugar	3 c. cornflakes
1 c. white syrup	1/3 c. coconut
1/2 c. cream	1/2 c. black walnuts, chopped

Combine sugar, syrup, and cream in saucepan and mix well. Bring to a boil. Test to soft ball stage. Remove from heat and fold in cornflakes, coconut, and walnuts. Drop by teaspoonfuls on buttered cookie sheets.

Christmas Wreaths

30 large marshmallows
1/2 c. butter
1 t. vanilla
Cinnamon red hot candies

2 t. green food coloring
3-1/2 c. cornflakes
1/2 c. walnuts, chopped (optional)

Combine marshmallows, butter, vanilla, and food coloring in top of double boiler. When melted, stir well and add cornflakes (and, if desired, walnuts). Mix lightly. Drop by teaspoonfuls onto waxed paper. With hands, form into small wreaths or sprays. Decorate with cinnamon red hots as holly berries. Chill.

Coconut Mink   Ruby Phillips

2 boxes powdered sugar
2 sticks butter or margarine
1 can Eagle Brand sweetened
   condensed milk

1 box (4 to 6 oz.) Angel Flake
   grated coconut
1-1/2 c. nut meats, chopped fine

Melt butter and mix all ingredients together in large bowl. Add 2 t. vanilla. Chill overnight in refrigerator. Form into small balls (half the size of a walnut). Set on waxed paper on cookie sheet and refrigerate. When balls are cold and firm, insert a toothpick about 3/4 in. into each candy and quickly dip in coating.

Coating: Melt 2 c. chocolate chips and 1 bar paraffin over hot water. Use toothpick to dip each piece and set on waxed paper again to dry. Keep dipping chocolate over hot water to keep it fluid. Use care with hot paraffin. Keep in a cold place or refrigerator. Yield: 120 balls.

♣ *To ease dipping, use a small saucepan for the chocolate and paraffin mixture, and tilt it to give depth for dipping; set it into a pan of hot water. Quickly pass balls through the liquid coating, which dries in a few seconds. Mother always made these for Christmas.*

Lea's Cornflake Candy   Lea Harbour

1/2 c. sugar
1/2 c. white syrup

1 c. crunchy peanut butter
3 c. cornflakes

Cook sugar and syrup until firm ball stage. Add peanut butter and blend. Add cornflakes. Drop by teaspoonfuls on waxed paper. Yield: about 30.

Divine Divinity   Sarah Kossove

1 c. sugar	1 c. light Karo syrup
1/2 c. water	1/4 c. water
3 c. sugar	1 t. vanilla
3 large egg whites	1 c. chopped walnuts

Part 1: Cook 1 c. sugar and 1/2 c. water until it spins a thread.

Part 2: At the same time, in a heavy stainless steel saucepan, combine

3 c. sugar, Karo syrup, and 1/4 c. water and cook on medium heat, letting it boil to soft ball stage.

Part 3: Beat egg whites to a stiff froth. Using electric mixer, add first syrup slowly. Do not scrape pan. Continue beating until second syrup makes a firm soft ball in cold water. Pour the second hot syrup slowly into the egg white mixture while beating on medium high. Use spatula to keep sides cleared. Beat until candy loses shine and holds shape. Remove mixer beaters. Fold in vanilla and chopped walnuts. Working quickly, drop by teaspoonfuls on waxed paper. One may also pour divinity into a 9 x 12 in. buttered pan and cut into squares. Yield: 70 dropped pieces.

Variation: Dip bottom of each piece in melted chocolate, or color candy with red or green food coloring. Omit nuts.

This recipe was given me by a dear friend, Sarah Kossove, and it has been my signature candy for fifty years. This mellow, tender confection melts in one's mouth. It is perfect for dropping into one-inch puffs that dress up the dessert plate.

♣ *Avoid making candy on stormy, humid or cloudy days.*

Mother's Cream Fondant   Anna M. Petersen

2 c. white sugar	Halves of pecans or walnuts
1 T. white corn syrup	Peppermint or other flavoring
1 c. sweet cream	

Mix ingredients well and place over low heat to dissolve sugar. Increase heat and boil to soft ball stage. Pour out on damp platter or marble slab. Work with spatula until creamy. When cool enough, flavoring may be added and kneaded in. Shape into 3/4-in. balls. Top with a pecan or walnut pressed down to flatten candy. Or, make two smaller balls and place a nutmeat between, then press flat.

Variations: For *Filled Dates*, cut a slit in the side of a date and press half a teaspoonful of fondant into it. Roll the date in granulated sugar.

Dip pieces of fondant in melted chocolate or roll them in chopped nuts.

To make *Chocolate-Covered Cherries*, drain a small jar of maraschino cherries in a sieve for 4 hr. Take a teaspoonful of fondant, make a ball and slit one side to insert cherry. Smooth fondant to cover cherry. Chill overnight on a cookie sheet. In a double boiler, melt a package of chocolate chips and 1/4 slab of confectioner's paraffin. Cool. Dip each candy, held on a toothpick. Place on waxed paper and chill.

Making chocolate-covered cherries was an activity the whole family enjoyed. Fondants are a nice addition to a gift box of candy. Mother added red and green food coloring to different batches to create pretty variations for the holiday season.

No-Cook Fondant

1/3 c. soft butter	1 t. vanilla or other flavoring
1/2 c. Karo white syrup	1 lb. sifted powdered sugar
1/2 t. salt	

Blend butter, syrup, salt, and flavoring. Add sugar all at once. Stir, then knead. Turn onto board and knead until well blended and smooth. Form into 3/4-in. balls, top with walnut half, and press down to flatten.

Remarkable Fudge   Ruby Phillips

4 c. sugar	2 pkg chocolate chips
1 14-1/2-oz. can Carnation	1 pt. marshmallow cream
evaporated milk	1 t. vanilla
1/4 lb. butter	

Boil sugar, milk, and butter together until soft ball stage, stirring constantly to avoid scorching — about 45 min. Remove from heat, add chocolate chips, marshmallow cream, and vanilla. Stir until blended. Add chopped nuts if desired. Pour into a buttered 9 x 12 in. pan. Cool and cut into pieces. Store in tightly covered containers.

Variation: Substitute butterscotch chips for chocolate chips. Then add chopped pecans or brazil nuts. Half a pound of marshmallows may be substituted for the marshmallow cream.

♣ *Place pieces of chocolate fudge in layers separated by foil, in an airtight container. (A rectangular one with a plastic lid is fine.) This will result in creamy, softer fudge.*

Velvet Fudge   Birdie Gilman

3 T. butter   1 c. milk
3 T. cocoa   1 t. vanilla
3 c. sugar   1 c. nuts, chopped

Combine butter, cocoa, sugar, and milk in a saucepan. Cook over medium heat to soft ball stage. Cool. Add vanilla and nuts. Beat until thick and creamy. Drop by teaspoonfuls on waxed paper.

Jan's Fudge   Jan Harbour

2 c. sugar   1/2 c. cocoa
1/3 c. corn syrup   1 t. vanilla
1/2 c. milk   2 T. butter

Boil sugar, syrup, milk, and cocoa to the soft ball stage (check by dropping teaspoonful into clear glass of cold water). Remove from heat, add butter, vanilla, and a little salt to taste. Beat until candy loses its gloss. Turn into buttered 8-in. square pan. Cut when set.

From an early age, Jan was able to make perfect fudge every time. Thus, Anne turned to her whenever the junior or senior class needed homemade fudge for the concession stand at football or basketball games at Correctionville High School. Of course, Jan made it when her own class ran the stand as well!

My Peanut Butter Fudge

2 c. sugar   1 c. marshmallow cream
2/3 c. milk or half and half   1 t. vanilla
1-1/2 c. creamy peanut butter

Cook sugar and milk until candy forms a soft ball when dropped in very cold water (about 230F). Add peanut butter, marshmallow cream, and vanilla. Mix well and pour into buttered pan 8-in. square. You may spread with 1 c. melted real chocolate morsels. Cut into 1-in. squares.

Pecan Fudge   Jan Harbour

2/3 c. Hershey's cocoa   1/4 t. salt
3 c. sugar   1/2 stick butter
1 c. milk   1 t. vanilla
1/2 c. evaporated milk   2 c. pecans, chopped

Sift cocoa and sugar together into saucepan. Stir in milk and evaporated milk slowly. Add salt. Cook on medium heat, stirring constantly until it comes to a boil. Reduce heat, stirring often, and cook until hard ball stage. Remove from heat. Add vanilla and butter. Stir until butter is melted. Add pecans, mix quickly, and pour into buttered 9 x 12 in. pan. Cool. Cut into squares.

White Fudge

2 c. sugar	1 c. marshmallows
1 c. evaporated milk	1/2 c. flake coconut
1/2 c. butter or margarine	1/2 c. chopped nuts
8 oz. white almond bark	1 t. vanilla

Butter the sides of a heavy 3-qt. saucepan. Combine sugar, milk, and butter. Cook to soft ball stage (234F). Remove from heat and add chopped almond bark and marshmallows. Stir until melted. Add remaining ingredients. Pour into a buttered 8-in.-square pan. Cool and cut in squares. Yield: 36 pieces.

Candied Grapefruit Peel   Anne Harbour

6 large grapefruit (or more)	Salt
Sugar	Unflavored gelatin

Peel as many grapefruit as you wish. Cut peels into 1/4-in. strips. Add water to cover peel. Boil 15-20 min. Drain and repeat twice — cover with water, boil 15-20 min.; drain, cover with water, boil 15-20 min. Measure drained peel. For every pint of peel, put 2 c. sugar, 1-1/2 c. water, and 1/8 t. salt into saucepan. Cook peel in mixture until syrup is heavy. Remove from heat. For each pint of grapefruit and syrup, soften 1/2 pkg of unflavored gelatin in 2 T. cold water; stir to dissolve. Add gelatin to hot peel and syrup, stir to distribute, and let stand until cool. Drain off syrup and roll peel in sugar. Store in layers separated by waxed paper in tightly covered container, Yield: about 100 pieces.

♣ *This is a good use for grapefruit and orange peel from a large batch of ambrosia or fruit salad.*

Party Mints

1 lb. powdered sugar	10 drops oil of peppermint
5 T. butter, softened	Food coloring as desired
2 T. evaporated milk	

Mix ingredients until very smooth and creamy. Press into rubber candy molds. Pop out of molds immediately onto sheets of waxed paper. Yield: 50 mints.

Party Patties

8 oz. cream cheese
1 lb. sifted powdered sugar
1 t. vanilla

1-1/2 c. chopped walnuts
   or pecans
Food coloring

Melt cream cheese in double boiler. Add sugar, nuts, and vanilla. Mix and knead until smooth. Drop immediately on waxed paper. Yield: 4 dozen.

Oriental Fruit Balls
Lucile Maddison

1-1/2 c. prunes, cooked
   and pitted
1-1/2 c. dates, pitted
3/4 c. dried apricots
1/2 c. golden raisins

1 c. walnuts
1/4 c. sugar
1 3/4 c. Angel Flake coconut
4 T. concentrated orange
   juice, thawed

Grind fruits and nuts with coarse blade of grinder. Add sugar and orange concentrate. Mix very well. Form into 1-in. balls and roll in coconut, pressing it in firmly. Keep refrigerated with waxed paper between layers. Yield: 9 dozen balls.

Attractive as part of candy plate.

Peanut Brittle

2 c. granulated sugar
1 c. white Karo syrup
1/2 c. water

2 c. peanuts (raw or salted)
2 T. butter
2 t. soda

Cook sugar, syrup, and water in a 3-qt. pan to the crack stage (290F). Add peanuts, cook until golden brown. Remove from heat. Add butter and soda. Stir briskly and pour out on a large buttered cookie sheet. When cool, crack into pieces. Yield: 2 pounds.

Jack's Peanut Brittle
Jack Stoddard

2 c. sugar
1 c. water
1/2 c. light corn syrup
2 c. raw peanuts

1 t. salt
1 T. margarine
2 t. vanilla
1 t. soda

Line electric skillet with heavy foil. Combine sugar, water, and corn syrup in skillet. Set control at 375F. Stir occasionally. When golden brown, add peanuts. When medium brown, add salt and margarine. Stir. Unplug skillet and add vanilla and soda. Stir. Remove foil from skillet and spread out peanut brittle. Let cool and break into pieces.

Jack was the Pierce School Engineer in Cedar Rapids. His recipe makes a very large amount of excellent brittle.

Peanut Butter Bonbons   **Charlotte Petersen**

1 c. crunchy peanut butter   1 c. chopped dates
1 c. powdered sugar   4 sq. almond bark, melted

Combine peanut butter, powdered sugar, and dates. Make into 1-in. balls. Using toothpick, dip into melted almond bark.

Variation: Substitute pkg of chocolate chips or butterscotch chips for almond bark.

Peanut Clusters

1 lb. pkg almond bark   1 16-oz. bag salted peanuts
1 12-oz. pkg real chocolate chips

In double boiler top, melt almond bark. Add chocolate chips. When melted, remove from heat and add peanuts. Drop by rounded teaspoonfuls on waxed paper. When set, store in covered container between sheets of waxed paper.

Penuche   **Anna M. Petersen**

3 c. brown sugar   1 t. vanilla
1 c. milk   1 c. nutmeats, chopped
2 T. butter

Cook sugar and milk in a saucepan to soft ball stage. Remove from heat, add butter and vanilla, and cool without stirring. When mixture is lukewarm, beat until it is creamy. Stir in the nutmeats. Pour into buttered 8-in. square pan. Yield: 36 pieces.

This was my dad's favorite candy.

New Orleans Pralines

3 c. light brown sugar,   1 c. evaporated milk
   firmly packed   1 T. butter
1/4 t. cream of tartar   1 t. vanilla
1/8 t. salt   2 1/4 c. pecan halves

Combine in large saucepan brown sugar, cream of tartar, salt, and milk. Stir over low heat until sugar dissolves. Cook to 236F or soft ball stage. Remove from heat and cool slightly. Add butter, vanilla, and pecans. Beat by hand until creamy.

Drop by teaspoonfuls on waxed paper and let harden. Humidity may cause pralines to become sugary. Yield: 24-30 pieces.

Creamy Texas Pralines

2-1/2 c. sugar
3/4 c. evaporated milk
2 T. butter

2 T. light corn syrup
2 c. pecan halves

Combine sugar, milk, butter, and corn syrup in large heavy saucepan. Mix well, bring to a boil, and add pecans. Cook until mixture reaches soft ball stage. Remove from heat; beat 2 to 3 min. Mixture should be thick and creamy. Working quickly, drop by rounded tablespoonfuls onto waxed paper. Let cool. Yield: about 18 pieces.

Coconut Strawberries

7 oz. flaked coconut
1 can Eagle Brand
  condensed milk
2 small pkg strawberry Jell-O

1/2 c. pecans, chopped
Red colored sugar
Green decorator icing

Mix coconut, condensed milk, 1 pkg Jell-O, and chopped pecans. Chill 4 hr. Then shape into 1-in. strawberries. Roll in dry strawberry Jell-O and red sugar. Top with green leaf of icing. Refrigerate and store in air-tight container. Yield: 3 dozen candies.

English Toffee   Bernice Peterson

2 c. sugar
1-1/2 c. butter
1/2 c. water

1/4 c. white corn syrup
1 c. pecans, chopped
4 oz. sweet chocolate

Boil sugar, butter, water, and corn syrup rapidly until it begins to change color. Lower heat. Stir continuously until syrup makes a firm ball in cold water. Add half the nuts and stir 1/2 min. Pour into buttered 9-in. square pan. When firm but still warm, scatter chocolate, chopped coarsely, over candy, and spread with a spatula. Sprinkle remainder of nuts over melted chocolate. When cold, break into small pieces.

Toffee Treats

Whole graham crackers
2 sticks butter or oleo
1 c. brown sugar

1 c. pecans, chopped
1 lb. Hershey's sweet chocolate

Line jelly roll pan with whole graham crackers. In saucepan combine butter and brown sugar. Boil about 4 min., stirring often. Pour over graham crackers. Scatter pecans over the top. Bake at 375F for 8 min. Remove from oven. Break up chocolate and scatter on top to melt. Cool in refrigerator. Break into pieces.

Truffles

24 oz. semisweet chocolate
1/2 pt. heavy cream
1 nip of Amaretto liqueur

2 large egg yolks
Cocoa, sifted

In top of double boiler melt chocolate, cream, and Amaretto over hot water. Stir until mixture is silky smooth. Remove from heat and let cool 5 min. Egg yolks should be at room temperature. Beat them well and stir into chocolate mixture. Chill mixture in refrigerator until it can be formed into small balls. Roll into 1-in. balls, place on waxed paper, and chill again. Roll balls in sifted cocoa. Store in refrigerator.

Caramel Corn

2 c. brown sugar
2 sticks margarine
1/2 c. corn syrup

1/2 t. salt
1 t. soda
8 qt. popped corn

Cook sugar, margarine, syrup, and salt for 5 min. Remove from heat; add soda, then pour over corn, mixing lightly. Spread in a deep, light aluminum pan or roaster. Bake at 200F for 1 hr. Stir every 15 min. Cool. Store in cool place. If desired, you may add peanuts.

My brother Tom enjoyed making caramel corn when he was 9 or 10, and I would make a simple batch of fudge. Our parents or younger brother might bring Jonathan apples from the cellar, and we all enjoyed the treats during a game of checkers or dominos.

Chow Mein Haystacks

2 pkg butterscotch bits   1 3-oz. can chow mein noodles

Melt butterscotch bits in top of double boiler over hot water, stirring often.
Remove from heat. Stir in chow mein noodles, covering all with butterscotch.
Drop on waxed paper with a teaspoon. Store in cool place.

Variations: Chocolate bits, or half butterscotch and half chocolate bits also make
excellent candies. If available, a combination of half chocolate and half cherry bits
is delicious.

Holiday Nibbler Mix   **Aunt Elta Petersen**

1 pkg Wheat Chex   1 lb. Planters mixed nuts
1 pkg Rice Chex   1 lb. butter
1 pkg Cheerios   1 t. garlic powder
1 pkg small pretzel sticks   1/2 t. celery salt
1 pkg pretzel curls   4 t. Worcestershire sauce

In large bowl combine cereals, pretzels, and nuts. In small saucepan, mix and melt
butter with seasonings. Add to dry mix, combine, and put in large aluminum pan
or roaster. Bake at 200F for 2 hr., stirring every 20 min. Cool. Store in clean coffee
cans. Freezes well.

Nut Clusters

2 6-oz. pkg butterscotch chips   3 c. salted peanuts *or*
1 6-oz. pkg chocolate chips   1-1/2 c. pecan halves

Melt chips in top of double boiler over hot water, add peanuts or pecans, and mix
well. Drop by teaspoonfuls on waxed paper. Let set.

Delicious!

Sugared Pecans I

1 egg white   1/8 t. salt
1 c. sugar   1/2 t. ginger
3/4 t. cinnamon   4 c. pecan halves
3/4 t. cloves

Egg white should be at room temperature. Beat it until stiff peaks form. Sift
together sugar, salt, and spices. Fold into egg whites. Then add pecans, stirring

until they are well coated. Pour onto large buttered cookie sheet. Bake at 250F for 2-1/2 hr., mixing lightly every 30 min. Break apart when cool. Store in air-tight container. Yield: 1-1/2 qt. pecans.

Sugar-Coated Pecans II

1 c. brown sugar	1 t. vanilla
1/2 c. granulated sugar	2-1/2 c. pecan halves *or*
1/2 c. dairy sour cream	walnut halves

Mix sugars and sour cream in heavy 6-c. saucepan. Cook, stirring until sugar melts, to soft ball stage (236F). Add vanilla and beat until mixture begins to thicken. Add pecans. Stir until well coated. Turn out on waxed paper. Separate nuts. Yield: about 3 cups.

Sugared Walnuts

2 c. shelled walnuts	1 t. cinnamon
1 c. sugar	1/4 t. salt
5 T. water	1 1/4 t. vanilla

Toast walnuts in moderate oven (350F) for 8-10 min. In saucepan, mix sugar, water, cinnamon, salt, and vanilla. Cover and bring to a boil. Uncover and boil to the soft ball stage when tried in ice water. Be careful not to cook too long. Add walnut halves a few at a time and keep stirring until all are coated with syrup and until they begin to sugar. Lift out and separate on waxed paper. When cool and dry, they are ready to eat. Store in covered tins.

Desserts and Pies

Cold and Hot Desserts ♣ Pies
♣ Pastry ♣ Meringues

Old Settlers' Reunion

The words "The Thirties" bring back memories of choking dust clouds hanging over fields where crops wilt in the relentless glare of the sun. Desperate gardeners carrying pails of water to soak tomatoes and beans and sweet corn search the sky for rain clouds that don't materialize. Old-timers recall folk sayings, "Red sky at morning, sailors take warning!" and "Red sky at night, sailors delight!" but unfeeling skies beat down both plantings and hope.

It was hard to give up the traditional July Old Settlers' Reunion picnic at Corley's Grove. But the community worried about the wells going dry, the pastures dusty and crisp, the scorched oats fields and stunted corn, and the prospect of selling livestock without feed. No one had any heart for celebration.

When the rain suddenly shattered the quiet, it was a shock — vast sheets of water sploshing from a dark, cold sky. Men hurried stock into shelter and led trembling horses to their stalls. Women shooed half-grown chickens out of the downpour into their coops. Daring children ran barefoot into the welcome wet, shouting and hopping until, soaked and shivering, they dashed screeching into the shelter of the porch. Farmers turned their faces toward the rain and let

131

themselves splash like boys in the rivulets that were gushing through the barnyard, for the moment forgetting fear.

The day after the big rain was Sunday. Refreshed and thankful, overflow crowds packed churches and meeting houses. After services the word spread: there would be an Old Settlers' Reunion picnic at Corley's Grove. It would celebrate over 50 years of Reunions. Most important, it would celebrate the merciful rain that had renewed hope and confidence for the heartland.

Every household became a hive buzzing with activity. Even the half-dozen bachelors and the least active elderly were conscripted as plans evolved. The bachelors were given the task of planning races and contests. The older folks were to plan prizes and award ceremonies. Someone volunteered to lend his brand new galvanized stock tank to hold the soda pop and watermelons. The icehouse manager followed with the promise of a load of ice. The men's quartet let it be known they were practicing barbershop harmony for the big day, and a whiskered fiddler allowed he could produce a trio to liven things up. On Wednesday a light, gentle shower shed its benevolence and was welcomed as a sign of well-being.

Soon the big day arrived. County maintenance men had guided their equipment back and forth over the narrow gravel roads leading to the Grove, leaving no trace of ruts and solid clods. Neighbors had pushed lawn mowers to cut somewhat skimpy grass and sprouting weeds, and the bachelors had laid out distances and placed markers for races and track. The grassy area looked neat, if not lush, when the Model T's and newish Model A's, the sporty roadsters with open rumbles, the staid and dignified coupes with their flower vases, and the kid-packed family cars arrived and parked in the designated rows.

Descending with baskets and grocery cartons filled to overflowing, the Old Settler ladies fell to the task of setting out food on the folding tables arranged in a shady area. There was a corps of roasting pans heaped with fried chicken, roasters of baked ham garnished with candied yams and platters of sliced roast beef. There were

132

fleets of deviled eggs, baked beans, cabbage slaws with fruit and with vegetables, casseroles of corn, baking dishes of scalloped potatoes, sliced tomatoes, green beans with bacon and with cheese sauce, pickled beets, potato salads, Dutch lettuce, three-bean and kidney bean salads, fluffy yeast rolls, buttered rye bread, corn muffins — as far as the eye could see, every celebratory dish they could imagine, these Old Settlers had baked, fried or cooked. Now they spread netting and clean tea towels over the display and turned to the important task of admiring and cutting the pies.

The bakers basked in the admiration and declared it was just good luck. The cutting went on: apple pie, apple with streusel topping; cherry with lattice top, cherry with meringue; blueberry, raspberry, boysenberry, gooseberry, strawberry; peach, raisin, rhubarb; and a pie for every kind and flavor of filling that could be poured into pastry — the pies were proof that the ladies could handle any culinary challenge.

After two egg-coffee makers had sampled and conferred, the dinner bell hanging from a venerable oak post rang. Children darted to their families. Folks quieted as they held hands and said Grace. Then the double lines waiting on either side of the tables surged forward. Each member of a family held an everyday plate and silver marked with loops of thread. They eyed the display, searching for a piece of Mom's fried chicken or Aunt Jessie's scalloped corn. The women settlers were poised for action. If one casserole or platter was empty, another took its place. There were cheerful compliments and smiling blushes. At last, when everyone had been served, a second helping of this or that temptation lured many back to the tables. When at last they had ambled away, the women turned to consolidate the leftovers into baskets and boxes, and the Old Settlers retired to be entertained.

The quartet sang with gusto and responded to calls for encores. The fiddler, banjo and accordion rolled out toe-tapping tunes. Next, the bachelors stepped up to announce contests and races. There was great excitement as children giggled so hard they forgot to run. Spry white-haired codgers showed skill tossing horseshoes and demonstrated their techniques to grandchildren. A few fellows sat on benches or lawn chairs and played pitch. The races continued, first the small fry, urged on by proud parents; then schoolchildren by size and age; and finally, teenagers.

The crowd-pleasers were the three-legged and sack races. Laughing and stumbling, the contestants were red-faced and hot, but triumphant as they hobbled to the finish line. Amid cheers, all the winners were called up to receive prizes — a half-dollar for first place and a quarter for second, with "silver" ribbons for everyone. The kids were jubilant — real money of their own! — and the elders who had contributed the prize money felt as warm and happy as the kids.

By now, the crowd was circling the oval stock tank where men were cutting the iced melons. They cut big round slices an inch thick and halved them into half-moons that one could bite into. When a kid held a piece to get a bite of the juicy, icy fruit, juice and seeds trickled down chin and hands, but the taste was worth the mess. A paper napkin helped mop his damp face, and he was soon biting into a quarter slice. If his mother saw his sticky face and stained shirt, she knew that, after all, this was the Reunion, and he was only nine.

As the kids slowed down, older folks saw the afternoon sun dropping in the west and began to round up their families. The bachelors collected horseshoes and stakes. The elderly twittered and recalled previous Reunions — none better than this. Men and boys helped police the ground, collecting litter. All the while, the women cleared. They folded the thin old tablecloths, working in an unconscious rhythm that might have been a ballet. They bent forward to speak in soft tones, dipped to pick up a basket or box, waved to their waiting family, and joined the procession moving toward the cars.

Laughing, calling farewells, the Old Settlers started the motors and rolled out. The cars moved slowly to the well-maintained gravel road. They dropped off to left and right. They were satisfied. The rain had come. It had made this the finest Old Settlers' Reunion at Corley's Grove, ever.

Recipes

Ambrosia

1 large ripe pineapple
  or 2 20-oz. cans
  unsweetened pineapple
  chunks in juice

8 or 9 large Sunkist seedless
  oranges
3 c. fresh or packaged coconut

Pare and core pineapple; cut into bite-size chunks. (Or use canned unsweetened pineapple chunks and juice.) Peel oranges; remove white pith, slice, and then quarter the slices. Layer pineapple, orange, and coconut in a large compote or bowl. Cover and chill 4-6 hr. Serve in glass compote. Sprinkle additional coconut on top. Serves 8 to 10.

This Southern dessert is traditionally served at Christmas.

Angel Supreme Dessert   Anna M. Petersen

4 egg yolks
1/2 c. lemon juice
1/2 c. orange juice
1-1/2 c. sugar
1/4 t. salt
2 env. Knox gelatin
1/4 c. cold water

1/2 c. hot water
2 egg whites
1 pt. whipping cream
1 angel food cake (bar)
Lemon or orange
  twists of rind
Additional whipped cream

Prepare two 5 x 9 in. bread tins by lining each with waxed paper strips. Set aside.

Step 1: Beat egg yolks, lemon and orange juice, sugar, and salt; cook in double boiler. Soften gelatin in cold water; add hot water to dissolve and add this to the first mixture. Cook in double boiler until mixture is of custard consistency. Cool completely. Beat egg whites to firm peaks and add to cooled custard. Whip 1 pt. cream. Fold into custard.

Step 2: Break bar angel food into 1-in. pieces and mix lightly with custard. Pour this mixture into prepared lined pans. Smooth tops so custard covers cake. Cover lightly with waxed paper and chill for 12-14 hr.

Step 3: To serve, remove each bar by turning it onto a 9 x 12 glass dish. Remove paper. Keep chilled. Cut into 1-in. slices and place on dessert plates. Top with whipped, sweetened cream and garnish with lemon or orange twists and 1/4-in. orange slices cut in half. Garnish with mint sprigs if available.

Variation: Add 1 c. drained crushed pineapple or crushed strawberries to cooled custard before adding whipped cream.

The lemon-orange combination gives a delicate citrus flavor that contrasts with the angel food cake. Mother served this dessert at our wedding supper.

Apple Crisp

3 c. tart apples	1/2 c. flour
1/2 c. butter	3/4 c. brown sugar
3/4 c. oatmeal	1/4 t. cinnamon

Peel and slice tart apples. Place in greased 9 x 9 in. pan and set aside. Cut butter into oatmeal, flour, brown sugar, and cinnamon with pastry blender. Sprinkle mixture over apples. Bake at 350F for 35-40 min. Serve warm or cold with cream or ice cream.

This topping may be used with other fruits, such as fresh cherries, peaches, or blueberries.

Bavarian Cream

1 env. Knox gelatin	1/2 t. almond extract
1/2 c. sugar, divided	1 c. whipping cream
1/8 t. salt	1/2 c. slivered almonds, toasted
2 eggs, separated	Chocolate sauce
1 1/4 c. milk	

Combine gelatin, 1/4 c. sugar, and salt in an 8-c. saucepan. Mix egg yolks with milk. Add to gelatin mixture and stir over low heat until gelatin is dissolved. Continue stirring on low until mixture thickens slightly. Add almond extract. Chill until mixture mounds.

Beat egg whites to soft peaks; beat in 1/4 c. sugar and beat until whites form stiff peaks. Fold into gelatin mixture. Whip and fold in cream. Pour into a 4-c. decorative mold that has been rinsed with cold water. Chill several hours. Unmold. Top with chocolate sauce and slivered almonds. Serves 6.

Strawberry Bavarian Parfait

1 pt. fresh strawberries	2 c. hot water
1 large (6-oz.) pkg strawberry Jell-O	1 pt. vanilla ice cream

Dixie Cheesecake

1 1/4 c. fine graham cracker crumbs	4 eggs, separated
1/4 c. melted butter	1 c. sour cream
3 8-oz. pkg cream cheese	1 T. vanilla extract
1 15-oz. can sweetened condensed milk	1 T. powdered sugar
Mandarin orange segments	1 T. grated lemon rind
	1/2 t. salt

Crust: Mix graham cracker crumbs with melted butter. Press firmly into a 10-in. springform pan. Set aside.

Filling: In large bowl of mixer, beat softened cream cheese and milk. Increase speed and add egg yolks one at a time, beating well after each addition until mixture is very smooth. On low speed, beat in sour cream, vanilla, sugar, and lemon rind. Beat egg whites with salt until stiff. Fold into cheese mixture and pour into pan. Bake at 275F for 1 hr. Turn off heat.

Do not open oven door for 45 min. Let cake cool slowly in oven. When cool, remove from oven and remove from pan. Garnish with mandarin orange segments. Serves 10 to 12.

Golden Glow Cheesecake

1 8-1/2-oz. pkg vanilla wafers	3 eggs, separated
1/2 c. melted butter	2 T. fresh lemon juice
1 20-oz. can Dole crushed pineapple	2 t. vanilla extract
2 env. Knox gelatin	1 t. grated lemon peel
3/4 c. sugar	2 8-oz. pkg cream cheese
1/8 t. nutmeg	1 c. whipping cream
1/4 t. salt	1 t. Knox gelatin
	1 T. sugar

Crust: Crush vanilla wafers and mix crumbs with melted butter. Press firmly into a 9-in. springform pan. Bake at 350F for 8 min. Chill.

Filling: Drain pineapple well, reserving 1 1/4 c. syrup. Mix 2 env. gelatin, 1/2 c. sugar, nutmeg, and salt in saucepan. Beat egg yolks with 1 c. reserved syrup; blend into gelatin mixture in saucepan and let stand 1 min. Stir over low heat until gelatin is dissolved, about 5 min. Stir in lemon juice, vanilla, and lemon peel. Pour into electric mixer bowl, and beat in cream cheese at moderate speed. Chill, stirring occasionally, until mixture mounds slightly when dropped from spoon.

Beat egg whites until soft peaks form; gradually add 1/4 c. sugar and beat until stiff peaks form. Fold into gelatin mixture. Then whip cream and fold into gelatin mixture. Turn into crust; chill until firm.

Mix remaining 1/4 c. syrup with water to equal 3/4 c.; heat to boiling. Mix 1 t. gelatin with 1 T. sugar; add hot liquid and stir until gelatin is dissolved. Add pineapple. Chill, stirring occasionally, until mixture is consistency of unbeaten egg whites. Spoon over cheesecake. Chill until firm. Serves 10 to 12.

Pineapple Cheesecake

1/2 stick margarine	6 T. sugar
3 t. sugar	1-1/2 T. flour
3/4 c. flour	1-1/2 c. milk
1 #2 can crushed pineapple	1/2 c. pineapple juice
1 pkg cream cheese	1 t. vanilla
3 eggs	Cinnamon

Crust: Cut margarine into 3 t. sugar and 3/4 c. flour; mix in 1 egg and 1 T. water. Roll out, and place in 9-in. pie pan. Drain pineapple, reserving juice. Cover crust with drained pineapple.

Filling: Separate 2 eggs, reserving whites. Combine softened cream cheese, 2 egg yolks, 6 T. sugar, and 1-1/2 T. flour. Mix well, then gradually add milk, 1/2 c. pineapple juice, and vanilla. Beat egg whites until they form stiff peaks; fold into cream cheese mixture. Pour over pineapple. Sprinkle cinnamon on top. Bake at 350F for 1 hr. Serves 6 to 8.

Cherries Jubilee   Laurel Harbour

1 15.6-oz. can dark cherries,	1 T. sugar
sweetened and pitted	1 T. cornstarch
1/2 t. lemon juice	2 strips orange peel
4 T. brandy	Ice cream to serve 6

Mix cornstarch and sugar. Drain cherries and add juice and orange peel to cornstarch and sugar. Mix well. Cook over medium heat until thick, stirring constantly. Add cherries and lemon juice. To serve, add warm brandy and ignite. Pour over vanilla ice cream. Serves 6.

Very festive for dessert with coffee.

George Washington Cherry Pudding

2 c. fresh pitted cherries	1 c. flour
2 c. sugar	1 t. baking powder
2 T. soft butter	1/2 c. milk

Combine cherries with 1 c. sugar and let stand while preparing the batter. Cream 1 c. sugar with soft butter. Sift together flour and baking powder. Add to creamed mixture alternately with milk. Pour batter into a buttered 6-c. baking dish and pour sweetened cherries with juice on top. Bake in 350F oven for about 35 min. Serve with light cream. Serves 4 to 5.

Pauline's Chocolate Sauce   Mrs. Roy Pitkin

1 c. sugar	2 T. flour
1 c. Karo syrup	2 T. cornstarch
1 c. milk	Vanilla
1 T. butter	Salt
1/4 c. cocoa	

Mix ingredients in saucepan and cook until slightly thickened. Sauce gets thicker when cold. Serve on cake or ice cream.

Rio Chocolate Sauce   Ardith Hohbach

2 large pkg semisweet	2 T. vanilla
chocolate pieces	1 lb. powdered sugar, sifted
1/2 lb. butter	2 c. light corn syrup
2 T. instant coffee	2 c. hot water
1/4 t. salt	

Melt chocolate with butter in double boiler over simmering water. Blend in coffee, salt, and vanilla; then add sugar alternately with corn syrup and hot water, stirring after each addition until smooth. Store in tight-fitting jars in refrigerator. Yield: 8 cups.

Hot Fudge Ice Cream Topping

2 oz. semisweet chocolate
  baking squares
1 c. evaporated milk

3/4 c. sugar
2 T. butter or margarine
1 t. vanilla extract

Combine chocolate, milk, and sugar in saucepan over low heat. Stir constantly 6 min. or until chocolate melts and mixture is smooth. Bring to a boil and stir constantly 6 min. Remove from heat; stir in butter and vanilla. Serve warm over ice cream. Store in refrigerator up to 3 wk.

Hot Fudge Topping

1/2 c. butter
4 sq. chocolate
1 tall can evaporated milk

3 c. sugar
1/4 t. salt

Melt butter in double boiler. Add chocolate and melt slowly. Stir in sugar and salt. Slowly add milk and cook until thick. Store in covered jar; heat needed amount before serving. Yield: 1-1/2 cups.

Cream Puffs

1 c. water
1/2 c. butter
1 c. sifted flour

1/4 t. salt
4 eggs

Heat water and butter to boiling in top of double boiler. Pour the flour and salt into hot mixture, beating hard. It will form a stiff ball. Remove from heat and add unbeaten eggs, one at a time, beating thoroughly after each egg until satiny. Drop by teaspoon or tablespoon, according to intended use, on ungreased cookie sheet, about 2-1/2 in. apart. Bake in preheated oven at 450F for 20 min. Reduce heat to 375F for 1 hr. Cool, slit one side, and remove soft part. Fill with whipped cream or custard and top with chocolate sauce. Yield: 8-16 puffs, depending on size.

For a luncheon main dish, you may fill large puffs just before serving with favorite chicken or seafood salad.

Basic Crepes

1 13-oz. can evaporated milk	1/2 t. salt
3/4 c. water	1 T. sugar
4 eggs	1-1/2 c. flour
1/4 c. butter, melted	

Put all ingredients into blender and mix for 1-1/2 min. Pour into container with cover and place in refrigerator for at least 3 hr. or up to 24 hr. before making crepes.

To cook, heat 1 T. oil in heavy 5- or 6-in. skillet. Pour oil out. Heat skillet to 375F. Pour a spoonful (about 1-1/2 T.) of batter into skillet; rotate skillet sidewise so batter covers bottom. When edges of crepe appear light brown, use a spatula to turn it over. Discard first crepe. As each crepe is made, lay it on a clean towel. Thin batter with milk if it gets too thick.

Suggested Fillings: Chopped chicken, ham, tuna, shrimp, or crabmeat may be added to basic white sauce with these optional ingredients: chopped green pepper, chopped mushrooms, finely diced shallots or spring onion, chopped celery, asparagus spears cut in thirds, 2 T. curry, chopped parsley or chives. Dry white wine enhances the seafoods. Salt and pepper.

White sauce may also be varied by adding 1/4 c. grated Swiss cheese or mild cheddar. Your choices depend on your preferences. Filling should be thick. Place a tablespoon of filling on each crepe, roll up, and fasten with pick. Place crepes in a buttered baking dish as you fill them and put dish in 300F oven to keep them hot. Serve 3 crepes to each person.

Dessert Crepes: Prepare 12 basic crepes. Soften 1 8-oz. pkg cream cheese with 3 T. powdered sugar, 1 c. sour cream, and a few drops of vanilla. Blend. Put 1 T. on each crepe, roll, and place in shallow baking dish. Cover. Heat at 350F for 20 min. Transfer crepes, 2 per serving, to dessert plates. Top each with 1/2 c. fresh strawberries, sliced and sugared. Serves 6.

Variations: Top with fresh raspberries, blueberries, or other seasonal fruit. Or try apricot puree, blueberry or boysenberry pie filling, or raspberry preserves.

Orange Filling: Combine 2/3 c. Eagle Brand sweetened condensed milk (half of 14-oz. can) with 1/3 c. thawed frozen orange juice concentrate; mix well. Stir in 1/2 c. chopped fresh orange and 2 T. chopped toasted almonds. Fold in 1 c. whipped cream. Spoon 2 tablespoonfuls into each crepe, roll, and place in shallow baking dish, as above. Top with chocolate almond sauce.

Chocolate Almond Sauce: Melt 2 oz. semisweet chocolate with 1 T. butter over low heat; stir in 2/3 c. condensed milk. Add 3 T. amaretto liqueur and remove from heat. Yield: 2/3 cup.

Curried Fruit

1 can pineapple chunks	1 can Bing cherries (optional)
1 can sliced peaches	1 c. brown sugar
1 can sliced pears	4 T. cornstarch
1 can apricot halves	1 T. curry powder
1 10-oz. jar maraschino cherries	1 stick butter

Drain fruit, reserving juice for another use, and mix in large casserole. Mix brown sugar, cornstarch, and curry powder. Sprinkle over the fruit. Melt butter and pour over fruit. Cover casserole and bake at 350F for 30 min. Uncover and bake 20 min. more. If you wish, add 1 T. sherry and stir lightly. Chill. Serves 10 to 12.

This spicy dish is a delicious and attractive accompaniment or garnish for roast fowl and baked ham. Experiment with the amount of curry you prefer. This amount is moderately spicy.

Baked Custard

4 eggs	1/4 t. salt
2 or 3 egg yolks	1 t. vanilla
2/3 c. sugar	4 c. whole milk
Nutmeg	

Beat eggs and egg yolks lightly with rotary beater. Add sugar, salt, and vanilla and beat 1 min. Add milk and stir to blend. Pour into 6 large custard cups or a 6-c. baking dish. Sprinkle with nutmeg. Set custard dish(es) into pan of hot water. Bake at 350F for 30-35 min. or until silver knife comes out clean. Serves 6.

Custard with Caramel Glaze / Flan

4 c. whole milk	1/4 t. salt
4 eggs	1 t. vanilla
2 egg yolks	1/2 c. light brown sugar
1/2 c. sugar	

With rotary beater, beat eggs and egg yolks. Add sugar, salt, and vanilla and beat 1 min. Add milk and stir to blend. Pour into 6 6-oz. custard cups. Set cups into 9 x 13 pan holding hot water to come up 1 in. on cups. Bake in 350F oven for 35-45 min. or until a silver knife comes out clean. Chill.

Before serving, sprinkle brown sugar generously over the custards. Return cups to large pan and place it beneath the broiler until the sugar browns and caramelizes. Remove from oven and cool. Place in refrigerator to chill. Caramel sauce will harden on top of custard. Serves 6.

Grandma's Danish Christmas Cake   Christena Paulsen

1 c. flour	3-4 T. ice water
1/2 t. salt	1 lb. cooked, pitted prunes
1/2 t. baking powder	1 c. sugar
1/4 c. sugar	1/2 t. cinnamon
1/2 c. butter, softened	

Sift together flour, salt, baking powder, and 1/4 c. sugar. Cut in soft butter with pastry blender. Add ice water and toss to make a loose ball. Chill 15 min. Meanwhile, prepare filling by combining prunes, 1 c. sugar, and cinnamon.

Roll pastry to 9 x 12 in. and place in 9-in. square pan with extra on sides to fold over filling. Pour filling down middle and 6 in. wide. Adjust and fold pastry on sides to make a cake about 9 x 7 in. Bake at 350F for 45 min. Cool. Drizzle top with thin white icing (powdered sugar, 1 t. soft butter, hot milk). Cut into 1 x 3 in. strips.

This cake is really a rich fruit-filled pastry that is delectable with coffee or with a glass of cold milk. It was always served at Christmas at Grandma's, but our family enjoys it often, and it is a good substitute for pie.

Danish Puff   Katie Bagenstos

1 c. flour	1/2 c. butter
1/2 c. butter	1 c. flour
1/2 t. salt	3 eggs
1-1/2 T. cold water	1 t. almond flavoring
1 c. water	1/2 c. chopped nuts

First layer: Cut 1/2 c. butter into 1 c. flour and salt as for pie crust. Add 1-1/2 T. cold water slowly. Shape dough into two 4 x 10 in. shapes 2 in. apart on ungreased cookie sheet.

Second layer: Bring to boil 1 c. water with 1/2 c. butter. Remove from heat and add 1 c. flour all at once; mix well. Add eggs one at a time, beating mixture smooth after each addition. Add almond flavoring. Pour half on each crust and spread to edges. Bake at 350F for 1 hr. If puff browns fast, cover lightly with aluminum foil. Cool and frost (powdered sugar and milk). Sprinkle with nuts. Serves 8 to 10.

This light pastry is equally welcome for mid-morning coffee or for the dessert tray after an evening of bridge.

145

Date Pudding   Marjorie Jansen

1 lb. dates, divided
1 t. soda
1-1/2 c. boiling water
1/2 c. butter
3 c. sugar, divided
Whipped cream

2 eggs, beaten
2-1/2 c. flour
1 t. baking powder
2 t. vanilla, divided
1 c. chopped nuts, divided

Chop dates. Add soda to boiling water and pour over half the dates. Add butter; let melt and cool. Add 1-1/2 c. sugar, eggs, and flour sifted with baking powder; mix lightly. Add 1 t. vanilla and 1/2 c. nuts. Pour into 9 x 13 in. pan. Bake at 350F for 35-40 min. Do not overbake.

Topping: Mix other half of chopped dates, 1-1/2 c. sugar, and 1/2 c. water; cook until thickened. Add 1/2 c. nuts and 1 t. vanilla. Spread over warm date cake. Serve with whipped cream. Serves 12 to 15.

A moist, flavorful dessert. May be frozen.

Devil's Float   Anna M. Petersen

1/3 c. sugar
1-1/2 c. water
12 marshmallows, quartered
1/2 c. sugar
2 T. butter
1 c. flour

1/2 t. salt
3 T. cocoa
1 t. baking powder
1/2 c. milk
1 t. vanilla
1/2 c. chopped nuts

Cook 1/3 c. sugar in 1-1/2 c. water 5 min. Put into a 9 x 9 in. baking dish with lid. Top with quartered marshmallows. Set aside.

Cream 1/2 c. sugar with 2 T. butter. Sift together flour, salt, cocoa, and baking powder. Add to creamed mixture alternately with milk and vanilla. Add nuts. Drop batter by spoonfuls over marshmallows. Cover and bake at 350F for 45 min. Top with whipped cream. Serves 5 to 6.

Two layers form, a chocolate sauce and a cake. A delicious 1920's treat — and still a treat today. Mother got this recipe from the women's column in the Chicago Daily Drovers Journal *about 1925. She also corresponded with other readers and exchanged recipes and household hints.*

♣ *Marshmallows stored in the freezer will not dry out.*

Dump Cake

1 can cherry pie filling	1 stick margarine, melted
1 20-oz. can crushed pineapple	1/2 c. broken nutmeats
1 box lemon cake mix	1/2 c. coconut (optional)

Pour pie filling into a 9 x 13 in. ungreased pan; then pour in undrained pineapple. Sprinkle the dry cake mix over the top. Drizzle melted margarine over cake mix. If desired, add nuts and coconut. Bake at
350F about 45-50 min. Yield: 15 servings.

Dutch Apple Cake with Lemon Sauce

1/2 c. butter	2 t. baking powder
1 c. sugar	1/2 t. salt
2 eggs	2 tart apples
1 c. milk	1/2 c. sugar
2 c. flour	1 t. cinnamon

Cream butter and sugar. Beat in eggs, one at a time. Add milk alternately with sifted flour, baking powder, and salt. Beat well. Pour into greased 8-in. square pan. Peel, core, and cut apples into 8 slices; press slices vertically into batter. Combine 1/2 c. sugar with cinnamon and sprinkle over top. Bake in 350F oven 30 min. Cut into squares and serve hot with lemon sauce. Serves 9.

Lemon Sauce: Combine 1 c. sugar, 2 T. flour, and 1/8 t. salt in saucepan. Add 2 c. boiling water gradually, stirring smooth. Boil 5 min., stirring constantly. Remove from heat and add 2 T. butter, 1-1/2 T. lemon juice, and 1/2 t. grated lemon peel. Serve hot over cake.

Served by the Amish in Lancaster County, Pennsylvania, where this is called Apple Pan Dowdy.

Fruit Cocktail Dessert   Gladys Casford

1 c. flour	1 t. vanilla
1 t. soda	1 #2 can fruit cocktail and juice
3/4 c. sugar	1 bottle maraschino cherries, drained
1 t. salt	1 c. brown sugar
1 egg	1/2 c. pecans

Sift together flour, soda, sugar, and salt. Beat egg, and add vanilla, fruit cocktail, and cut-up cherries. Stir in dry ingredients and mix well. Turn into greased 8-in. square pan. Mix brown sugar and pecans; sprinkle on top of batter. Bake at 350F for 45 min. Top with whipped cream or ice cream. Serves 9.

Hot Fruit Compote   Middie Mae Morf

1 can sliced peaches
1 can apricot halves
1 can pitted black cherries
1/4 c. orange juice

1/4 c. lemon juice
1 t. grated orange rind
1 t. grated lemon rind
2 T. brown sugar

Drain peaches, apricots, and cherries, reserving juice for other use. Arrange fruit in a baking dish. Combine orange juice, lemon juice, grated orange and lemon rind, and brown sugar. Pour mixture over fruit. Bake at 350F for 1 hr. Cool. Serve as dessert topped with soft custard sauce, or use the compote to complement baked ham or tenderloin.

Custard Sauce: Scald 2 c. milk. Beat 4 egg yolks and combine with 1/4 c. sugar and 1/8 t. salt. Gradually add hot milk, whisking with wire whip. Cook over boiling water, stirring constantly, until mixture coats a metal spoon. Add 3/4 t. vanilla and 1/4 t. almond extract. Cool. Serve over compote.

Indian Pudding

4 c. milk
1/2 c. sugar
3 eggs, slightly beaten
1/2 c. yellow cornmeal
1 c. dark molasses

1 t. grated orange peel
1/2 t. cinnamon
1 t. ginger
1 t. salt

Scald milk with 1/4 c. sugar. Add cornmeal very slowly, stirring constantly until mixture is blended and smooth and beginning to thicken. Remove from heat. Slowly add about half a cup of hot mixture to beaten eggs, stirring constantly; pour egg mixture into the first mixture, blending well. Add rest of sugar, cinnamon, ginger, salt, and molasses. Mix and pour into a 6-c. baking dish. Bake at 375F for 1 hr. Serve hot topped with vanilla ice cream. Serves 6.

Linda's Luscious Creamy Dessert   Linda Harmon

1 c. flour
1/2 c. margarine
1/2 c. pecans, finely chopped
1 8-oz. pkg cream cheese
1 c. powdered sugar

2 c. Cool Whip, divided
2 pkg instant pudding — butter
   pecan, coconut cream, or lemon
3 c. milk
Butter brickle or toffee bits

First layer: Cut margarine into flour and half the pecans (1/4 c.) . Pat into 9 x 13 in. pan and bake at 350F for 15-20 min. Cool completely.

Second layer: Mix cream cheese, powdered sugar, and 1 c. Cool Whip. Spread over cooled crust. You may drop it by teaspoonfuls; the crust is very tender. Chill.

Third layer: Mix instant pudding with milk. Spread over second layer. Chill.

Fourth layer: When pudding layer is set, spread 1 c. Cool Whip atop. Garnish with butter brickle or toffee bits and the other half of the pecans. Serves 12.

This dessert was an instant hit when it was introduced in the 1970's. Today, variations suggest different flavors, but the appeal is the same: rich, creamy, definitely a "Luscious — MORE" bell-ringer.

Jelly Roll Cake

4 eggs	3/4 c. sifted cake flour
3/4 c. sugar	3/4 t. baking powder
1 t. vanilla	1/4 t. salt
Sugar	Filling

In large mixer bowl, beat eggs on medium speed 7-8 min. Add sugar and vanilla and beat 1 min. more. Sift cake flour, baking powder, and salt together. Fold into egg mixture with wire whisk. Spread batter on greased, waxed-paper-lined 9 x 15 in. jelly roll pan. Bake at 375F for 13-15 min.

When cake is done, turn onto tea towel that has been sprinkled with sugar. Remove waxed paper, roll in towel, and let cool before filling. Fill with grape jelly, seedless raspberry jam, or 7-minute frosting. Cut into 1-in. slices and serve. Can be garnished with a few fresh berries or mint leaves. Serves 8 or 9.

Pavlova

4 egg whites, room temperature	Whipped cream
1/4 t. cream of tartar *or*	1 c. pecan halves
1 t. vinegar	Fresh fruit: sliced peaches,
Pinch of salt	pineapple chunks, cherries
1 t. vanilla	1-1/2 c. green grapes, halved
1-1/2 c. sugar, divided	

Combine egg whites, cream of tartar, and salt in large mixer bowl. Beat on low until mixture is frothy. Increase to medium until egg whites hold soft peaks. Beating at high speed, gradually add sugar 1 t. at a time. Beat until meringue is very stiff and dull. Gently fold in balance of sugar and vanilla. Shape meringue into two buttered 9-in. cake pans. Bake in slow 300F oven for 1 hr. Turn off heat and let dry 4-6 hr. (Do not open oven door.)

When cool, fill first layer with whipped cream and one fruit. Top with second layer. Frost with whipped cream; garnish with halved green grapes and pecans.

Elegant!

Peanut Buster Bars

1 small pkg Oreos	1-1/2 c. hot fudge sauce
1 stick margarine	1-1/2 c. salted peanuts
1/2 gal. vanilla ice cream	1 8-oz. carton Cool Whip

Melt margarine. Crush Oreo cookies, reserving 1 c. for topping. Combine margarine with rest of cookie crumbs and press into bottom of 9 x 13 pan. Spread softened ice cream over crust. Freeze until firm. Spread hot fudge over ice cream. Sprinkle peanuts over sauce. Cover with Cool Whip (spreads best at room temperature). Sprinkle reserved cookie crumbs on top. Cover with wrap and freeze. Remove from freezer 10 min. before serving. Cut with knife dipped in water. Serves 12 to 15.

Fruit Pizza

1 roll Pillsbury sugar cookie dough	Blueberries
1 8-oz. pkg cream cheese	Strawberries
1/3 c. sugar	Kiwi fruit
1/2 t. vanilla	Bananas
1 T. water	Cantaloupe
1/2 c. peach or apricot	Apricots
marmalade	Mandarin oranges

Crust: Slice cookie dough about 1/4 in. thick and press into thin layer in 9 x 13 in. pan. Bake at 350F for 12-15 min. Cool.

Second layer: Combine cream cheese, sugar, and vanilla; spread on cooled crust. Prepare fruit in bite-sized pieces; arrange on cream cheese layer in rows, squares, or designs.

Glaze: Thin marmalade with water; spread on top of fruit. Cut into squares to serve. Yield: 12-15 servings.

Variations: Crust 2: Cut 1/2 c. margarine into 1 c. flour and 1/2 c. nuts. Bake at 350F for 15 min.

Glaze 2: Combine 2 T. sugar, 2/3 c. apricot juice, and 2 T. cornstarch; cook over medium heat, stirring constantly, until thickened.

Glaze 3: Combine 1/2 c. sugar, 2 T. cornstarch, 1/4 c. water, 1/4 c. lemon juice, and 1/2 c. orange juice; cook over medium heat, stirring constantly, until thickened.

Prune Compote

1 l-lb. pkg medium-size prunes	2 whole cloves
Water	1 cinnamon stick
1/2 c. sugar	Juice of 1 lemon

Soak prunes overnight in water to cover. Next morning, drain prunes, reserving water, and put in 2-qt. saucepan with 1-1/2 c. of the drained water. Add sugar, cloves, and cinnamon stick. Simmer on low heat until prunes are soft. Remove from heat and add lemon juice. Chill. Serve for breakfast fruit or as garnish for meat dishes.

Chocolate Pudding Cake   Jan M. Harbour

1 c. sugar, divided	1 c. flour
8 T. cocoa, divided	1 t. baking powder
1 2/3 c. boiling water	1/2 t. salt
6 T. margarine or butter	1/2 c. milk
1 t. vanilla	

Combine 1/2 c. sugar, 5 T. cocoa, and boiling water. Cream butter, 1/2 c. sugar, and vanilla. Sift dry ingredients together (including remaining cocoa) and add alternately to creamed mixture with milk. Spoon the water mixture over this batter in 9-in. square pan. Bake at 350F for 40 min. Serves 9.

This is one of Daughter Jan's favorite desserts.

Aunt Myrtle's Lemon Cake Pudding   Myrtle Harbour Mincer

3/4 c. sugar	3 T. flour
1 T. soft butter	1/8 t. salt
1/2 t. lemon rind, grated	3/4 c. lemon juice
3 eggs, separated	1-1/2 c. milk

Cream flour, sugar, butter, and lemon rind. Add lemon juice and mix. Beat egg yolks well and add milk. Combine with sugar mixture. Beat egg whites until they form stiff peaks; fold into sugar mixture. Pour into 6 custard cups or 4-c. baking dish. Place in shallow pan of hot water and bake at 350F for 45 min. or until a silver knife comes out clean. Serves 6.

Aunt Myrtle served this often and our family requests it. They like its light lemony custard.

Mrs. Truman's Ozark Pudding

1 egg	1/8 t. salt
3/4 c. sugar	1/2 c. walnuts, chopped
2 T. flour	1/2 c. finely chopped apples
1 1/4 t. baking powder	1 t. vanilla

Beat egg and sugar together until very smooth. Sift flour, baking powder, and salt; stir into egg mixture. Add nuts, apple, and vanilla. Bake in greased pie tin at 350F for 35 min. Serve with whipped cream. Serves 4 to 6.

This was Mrs. Truman's favorite dessert. It came into our family through Aunt Millie Paulsen (Mrs. R. W. Manning).

Martha Washington Pudding

1 c. sugar	1/2 c. milk
2 c. boiling water	1/2 c. raisins
1/2 c. sugar	1 T. cinnamon
2 T. soft butter	1 c. flour
1/8 t. salt	2 t. baking powder
1 T. cocoa	

Mix syrup of 1 c. sugar and boiling water in 9 x 13 in. pan. Combine and add 1/2 c. sugar, butter, salt, cocoa, milk, raisins, and cinnamon. Add flour sifted with baking powder and stir smooth. Drop by tablespoonfuls into pan with syrup. Bake at 350F for 20-25 min. until cake is browned. Serve warm or cold with milk or cream. Serves 8 to 10.

Alexis's Pumpkin Pudding

Alexis Harbour Crowley

1 #2-1/2 can pumpkin (3 c.)	1 t. cinnamon
1/4 c. butter	1/2 t. nutmeg
2 c. sugar	1 t. ginger
4 eggs	1/2 t. cloves
2 T. flour	1/2 t. salt
1 c. evaporated milk	2 t. vanilla
1 c. pecan halves	

Melt butter. Combine with sugar. Beat and add eggs; mix well. Stir in flour, then milk; blend thoroughly. Add pumpkin, spices, and vanilla and mix thoroughly. Pour batter into a greased 9 x 9 in. pan. Set in a larger pan with 1 in. water and bake at 350F for 1 hr. or until firm. Place pecan halves evenly over pudding after 30 min.; return to oven. The center may seem slightly underdone, but will continue to cook. (Test with a silver knife.) Remove from oven to cool. Very good with whipped cream; tastes even better the next day. Serves 8 to 10.

Alexis is ten years old and likes to cook. Her first cooked dish is a typical American sweet pumpkin dessert. She learned to measure carefully when she was six. There is a real thrill when one prepares the Thanksgiving dessert, especially when celebrating the traditional American holiday in another country!

Summer Pudding

1 loaf day-old firm white bread	1 c. strawberries
2 c. red raspberries	1 c. sugar
2 c. blueberries	1/4 c. lemon juice
1 c. red currants	1 c. whipping cream

Remove crusts and lightly toast bread; then crumb it finely into a large mixing bowl. Working with 2 c. at a time, mash berries in a separate bowl. Sprinkle with 1/3 c. sugar. Pour berries over crumbs. Repeat until all berries are mashed. Sprinkle lemon juice over fruits topping bread. Fold together the bread crumb and fruit mixture lightly until all crumbs are colored with juices. Cover bowl and refrigerate until well chilled.

Set out 8 clear glass goblets that will hold 1 c. Remove fruit mixture from refrigerator. With a potato masher, press firmly so that juices mingle. Toss mixture — do not stir. Taste to see if it needs more sugar and adjust. With a tablespoon, fill the goblets half full and gently press mixture so it is firm. Repeat to fill goblets, dividing fruit mixture evenly. The mixture should be firm and juicy. Place goblets on a tray, lay a sheet of waxed paper over them, and return to chill. About 2 hr. later, puddings will be ready to serve. Top each with a spoonful of whipped cream. Serves 8.

Summer pudding is a specialty of many country restaurants in England. Fine-quality seasonal berries are available locally. We were served this fragrant, flavorful dessert on a high plain on which, we were told, Princess Anne exercises her horses.

Rhubarb Cake Dessert   **Madge Petersen**

1 c. sugar	1 c. sour cream
1/2 t. salt	1 t. soda
1/2 t. nutmeg	2 c. rhubarb
2 c. flour	

Sift together sugar, salt, nutmeg, and flour. Add soda to sour cream; stir into flour mixture. Cut rhubarb fine; stir into mixture. Spread in 9 x 9 in. cake pan. Bake at 350F for 25-30 min. until golden brown and a toothpick comes out clean. Serve warm with cream.

Variation: Fresh peaches may be used instead of rhubarb.

Glorified Rice

2 c. cooked rice	1/2 c. sugar
1 20-oz. can crushed pineapple	1/2 c. maraschino cherries
2 c. miniature marshmallows	1 c. whipping cream

Drain pineapple. Combine with rice, marshmallows, and sugar. Cover and chill 4 hr. Drain cherries and chop fine. Whip the cream until it holds soft peaks. Fold whipped cream and cherries lightly into rice mixture. Chill. Serve in sherbet glasses. Serves 6.

Rice Pudding

1/4 c. rice	2 c. milk
1-1/2 c. milk	Whipped cream
1 4-oz. pkg cook-and-serve vanilla pudding mix	Coconut

Cook rice and 1-1/2 c. milk in double boiler until rice is tender. Combine pudding mix with 2 c. milk. Add to rice, stir well, cook 7 min. Put in serving dish and chill. Serve with whipped cream and top with coconut. Serves 6.

Aunt Myrtle's Suet Pudding   Myrtle Harbour Mincer

1/2 c. cut suet (add butter to 1 c.)	1 egg
1/2 c. molasses	Pinch salt
1 c. sugar	1 t. cinnamon
1 c. milk	1 c. raisins
3 c. flour	1 c. chopped apple
1 t. soda	

Butcher can supply suet. Chop into small pieces and pack into 1/2 c., filling cracks with soft butter; add butter to fill 1 c. Combine with molasses and sugar. Beat; add egg, beating well. Sift together flour, soda, salt, and cinnamon. Add to mixture alternately with milk. Stir in raisins and chopped apple. Pour into 1-lb. coffee cans, leaving space at top. Cover with aluminum foil or cloth tied down with string. Steam 4 hr. Serve warm with lemon sauce, whipped cream, or vanilla ice cream.

Strawberry Shortcake (Biscuit)

2 c. flour	3/4 c. milk
4 t. baking powder	Strawberries
1/2 t. salt	Sugar
8 T. half butter/shortening	Whipped cream

154

Sift together flour, baking powder, and salt. Cut in shortening. Mix milk in with a fork. Roll or pat out dough, cut with 2-1/2 or 3-in. cutter. Bake at 450F for 12-15 min.

Prepare strawberries: stem, wash, and crush with a pastry blender or potato masher. Add 2 T. sugar per 4 c. crushed berries. Let stand until ready to serve. Split biscuits, add a generous half cup of berries, top with the biscuit top and then more berries. Pass a bowl of sweetened whipped cream. Serves 6.

♣ *If you have leftover whipped cream, spoon it into small rosettes on a cookie sheet and freeze. Store rosettes in a plastic freezer bag. Defrost for 20 min., then use as a garnish.*

My Shortcake for Berries

1-1/2 c. flour	2 T. shortening
3/4 c. sugar	1-1/2 T. butter
3/4 t. salt	3/4 c. milk
3 t. baking powder	1 t. sugar

Sift together flour, 3/4 c. sugar, salt, and baking powder. Cut in shortening and butter. Add milk, tossing with fork to make a loose mixture that can be dropped by spoonfuls to make 8 individual shortcakes on a cookie sheet or spread in a 9-in. cake tin to make one large cake. Sprinkle with 1 t. additional sugar. Bake at 400F about 20-25 min. Cool.

To serve: Transfer large cake to a platter. Split in two layers. Fill generously with fresh crushed strawberries. Put second layer on top. Top with more berries and whipped cream or vanilla ice cream. Prepare individual shortcakes in same manner on dessert plates. Serves 8.

This is also delicious with fresh raspberries — all you can pick! Yummy!

Orange Cream Tarts

1/2 c. butter	1/4 c. orange juice
1/4 c. powdered sugar	1 T. lemon juice
1/2 t. salt	1/2 c. sugar
1-1/2 c. flour	1/8 t. salt
2 T. milk	1 c. whipping cream
3 egg yolks	1 T. grated orange rind
Orange slices	

155

Cream butter thoroughly. Add sifted powdered sugar and salt; blend. Add sifted flour and milk. Mix with fork to form a ball; flatten to 1/2-in. ball. On a floured pastry cloth, roll out to 1/8-in. thickness. Cut 4-in. circles, using a saucer. Fit loosely into tart pans or over inverted muffin pans, pinching dough to shape. Prick generously. Bake in hot oven 425F for 8-10 min. until light golden brown. Cool.

Orange Filling: Slightly beat egg yolks. Blend in orange and lemon juice. Add sugar and salt. Cook over boiling water, stirring constantly, until thickened. Cool. Beat cream until very thick. Fold lightly into cooled orange mixture. Fold in grated orange rind. Just before serving, divide filling into cooled tart shells. Garnish each with a quarter orange slice. Yield 8-10 tarts.

♣ *Grate lemon or orange zest, freeze, and store in a plastic bag. If squeezing for juice, wash lemon or orange, then grate only the colored portion of the rind. Store zest in plastic bag and freeze to have on hand when recipe calls for zest or grated peel.*

Apple Torte   **Ruth Lowell**

1 pkg yellow or white cake mix	1 t. cinnamon
1/2 c. Angel Flake coconut	1/2 c. sugar
1/2 c. margarine	1 c. sour cream
2-1/2 c. tart apples	1 egg

Cut margarine into cake mix as for pie crust. Add coconut. Pat into 9 x 13 in. cake pan, building up sides slightly. Bake at 350F for *only* 10 min. Slice tart apples and arrange on crust. Sprinkle cinnamon and sugar over apples. Beat together sour cream and egg. Drizzle this over apples and bake for 25 min. Serve slightly warm. Can be cut into 2 x 4 in. bars or 4-in. squares for dessert.

Unusually easy and good!

Mocha Chocolate Torte

3 egg whites at room temperature	1 c. sugar
1/2 t. baking powder	1 12-oz. pkg semisweet chocolate chips
1/8 t. salt	1 T. instant coffee
2 t. vanilla extract, divided	1 c. whipping cream
1 t. water	Extra whipped cream
1/4 c. boiling water	

Meringue: Beat egg whites, baking powder, and salt until soft peaks form. Combine 1 t. vanilla and 1 t. water. Add small amount of sugar and drops of liquid alternately, beating after each addition until whites form firm peaks. Make four 8-in. circles on buttered brown paper. Divide meringue into four equal parts and spread on circles. Place on oiled cookie sheets. Bake in 250F oven 1 hr. Turn off heat and leave in oven 1 hr. longer.

Filling: Melt chocolate. Stir instant coffee into boiling water; blend with chocolate until creamy. Cool slightly. Whip cream and add 1 t. vanilla. Fold into chocolate mixture.

Remove paper from meringue layers. Spread chocolate filling over tops, spreading to edges. Stack layers on a large cake plate to make a four-layer torte. Score top with knife to serve 12 to 16. Decorate with whipped cream and shaved chocolate curls. Chill overnight. Cut into wedges to serve. Serves 12 to 16.

Lemon Meringue Torte

4 egg whites at room temperature	2 c. whipping cream
1 c. sugar	1/4 c. sugar
1/2 t. vanilla extract	2 t. vanilla extract
4 egg yolks	Additional whipped cream
1/2 c. sugar	Strawberries, cherries, or
3 T. lemon juice	mint leaves
2 t. grated lemon peel	

Meringue: Beat egg whites until soft peaks form. Add 1 c. sugar very slowly, beating constantly until stiff peaks form. Fold in 1/2 t. vanilla. Make three 8-in. circles on buttered brown paper. Divide meringue into three equal parts and spoon on paper circles, leveling with knife. Place on oiled cookie sheet. Bake in 250F oven about 1 hr. Turn off heat and leave in oven 1 hr. Meringues may be baked a day ahead.

Filling: Beat egg yolks with 1/2 c. sugar until smooth. Add lemon juice and grated peel. Cook in double boiler, stirring constantly until smooth and thick. Cool. Whip cream until it holds stiff peaks. Gradually add 1/4 c. sugar and 2 t. vanilla. Fold into lemon mixture.

Remove paper from meringues. Spread lemon mixture between meringue layers and refrigerate several hours. Garnish with whipped cream and strawberries, cherries, or mint leaves. Serves 8 to 12.

Aunt Alice's Forgotten Torte   Alice McDermott

5 egg whites at room temperature   1 t. vanilla
1/2 t. cream of tartar   2 c. fresh fruit
1/4 t. salt   Whipped cream
1-1/2 c. sugar

Beat egg whites in electric mixer with cream of tartar and salt until soft peaks
form. Slowly add sugar, 1/4 c. at a time, with mixer at medium speed. Increase
speed until mixture forms stiff peaks. Fold in vanilla.

Spread meringue in two 9-in. buttered pie tins, forming a high outer edge and
shallow center. Place tins into preheated 500F oven and *turn off heat at once*. Let
meringues stay in oven overnight or at least 8 hr. Do not open oven door.

Fill each meringue with 2 c. or more prepared fruit and top with whipped cream.
Each serves 6. You may use raspberries, stemmed and sliced strawberries, sliced
peaches, or a mixture of fruits. Refrigerate leftovers.

This meringue is crisp on the outside and firm and tender underneath.

Trifle — American Style

1 5 x 9 in. pound cake   1 pkg strawberry Jell-O
1 pkg French vanilla Jell-O   2-1/2 c. boiling water
  instant pudding   1 c. whipping cream
3 c. whole milk   3 t. sugar
3 pt. fresh strawberries   Cream sherry

Cake: Cut homemade or purchased pound cake into 1/3 in. slices. Arrange slices
to cover bottom and sides of a deep 2-1/2-qt. compote. Sprinkle cake liberally
with cream sherry.

Custard: Mix instant pudding with cold milk according to package directions. Set
custard aside for 10 min.

Fruit: Prepare strawberry Jell-O with boiling water. Cool until beginning to
congeal. Then combine slightly crushed strawberries with Jell-O, reserving 10 or
12 whole berries for garnish.

Whip cream to soft peak stage. If desired, stir in 3 t. sugar.

To assemble: Pour half the custard onto the pound cake. Use a large spoon to ladle
half the fruit mixture on top of custard. Place a few half-slices of pound cake on
berries. Repeat layers, using all custard and fruit mixture. Spread each layer out to
the pound cake lining the compote. Spread whipped cream decoratively over all. Top
with reserved whole berries. Cover compote with cling wrap and refrigerate 8-12 hr.

To serve: Use two large spoons to remove a serving including part of all layers, about 3/4 c.

Variation: Substitute fresh raspberries and raspberry Jell-O.

The contrasting textures and colors make this a delicious and festive dessert that compares favorably with a true English trifle. It is less sweet. (One could add 1-2 T. sugar to the berries or whipped cream if desired.)
This is an original adaptation, family endorsed. It has become a favorite dessert for summer birthday parties.

Pineapple Upside Down Cake

1 #2 can sliced or crushed pineapple in juice	2 eggs
4 T. soft butter	1 c. flour
1 c. brown sugar	1 t. baking powder
1/4 c. Crisco	1/2 c. milk
3/4 c. sugar	Whipped cream
	Maraschino cherries (optional)

Drain pineapple, saving juice. In a 9 x 9 in. baking pan, spread butter, brown sugar, and pineapple. Blend Crisco with sugar. Add eggs and beat until fluffy. Add flour sifted with baking powder alternately with milk (or substitute 1/2 c. pineapple juice). Beat until smooth. Pour over prepared fruit. Bake at 350F for 30-40 min.

While warm, turn pan upside down on serving plate. May be served with whipped cream. You may center each pineapple slice with a maraschino cherry. Serves 8.

Variation: Substitute #2 can of apricot halves for pineapple.

American Apple Pie

Unbaked pastry for double-crust 9-in. pie	3/4 t. cinnamon
6 c. Granny Smith or other firm, tart apples, peeled and sliced	1/4 t. nutmeg
	1/2 t. salt
	1 t. lemon juice
1 c. sugar	1 T. butter

Fill the prepared pastry crust with apples that have been mixed with sugar, cinnamon, nutmeg, salt, and lemon juice. Apples should be firmly packed. Dot with butter. Fit on top crust. Brush with milk and sprinkle with 1 t. sugar. Moisten lower crust and crimp edges. Slit top. Bake in hot oven 425F for 40-50 min. or until brown and apple juice is bubbling. Serve slightly warm with a triangle of cheddar cheese or dip of vanilla ice cream.

Early settlers often planted fruit trees, grapes, rhubarb, and berry bushes as soon as they cleared space for an orchard. Plums, pears, and apples were favored because they were hardy. One orchard planted in 1904 had Dutchess, Greening, Wealthy, and a late variety. Another earlier apple, the Whitney, was prized for pickling. Later, Winesaps, Jonathans, and Granny Smiths were introduced.

♣ *Handle pastry lightly and as little as possible. When the dough holds together, form a ball and flatten it to about 6-in. diameter. Roll out to size needed and make crust. At this point, crust may be refrigerated until needed.*

English Apple Pie

1 egg	1-1/2 c. chopped apples
3/4 c. sugar	1/2 c. chopped nuts
1/2 c. flour	1/2 t. vanilla
1 t. baking powder	

Mix all ingredients together. Pour into a well-greased pie pan. Bake at 350F for 25 min. Serve with cream or soft custard. Serves 6.

Most English apple pies have two pastry crusts, as do their American counter-parts. This delicious variation is quick and easy to prepare.

Lazy Day Banana Pie

12 to 14 graham crackers	3 medium bananas, sliced
1 small pkg Jell-O French	1 c. whipping cream
vanilla pudding mix	1 t. sugar
2 c. milk (may be 2%)	

Break (do not crush) graham crackers into bite-size pieces to cover bottom and sides of 9-in. pie plate.

In a saucepan, whisk pudding mix into milk. Cook on medium heat, whisking constantly, until pudding starts to boil. Remove from heat, cover, and let cool to room temperature. Pour half the pudding into cracker-lined plate. Slice half the bananas over pudding. Stir remainder of sliced bananas into the second half of pudding and pour mixture onto banana layer in pie plate. Chill. Whip cream with sugar until it reaches firm peaks. Pour whipped cream over pie filling, spreading out to cover crackers. Chill an hour. Serves 6.

This pie can be made in 10 min. and served warm. It has very little sugar and fat, but has the flavor of a luscious dessert.

Very Berry Pie

Unbaked pastry for double- crust 9-in. pie	2 T. butter
	Dash of salt
1 pt. fresh blueberries	1-1/2 T. cornstarch
6 oz. fresh red raspberries	1/4 c. water
6 oz. fresh blackberries	1 t. Minute tapioca
6 oz. fresh boysenberries	2 T. lemon juice
1 1/4 c. sugar	Boysenberry juice

Crust: Prepare pastry for two-crust 10-in. or deep-dish 9-in. pie. Allow at least 1/2-in. overhang on bottom crust. Sprinkle bottom crust with tapioca. Set aside.

Filling: Rinse, drain, and pick over fresh berries. Put in a large bowl with sugar and salt and mix. Set aside for 20 min. to let juices accumulate. Drain and measure juice from combined berries. Add boysenberry juice to make 1 c. Combine cornstarch and water; add to 1 c. juice and cook until thick, stirring constantly. Add 1-2 T. extra juice if needed. Remove from heat and stir in all berries. Add butter and lemon juice, stir. Pour berry mixture into prepared crust. Moisten edge of bottom crust overhang well. Slash a design in top crust and arrange it atop berries. Press firmly to seal crusts. Trim neatly and fold overlap up over top crust to make a high crimped edge. If desired, sprinkle a scant teaspoonful of sugar over crust.

Bake at 450F for only 10 min. Reduce heat to 375F and bake 35 min. or until juices bubble through slits. Cool completely before serving. Put a foil collar around outer edge to avoid over-browning. Serves 8.

Variation: Canned and frozen fruit can be substituted out of season — 2 c. frozen blueberries, 6 oz. frozen raspberries, canned or frozen black- berries, and 1 can boysenberries, drained to obtain extra boysenberry juice.

This berry pie is my version of a four-berry pie my mother and I were served in 1981 in a Carmel, California, shop specializing in pie. The deep berry-red color, delectably juicy filling, and flaky crust were simply perfect, and the blend of berry flavors indescribably delicious.

Five years later my daughter Anne and I came across another memorable four-berry pie at Moody's Diner in Waldoboro, Maine. Moody's is justly famed for its pies; whether the four-berry pie is available depends on what was made that day — and what was already consumed before the traveler arrived.

Throughout the United States, and certainly wherever one travels in the Middle West, small restaurants in small towns invariably serve great pie, usually baked by a pastry chef whose skills have been perfected through years of practice. These pies aren't nouvelle cuisine with fancy ingredients. They are honest, delicious, and make you want seconds.

Blueberry Cream Pie

Graham cracker crust
   for 9-in. pie
1 8-oz. pkg cream cheese
1/2 c. sugar

2 eggs
1 can blueberry pie filling
8 oz. Cool Whip

Blend cream cheese with sugar. Beat and add eggs. Pour into crust and bake at 325F for 25-30 min. Cool. Pour blueberry filling evenly on baked mixture when cooled. Top with softened Cool Whip. Chill 2-3 hr. before serving. Serves 6 to 8.

Blueberry Mystery Pie

Unbaked pastry for double-
   crust 8-in. pie
1 can blueberry pie filling

1 T. butter
3 T. brown sugar
Juice of 1/2 lemon

Pour blueberry filling into unbaked crust. Dot blueberries with butter, cut into six slivers and distributed evenly. Sprinkle brown sugar evenly over filling. Squeeze lemon juice over all. Arrange top crust, slit in several places to allow steam to escape. Moisten lower crust and crimp edges together. Bake pie for 10 min. at 425F, then for 30 min. at 375F until filling bubbles and crust is golden brown. Serves 6.

This has a tempting difference, the brown sugar and lemon flavors.

Fresh Blueberry Pie

1 baked 9-in. pie shell
5 c. blueberries
1 c. water
3/4 c. sugar

1 t. grated lemon peel
3 T. cornstarch
Whipped cream

Wash berries, drain thoroughly, and allow to dry on paper towels. Place 4 c. berries in pie shell. Combine 1 c. berries, 3/4 c. water, sugar, and grated lemon peel in saucepan. Bring to rolling boil. Add remaining water, sugar, and cornstarch, mixing well. Cook over lower heat, stirring constantly, until thick and clear. Pour over blueberries in pie shell, spreading glaze evenly. Chill completely. Serve with sweetened whipped cream. Serves 6 to 8.

♣ *Avoid messy oven spills by slipping a sheet of foil under a fruit pie or casserole to catch drips. If you do have oven spills, toss 1/2 t. salt on the spill to control smoke and odor.*

Butterscotch Cream Pie

1 baked 9-in. pie shell	1/4 c. cornstarch
3/4 c. packed brown sugar	2 eggs, separated
1/3 c. whipping cream	1 t. vanilla
2 T. butter	1/4 t. cream of tartar
2 c. milk, divided	1/4 c. sugar

Combine brown sugar, cream, and butter in a heavy saucepan. Cook over low heat until butter melts, stirring often. Add 1-1/2 c. milk. Cook until mixture is hot. Combine cornstarch and remaining 1/2 c. mulk; set aside. Beat egg yolks until lemon colored. Stir about 1/4 of hot mixture into egg yolks; then stir this into remainder of hot mixture. Cook 3 min., stirring constantly. Add cornstarch-milk mixture, stirring briskly; cook for 5 min. Remove from heat. Stir in vanilla and cool partially. Pour filling into baked crust. Spread meringue over filling to crust edge. Bake in 350F oven for 12-15 min. until meringue is golden. Serves 6 to 8.

Meringue: Beat egg whites with cream of tartar until stiff but not dry. Beat in sugar gradually until meringue is stiff and glossy.

My Cherry-Ripe Pie

Unbaked pastry for double- crust 9-in. pie	1 T. soft butter
	1/2 c. cherry juice
1 t. Minute tapioca	2 t. lemon juice
1 1/4 c. sugar	3 c. fresh pitted cherries,
3 T. cornstarch	drained in a colander
1/4 t. salt	Cherry juice (saved)

Sprinkle tapioca into lower pastry crust. Combine sugar, cornstarch, and salt. Stir in butter. Combine cherry juice and lemon juice and stir into dry ingredients. Add cherries and mix lightly. Pour cherry mixture into prepared unbaked pastry. Make lattice top, flute edges. Cut a strip of aluminum foil 3 in. wide and fold the collar around edge of pie to prevent over-browning. Bake at 400F for 50-55 min. until crust is golden and filling is bubbling. Cool. Serves 8.

Bakers who owned a china "bird," intended to vent the steam and bubbling juice of a cherry pie, might amuse their guests by placing it under the second crust before baking. Are you lucky enough to own an antique bird?

Tiptop Cherry Pie

Unbaked pastry for double- crust 9-in. pie	1 c. sugar 3 T. Minute tapioca
3 c. fresh pitted cherries with juice	1/2 t. salt 2 T. butter

Combine cherries, juice, sugar, salt, and tapioca in a bowl; let stand 15 min., stirring occasionally. Pour into prepared bottom crust. Dot with butter. Moisten edges. Slit top crust and arrange over cherries, flute to a high edge. Bake 15 min. at 400F; lower heat to 350F for 30 min. more or until filling is bubbling. Serves 6 to 8.

♣ *Using tapioca produces a juicy but firm filling that cuts well and holds its shape.*

Chocolate Pie

1 baked 9-in. pie shell	3 eggs
1 c. sugar	2-1/2 c. milk
1/2 c. cocoa	2 T. butter
4 T. flour	2 t. vanilla
1/2 t. salt	

Mix together cocoa, sugar, flour, and salt. Beat eggs until completely blended and add to milk. Blend egg-milk mixture with dry mixture. Cook in double boiler over hot water, stirring constantly until thick. Stir in butter and vanilla. Cool slightly, then pour into baked crust. Chill. Top with whipped cream or meringue. Serves 6 to 8.

♣ *Press plastic wrap on surface of puddings, etc., to prevent a skim from forming.*

Choco-Chip Pie

1 baked 9-in. pie shell
1 6-oz. pkg chocolate chips
3 eggs, separated
1/4 c. water

1/8 t. salt
2 t. vanilla
1/3 c. brown sugar

Melt chocolate chips over hot water. Add egg yolks, one at a time. Stir in water. Beat egg whites, salt, and vanilla until stiff but not dry. Gradually add brown sugar. Fold chocolate mixture into egg whites. Pour into baked pie shell. Garnish with whipped cream and chocolate curls. Chill. Serves 6 to 8.

Bishop's Chocolate Marshmallow Pie

Graham cracker crust for
  9-in. pie
1/2 lb. large marshmallows
1/2 bar German sweet chocolate

3/4 c. milk
1/2 pt. whipping cream
1 t. vanilla

Put marshmallows, chocolate, and milk in top of double boiler. When melted, set aside to cool. Stir only to blend. When completely cooled, whip cream to stiff peaks, add vanilla, and fold into chocolate mixture. Pour into prepared graham cracker crust. Decorate with grated chocolate and additional whipped cream around edges. Chill 2 hr. Serves 6 to 8.

Bishop's Cafeterias were famous for their pies. This chocolate marshmallow pie was a favorite with customers for many years.

Fantastic Fudge Pie

2 oz. German sweet chocolate
1/2 c. butter
3 large eggs
1/2 c. sugar

1/2 c. brown sugar, firmly packed
1/2 c. flour
1 t. vanilla

Combine chocolate and butter in medium saucepan. Melt over low heat (325F), stirring until butter is melted. Remove from heat and cool. In large mixer bowl, beat eggs at high speed for 2 min. Add white and brown sugar; beat 1 min. at high speed. At low speed, add flour and beat 1 min. Add cooled chocolate mixture and vanilla; beat 1-1/2 min. at medium speed. Pour into well-greased 9-in. pie pan. Bake at 325F for 40 min. Cool. Serve with whipped cream. Serves 6 to 8.

Coconut Meringue Pie

Anna M. Petersen

1 baked 9-in. pie shell
1 c. sugar
1/2 c. cornstarch
1/4 t. salt
3 1/4 c. whole milk

3 eggs, separated
2 T. butter
1 t. vanilla
1/2 c. flaked coconut

Combine sugar, cornstarch, and salt in 2-qt. saucepan. Stir in milk and cook over medium heat, stirring constantly, until thick and smooth. Beat egg yolks until lemon colored. Stir a cup of the hot milk mixture into yolks, stirring steadily. Add this to the hot milk mixture, stirring constantly; and cook 5 min. Remove from heat. Add butter and vanilla. Cool. Stir coconut into filling and pour into baked pastry shell. Cool.

Meringue: Beat egg whites with 1/4 t. salt and 1/4 t. cream of tartar to soft peaks. Add 1/2 c. sugar slowly, beating until egg whites form stiff peaks. Spread the meringue over the pie, covering where the edge of pastry meets filling. Sprinkle meringue liberally with 1/3 c. additional coconut. Bake in 375F oven about 12 min. until meringue and coconut are a delicate brown. Remove from oven and cool on rack. Store in refrigerator until served. Serves 6 to 8.

♣ *Dip knife in hot water when cutting meringue to prevent ragged cuts.*

Coconut Supreme Pie

3 T. melted butter
1 1/4 c. flaked coconut
1 can sweetened condensed
    milk (Eagle Brand)
1/2 c. brown sugar

1/4 c. chopped pecans
1/4 c. whole pecans
Whipped cream or topping
Toasted coconut

Crust: Mix together melted butter and coconut. Press into a greased 9-in. pie pan. Bake at 300F for 15 min. Cool.

Filling: Mix condensed milk and brown sugar in top of double boiler. Cook, stirring constantly, until thick. Fold in chopped pecans. Cool. Spoon filling into coconut crust. Sprinkle whole pecans over top. Frost with whipped cream or softened topping; sprinkle toasted coconut over the top. Refrigerate until served. Serves 6 to 8.

Custard Pie

1 unbaked 9-in. pie shell	1/4 t. salt
4 large eggs	1/2 t. nutmeg
1/2 c. sugar	2 t. vanilla
2-1/2 c. whole milk	

Beat eggs to blend; add sugar and beat about 1 min. Add milk, salt, and vanilla; blend well. Pour into prepared crust and sprinkle with nutmeg. Place pan in preheated 400F oven and bake 20 min. Reduce heat to 350F and bake another 25 min. or until a silver knife is clean when tested. Cool. Refrigerate until serving. Serves 6 to 8.

Lemon Pie

1 baked 9-in. pie shell	3 T. butter
1 1/4 c. sugar	1-1/2 t. lemon extract
6 T. cornstarch	2 t. vinegar
2 c. water	1 T. grated lemon rind
3 eggs, separated	1/3 c. sugar
1/3 c. lemon juice	

Mix 1 1/4 c. sugar, cornstarch, and water in top of double boiler; blend well. Combine egg yolks with lemon juice; beat well. Stir egg yolk mixture into sugar mixture in top of double boiler. Cook over boiling water 25 min., stirring constantly. Add butter, lemon extract, and vinegar. Stir well. Pour into baked pie shell and allow to cool. Preheat oven to 350F.

Meringue: Beat egg whites stiff. Add 1/3 c. sugar gradually, beating until meringue is very stiff and glossy. Spread meringue on pie, sealing up to edges. Bake at 350F about 10-12 min. until golden brown. Cool, then chill several hours.

To serve, sprinkle grated lemon rind over meringue. Cut into 6 or 8 pieces.

♣ *Wash lemons, then press and roll on hard surface until lemon yields to pressure. Then squeeze (ream) to get more juice.*

Irene's Lemon Pie   Irene Heritage

1 baked 8-in. rich pastry	1 T. cornstarch
2 lemons	2 eggs, separated
1/2 c. sugar (or less)	1/2 c. cold water

Grate peel of both lemons. Squeeze lemons for juice. Mix cornstarch with water; add sugar, grated lemon rind, and lemon juice. Stir over heat until boiling; boil 5 min. Cool a little before stirring in beaten egg yolks. Pour into baked pastry case. Whip egg whites stiffly; add 2 T. sugar and beat well. Pile on pie to edges. Decorate with cherry and angelica. Brown meringue lightly in 400F oven. Cool. Serves 6 to 8.

This English recipe makes a tarter lemon pie, contrasting with the rich pastry and meringue.

Stone's "Mile High" Lemon Pie

1 baked 9-in. pie shell	Salt to taste
8 eggs, separated	2 T. Knox unflavored gelatin
1 c. sugar	1/2 c. cold water
Juice of 2 lemons	1 c. sugar
Grated rinds of 2 lemons	

Slightly beat egg yolks and blend with 1 c. sugar, lemon juice and grated rind, and salt in double boiler. Cook, stirring frequently, until mixture reaches the consistency of thick custard. Soak gelatin in cold water until dissolved. Add to hot custard and cool.

Beat egg whites stiff but not dry in the large bowl of electric mixer. Beat 1 c. sugar in gradually, using spatula to push whites toward beaters. Fold cool custard into beaten egg whites; blend but do not overmix. Pour into baked pie shell and chill 3 hr. Serve with whipped cream. Serves 8.

As long as I can remember, going to Stone's Restaurant in Marshalltown, Iowa, was an extra-special occasion, especially for Sunday dinner. The fried chicken and baked ham were gourmet treats. But we had all made the trip for their signature dessert — "Mile High Lemon Pie."

Lemon Chess Pie

1 unbaked 9-in. pie shell	1 T. white vinegar
1 T. flour	1/2 c. butter, melted
1/4 t. salt	1/3 c. buttermilk
2 T. cornmeal	2 t. lemon zest
2 c. sugar	1/3 c. lemon juice
4 large eggs	

In a large bowl, blend dry ingredients, vinegar, and buttermilk. Beat eggs 1 min. Stir into first mixture. Blend in lemon juice and zest. Pour into prepared pie crust. Bake at 400F for 10 min. Reduce heat to 350F and bake for 40 min. Cool on a wire rack. Serves 6-8.

Key Lime Pie

Graham cracker crust
   for 9-in. pie
1 can Eagle Brand
   condensed milk

1/2 c. lime juice
8 oz. Cool Whip
Fresh limes

Beat milk together with lime juice. Fold in Cool Whip. Pour mixture into graham cracker crust. Garnish with very thin slices of fresh lime. Refrigerate. Serves 6 to 8.

Fresh Peach Pie

1 unbaked crust for 9-in. pie
5 large ripe peaches
1 c. sugar

1/4 c. flour
1 c. half and half

When preparing crust, crimp edges to be high. Peel and slice peaches; put in raw crust. Mix sugar, flour, and half and half. Pour evenly over peaches in crust. Bake at 450F for 10 min. Turn heat down to 350F for 45 min. Cool. Serve warm or cold with vanilla ice cream. Serves 6 to 8.

Rich peach flavor.

♣ *When buying peaches or nectarines, look for the small, heavy paper bags grocers offer to improve the fruits' ripening.*

Waid's Peanut Butter Pie

1 baked 9-in pie shell
1 c. plus 2 T. sugar
2-1/2 c. milk
1 t. vanilla
Pinch salt
1 T. margarine

2 eggs
3-1/2 T. cornstarch
1/2 c. water
1/3 c. peanut butter
Whipped cream
Peanut butter chips

Combine sugar, milk, vanilla, salt, and margarine in top of a double boiler. Cook over medium heat, stirring frequently, until custard mixture is hot. Beat eggs; add cornstarch and water, stirring until cornstarch is dissolved. Stir into hot milk mixture. Cook, stirring frequently, until hot and slightly thickened. Add peanut butter, stirring until it is melted; cook until mixture is thickened. Remove from heat and cool slightly. While still warm, pour into baked pie shell. Refrigerate several hours until set. Top with sweetened whipped cream and sprinkle with peanut butter chips. Serves 8.

Lady Bird's Pecan Pie   Lady Bird Johnson

1 unbaked 9-in pie crust   1/2 t. salt
1 c. sugar   3 eggs, beaten
1 c. dark Karo syrup   2 c. pecans, coarsely chopped
1-1/2 t. vanilla   Whipped cream
1 stick butter, melted

Mix sugar, syrup, vanilla, melted butter, salt, and beaten eggs. Blend thoroughly. Fold in pecans. Pour into unbaked pastry shell. Bake at 375F for 15 min. Reduce heat to 325F for 30-40 min. or until silver knife comes out clean. Cool. Serve with whipped cream. Serves 8.

Mrs. Johnson has earned a special place in our hearts for her leadership in years of planting wildflowers to beautify America. Thank you, dear Lady Bird! In our family, her recipe for pecan pie has been used for 40 years, and we thank her.

Pineapple Pie

Unbaked double-crust pastry   1/2 c. sugar
   for 9-in. pie   1/2 c. evaporated milk
1 20-oz. can crushed pineapple   2 T. soft butter
2 T. cornstarch   2 T. lemon juice
1/4 t. salt

Prepare pastry; roll and fit the bottom crust. Combine crushed pineapple and juice with cornstarch, salt, sugar, and milk. Cook over low heat, stirring constantly, until thick. Add butter and lemon juice and stir until blended. Pour into pastry-lined pan.

Roll out second pastry 1/8 in. thick. Cut into ten 1/2-in. strips to make lattice design. Moisten edge of under crust. Trim overhang. Flute edges. Bake at 400F for 40-45 min. until crust is golden brown. Serves 6 to 8.

Libby's Famous Pumpkin Pie

Libby's

1 unbaked 9-in. pie shell
2 eggs
1 16-oz. can Libby's solid
  pack pumpkin
3/4 c. sugar
1/4 c. brown sugar
1/2 t. salt

1 t. ground cinnamon
1/2 t. ground ginger
1/4 t. ground cloves
1 tall can (13 oz.) Pet
  evaporated milk
1 T. vanilla
Whipped cream

For this recipe, the pie shell should have a high fluted edge; filling will puff above the edge of the pie pan. Preheat oven to 425F. Slightly beat eggs. Mix in other filling ingredients in order given. Pour into pie shell. Bake 15 min. at 425F. Reduce heat to 350F and bake 45 min. or until a silver knife inserted near center comes out clean. Cool completely on a wire rack. Before serving, garnish with whipped cream or, if preferred, whipped topping. Serves 6 to 8.

Variation: Chop 1/2 c. pecans and sprinkle on unbaked pie.

Mamie's Pumpkin Chiffon Pie

Mamie Eisenhower

1 baked 9-in. pie shell
1 env. (1 T.) unflavored gelatin
3/4 c. brown sugar, firmly
  packed
1/2 t. salt
1 t. cinnamon
1/8 t. nutmeg

1/2 c. milk
1/4 c. water
8 eggs, separated
1-1/2 c. cooked pumpkin, mashed
1/4 c. sugar
Whipped cream

Mix gelatin, brown sugar, salt, cinnamon, and nutmeg in top of double boiler. Stir in milk and water. Beat in egg yolks with a fork or whisk. Add the pumpkin and stir well. Place over boiling water and cook, stirring often, until mixture is heated through, about 10 min. Remove from heat and chill until mixture begins to set (a spoonful of it dropped back will hold its shape well in a mound). Beat egg whites until stiff but not dry; gradually beat in granulated sugar until very stiff. Fold gelatin mixture into egg whites. Turn into pie shell and chill until firm. Garnish with whipped cream. Serves 6 to 8.

Pumpkin Chiffon Pie

1 baked 9-in. pastry crust	1 c. sugar, divided
1 T. Knox gelatin	1/2 t. salt
1/4 c. cold water	1 t. pumpkin pie spice *or*
1 #2 can pumpkin	1/2 t. cinnamon and 1 t. ginger
3/4 c. milk	1/2 t. vanilla
2 eggs, separated	2 c. whipped topping

Soften gelatin in water. In top of a double boiler, combine pumpkin, milk, egg yolks, 1/2 c. sugar, salt, and spices; cook over boiling water for 10 min., stirring constantly. Stir in gelatin. Cool until thick but not set. Beat egg whites until stiff, adding remaining 1/2 c. sugar. Fold pumpkin into beaten egg whites. Pour into pastry shell and chill until firm. If desired, decorate with 1/3 c. chopped pecans or walnuts, and top with whipped cream, Cool Whip, or other topping. Serves 6 to 8.

Sour Cream Raisin Pie

Unbaked pastry for double- crust 9-in. pie	1/8 t. salt
	2 eggs, separated
1 c. raisins	1 t. cinnamon
1 c. sugar	1/2 t. nutmeg
1 c. sour cream	1/2 t. cloves

Mix raisins with sugar. Add sour cream, salt, and slightly beaten egg yolks. Beat egg whites stiff and fold into raisin mixture. Pour into prepared pastry. Moisten edges of bottom crust, and put top crust in place. Crimp edges, slit top. Bake at 425F for 10 min. Reduce heat to 350F and bake 30 min. until light brown. Serve slightly warm. Serves 6 to 8.

Red Raspberry Pie

1 9-in. graham cracker crust	2 c. fresh red raspberries
1 T. Knox gelatin (1 env.)	1-1/2 T. lemon juice
3 T. cold water	1 c. heavy cream, whipped
1/2 c. sugar	

Reserve 1/4 c. raspberries for garnish. Soften gelatin in cold water; dissolve over hot water in a double boiler. Add sugar, raspberries, lemon juice, and a dash of salt. Chill until partially set. Fold in half the whipped cream and pour into the graham cracker crust. Chill until firm. Spread with remaining whipped cream, and garnish with reserved berries.
Serves 6.

Graham Cracker Crust: Combine 1-1/2 c. crushed crumbs (12 graham crackers), 1/3 c. sugar, and 1/3 c. melted butter. Mix well, and press into a 9-in. lightly greased pie pan. Chill until set.

♣ *Sort berries but do not wash before refrigerating. Hull and wash just before serving.*

Creamy Rhubarb Pie

1 unbaked 9-in. pie shell
2 eggs
3/4 c. sugar
2 T. flour

1/2 t. salt
1 T. very soft butter
3 c. prepared rhubarb

Clean rhubarb and chop into 1-in. pieces. Beat eggs until light. Gradually add sugar, flour, and salt. Beat until thick. Add butter and rhubarb. Combine. Turn into pie crust. Roll out remaining crust to 1/8-in. thickness. Cut into ten 1/2-in. strips and make lattice crust. Seal ends to bottom crust and flute. Bake at 375F for 15 min. Reduce heat to 325F for 30-35 min. until golden brown. Serve warm with cream or ice cream. Serves 6 to 8.

Rhubarb Custard Pie   Amanas

1 unbaked 9-in. rich crust
2-1/2 c. prepared rhubarb
1-1/2 c. sugar
3 T. flour

2 eggs, separated
1/2 c. sour cream
3 T. sugar

Wash and cut rhubarb in small pieces. Combine sugar, flour, beaten egg yolks, and sour cream. Add rhubarb, mix well, and pour into rich crust. Bake at 375F about 45 min. until firm when tested with silver knife. Cover with meringue made of egg whites beaten to stiff peaks, then folding in 3 T. sugar. Bake at 350F for 10 min. until meringue is golden. Serves 6 to 8.

We look for this spring dessert at the Amana Colonies in Iowa — simultaneously tart and sweet!

Shoo-Fly Pie

1 unbaked 9-in. pie shell	1/8 t. cloves
3/4 c. molasses or dark	1/2 t. cinnamon
corn syrup	1/4 t. ginger
3/4 c. boiling water	1-1/2 c. flour
1/2 t. soda	1/4 c. soft shortening
1/3 t. nutmeg	1/2 c. brown sugar

Mix syrup, boiling water, soda, and spices together. Set aside. Put flour, shortening (butter or oleo), and brown sugar into a bowl and blend thoroughly with pastry blender. Sprinkle half a cup of these crumbs in the bottom of the unbaked crust. Then add half a cup of the liquid mixture, then a layer of crumbs, alternating layers with the final layer being crumbs. Bake at 375F for 35 min. and filling is set. Serves 6 to 8.

An early settler might have brought this recipe for a pie still popular in the East Central States. It's spicy and sweet.

Jean's Fresh Strawberry Pie   Jean Petersen

1 baked 9-in pie shell	1-1/2 c. cold water
1 c. sugar	2 c. prepared strawberries
3 T. strawberry Jell-O	Extra berries, quartered
4 T. cornstarch	Whipped cream
1/2 t. red food coloring	

Combine sugar, Jell-O, and cornstarch. Stir in cold water and bring mixture to a boil, stirring constantly. Cook until clear. Add food coloring. Cool. Stir strawberries into sauce. Put into baked crust and chill. Top with whipped cream and quartered berries. Serves 6 to 8.

Fresh Strawberry Pie

1 9-in. graham cracker or	1/4 c. white Karo syrup
pastry crust	1 T. lemon juice
4 c. fresh strawberries	3 T. cornstarch
Extra berries	3/4 c. sugar
3/4 c. water, divided	Whipped cream
Red food coloring	

Wash, stem, and halve strawberries. Mix 1/4 c. water and cornstarch. Add remaining water, syrup, sugar, and lemon juice. Cook until thick. Add drop of red food coloring. Cool. Place berries in pie shell. Top with cooled mixture. Chill. Cover with whipped cream and a few berries. Serves 6.

Strawberry Glaze Pie

1 baked 9-in. pastry shell	2 c. strawberries, sliced
1 1/4 c. sugar, divided	2 c. crushed strawberries
3 T. cornstarch	8 whole strawberries
1/2 c. water	for garnish

In medium bowl, sprinkle 1/4 c. sugar over 2 c. sliced strawberries; mix very gently and arrange in pie shell. Set aside.

Glaze: In saucepan, blend cornstarch, water, and 1 c. sugar. Mix in 2 c. crushed strawberries. Cook until thick, stirring constantly. Cool for 3 min., then pour glaze over berries in the pie shell. Chill several hours. Top with whipped cream and whole berries. Serves 6 to 8.

Strawberry-Rhubarb Pie

Pastry for double-crust	1-1/2 c. strawberries, halved
9-in. pie	2 c. rhubarb, diced
1 1/4 c. sugar	2 T. butter
1/4 c. flour	

Crust: Prepare pastry for two-crust pie. Fit one crust into 9-in. pie pan. Roll out second crust and cut into 1/2-in. strips.

Filling: Sift flour and sugar together and combine 3/4 of it with strawberry and rhubarb mixed together. Sprinkle remaining dry mixture over bottom of crust in pie pan and add filling. Dot with butter. Arrange pastry strips over filling in lattice design. Moisten ends of strips and crimp around edge. Bake in hot oven (450F) for 10 min. Reduce to moderate (350F) and bake 30 min. longer or until fruit is tender. Serves 6 to 8.

Sweet Potato Pie

1 unbaked 9-in. pie shell	1/2 c. fresh orange juice
2 c. mashed orange sweet	1 t. grated orange peel
potatoes or yams	1/2 t. salt
1 stick butter or margarine	1 T. lemon juice
2 eggs, well beaten	1/2 t. cinnamon
3/4 c. brown sugar, packed	

Cream butter and sugar. Add beaten eggs, salt, and cinnamon; blend well. Stir in mashed sweet potatoes until smooth. Add orange juice, orange peel, and lemon juice; stir to blend. Pour mixture into unbaked, crimped pie shell. Bake at 325F for 35-40 min. or until a silver knife inserted comes out clean. Cool entirely. Serve with sweetened whipped cream. Serves 6 to 8.

Toll Crest Pie   Fern Petersen

1 baked 9-in. pie shell	3 eggs, separated
5 T. flour	2 T. margarine
1/4 t. salt	1 t. orange (or lemon) extract
1 c. dark corn syrup	6 T. sugar
1 1/4 c. milk	1/4 c. pecans
1 c. raisins	

Mix flour, salt, and syrup in top of double boiler, add milk, and cook until thick. Add raisins and beaten egg yolks. Add margarine; cool. Add orange or lemon flavoring. Pour into baked shell. Cover with meringue made by beating egg whites to stiff peaks, then adding 6 T. sugar. Sprinkle with pecans. Brown at 400F for 12-15 min. Serves 6 to 8.

White Christmas Pie   Alice Volkert

1 baked 9-in. pastry shell	1 c. whipped cream
1 T. Knox gelatin	3 egg whites
1/4 c. water	1/2 c. sugar
1-1/2 c. milk	1 c. + 3 T. flake coconut
1/2 c. sugar	Red and green candied
4 T. flour	cherries for garnish (optional)
1/2 t. salt	

Soften gelatin in water. In saucepan, mix sugar, flour, salt, and milk. Boil 1 min., add gelatin, mix, and cool. Beat egg whites with 1/2 c. sugar until firm peaks form. Fold egg whites into cooled mixture, then fold in whipped cream. Fold in 1 c. coconut and pour into baked pastry shell. Sprinkle 3 T. coconut on top. If desired, decorate with candied cherries cut to resemble holly leaves and berries. Chill several hours. Serves 6 to 8.

A very festive dessert.

Pastry for a Double-Crust 9-in. Pie

2 c. sifted flour	2/3 c. shortening, divided
1/2 t. salt	4 T. ice water

Sift together in a bowl sifted flour and salt. Cut in 1/3 c. shortening with a pastry blender. Then cut in a second 1/3 c. shortening until crumbs are the size of peas. Sprinkle with ice water. Mix with fork and round into a ball. Divide in half for two crusts. Roll on floured board. Chill. Yield: two 9-in. crusts.

♣ *Home-rendered lard makes excellent shortening for pie crust. Home rendering is now rare, but you may be fortunate enough to be able to purchase home-rendered lard from a local butcher. Good alternatives are Crisco, commercial lard, or corn oil. Butter and margarine produce a richer pastry, which may be desired for tart fillings.*

One secret to a perfect crust is minimal handling of the dough. One also needs to work quickly. Lots of practice helps in mastering the art.

Fluted or crimped edges make a more attractive pie. To finish a single crust, prick bottom liberally with fork. For a double-crust pie, moisten the edge of the bottom crust before arranging the upper crust over the filling; flute the edges carefully, since a tight seal will prevent filling from bubbling out.

The upper crust should be slit to vent steam. You can do this by lightly folding the crust in half on the pastry cloth and slashing at the half and quarter points. Lift the top onto the filled lower crust (which has moistened edges) and carefully unfold to cover the whole pie; flute edges and trim neatly.

A lattice effect is an attractive alternative upper crust, especially for fruit pies. Place bottom pastry in pie tin as usual and fill. Roll out second pastry 1/8 in. thick. Cut into ten 1/2-in. strips to make lattice design. Moisten edge of under crust. Trim overhang. Flute edges.

Pie Crust I

3 c. sifted flour	5 T. cold water
1/2 t. salt	1 t. vinegar
1 c. lard	1 egg

Sift flour and salt into a bowl. Cut in lard with pastry blender. Mix cold water with vinegar and whole egg. Beat thoroughly and blend into flour mixture. Continue as with any crust. Yield: two 9-in. crusts.

Flaky and tender.

♣ *To make pie crust flaky, measure flour and shortening into bowl and chill for an hour before mixing.*

Basic Pie Crust II

2 c. sifted flour
1 t. salt

2/3 c. Crisco
4 T. ice water

Sift flour and salt together in a bowl. Use a pastry blender to cut Crisco into flour until it is the consistency of coarse meal. Add ice water slowly, tossing with a fork until dough forms a ball. Roll out half on lightly floured pastry cloth or board. For one crust, prick with a fork and bake at 450F for 10-12 min. This amount will make two 9-in. crusts.

Pie Crust with Egg and Vinegar

3 c. flour
1 egg
1-1/2 c. Crisco

1 t. vinegar
3/4 t. salt
2 to 4 T. water

Cut shortening into sifted flour until it forms coarse crumbs. Beat egg and mix with vinegar, salt, and 2 T. water. Add to flour-shortening mixture. Toss lightly. Add more water as needed so mixture can be gathered into a ball. Take half and roll on slightly floured board to make a 9-in. crust.

For single crust, fit into pie tin, and crimp edges. Prick bottom liberally with fork. Bake at 450F for 10-12 min. If desired, line crust with foil and fill with dry beans. Bake, remove beans.

For two-crust pie, fill lower crust. Moisten edges of lower crust, slash and fit upper crust, and crimp. Yield: two 9-in. crusts.

Wrapped in foil, this dough keeps in refrigerator or frozen for weeks.

Graham Cracker Crust

1-1/2 c. graham cracker crumbs
1 T. brown sugar

6 T. melted butter

Crush graham crackers in a sealed freezer bag to make 1-1/2 c. crumbs. Mix with brown sugar and melted butter. Press mixture on sides and bottom of a 9-in. pie pan. Bake at 350F for 10-12 min. Cool. Fill with chosen filling. Yield: one 9-in. crust.

Variation: Substitute vanilla or chocolate wafers for graham crackers, omitting brown sugar.

Meringue — Tried and True

3 egg whites at room temperature   6 T. sugar
1/4 t. cream of tartar   1/2 t. flavoring if desired

Beat egg whites with cream of tartar until frothy. Gradually beat in sugar, beating until stiff and glossy. Pile meringue onto pie filling, being careful to seal the meringue onto the edge of crust to prevent shrinking. Bake at 400F for 8-10 min. until meringue is golden.

Main Dishes

Beef ♣ *Fowl and Dressing* ♣
Lamb ♣ *Pork* ♣ *Meat Hot Dishes*
♣ *Seafood* ♣ *Pasta* ♣ *Miscellany*

<u>Threshing</u>

In the Midwest, planting and cultivating are a time of hope and anticipation. When glaciers covered the region thousands of years ago, the ice retreated northward as the earth warmed. Their weight and the load of rock the glaciers pushed ground the rock to powder or gravel, leveled the hills and filled in valleys to form gently rolling prairies. Great winds blew, depositing deep clay soils and shaping loess bluffs along the Missouri and Mississippi Rivers. These soils form the huge fertile area that produces bumper crops. The Midwest explodes with energy at harvest season.

The early settlers needed everyone's cooperation and pooled resources of man and beast. Men and women wielded sickles and scythes to cut grain. They tied it by hand and juggled the bundles into shocks that would shed rain. Women and half-grown children helped shock, and younger children fetched pails of water or coffee. They worked until all the grain was separated from the straw, and all celebrated when the task was finished.

Rituals of cooperative harvesting continued well into the mid-twentieth century. Working with neighbors in a threshing "ring" of 15 to 20 men, the ring boss was usually the owner-operator of the huge rig that moved from farm to farm. The boss was responsible for keeping the engine and separator in topnotch condition, for setting up the rotation among the farms, and for settling the price for the job. His competence and fairness earned respect and made his ring successful.

The evening before work began, the threshing machine lumbered along the countryside to the farmstead. In a level clearing where the straw would be stacked, the rig was made ready. The next morning, the boss was checking at 6:30. The farmer had gone to the butcher to get the huge roast of beef that had been ordered. His sons had fed and harnessed their teams and were off to the farthest grain field to load their racks. Soon neighbors drove in, greeted one another, and headed to the field. By 7:00, everyone was in place, the machinery was operating, and the loaders were in line. The sound of the engine's whistle filled the air. Everyone within miles knew this was threshing day.

Another well-organized team had started work in the farmhouse before dawn. The dining table had been extended to seat 12, and a second table was set up in the living room. China and silver were laid on everyday table coverings — oilcloth or brightly patterned second-best cloth. In the workroom, a table displayed half a dozen fruit pies — apple, cherry, rhubarb cream and fresh peach, along with lemon meringue and chocolate cream. Chocolate fudge and caramel nut sheet cakes were ready to cut.

The lady of the house was supervising the kitchen, and her helpers each had a task. Meanwhile, the 18-pound beef roast was almost done, the scent of bay leaf and onion filling the air. Huge kettles of peeled potatoes — the early crop from the garden — waited. A neighbor lady sliced ripe tomatoes onto a platter heaped with their goodness. Grandma opened beet and cucumber pickles brought from the cellar and filled bowls. She added a jelly dish of strawberry jam to top golden brown pan rolls. There were green beans cooked with bacon and calico coleslaw dotted with flecks of red and green peppers. The big coffee pot was steaming hot. Soon the mistress would move the roast to a rack to rest before she sliced it. Meanwhile, she stirred gravy, put the potatoes on to boil, cooked a pan of sweet corn to creamy perfection, checked the tables for coffee cream, saw the baskets of rolls in place, the butter beside them, the pitchers of cold water nearby — and now to whip the potatoes, slice and pile high the roast on platters. Was that the first of the threshers washing up at the stand on the porch? Come right in! Sit down, everybody!

Neighbor lady and Grandma pass the bowls and platters and fill the coffee cups. Refills are brought. Which kind of pie would you like? They all do look good! Maybe one of each? Before long the men lean back with broad smiles, the ladies accept the praise they deserve, and the men move out to rest under the trees.

The three women hurry about clearing the tables and washing up. They talk about the supper: cold meats, potato salad, baked beans, tomatoes, rolls, warm green beans, pickles, pies and cake. Iced tea and coffee.

The farmer comes in, dusty and prickly with straw. He eats a second piece of pie. The boss says things are going well and he plans to work until dusk. But this is a big job. There may be another half-day. Midwesterners have learned to be philosophical. Another day? The lady of the house has been a farm wife for many years. Farm women take it one day at a time. Tomorrow — maybe chicken?

January 1920 — This wagon box put on sled runners took a family and friends on winter trips to visit or attend to shopping. The team was stabled in the large "tie barn" during trips to the village. Here, friends got dressed up for Sunday dinner with neighbors three miles away.

Ruth, nine months old, in the family car, 1918. Heavy curtains were snapped in place to shield passengers from bad weather. The car was put up on blocks during winter. This big touring car seated six.

Farmers took great pride in their horses, which provided the power to do farm work and transportation for trips to town to transact business. The farm scene, 1916 (above). A couple ready for a trip to the village, 1915 (below).

A two-row corn planter, May 1943. Dad paused for a snapshot with his baby daughter.

Corn husking with a team of horses and a wagon with "bang boards," fall 1943. The goal was to pick 100 bushels per day.

A team of mules was valued for its endurance and quickness. Jewel and Minnie pose with a cultivator, 1921.

The last haystack built during threshing, 1951. Later, oats were combined and straw was baled.

Threshing machine with two men in hayracks on either side. The men alternated pitching oats bales into the machine. The straw was built into a rain-resistant stack by two men. It was a hot, dusty job requiring great skill.

Northwest Iowa – the last harvest for this threshing ring in 1950. Combines eventually took over grain harvesting.

Our Danish Grandma stood tall and straight as she tended a large garden, canned fruits and vegetables, cooked, baked, served and cared for the sick among her neighbors.

Dressed just like Grandma Petersen in the yard in Anthon, Iowa, where she lived.

1961 — Gardening was a favorite 4-H activity. In August, one of Laurel's cabbages had grown to become the county fair champion.

1928 – The extension service provided education for rural families in the 1920s. Here, a group of women is making laundry soap using pork cracklings and lye, for an economical and effective product.

Laurel and Mother are taking straw to fill the hens' nests, 1952. In winter, they hayed about 150 ewes and checked out new lambs.

Ruth was excited to find eggs on the ground, but was timid around the watchful hens.

Every generation of women in the family took care of a large flock of poultry. These are white Leghorns, a good breed for producing fine eggs.

Recipes

Beef Burgundy

3 lb. round or sirloin steak, 2 c. Burgundy wine
   cut into cubes   1 10-oz. can beef broth
1/2 c. margarine, melted   1 onion, chopped
6 T. flour   1 8-oz. can sliced mushrooms
1/4 t. pepper   Cooked rice
3/4 t. thyme

Brown meat in melted margarine and put in a 2-1/2-qt. baking dish with cover. Mix flour and seasonings, blend slowly with wine and broth. Pour over meat. Cover and bake at 325F for 2 hr. Add onion and mushrooms. Cover and continue cooking 1 hr. more. Serve over hot rice. Serves 6-8.

Tender beef and rich sauce make this a special occasion entrée.

Beef Burgundy / Crockpot

2 lb. round steak   1 can mushroom soup
1/2 c. burgundy wine   1 4-oz. can mushrooms
1 packet (1 3/8 oz.) dry onion   pieces and juice
   soup mix   3 or 4 sliced carrots
Rice or noodles to serve 5-6   1/2 c. sour cream (optional)

Cut beef into serving pieces. Mix all ingredients together and put into Crockpot. Cook on high 1 hr. and on slow 6 hr. Stir two or three times, and add liquid if meat seems dry. Serve over hot cooked noodles or rice. If you wish, stir in 1/2 c. sour cream just before serving. Serves 5 or 6.

Burgundy Beef Casserole   **Karen Pickett**

6 slices bacon   12 fresh mushrooms
2 cloves garlic   6 to 8 carrots
3 lb. beef stew meat or   8 to 10 small onions
   round steak   1 bay leaf
1 oz. brandy (unflavored)   2 T. parsley
Salt   6 peppercorns
1 can beef bouillon   4 whole cloves
1-1/2 c. burgundy wine   Pinch of marjoram
   (or other dry red)   Pinch of thyme

Cut beef into bite-sized pieces. Fry bacon, not crisp, and cut into bite-sized pieces. Remove from pan. Press garlic into pan. Coat beef with salt, cover with flour, and brown in bacon fat. Place bacon in casserole and place browned beef on top of it. Pour brandy into frying pan; add bouillon and 1 c. wine. Allow to boil and add mushrooms. Pour mixture over meat in casserole. Add carrots, whole or cut into chunks. Add onions, remaining spices, and 1/2 c. wine. Cover casserole and refrigerate for one day. Bake at 350F for 5 hr. Serves 8-10.

Beef Burney   Anne Harbour

1 lb. beef chuck or round steak,	Salt and pepper
cut in cubes	Dried herbs, ground together, with
3 or 4 medium potatoes	rosemary predominating: basil,
4 or 5 carrots	marjoram, oregano, rosemary,
3 or 4 medium onions	sage, savory, thyme — use the
2 T. butter	ones you prefer, omit others
2 T. olive oil	

Prepare vegetables, cutting into large bite-sized chunks; just cover with salted water and set aside. In large cast-iron skillet or Dutch oven, brown beef in oil and butter. Add vegetables, water (will probably be 3-4 c., but more can be added later if needed), ground herbs, and a dash of salt. Cover and cook over low flame or in oven at 325F until everything is tender — about 1 hr. Stir occasionally and add water if necessary. Adjust salt and pepper to taste. If there is too much liquid when vegetables are tender, thicken with 1 T. cornstarch. Serves 4. Reheats well.

A mortar and pestle makes a good wedding or shower present. A wooden one is best for dry herbs; a ceramic or pottery one can be used for both dry and fresh. Children enjoy helping to grind.

Marinated London Broil

2-1/2 to 3 lb. London broil	2 T. orange or ginger marmalade
1 can beer	1 t. garlic powder
1/2 c. vegetable oil	Salt and pepper
1 t. dry mustard	3 or 4 green peppers
1/2 t. ginger	1 #2-1/2 can pineapple chunks,
1/2 t. Worcestershire sauce	drained, or fresh pineapple chunks
1 T. sugar	12 medium mushrooms

Cut London broil into bite-sized pieces and place in covered glass casserole. Prepare marinade with beer, oil, and seasonings, including marmalade. Pour marinade over meat, cover glass casserole, and refrigerate overnight.

Prepare barbecue grill or broiler. Cut peppers into squares. On skewers, alternate cubes of beef with pepper squares, pineapple chunks, and mushrooms. Brush vegetables lightly with marinade. Turn skewers to cook evenly. Serves 4-5.

If you use your grill a lot and would like to enlist the family's help, look at the recipes for Shish Kabobs, Satay, and Souvlakia — the Middle Eastern, Southeast Asian, and Greek recipes for skewered lamb and vegetables. Everyone likes putting chunks of meat and veggies on skewers to grill. Reminds one of an old-time weiner roast, but much healthier!

Baked Brisket

4 or 5 lb. beef brisket, untrimmed
4 T. olive oil
1/4 c. white wine vinegar
1 c. water
2 T. ketchup

1 t. salt
2 t. pepper
2 t. garlic powder
1 pkg dry onion soup mix

Brown brisket in 2 T. olive oil. Place in greased 2-1/2-qt. casserole. Combine 2 T. olive oil, vinegar, ketchup, seasonings, and soup mix; gradually stir in water and pour over brisket. Cover and bake at 350F for 2 hr., basting every hour. Reduce heat to 300F and bake 1 hr. more. Skim fat. Use drippings as base for sauce (add 1 or 2 T. flour and hot water, season to taste). Serve sauce on side with brisket. Serves 4-6.

Spicy Brisket

3 to 4 lb. beef brisket, trimmed
2 T. liquid smoke
1 t. pepper
2 T. Worcestershire sauce

2 T. Lawry's seasoning salt
1 t. garlic powder
1/2 c. water
1-1/2 c. barbecue sauce

Place brisket in glass 9 x 13 in. baking dish. In small bowl, combine liquid smoke with seasonings and coat all sides of meat with mixture. Cover dish with foil and marinate overnight in refrigerator.

Remove from refrigerator and bake, still covered with foil, at 325F for 40 min. Add water and continue baking, covered, for 4 hr. Pour your favorite barbecue sauce over meat and bake, uncovered, 30-45 min. Add water if needed. Let stand 20 min. before slicing. May be shredded for buns. Serves 8-10.

Savory Beef Loaf

2 lb. ground beef chuck	2 T. prepared horseradish
2 eggs, slightly beaten	1 t. salt
2 c. fine dry bread crumbs	1/8 t. pepper
1 c. onion, finely chopped	1 t. dry mustard
1/2 c. green pepper, chopped	1/2 c. ketchup
1/4 c. milk	

Mix all ingredients except ketchup. Shape into loaf and place in greased bread pan or 6 x 10 in. baking dish. Brush half the ketchup over the top and bake at 350F for 45 min. Drain excess fat. Spoon remainder of ketchup over top and bake 20-25 min. longer. Let rest 10 min. before slicing and serving. Serves 8.

Snappy Beef Short Ribs (Crockpot)

2 to 3 lb. boneless beef short ribs, cut in 6 to 8 servings	1/2 c. ketchup
	3/4 c. cider vinegar
2 T. shortening	Dash of Tabasco sauce
1 t. salt	1 c. water
1/2 t. pepper	2 T. Worcestershire sauce
2 T. brown sugar	1 t. dry mustard
1 clove garlic	

Brown beef in shortening. Combine all other ingredients in a slow cooker. Place beef on top. Cook on low for 4 hr. Remove cover and use a long-handled fork to stir sauce ingredients to cover meat. Replace cover and cook 2-3 hr. longer. Thicken juice with 1 T. cornstarch. Serve with hot rice or buttered noodles. Serves 4-6.

Beef Stew (Crockpot)

2 lb. chuck or sirloin beef	4 medium potatoes
3 T. flour	1/2 c. celery, chopped
1/2 t. salt	1 t. Worcestershire sauce
3/4 t. pepper	1 t. paprika
1 #2 can tomatoes	2 bay leaves
6 carrots	1 clove garlic, crushed
1 large onion	

Cut beef into cubes. Dredge with flour; season with salt and pepper. Place in large Crockpot or slow cooker. Prepare vegetables, cutting into bite-size pieces. Add to meat in cooker. Pour tomatoes over all, slicing tomatoes with spatula. Stir in seasonings. Cover and cook on low for 8-10 hr. Remove bay leaves, and stir. Serve with hearty bread and crisp relishes. Serves 8.

St. Pat's Casserole

1 pkg scalloped potatoes	1 1-lb. can corned beef, diced
2 T. horseradish	1 15-oz. can sliced carrots, drained

Prepare scalloped potatoes in 2-qt. casserole according to directions, increasing water to 2 2/3 c. Stir in remaining ingredients. Bake at 375F for 50-60 min. and potatoes are tender. Serves 4-6.

Ingredients for this dish can be kept in the pantry to make an inviting dinner that is easy to prepare when you have unexpected visitors.

Corned Beef Casserole I

1 12-oz. can corned beef, diced	1 c. Velveeta cheese, cubed
1 can cream of chicken soup	1/2 c. onion, minced
1/2 c. evaporated milk	Pepper
8 oz. noodles, cooked without salt	1/2 c. crushed potato chips

Mix ingredients except for potato chips. Pour into a greased 2-qt. casserole. Top with potato chips. Bake at 350F for 20 min. Serves 4-6.

Corned Beef Casserole II   Joann Gorman

3 c. cooked elbow macaroni (1-1/2 c. uncooked)	1 small onion, chopped
1/2 lb. sharp cheddar cheese, shredded	1 can corned beef, broken up
	1 can cream of chicken soup
1/2 c. green pepper, chopped	1/2 c. half and half
	Buttered cracker crumbs

Combine ingredients gently, place in 2-qt. casserole, and top with buttered cracker crumbs and a little grated cheese. Bake at 350F about 40 min. Serves 8.

This recipe comes from Hollywood, California, where Joann served it with a crisp green salad with oil dressing.

Cheesy Beef Casserole

1-1/2 lb. lean ground beef	2 eggs
1 c. bread crumbs	1 t. salt
1/2 c. longhorn cheese, grated	1/2 t. pepper
1 onion, chopped	1 T. sugar

Mix all ingredients and form into 1-1/2-in. balls. Roll in flour. Place in a covered 2-1/2-qt. casserole containing sauce. Cover and bake at 350F for 1-1/2 hr. Serves 6 to 8.

Sauce: Combine 1 can tomato soup, 1 can water, 1 large chopped onion, and 1 t. paprika; mix well and pour into casserole. Add meatballs.

Serve with a green vegetable and garlic bread.

Grillade and Grits   **Mary Jane Kahao**

2 lb. round steak, cut	2 c. stock
1-1/2 in. thick	2 t. tomato paste
2 to 3 T. flour	1 t. Lea & Perrin's
3 to 4 T. bacon drippings	Worcestershire sauce
1 medium onion	1/4 t. thyme
1 rib celery	1 bay leaf
1/2 bell pepper	Pinch of allspice
2 cloves garlic	Dash of Tabasco sauce
4 T. olive oil	Dash of Angostura bitters
3 T. flour	

Pound steak and cut into bite-size pieces. Roll lightly in flour, add salt and pepper, and brown in bacon drippings. Watch and turn to avoid burning. Remove beef from pan and set aside. Chop onion, celery, bell pepper, and garlic fine; add all to drippings in pan and wilt. Remove from pan and add to beef.

Add olive oil to what's left in pan and make a roux, using 3 T. flour, stock, and tomato paste. Add seasonings. Put beef and vegetables in roux. Cover and cook on slow fire until beef is tender, adding water or stock as necessary. Allow 2-3 hr. Serve over grits. Serves 8 to 10.

Grits

8 c. boiling water	2 sticks butter
1 t. salt	1 roll Garlic Cheese
2 c. quick-cooking grits	2 c. sharp cheddar, grated

Stir grits into boiling water slowly. Cook 2-3 min., stirring. Take off fire, add butter and cheese. Stir until dissolved, put in casserole and cover. Keep warm until ready to serve.

Mary Jane introduced my daughter Anne to this delicious recipe at a dinner in Baton Rouge. It makes an excellent entrée for a special dinner, accompanied by fresh peas or green beans, a large green salad, and homemade rolls.

Amana Hamburgers   Sarah Kossove

1 lb. ground beef	2 tart apples, cored and chopped
1/4 lb. ground cured ham	3/4 c. mild onion, sliced
1/2 t. salt	1/2 c. hot water
1 egg, beaten	

Combine ground beef and ground ham with salt, egg, and apples. Form into eight flat cakes. Sauté onions in a greased skillet. When onions are soft, push to one side and brown the meat cakes on both sides. Add hot water. Cover and simmer slowly for 20 min. Serves 6 to 8.

Serve with mustard, relish, or chili sauce on whole wheat bread or buns. These portions can also be served as a main dish with scalloped potatoes.

Malayan Beef   Anne Harbour

1 lb. ground sirloin steak or	1/4 t. pepper
extra lean ground beef	1 slice firm white bread
1 small onion, chopped	3 T. water
1 T. olive oil	1 T. vinegar
1 T. chutney	1 T. raisins
1 T. apricot jam	1 egg
1 t. turmeric	1/2 c. milk
1 t. curry powder	Salt and pepper
1 t. salt	2 bay leaves

In large skillet, sauté onion in olive oil until transparent. Remove from heat and stir in jam, spices, chutney, and salt and pepper. Add meat and mix well. Soak bread in water; then squeeze out water. Add bread, vinegar, and raisins and mix well. Turn into greased deep 9-in. pie pan or casserole and level off top. Beat egg, milk, and salt and pepper until frothy. Pour over meat, placing bay leaves in the center. Bake at 350F for 1 hr. Serves 6 or 8.

Serve with fluffy rice, chutney, and green salad.

Minute Steak Español

4 large minute steaks, each	2 cloves garlic, bruised
cut into 3 strips	4 potatoes, peeled and cubed
2 T. flour	4 carrots, sliced
1 t. salt	1 #2 can tomatoes
1/4 t. pepper	1 8-oz. can tomato sauce
1 large onion, chopped	1 green pepper, chopped
2 T. Mazola oil	

Dredge meat strips in seasoned flour. Brown with onion and green pepper in oil. Add rest of ingredients. Mash tomatoes if whole. Mix and bring to a boil. Cover and simmer at 325F for 30 min. or until vegetables are tender. Serves 4 or 5.

Serve with tossed green salad and garlic bread or bread sticks.

Grandpa Ben's Pot Roast
Ben Petersen

2 large T. lard	Salt and pepper
1 T. butter	4 or 5 medium potatoes
1 medium onion	6 or 8 carrots
3-1/2 to 4 lb. boneless beef roast	4 parsnips
1 to 1-1/2 c. hot water	4 or 5 medium onions
2 bay leaves	2 or 3 T. flour

Put lard and butter into heated heavy Dutch oven or an electric frying pan with a high dome. Slice medium onion into hot fat (325F) and cook until well browned. Remove onion and discard. Put roast into pan and brown on all sides, turning often. When well browned, add hot water. Salt and pepper to taste; add bay leaves. Let meat simmer about 2 to 2-1/2 hr. with cover partially off. Keep adding a small amount of water to keep meat moist. You may prepare and add potatoes, carrots, parsnips, and onions 45 min. before meat is done.

When ready to serve, remove all vegetables to a heated serving platter, and make gravy with drippings, 2-3 T. flour, and hot water; season to taste. Serves 8 or 10.

Grandpa prepared his famous beef pot roast with vegetables — potatoes, onions, carrots, and parsnips — from his kitchen garden. To complete the Sunday dinner, Grandma would add fresh peas in a creamy sauce, cucumbers in sour cream with dill, tomatoes sliced thin and sprinkled with herbs, her own thinly sliced rye bread, and a tall compote of jelly. The vegetables were placed around the roast on an ample ironstone platter. Grandpa carved the roast at the table, adding vegetables to each plate.

Somehow, roast beef that Grandpa made was always more delicious and succulent than any other. Grandma had given him the task when they retired because she thought he had a great knack for cooking.

♣ *Take meat from refrigerator to stand at room temperature an hour before roasting.*

♣ *When meat has been roasted (ham, beef, fowl), allow it to rest at room temperature 15-20 min. before carving.*

Pot Roast (Crockpot)

3 lb. beef rump roast
1 pkg onion soup mix
1 can beef broth
Salt and pepper
2 T. shortening

5 or 6 medium potatoes
4 large carrots
2 large onions
4 medium parsnips

In a large skillet, melt shortening. When very hot, brown roast on all sides. Remove roast to Crockpot, set on high. Sprinkle onion soup over roast. Pour undiluted beef broth along side. Sprinkle a little salt and pepper over meat. Cook beef on high setting 1 hr., then reduce to low for 3 hr.

Peel potatoes and cut into quarters. Scrub carrots and cut into 2-in. chunks. Peel and quarter onions. Peel parsnips and cut into four pieces each. Uncover Crockpot and place vegetables around meat. Cook at medium heat 2 hr. or until vegetables are tender.

Remove roast, let stand 10 min., and slice. Use a slotted spoon to remove vegetables; arrange around roast or in a serving dish. Thicken meat juices in the Crockpot with 2 or 3 T. flour, adding hot water as needed. Pour over the roast or serve in gravy boat. Serves 8.

♣ *Add 1/2 t. instant coffee powder when making gravy to give rich brown color and extra flavor.*

Grandpa's Sauerbraten   Ben Petersen

3 lb. bottom round steak
3/4 c. vinegar
1-1/2 c. water
2 bay leaves
1 t. mixed spices
Shortening for browning

3 T. flour
1-1/2 t. salt
Sprinkle of pepper
1 c. hot water
2 or 3 medium onions, sliced
Browned flour

Cut steak into serving-size pieces and mix with vinegar, water, bay leaves, and spices in a 9 x 13 in. glass baking dish. Cover tightly and place in refrigerator for 2 days. Stir, turn, and pour marinade over the meat each day.

Drain meat, and discard spices, saving liquid. Sprinkle meat with the flour, salt, and pepper, and brown in hot fat (lard is best). Add marinade saved, hot water, and sliced onions. Cover. Cook over slow heat (300-325F) for 1 hr. 45 min. or until meat is tender. Remove meat. Strain liquid. Add browned flour to make gravy. Add meat to gravy and serve with noodles or mashed potatoes. Serves 6-8.

Browned Flour: Sift 1/2 c. flour over the bottom of a pie tin and place it in the oven the last 10-15 min. the meat is roasting, stirring once, until flour turns light brown. Do not let it burn. May be stored, covered, in refrigerator. Browned flour improves the color and flavor of gravy.

This dish is served at German-American dining spots in the Midwest — wonderful!

Chicken Fried Steak

4 5-oz. beef cube steaks	3-1/2 c. milk, divided
1-1/2 t. salt, divided	2 eggs
1 t. pepper, divided	2 T. canola oil
1-1/4 c. flour, divided	Dash of paprika
2 c. crackers, crushed	

Combine 1/2 t. salt, 1/2 t. pepper, 1 c. flour, and finely crushed cracker crumbs. Beat eggs slightly, and whisk together with 1/2 c. milk. Press each steak into cracker mixture on all sides. Dip into egg mix, then dredge in crackers again. Heat oil in 10-in skillet or electric frying pan to 375F. Fry steaks 8-10 min.; turn and fry 5 min. on second side.

Remove steaks to pan in oven at 225F. Drain hot oil from skillet, keeping cooked bits and 2 T. drippings in skillet. Combine 1/4 c. flour, 1/2 t. salt, and 1/2 t. pepper, and whisk into 3 c. milk. Stir mixture into drippings in skillet and cook over medium high heat, whisking steadily, 10-12 min. or until gravy has thickened. Adjust seasoning. Serve gravy with steaks and mashed potatoes. Serves 4.

Pepper Steak   Anne Harbour

1 lb. chuck or round steak	1 #2 can tomatoes *or, in season,*
2 T. olive oil	3 very ripe tomatoes
3 medium green peppers	1 cube beef bouillon in 1 c. hot water
2 large onions	1 t. basil, ground fine
2 cloves garlic	Salt and pepper

Seed peppers and slice thin. Peel and slice onions thin. Chop garlic. In large skillet, sauté these vegetables in olive oil until tender. Remove and set aside. Cut meat into equal pieces, and sear in same skillet, adding a little more oil if needed. Remove meat and set aside.

Pour bouillon into skillet, sprinkle basil in, and bring to boil. Simmer to reduce by half. Remove from heat, add sautéed vegetables and tomatoes. Use fresh tomatoes only if locally grown and ripe. Prepare by pouring boiling water over fresh tomatoes in colander, peel, and cut into pieces. The rest of the year, use drained, canned whole tomatoes; reserve tomato juice. Return meat to skillet, cover, and cook 20 min. or until meat is tender.

Remove meat to platter. Remove vegetables with slotted spoon and arrange over meat. Add tomato juice to skillet, bring to boil, and thicken with 1 T. cornstarch. Pour into gravy boat. Serves 6.

This dish can also be prepared to serve over rice. If that is desired, cut meat into strips about 1/2 in. x 2 or 3 in. before browning. Prepare a thicker sauce (do not add tomato juice; use more cornstarch if needed), and return meat and vegetables to sauce before serving.

Spanish Steak

2 lb. top round steak	2 medium onions
2 T. lard or Mazola oil	1 t. paprika
1 qt. canned tomatoes *or*	Salt and pepper
2 #2-1/2 cans	Flour

Pound steak full of flour on both sides. Cut into serving size pieces. Brown in iron frying pan in hot lard or Mazola oil. Salt and pepper to taste. Peel and slice onions. Add onions and tomatoes, mashing or cutting large pieces of tomato. Sprinkle with paprika. Cover and simmer at 325F about 1 hr. If needed, mix 2 T. flour and 1/4 c. cold water to thicken sauce. Serves 8.

Swiss Steak

2 to 2-1/2 lb. round steak	1 pkg Lipton's onion soup
1/4 c. flour	1 large can tomatoes and juice
3 T. shortening or oil	Salt and pepper
6 carrots, sliced	

Pound flour into both sides of steak. Cut into serving size pieces. Brown in hot fat in large skillet. Put onion soup in pan with 1 c. hot water. Mash tomatoes and add carrots and drippings from skillet. Transfer all ingredients to a roaster or large casserole. Cover and bake in oven at 325F until meat is tender, about 1-1/2 hr. Serves 6.

Serve the meat and sauce with baked or mashed potatoes. A terrific Sunday-after-church oven dish.

Beef Stroganoff

2 lb. boneless sirloin steak	1 clove garlic, crushed
3 T. margarine	1 4-oz. can mushrooms, drained
1/2 t. salt	2 10-1/2-oz. cans mushroom soup
1/4 t. pepper	1 T. Worcestershire sauce
1/2 c. onion, minced	1 c. dairy sour cream

Cut sirloin into serving-size pieces. Brown quickly in hot fat. Season to taste. Combine onion, garlic, mushrooms, soup, and Worcestershire sauce; add to meat. Cook covered until tender, 30-40 minutes. Add sour cream before serving over hot, cooked noodles. Serves 6.

♣ *Fresh mushrooms can be used in this recipe. Use an egg slicer to slice fresh mushrooms faster.*

Veal Birds

2 c. bread cubes	6 veal cutlets
1/2 c. onion, diced fine	1/4 c. additional butter
1/4 c. butter	1/2 lb. fresh mushrooms, quartered
Pinch of thyme	Flour
Salt and pepper	1 c. dry sherry
1/4 c. cream	2 c. beef bouillon

In large skillet, sauté onions in butter. Then add bread cubes and thyme to pan, seasoning with salt and pepper to taste. Remove from heat and add cream.

Pound veal cutlets between sheets of waxed paper until thin. Salt and pepper and roll in flour. Put 2 T. filling in each cutlet, roll up, and fasten with a toothpick. Brown veal rolls in additional butter in second large skillet.

Arrange rolls in greased baking dish and cover with mushrooms. Add 1 T. flour to drippings in skillet, then stir in sherry and bouillon. Cook, stirring, until thick. Pour over veal rolls. Bake at 325F for 40-45 min. Serves 6.

Veal Marsala

2 lb. veal cutlets, 1/4 in. thick	1/2 c. Marsala wine
4 T. butter	Salt and pepper
Flour	Wide egg noodles, cooked
1/2 c. beef broth	1/2 c. parsley, chopped

Pound veal cutlets to flatten. Cut to serving size. Brown quickly on both sides in butter. When all are browned, add broth slowly. Salt and pepper to taste. Sift 1 T. flour over meat, turn meat, and sift 1 T. flour over other side. Let flour brown. Add sherry. Cover and simmer 5 min. Serve over cooked noodles; sprinkle with chopped parsley. Serves 6.

Chicken à la King

1 c. sliced mushrooms	2 c. chicken stock or milk
4 T. butter	3 c. cooked chicken, diced
4 T. flour	in 1/2-in. pieces
1/2 t. salt	1-1/2 c. cooked peas,
1/4 t. white pepper	fresh or frozen
1/2 t. curry powder, if desired	Small jar pimiento, diced

Sauté mushrooms in butter. Blend in flour, salt, and pepper. Stir in stock or milk and stir until thickened. Add chicken, peas, and pimiento. Lower heat to 325F and heat, but do not allow to boil. Serve in patty shells or toast cups. Serves 8.

Toast Cups: Cut crusts from slices of fresh medium- to thin-sliced bread. Press slices into standard muffin cups so the four corners of bread stand to form points. Bake at 400F about 10 min. or until toasted and light brown. Cool in muffin tin to hold shape. Fill with chicken mixture. Garnish with parsley beside the toast cup.

In the 1940s and 1950s, this was the entrée one served for ladies' bridge luncheons — light, delicious, and very attractive. A favorite fruit salad, often "congealed" with Jell-O or Knox gelatin; petite homemade rolls; and something chocolate completed the menu that drew raves.

Chicken à la King was a prime favorite for banquets and large luncheons too. It could be prepared and chilled, then heated to serve in patty shells or toast cups, and I recall its being served over hot rice. Today's luncheons are more likely to feature salads and, again, "something chocolate." This basic chicken dish is one every hostess and homemaker can prepare easily at low cost; it looks good and tastes delicious. Try it for a light family supper.

Baked Favorite Chicken   Stevenson's Apple Farm

1 frying chicken, cut up	1/4 t. pepper
1/2 c. flour	1 14-1/2-oz. can evaporated milk
1-1/2 t. salt	1/2 c. hot water
1/2 t. paprika	2 T. butter

Choose meaty parts of chicken for baking; set aside ribs and backs for making stock. Mix flour, salt, pepper, and paprika. Dip chicken into water. Coat with flour mixture, and place skin side up into 9 x 13 in. baking dish. Dot with butter. Bake at 325F for 30 min. Remove from oven. Mix evaporated milk with hot water, and pour around chicken. Cover with aluminum foil. Return to oven and bake at 350F for 45 min. Serves 4.

♣ *Fill orange shells with cranberry sauce or relish as a colorful garnish for baked fowl or ham.*

Barbecued Chicken

3 to 3-1/2 lb. frying chicken	1/4 c. lemon juice
2 T. shortening and butter, mixed	1 c. ketchup
1/2 c. flour	2 T. vinegar
1 t. salt	2 T. brown sugar
1/2 t. black pepper	1/2 t. dry mustard
1 medium onion, chopped	Dash of red pepper
1 c. hot water	2 T. Worcestershire sauce
1 t. liquid smoke	

Cut chicken into serving pieces. Mix flour with salt and pepper. Dredge chicken in flour mixture, and brown in hot fat. Remove chicken from skillet and place in 9 x 13 in. baking pan. Combine remaining ingredients in saucepan and simmer, stirring frequently, for 30 min. Pour over chicken in baking pan, cover with foil, and bake at 350F for 1 hr. 30 min. Remove foil after 1 hr. and spoon sauce over chicken. Serves 6.

♣ *When breading or dredging meats or croquettes, lay dredged pieces on waxed paper for 15-20 min. The pieces will retain the coating and not stick to the pan.*

Chicken with Biscuits

Plump year-old hen (4-5 lb.)	1 t. poultry seasoning *or*
5 c. Bisquick mix	1/2 t. rubbed sage
2 T. butter or chicken fat	1/2 t. salt
3 c. warm chicken stock	4 T. flour
2 c. celery, finely diced	2 c. peas, fresh or frozen
1 t. onion, finely cut	

Cook a plump hen, the kind sold as "roaster," with water to cover in large pot. When cooked and cooled, bone and dice chicken into medium chunks, discarding skin and bones. Strain, skim, and save stock. Make basic sauce with butter and flour, slowly adding warm chicken stock, stirring steadily until medium thick. Add celery, onion, poultry seasoning, salt, and pepper.

Place diced chicken evenly into a lightly greased 9 x 13 x 2 in. baking pan. Pour sauce over evenly. Prepare double batch of biscuits with Bisquick mix, following recipe on box. Place prepared biscuits on sauce in pan. Bake at 400F for 30-40 min. Serves 8 to 10.

Buffalo Wings

2 lb. chicken wings	2 T. honey
1 c. flour	2 T. orange juice
2 T. butter and shortening, mixed	Celery sticks
1/2 c. hot sauce	Carrot sticks
1/4 c. butter, melted	1 8-oz. bottle blue cheese dressing

Cut off wing tips and reserve for making stock. Roll wings lightly in flour and brown in hot fat until golden brown. Drain on paper towels or brown paper. Combine hot sauce, melted butter, honey, and orange juice. Dip wings in marinade; arrange on rack in baking pan (or use broiler pan). Bake at 350F for 20 min. Bring remaining marinade to boil for 1 min. Serve wings on a platter with celery and carrots; accompany with marinade and blue cheese dressing in small bowls for dipping. Serves 6 as main dish; 12 as appetizers.

Chicken Cacciatore   Lea C. Harbour

3-lb. frying chicken	1 small can tomato paste
2 4-oz. cans mushroom pieces	1 8-oz. can tomato sauce
1 medium onion, chopped	1/8 t. oregano
1 green pepper, seeded and	1 t. Italian herbs
cut into strips	2 c. water
1/2 c. shortening or oleo	Salt and pepper
1 can tomato soup	

Cut frying chicken into serving pieces. You may reserve neck and back for another use. Cut breast into four or six pieces. Flour chicken well and brown in shortening. Salt and pepper to taste. Remove chicken from pan. In the same fat, cook onion and pepper about 8-10 min. Add tomato soup, paste, and sauce. Stir. Add mushroom pieces with juice, herbs, and water. Bring to a boil. Put the browned chicken into a buttered casserole and pour the sauce over. Cover and bake at 350F for 1 hr. Serve with cooked long spaghetti or over rice. Serves 6 to 8.

Chicken Chow Mein

1 c. onion, chopped	1 can bean sprouts, drained
2 large chicken breasts	1 can sliced water chestnuts, drained
1 c. fresh mushrooms, sliced	1 T. cornstarch
2 c. celery, diced	6 T. soy sauce
1 can beef bouillon, divided	1/3 t. ginger

Skin chicken breasts and cut into strips. In large frying pan, sauté onions in 2-3 T. butter until tender. Push onions to side of pan, and brown chicken strips. Add mushrooms, celery, and 1/2 can beef bouillon. Cover and simmer 20 min. Make sauce of cornstarch, soy sauce, ginger, and 1/2 can beef bouillon. Stir into skillet, along with drained bean sprouts and water chestnuts. Bring to boil. Serve over rice. Serves 6.

♣ *3 c. cooked turkey can be substituted for the chicken breasts—a good way to use roast turkey left from Thanksgiving or other occasions.*

Corn Crisp Oven Chicken

3 lb. frying chicken	1 t. salt
1-1/2 c. cornflake crumbs	Pepper
1/2 c. evaporated milk	2 T. melted butter

Cut chicken into serving pieces. Dip in evaporated milk. Roll in mixture of crushed cornflakes, salt, and pepper. Place chicken skin side up in shallow foil-lined 9 x 13 in. pan. Drizzle chicken with melted butter. Do not cover pan. Bake at 350F for about 1 hr., turning pieces when chicken has browned. Scrape drippings from foil into a small saucepan. Add flour and milk to make gravy. Serves 6.

Curried Chicken   Anne Harbour

2 medium onions, chopped	1 T. curry powder
2 Granny Smith apples, chopped	1 t. salt
3 or 4 T. butter	Pepper
3 lb. frying chicken	2 c. chicken stock
3 T. flour	1/2 c. heavy cream

Sauté onion and apple in butter. Remove from pan. Combine flour, curry powder, salt, and pepper in shallow dish. Cut chicken into serving pieces and roll in seasoned flour. Brown in pan, adding more butter if needed. Place chicken pieces skin up in 9 x 13 in. pan. Sprinkle onion and apple over pieces. Pour chicken stock over all, adding water if needed to cover. Bake at 325F for 1 hr. or until chicken is tender. Remove chicken from pan. Make sauce with 1 to 3 T. flour and heavy cream. Serve with rice. Serves 6.

My Chicken Divan

3 large chicken breasts	1/4 c. half and half
1-1/2 lb. fresh broccoli	1/2 t. salt
2 T. butter	1/8 t. white pepper
Flour	1 c. Ritz cracker crumbs
2 cans cream of mushroom soup	1/2 c. toasted slivered almonds

Split and debone chicken breasts. Roll each half in flour, and sauté in hot butter until lightly browned. Arrange in buttered 2-qt. casserole. Wash broccoli and break into florets; parboil about 2 min. (broccoli should remain bright green). Arrange broccoli over chicken. Combine mushroom soup with half and half, salt, and pepper, and mix until smooth. Pour over chicken-broccoli mixture. Crush crackers on waxed paper. Melt 1/2 t. butter and sprinkle over crumbs, mixing with fork. Sprinkle buttered crumbs on top of casserole. Bake at 350F for 45 min. or until bubbling and golden brown. Sprinkle almonds on top for last 10 min. of baking.

Original Farm Bureau Chicken   Anna M. Petersen

1 qt. chicken, cooked and cubed	1/4 c. chicken broth
1 qt. chicken broth, strained	3/4 c. butter or chicken fat
and skimmed	1-1/4 t. sage
4 T. flour	3/4 t. salt
4 T. chicken fat	Dash of pepper
1-1/2 qt. bread cubes	2 T. onion, chopped

Prepare gravy by blending flour and 4 T. hot chicken fat; add 1 qt. broth and cook until thickened. Sauté onion and add to bread cubes, 1/4 c. broth, sage, salt, and pepper; mix thoroughly. Layer chicken and dressing in casserole. Pour gravy over top and bake at 350F about 1 hr. until lightly browned.

Glazed Cornish Hens

6 Cornish hens	1 t. nutmeg
4 c. wild rice, cooked	1 t. salt
2 c. tart apple, chopped	1/3 c. melted butter
3/4 c. dried apricots, chopped	1/4 c. orange juice concentrate
1 c. walnuts, chopped	1/2 c. orange marmalade
1-1/2 t. ginger	

Thaw hens in refrigerator. Wash, pat dry, and sprinkle with salt. Combine wild rice, apple, apricots, nuts, spices, and salt. Pour melted butter over all, and fold in. Spoon into cavities. Place extra dressing in buttered baking dish; cover and bake separately 30 min.

Arrange hens breast side up in large, shallow baking pan. Use soft butter to coat the skin lightly. Roast at 350F for 30 min. Baste with juices and butter every 10 min. for another 25 min. Combine orange concentrate and marmalade; brush over hens and continue to roast 15-20 min. until glazed and brown. Serves 6.

Honey Comb Chicken

3-1/2 to 4 lb. chicken
1 #2 can peas, drained
2 c. cooked noodles
1 small jar pimientos

1 c. cheddar cheese, grated
2 c. chicken broth
4 heaping T. flour
1 c. light cream

Cook chicken. Cool and remove skin and bones; reserve chicken stock. Cut chicken into pieces and place in one layer in buttered 9 x 12 in. pan. Combine peas, noodles, pimientos, and grated cheese in large bowl. Make paste of flour and a little chicken broth; beat in 2 c. broth until smooth. Fold into noodle mixture and spread evenly over chicken. Pour light cream over all. Bake at 350F for 1 hr., until set and browned. Serves 6 to 8.

Mrs. Nixon's Hot Chicken Salad   Pat Nixon

4 c. cooked, cut up chicken
3/4 c. mayonnaise
1/2 t. Accent
4 hard-cooked eggs, sliced
1 t. onion, minced
1 c. cheddar cheese, grated
2/3 c. toasted almonds, chopped

2 c. celery, chopped
3/4 c. cream of chicken soup
2 T. lemon juice
1/2 t. salt
2 pimientos, cut fine
1-1/2 c. potato chips, crushed

Combine all ingredients except cheese, chips, and almonds in 9 x 12 in. pan. Top with cheese, chips, and almonds. Cover with foil and refrigerate overnight. Let come to room temperature. Bake at 400F for 20-25 min. Serve hot. Serves 8-12.

My Pheasant Fricassee

Pheasant, plucked, singed, and
  drawn
Water to cover
2 T. salt
2 T. butter
2 T. oil

1 c. flour
1/2 t. salt
1/2 t. pepper
1 t. poultry seasoning
1 c. hot water
1 c. dairy sour cream

Cut pheasant into 6-8 pieces. Soak in salted cold water to cover for 2 hr. Make sure all lead shot is removed if bird was shot.

Drain pieces on paper toweling. Combine flour, salt, pepper, and poultry seasoning in paper bag. Place one or two pieces of pheasant at a time into bag and shake well. Repeat until all pieces are floured. In 10-in. frying pan, heat butter and oil. When very hot, put in floured pieces with space around each. Brown well on both sides, sprinkle with salt and pepper.

Transfer browned pieces of pheasant to a casserole. Place meaty pieces on the bottom and bony pieces on top. Add hot water, cover, and bake at 350F for 1-1/2 hr. or until meaty pieces are tender. Before serving, pour sour cream over meat, leave uncovered, and reduce heat to 300F for 20 min. Serve with rice, noodles, or mashed potatoes. Serves 4.

Together with neighboring Nebraska, South Dakota, and southwestern Minnesota, western Iowa has long been a Mecca for pheasant hunters, who invade the area from places as much as 1,000 miles away. They arrive singly and in caravans, descend on posted and unposted areas alike, and sometimes shoot farm animals in their eagerness to bag the wily birds. In recent years, the thickets, brambles, cornstalks, and other protective cover have gotten scarce, but game laws have been enforced more vigorously. Nevertheless, only a few farmers hunt and bring home a bird or two. Fortunately, my husband did so often in pheasant season.

Pheasant makes a delicious entrée if cooked simply or with an array of embellishments. We preferred this straight-forward method that results in keeping the fowl's natural flavor and moisture. The sauce may be spooned over the meat or side dish. Fresh green or root vegetables and wild rice are tasty side dishes.

♣ *When dredging meat or fish with flour or rolling in cracker crumbs, use waxed paper and sift flour or sprinkle cracker crumbs thickly on it. Save leftover flour to make gravy.*

Pheasant Breasts with Mushrooms   Anne Harbour

Breasts of 3 large pheasants	1/2 lb. fresh mushrooms, sliced
1 t. salt	4 small green onions, chopped
1/2 t. pepper	1/2 c. cooking sherry
1 c. flour	1-1/2 c. chicken stock, divided
1/3 c. butter, melted	1/2 c. heavy cream

Soak pheasant breasts in salt water for 2 hr. Rinse and dry on paper toweling. Debone and cut each breast in two. Combine flour, salt, and pepper in paper bag.

209

Shake a piece or two of pheasant at a time to coat with flour. Heat 10-in. skillet, add butter and then pheasant. Brown both sides. Add 1 c. chicken stock, cover, and simmer on top of stove or in 350F oven for 1-1/2 hr. or until breast meat is tender. Remove pheasant and set aside.

Add mushrooms and onions to skillet; sauté until tender. Add sherry and reduce until sherry is nearly evaporated. Add stock; reduce again. Add cream and pheasant. Simmer 20 min. or until heated through. Remove pheasant. Heat sauce until thickened (add 1 T. cornstarch and a little more cream if more sauce is needed). Pour sauce over pheasant on individual plates; serve with wild rice, and green beans or peas. Extra sauce may be passed. Serves 6.

This recipe is also good with wild duck.

Chicken Paprika

4 boneless chicken breast halves,
   cut crosswise in 1/2-in. strips
1/4 c. paprika, preferably
   Hungarian sweet
3 T. butter
Salt and pepper

1-1/2 c. chicken broth
1/2 c. sour cream
1 c. onion, chopped
2 large plum tomatoes, chopped
Poppy seeds
Green onions, thinly sliced

Season chicken with salt, pepper, and a sprinkling of paprika. Melt butter in large skillet. Sauté chicken for 5 min. Transfer chicken to serving platter. Sauté onion. Add rest of paprika and tomatoes. Cook 2 min. Add broth and boil to thicken. Mix in chicken, reduce heat to low. Add sour cream. Heat but do not boil. Serve over buttered, wide noodles with poppy seeds and thinly sliced green onions. Serves 4.

Baked Parmesan Chicken

1/2 c. butter or margarine
Meaty pieces from 2 broiler-
   size chickens, cut up
1 t. salt
1/2 t. pepper

2/3 c. flour
1/2 c. grated Parmesan cheese
1/2 t. paprika
1/2 c. buttermilk

Line broiler pan (about 10 x 15 in.) with foil. Melt butter. Combine flour, paprika, salt and pepper, and Parmesan cheese in a paper bag or large plastic freezer bag. Roll chicken pieces in buttermilk and then put one or two at a time into the bag holding flour mixture. Shake gently to coat chicken. Place chicken pieces skin side up in foil-lined pan. Bake at 425F for 50 min. Turn once — with tongs to avoid losing juices. When chicken is golden brown, pour additional butter over if desired. Serves 6.

Variation: Substitute 3/4 c. finely crushed cracker crumbs or 3/4 c. crushed potato chips for the Parmesan cheese. Or add 1-1/2 t. poultry seasoning or rubbed sage and 1/2 t. onion powder to the flour mix.

The browned bits and butter on the foil are a good addition to sauce or gravy. Just scrape the foil tidbits into a saucepan, blend in 1 t. flour and milk to make sauce to serve with the chicken.

Pepper Chicken   Anne Harbour

2 chicken breasts   3 t. rosemary
3 T. olive oil   Juice of 1 large lemon
1 large Bermuda onion   Salt and pepper
1 large red pepper   3 c. water
1 large yellow pepper

Debone chicken and halve to get four serving pieces. Sauté lightly in olive oil. Place in Dutch oven or casserole. Pour lemon juice over chicken. Peel onion and slice 1/4 in. thick. Seed peppers and cut into large pieces, about 1-1/2 in. wide. Add vegetables to casserole. Grind rosemary and sprinkle over all; salt and pepper to taste. Add 3 c. water.

Cover and bake at 350F about 1 hr. or until chicken is tender. Using large slotted spoon, gently rotate ingredients every 20 min. or so, so that all are cooked evenly. Onion rings will separate. Add water as needed. Arrange on four plates so that each serving contains chicken topped by red and yellow pepper pieces and onion rings. Strain out rosemary and use juice as soup base. Serve with green salad and bread or rolls. Serves 4.

Chicken Tarragon   Vivian Smith

2 frying chickens *or*   1/2 t. thyme
   8 chicken breasts   1 bay leaf
3 T. butter   1 T. parsley, finely chopped
2 T. oil   2 T. flour
1/4 c. shallots, chopped   1/2 c. dry Vermouth
1 t. salt   Chicken broth
1/2 t. pepper   1/2 c. heavy cream
1/4 t. tarragon   4 T. parsley, finely chopped

Dry chicken pieces on a towel. Brown in hot butter and oil in skillet. Add shallots; cook until soft. Grind tarragon and thyme; sprinkle over chicken. Add salt and pepper, 1 T. parsley, and bay leaf. Sprinkle in flour; stir. Add Vermouth and add chicken broth to cover pieces. Cover and simmer 20 min. Remove breasts; simmer rest of pieces another 25 min.

Remove chicken to a hot baking dish. Stir heavy cream into skillet, and serve in gravy boat. Alternatively, place chicken pieces in preheated oven for 30 min. Add cream and heat. Garnish with 4 T. freshly chopped parsley. Serves 6.

Delicious!

Chicken or Turkey Tetrazzini

2 c. or more cooked turkey *or*
  chicken, diced
1/2 8-oz pkg noodles *or*
  spaghetti, cooked and drained
1/4 c. butter or margarine
6 T. flour
1/2 t. salt
1/4 t. pepper
Cherry tomatoes

3 T. parsley, minced
1 T. green pepper, chopped
2 c. chicken broth
1 c. half and half
1 T. cooking sherry
1-1/2 c. mushrooms, sliced
1/2 c. Parmesan cheese, grated
1/3 c. toasted slivered almonds

Melt butter in large skillet; add green pepper, parsley, and mushrooms; and sauté for 5 min. Blend in flour. Add broth and, over low heat, stir until thickened. Add half and half, sherry, salt, pepper, and chicken or turkey. Fold in drained noodles or spaghetti. Place in shallow 2-qt. buttered casserole. Sprinkle with Parmesan cheese and almonds. Bake at 350F for 30 min. Garnish with halved cherry tomatoes added on top 10 min. before removing from oven. Serves 6.

Chicken Tetrazzini   **Madge Petersen**

2 T. margarine
3 T. flour
1 big c. chicken broth
  or 1 can condensed broth
1 c. half and half
1 pkg (4-1/2 oz.) shredded
  mozzarella cheese

2 c. cooked chicken, chopped
1 2-1/2-oz. jar sliced mushrooms,
  drained
2 T. pimiento, chopped
1 pkg Italian style spaghetti dinner
2 eggs, beaten

Melt margarine over low heat. Blend in flour and the herb-spice mix from packaged dinner. Gradually add broth and half and half. Cook, stirring constantly, until thickened. Add chicken, mushrooms, and pimiento. Heat thoroughly before serving over spaghetti.

Spaghetti: Heat oven to 350F. Prepare spaghetti as directed on package. Add eggs and Parmesan cheese packet from dinner mix. In buttered 9-in. pie pan, layer half of spaghetti mixture, and sprinkle with half of mozzarella; repeat layers. Bake at 350F about 15 min. until set.

Chicken Tortilla Casserole   Jean Grochowski

1 chicken, cooked and shredded	2 7-oz. cans green chili salsa
1 can mushroom soup	12 corn tortillas
1 c. milk	1/4 c. onion, chopped
1 c. chicken broth	1-1/2 c. cheddar cheese, shredded

Butter a 9 x 12 in. casserole. Cut tortillas into bite-sized pieces. Line dish with half the tortillas. Layer on all chicken. Separately, combine soup, milk, broth, chili salsa, and onion. Pour half of this mixture over the chicken layer. Add rest of tortillas. Pour remaining liquid over evenly. Sprinkle cheese on top. Cover and refrigerate at least 5 hr. or overnight. Bake uncovered at 350F for 1 hr. 15 min. Serves 8.

This delicious casserole can be prepared ahead and baked while the rest of the meal is being assembled. Serve with green salad.

Chicken–Wild Rice Casserole   Anne Harbour

1 c. uncooked wild rice	1 c. celery, chopped
3 c. water	1/4 c. green pepper, chopped
2 c. chicken, cooked	2 T. butter or olive oil
3 c. chicken broth	Dash of garlic powder
2 T. cornstarch	2 T. pimientos
1/4 c. onion, chopped	4 oz. toasted slivered almonds
1 c. mushrooms, sliced	

Rinse wild rice. Place in heavy saucepan with water; bring to boil. Cover and simmer about 45 min. until tender and rice grains have popped open. Drain and set aside.

Cut chicken into bite-sized pieces. In small skillet, sauté onion until soft. Remove from skillet and sauté celery, green pepper, and mushrooms until soft. Heat chicken broth. Combine a little with cornstarch to make a paste; stir into rest of broth and heat until thickened. Stir garlic powder, sautéed vegetables, and chicken into sauce. Fold in wild rice. Pour into buttered 2-qt. casserole. Sprinkle with toasted almonds. Bake at 350F for 1 hr.

This recipe is a good way to use parts of chicken not needed in other dishes. It is also delicious with turkey after the holidays.

Turkey Casserole

1-1/2 c. wild rice
4 c. water
1 t. salt
1 lb. pork sausage
1 3-oz. can mushrooms

2 cans cream of mushroom soup
1 t. Worcestershire sauce
3 c. cooked turkey or chicken
1-1/2 c. day-old bread crumbs
1/4 c. butter or margarine, melted

Rinse wild rice. Place in heavy saucepan with 4 c. water and 1 t. salt. Bring to boil; cover and cook 30-40 min., until tender. Drain and set aside.

Brown pork sausage; drain. Cut turkey into bite-sized pieces. In large bowl, combine mushrooms and juice, cream of mushroom soup, and Worcestershire sauce. Fold in wild rice, drained sausage, and turkey. Salt and pepper to taste. Pour into buttered 2-qt.casserole. Spread bread crumbs mixed with melted butter on top. Bake at 375F for 30 to 45 min.

Mrs. Reagan's Cornbread Dressing   Nancy Reagan

1 box cornbread stuffing mix
1 pan homemade cornbread
1 pkg chicken livers
Parsley
1 small stalk celery
2 c. chicken broth

3 large onions
Turkey giblets, cooked
Poultry seasoning
Salt
White pepper

Chop chicken livers and sauté in butter. Add finely chopped parsley, celery, and onions. Chop turkey giblets fine and add. Season to taste. Crumble homemade cornbread into large bowl and add box of cornbread stuffing mix. Mix in chicken liver mixture. Add 2 c. chicken broth and mix to moisten. Stuff turkey, piling extra stuffing, if any, around bird.

♣ *After cooking turkey giblets, divide broth in half. Use half for basting, after adding 1 chicken bouillon cube plus one cube butter. Baste frequently with this mixture. Reserve the remaining broth for gravy.*

Dressing for Fowl

1 lb. loaf of two-day-old bread
2 c. hot broth
1 t. salt
1 t. pepper

1 t. sage
2 eggs, beaten
1/2 c. onion, chopped
1/2 c. butter, melted

214

Cube the two-day-old bread into a large mixing bowl. Pour hot broth over it, and toss lightly. Add salt, pepper, sage, eggs, onion, and butter. Mix. Pour into roaster beside fowl when fowl is about three-quarters done. Cover dressing lightly with foil.

Broth: When fowl has roasted about 1-1/2 hr., drain all or part of liquids to provide broth for dressing. Otherwise, make broth with 2 Knorr chicken bouillon cubes and 2 c. hot water. Reduce salt to 1/2 t. This is light and flavorful.

♣ *Always remove dressing from roasted fowls and refrigerate separately at once.*

Dressing for Turkey or Chicken

1 qt. toasted bread cubes	1 t. sage
1 t. salt	4 T. melted butter
2 T. onion, chopped	1/2 t. black pepper
Juice and grated rind of 1 lemon	1 c. chopped oysters *or*
1 T. parsley, chopped	sliced water chestnuts

Mix ingredients lightly with hot water to moisten (not too much). Loosely stuff cavity of fowl that has been washed and wiped dry, truss legs and wings, and roast. The wrapper will give correct time and directions. When done, bird should rest 15 min. before carving.

Fruit Dressing   Christena Paulsen

3 T. melted butter	2 c. dried apples
2 T. onion, finely diced	1-1/2 c. pitted prunes
1 c. celery, finely diced	1 c. dried apricots
3 c. dry bread cubes or mix,	2 c. hot water
such as Pepperidge Farm	3 T. lemon juice

Pour hot water over dried fruit and let it soak 30 min. Drain, saving juice. Cut fruits in quarters. Set aside.

Sauté onion and celery in butter. Mix with bread cubes, apples, prunes, apricots, lemon juice, and if needed, reserved juice from soaking fruit, to make a fairly moist dressing. Salt lightly.

This is the fruit dressing my Danish grandmother used 80 years ago to stuff the Christmas goose. It may be used to stuff ducks or roasting chicken or baked separately in a covered casserole to serve with baked ham.

Oyster Stuffing

1 c. oysters, cooked and chopped	8 c. fresh bread cubes
1 c. celery, chopped	2 eggs, beaten
1 medium onion, chopped	1/2 to 1 t. tarragon or parsley flakes
1/4 c. butter or margarine	1 to 2 t. lemon juice
1 c. chicken or turkey broth	1/2 t. salt

Sauté oysters, celery, and onion in butter. Combine with remaining ingredients. Stuff cavity of turkey, or bake separately in 2-qt. casserole at 325F for 30 min. Yield: 6 cups.

Pecan Stuffing for Turkey   Elizabeth Brandt

1/2 c. butter	1/2 t. sage
1 c. celery, chopped	3/4 t. salt
1 c. onion, chopped	1/4 t. seasoned salt
2 T. parsley, minced	1-1/2 to 2 qt. cubed dry white bread
1 t. thyme	3 c. hot chicken or turkey broth
1/4 t. pepper	1/2 c. pecans, chopped
1/4 t. nutmeg	

Sauté celery, onion, and parsley in butter 5 min. over low heat. Stir. Add seasonings. Add mixture to bread cubes in large bowl. Pour hot broth over. Add pecans. Mix lightly. Place stuffing in a well-greased 9 x 12 in. dish. Bake at 325F for 40-45 min. until somewhat puffy. Yield: 8-10 servings.

Sage Dressing

1 c. celery, chopped	1 t. sage
1 c. onion, finely cut	1 qt. hot broth
1/2 c. butter	1 t. salt
1 loaf day-old white bread	

Sauté celery and onion in butter. Cut bread into cubes, place on cookie sheet, and toast lightly in oven. Place toasted cubes in large bowl. Pour sautéed vegetables and butter over bread. Sprinkle on sage. Pour hot broth over mixture. Toss lightly with fork. Salt to taste. Pack lightly into washed and dried bird, or bake in side pan.

Beef Kabobs I

Juice of 1-1/2 lemons
3 T. oil
1 onion, grated
1/2 t. salt
1/2 t. dry mustard
1/2 t. ginger
2 t. Worcestershire sauce
1 clove garlic

2 lb. sirloin, steak, cut into
   1-in. cubes
Mushroom caps
2 green peppers, cut in
   1-1/2-in. squares
2 red peppers, cut in squares
Cherry tomatoes
Small onions, parboiled

Prepare marinade by combining first 8 ingredients; add sirloin cubes. Refrigerate overnight. When ready to grill, alternate steak cubes with vegetables on skewers. Grill over glowing coals about 20 min. Serve with steak sauce if desired. Serves 4.

Beef Kabobs II

1 clove garlic, chopped fine
1/2 t. salt
1/4 t. pepper
1/2 c. cooking sherry
1/4 c. olive oil
2 T. soy sauce
1 lb. sirloin steak, cut
   into 1-in. cubes

8 mushroom caps
1 green pepper, cut into
   1-1/2-in. squares
1 red pepper, cut into
   1-1/2-in. squares
8 cherry tomatoes
8 small onions, parboiled

To prepare marinade, combine garlic, salt, pepper, sherry (or beef broth), olive oil, and soy sauce in baking dish; add steak and vegetables. Cover and refrigerate overnight, turning occasionally. When ready to grill, alternate steak cubes with vegetables on skewers. Grill over medium heat 7 min. a side or until done. Can be covered with lid to cook. Serves 4.

Kabobs III

1-1/2 lb. boneless beef sirloin
2/3 c. white wine or beef broth
2 T. canola oil
1/3 c. soy sauce
1/4 t. ground ginger

1 clove garlic, minced
1/2 t. dried tarragon
Small whole onions
Zucchini, cut in 1-in. cubes
Sweet red pepper, cut in squares

Cut sirloin into 1-1/4-in. cubes and place in gallon plastic bag. Prepare marinade by combining wine or broth, oil, soy sauce, and seasonings in bowl. Blend well and pour over meat in bag. Seal bag and turn to coat beef. Let stand at room temperature 45 min. Drain meat, reserving marinade.

Thread piece of sirloin, onion, zucchini, and red pepper on skewer, repeating three times on each of six skewers. Grill over medium hot coals about 12 min., turning and basting with reserved marinade. The kabobs may be broiled in the oven if desired. Serves 6.

Chicken Kabobs

1/4 c. brown sugar, packed	1/2 t. coriander *or* 1 T. fresh
1/4 c. soy sauce	cilantro, chopped
1 T. oil	4 chicken breasts, cut into strips
1/4 t. ground ginger	1 small pineapple, cut into 1-1/2-in.
1/2 t. paprika	pieces *or* 1 can pineapple chunks
2 cloves garlic, minced	in own juice, drained

Prepare marinade by combining brown sugar, soy sauce, oil, and seasonings in gallon plastic bag. Add chicken and cover or seal. Refrigerate 2 hr., turning bag occasionally to coat chicken.

Remove chicken from marinade. Thread onto three 6-in. skewers. Separately, thread pineapple onto three skewers. Grill chicken over medium heat for 15-20 min. or until done, turning and basting with marinade. Grill pineapple 5-7 min. or until well heated. Serve over rice. Garnish with slice of orange or fresh cilantro. Serves 6.

Skewered Pork

2 lb. pork tenderloins	1/2 c. French dressing
3/4 c. brown sugar, packed	1/2 c. Italian dressing
3/4 c. water	1/3 c. red wine vinegar

Cut pork tenderloins in half crosswise; then cut lengthwise into thin strips. Prepare marinade by combining brown sugar, water, dressings, and wine vinegar in gallon plastic bag, reserving 1/2 c. marinade for basting. Add pork strips. Cover or seal and refrigerate for 8 hr. or overnight.

Remove pork from marinade. Thread strips onto 12-in. skewers. Grill over medium heat covered with grill lid for 5-7 min. on each side or until done, basting with reserved marinade. Pork must be completely cooked and no longer pink. Serves 6.

Satay

1-1/4 lb. lean pork, lamb,
   beef, or chicken, cut into
   1-in. cubes

1-1/4 c. satay sauce
1/4 c. peanut or corn oil

Prepare charcoal grill or use an electric broiler. Combine cubed meat with 6 T. satay sauce. Blend well. Arrange equal amounts of meat on skewers and brush with oil. Grill, turning as needed, until done — about 10 min. or longer for pork (which must be completely cooked), less for other meats. Heat sauce and serve with skewered meats, rice, and green salad. Serves 6.

Satay Sauce:

3/4 c. smooth peanut butter
1 T. brown sugar
1 T. garlic, minced fine
2 T. onion, minced fine
2 T. lime juice

1 t. ground coriander
1/2 t. ground cumin
1/4 t. pepper
1/2 t. chili powder
4 T. light cream

Combine all ingredients in food processor or blender. Blend thoroughly. May be kept several days in a tightly covered jar in refrigerator. Yield: 1-1/4 cup.

Satay originated in Indonesia and Malaysia. This is an Indonesian recipe popular in The Netherlands. It serves 6 as an entrée, but makes an appealing appetizer for 12.

Shish Kabob Marinade

3/4 c. hot water
1/4 c. honey
1/2 c. soy sauce

2 T. salad oil
2 T. lemon juice
4 cloves garlic, split

Combine all ingredients and use to marinate meats overnight in covered glass container.

Skewered Lamb / Souvlakia

2 lb. lamb, cut into 1-1/2- to
   2-in. cubes
1/2 c. lemon juice
1-1/2 t. oregano

2 T. olive oil
1 t. salt
Pepper
1/2 c. onion, sliced thin

Place lamb pieces into gallon plastic bag or baking dish. Prepare marinade by combining all other ingredients in bowl; whisk to blend and pour over lamb. Seal bag or cover dish tightly and marinate overnight in refrigerator. Stir or turn several times.

Drain off marinade. Push the meat onto skewers. Preheat broiler. Put broiler pan about 1 in. from heat. Arrange meat on broiler pan leaving 1/2 in. between skewers. Broil 4-5 min. on each side. Serve on fluffy rice. Skewers may be barbecued outside on a hot grill close to the coals.

Skewered lamb makes a good hot appetizer. Cut the lamb into smaller pieces and use smaller skewers. Provide a small bowl of mint sauce or mint jelly for dipping.

Leg of Lamb

1 leg of spring lamb	1 t. rosemary (or 1 sprig fresh)
6 T. butter	Salt and pepper
3 cloves garlic	1 to 2 T. flour or cornstarch

Heat butter in roasting pan or Dutch oven. Brown lamb on all sides, and remove from pan. Using a sharp knife, cut slits into meat evenly. Peel garlic cloves, slice in half, and press pieces into slits in meat. Add 1 c. hot water to pan. Grind rosemary and sprinkle over water. Salt and pepper generously. Stir seasonings into water, return lamb to pan, and cover with lid or foil. Bake at 350F for 2 hr. Remove lamb to heated serving platter. Let rest 15 min., remove garlic, and carve. Serve with new potatoes, young peas, and cooked carrots or carrot soufflé. Pass mint sauce and lamb gravy.

To prepare gravy, place roasting pan over medium heat. Add a little drippings to flour or cornstarch, make a paste, and stir into juices in pan. Add a little hot water. Cook, stirring constantly, until gravy thickens.

Lamb Ragout   **Anne Harbour**

1 lb. lean shoulder or	2 t. rosemary
leg of lamb	1/2 t. thyme
3 T. butter	1 c. tomato sauce
2 medium onions, chopped	6 carrots
1 clove garlic, minced	1 or 2 zucchini
1 t. salt	1 c. celery
1/2 t. pepper	1 c. okra or cauliflower
2 T. parsley, chopped	

Cut lamb into bite-sized pieces. In large skillet, brown lamb in butter. Remove from pan and set aside. Sauté onion, garlic, and parsley. Return lamb to pan. Grind rosemary and thyme; sprinkle over all. Add salt and pepper. Add tomato sauce. Combine thoroughly, cover, and simmer 1 hr. Chill and skim off fat.

Prepare vegetables, cutting into bite-sized pieces. Heat meat and sauce, add vegetables, and cook until vegetables are tender. Serve with rice. Serves 6 to 8.

Braised Lamb Shanks

1/4 c. Mazola oil
1/4 c. butter
5 or 6 lamb shanks
Bay leaf
1 c. celery, diced
6 small carrots, sliced
3 medium onions, sliced
Salt and pepper

2 cloves garlic, crushed
1 t. rosemary
1 t. thyme
1 c. red wine
2 T. tomato paste
6 c. beef bouillon
1/3 c. flour

Preheat oven to 400F. Heat oil and butter in heavy skillet or Dutch oven. Brown shanks and place in oven in roasting pan with celery, carrots, onion, garlic, and bay leaf. Grind rosemary and thyme and add with salt and pepper to taste. Combine and add red wine, tomato paste, and bouillon. Cover and braise until tender, about 1 hr.

Remove from oven. Lift shanks onto a platter and keep warm. Skim fat from the stock and strain. In medium saucepan, combine reserved fat and 1 T. flour. Add the strained stock and whisk until smooth. Return shanks to pan, pour over sauce, and simmer for 15 min. Correct seasonings. Serve with rice or potatoes. Serves 6.

Olga's Lamb Stew   Olga Schley

1/2 lb. lamb (2 lamb steaks)
2 T. flour
1/4 c. wine
2 T. oil
1 t. rosemary

3 carrots
1 c. canned tomatoes, diced
4 small onions
1/2 c. celery

Cut lamb into chunks 1 x 2 in. Roll in flour. Brown in hot oil. Remove lamb from pan and deglaze pan with the wine. Grind and sprinkle in rosemary. Replace lamb and add water to cover. Simmer for 1 to 1-1/2 hr. (After 1 hr. the lamb may be refrigerated and fat skimmed off the next day.) Cut carrots and celery into bite-sized pieces. Add carrots, celery, onions, and tomatoes. Return to oven and simmer until vegetables are tender. Serve piping hot with mint jelly and pear salad. Serves 2.

Lamb Shanks Stew

4 or 5 shanks of lamb, trimmed
1 large onion, sliced thin
1 T. garlic, minced
1 large green pepper, seeded
and chopped
2 c. carrots, diced
1 T. crumbled dill weed

1/2 t. oregano
1 t. thyme
1/2 t. red pepper flakes
1 12-oz. can tomato sauce
1 c. white wine
1/2 t. black pepper

Place lamb shanks in a Dutch oven or a deep casserole. There should be one layer. Scatter the onion, garlic, green pepper, and carrots over the lamb. Combine remaining ingredients, mixing well, and pour over the lamb.

Place the Dutch oven on the stove and bring the liquid to boil. Cover and bake at 375F for 1 hr. Lower heat to 350F and continue baking 30 min. Uncover. Turn lamb, and stir sauce. Increase oven heat to 400F and bake lamb, uncovered, for 20 min. Remove from oven and transfer meat to heated serving platter. Skim excess fat off the sauce. Serve lamb surrounded by fluffy rice; pass the herb-flavored sauce.

McGonigle's Glazed Ham Loaf   McGonigle's Food Store

1-1/2 to 2 lb. ham loaf mix
1/2 c. fine bread crumbs
3 T. onion, chopped fine

1 egg, beaten
1/4 t. liquid smoke
3/4 c. milk

Combine loaf ingredients and mix well. Shape into an oval, flat loaf in glass baking dish. With a large knife, make three wide slashes at an angle across the top. Bake at 350F for 1 hr. Spoon off drippings and baste all of Brown Sugar Glaze over the loaf. Continue baking 30 min, basting often with the glaze accumulated in pan.

Brown Sugar Glaze: Combine 3/4 c. brown sugar, 1-1/2 t. dry mustard, 1/4 c. vinegar, and 1/4 t. liquid smoke in small bowl; blend well.

McConigle's Food Store is a landmark in Kansas City, famed for its excellent old-fashioned meat counter. McGonigle's blends its own ham loaf mix — a unique combination of ground pork, veal, and ham.

Ham Loaf
Anna M. Petersen

1 lb. ground ham	2 eggs
1/2 lb. ground pork (not sausage)	1-1/2 c. milk
1/2 lb. ground beef	1/2 t. salt
1-1/2 c. cracker crumbs	1/8 t. pepper
1 small onion, cut fine	1 can condensed tomato soup

In large bowl, mix ground meats with hands or potato masher. In small bowl, pour milk over cracker crumbs. Stir in eggs, salt, pepper, and onion. Combine with meat and mix well. Form into loaf and place in greased 9 x 4 in. bread pan. Pour tomato soup over loaf. Bake at 350F for 1 hr. Skim fat that accumulates after the first half hour. Let stand 10 min. before cutting. Serves 6.

Variation: Omit tomato soup. Baste with this sauce: 1 c. brown sugar, 2 t. dry mustard, and 1/2 c. vinegar mixed well. Bake at 350F for 1 hr. Skim fat after first half hour, then baste with sauce every 15 min.

Meatballs: If you prefer, form the mixture into 2-1/2-in. balls instead of a loaf. Bake at 325F a total of 1-1/2 hr. Skim fat. Then baste with sauce every 15 min. Makes 16 balls.

Ham and Broccoli Bake

2 c. cooked ham, diced	3-1/2 c. milk
3 c. broccoli, cooked and	1/2 t. dry mustard
cut into pieces	1 T. instant minced onion
10 slices day-old white bread	12 oz. sharp cheddar cheese, grated
6 eggs	Paprika

Remove bread crusts and cut into 1/2-in. cubes. Line well-buttered 9 x 12 x 2 in. baking dish, layer half the bread cubes, then all the ham cubes and broccoli pieces, then other half of bread cubes. Slightly beat eggs in bowl. Add milk, mustard, onion, and cheese. Blend and pour over casserole. Cover with foil and refrigerate overnight.

Remove from refrigerator and let stand 30 min. Bake, uncovered, at 325F for 1 hr. Sprinkle with paprika. Serves 12.

Creole Ham

2 c. cooked ham, diced	1 #2-1/2 can tomatoes and juice
3/4 c. rice, uncooked	1/4 t. pepper
1 green pepper, chopped	1 c. ripe olives, diced
1 c. onion, chopped	1 bay leaf
2 T. salad oil	

Sauté pepper, onion, and bay leaf in oil. Combine with other ingredients in a 2-1/2-qt. casserole. Remove bay leaf. Cover and bake at 300F for 1 hr. or until rice is tender. Stir and bake uncovered at 350F another 30 min. Serves 8.

Ham and Asparagus Casserole

1/2 lb. fresh asparagus	1/4 lb. Velveeta cheese, cubed
6 hard-cooked eggs, sliced	1 c. milk
1 to 2 c. cooked ham, diced	3 c. potato chips, not crushed
2 cans cream of chicken soup	

Clean and steam asparagus spears; drain. In large casserole, arrange half the potato chips. Layer first asparagus, then eggs, ham, and cheese. Mix soup with milk and pour over layers. Top with rest of potato chips, not crushed. Bake uncovered at 350F for 30-40 min. Serves 6.

Iowa Pork Chops with Stuffing

4 1-in. Iowa pork chops	1 t. salt
2 T. butter or oil	1/4 c. water
3 c. soft bread crumbs	1/2 t. poultry seasoning
2 T. onion, chopped fine	1 can mushroom soup
1/2 c. celery, chopped	1/3 c. water
1/4 c. melted butter	Pepper

Brown chops on both sides in butter. Place in shallow baking dish. In large bowl, mix together bread crumbs, onion, celery, melted butter, 1/4 c. water, salt, and poultry seasoning. Place a mound of stuffing on each chop. Blend soup and 1/3 c. water; pour over chops. Cover with foil. Bake at 350F for 1 hr. or until tender.

Pork Chops Hawaiian

6 meaty pork chops, 1/2 in. thick	3 T. vinegar
1 T. vegetable oil	1 T. soy sauce
1 large green pepper, cut into 1-in. pieces	1/2 c. brown sugar, packed
	3 T. cornstarch
1 20-oz. can pineapple chunks	Hot cooked rice
1/3 c. water	

Heat oil in skillet; brown pork chops on both sides. Remove from skillet and set aside. Drain pineapple, saving juice; set pineapple aside. Add water to pineapple juice to make 1 c.; pour into skillet. Add brown sugar, vinegar, and soy sauce. Blend cornstarch in water, add to skillet, and heat, stirring constantly, until sauce is smooth and thickened. Add pork chops, green pepper, and pineapple chunks. Simmer 20-25 min. until thoroughly heated. Serve over hot cooked rice. Garnish with chopped black olives. Serves 6.

Laurel's Pork Chops   Laurel Harbour

4 Iowa pork chops, cut thick	1 t. salt
2 T. butter or oil	6 carrots
1 t. Worcestershire sauce	3 or 4 medium onions
1 t. thyme	2 medium potatoes
1/2 t. rosemary	1 stalk celery
1/2 t. black pepper	1 T. cornstarch

Heat butter in heavy skillet or electric frying pan. Brown pork chops well on both sides. Grind thyme and rosemary; sprinkle over pork chops, add salt, pepper, Worcestershire sauce, and 1 c. water. Simmer for 1 to 1-1/2 hr., adding water to keep moist. Clean vegetables, peel potatoes and onions, and cut into chunks. Add to pork chops with 1 c. water and cook until vegetables are tender. Remove pork chops and vegetables to serving platter. Add a little pan liquid to cornstarch to make paste, stir into pan, and add water if needed. Heat, stirring constantly, until sauce is thickened. Pass in separate bowl. Serves 4.

Pork Chops Supreme   Agnes Lester

6 center-cut pork chops	1 can cream of chicken or
1/4 c. prepared mustard	mushroom soup
1/2 c. water	1 soup can of water
Flour to coat	Salt and pepper
2 T. shortening	

Combine mustard and water. Roll chops first in this mixture and then in flour to coat well. Place in frying pan with shortening to brown slowly on both sides. Salt and pepper to taste. Transfer to casserole. Drain off excess fat from frying pan. Add soup and water, blend well, and cook a few minutes. Pour over the chops. Bake at 350F for 1 hr. Serves 6.

Slow Cooker Roast Pork

3-1/2 to 4 lb. pork butt roast	1/2 t. salt
Worcestershire sauce	4 to 6 large sweet potatoes,
3/4 c. brown sugar, packed	scrubbed
1 c. apple juice	

Put roast in slow cooker. Sprinkle Worcestershire sauce all over meat. Press as much brown sugar as possible on top and sides of pork. Carefully pour apple juice directly to the bottom of the cooker, not over roast. Cover. Set on high for 30 min. Then turn to low for 5-6 hr. Place sweet potatoes around and on pork. Cover and cook another 2-3 hr. To serve, cut meat in serving pieces, removing bone. Cut potatoes in halves. Ladle hot juice over pork. Serves 6 to 8.

Broccoli, Chicken, and Rice Bake

2 10-oz. pkg frozen broccoli
3 chicken breasts
1 c. uncooked rice
1 can cream of chicken soup
1 c. light cream

1 can cream of mushroom soup
1/2 c. celery, chopped
2 T. onion, chopped
1 c. cheddar cheese, shredded

Butter a 2-1/2-qt. baking dish or use a nonfat spray. Cook broccoli 2 min. less than recommended (it will cook in casserole); drain. Cut chicken breasts in half, removing bone and skin. In a bowl, combine soups and cream; blend well.

Sprinkle uncooked rice in casserole. Add onion and celery. Arrange pieces of chicken and broccoli on rice and vegetables. Pour soup mixture over this, using a fork to allow soup to fill all spaces around chicken. Soup should cover all ingredients. Cover dish and bake at 350F about 1 hr. Uncover and continue baking until chicken is tender. Sprinkle with shredded cheese and broil a few minutes. Serve a piece of chicken with broccoli and rice, and top with a spoonful of the soup-cheese sauce. Serves 6.

Cabbage Roll-Ups

1 lb. ground pork
1 lb. ground beef
2 c. ketchup
1/2 t. salt
1/2 c. onion, chopped
1/2 t. pepper
1/2 c. rice

12 leaves of fresh green cabbage
2 c. tomato juice
1/2 t. Italian herb seasoning
1 t. basil
1 bay leaf
1 T. paprika

Mix together ground meats, ketchup, salt, pepper, onion, and rice. Separate 12 outer leaves of fresh green cabbage and pour boiling water over to wilt the leaves. Roll about 3 T. of the meat mixture into a cabbage leaf, folding leaf snug. Pin with a toothpick. Put in small roaster or 9 x 12 baking dish, fold side down. Place rolls in two layers.

Combine tomato juice with Italian herb seasoning, basil, bay leaf, and paprika. Pour over cabbage rolls. Cover with foil and bake at 325 F for 2-1/2 hr. Uncover and bake 30 min. longer. Serves 8 or 9.

Chow Mein Casserole

1 can chow mein vegetables, drained
1 can chow mein noodles
1 can sliced water chestnuts, drained
2 c. cooked rice
1 lb. ground chuck steak

1 onion, chopped
1 c. celery, cut fine
Salt and pepper
1 can cream of chicken soup
1 can cream of mushroom soup
1 t. soy sauce

Brown ground chuck; add onion, celery, salt, and pepper and simmer 3 min. Add rice, vegetables, water chestnuts, soy sauce, and soups. Mix well. Pour into a large buttered or sprayed casserole. Bake at 350F for 20 min. Top with chow mein noodles and bake 15 min. more or until bubbling. Serves 10 to 12.

Cornish Pasties

3 c. flour
1-1/2 t. salt
1-1/2 c. shortening or lard

1 T. vinegar
1 egg, beaten
4 T. ice water

Cut shortening into flour and salt until crumbs are the size of peas. Add vinegar, egg, and ice water. Toss together with fork. Gather into two equal balls. Chill 1 hr. Roll each ball out into a rectangle about 8 x 12 in. Cut in 4 x 4 in. squares, or into circles about 4 in. in diameter. To fill, put 1/3 cup of the meat mixture on half of the pastry square or circle. Put a little milk on edges to help seal, fold the other half of pastry over, and crimp edges with a fork. Brush tops with beaten egg. Bake in a 350F oven for 1 hr. Serves 12.

Filling: Combine 3 c. diced roast beef, 2 c. grated potatoes, 1 diced medium onion, 1 diced large turnip, 1/2 t. salt, pepper to taste, and 1 c. leftover gravy or gravy made from mix. Add a little soft butter or bacon drippings to moisten.

When miners from Cornwall in the West Country of England migrated to work tin mines in southern Wisconsin, their womenfolk brought recipes for Cornish pasties. Filled with meat, potatoes, and other vegetables, the pasty provided a hearty, nutritious meal-in-one package for the men's tin lunch pails. Today, the tradition becomes the basis for a worker's lunch, a snack, or alfresco picnic. The pasty is a great way to use leftover roast beef, pork, or lamb, and it is simply delicious.

Iowa Goulash

1 medium onion, chopped
1 lb. or more ground beef
1 T. lard
1 green pepper, chopped
1 qt. tomatoes, home canned, or
    1 #2-1/2 can tomatoes

2 c. medium macaroni *or*
    1 small pkg spaghetti, broken
    into 2-in. lengths, *or*
    4 oz. egg noodles
    (all uncooked)
Salt and pepper

In large skillet, brown onion and pepper in lard until slightly brown. Push to one side, and brown beef until pink color is gone. Salt and pepper. Add the tomatoes. Break them up with edge of mixing spoon or spatula. Add uncooked pasta and stir to cover it. Cover pan and cook on medium low heat (325F) for 30 min. Uncover and stir. Add some hot water if it seems dry. Cover and cook 15 min. longer. Serve with slaw or leaf lettuce dressed with sour cream and vinegar. Takes care of 6-8 country appetites!

This was a favorite supper on the farm — fast, filling, and fine for a frugal budget! Easy to expand for unexpected guests and delicious the next day. A good recipe for a 10-year-old beginning chef.

Danish Baked Liver Sausage   Christena Paulsen

Pork liver
Pork side meat
1 medium onion
1 T. salt
1 t. pepper

1 t. allspice
1 t. cloves
1 t. ginger
3 eggs, beaten

Take half a pork liver and weigh it. Then take half that weight of pork side meat. Cook the side meat until half done when tested with a fork. Scald and drain the pork liver. Put the cooked pork and liver through a fine grinder with onion. Into this mixture add seasonings, and mix well. Add eggs, and mix well. Put into well-greased pan or pans and bake at 350F for 1-1/2 hr. Skim off fat. Cool. Wrap in foil; will freeze up to 6 weeks.

This liver sausage is very good for open-faced rye sandwiches.

Beef Liver and Onions

4 bacon strips
1 lb. beef liver, cut up
2 T. flour

2 large mild onions, sliced thin, *or*
    1 can Campbell's onion soup
Salt and pepper

228

Cook bacon until crisp, remove from pan and drain on paper towels. Dredge pieces of liver in flour. Brown in bacon drippings, turning once after 7-8 min. Salt and pepper. Crumble bacon over liver, add onions, and add water as needed to get about 1/2 in. in bottom of pan. Cover and simmer 20 min. or until liver is fork tender and onions are soft. Uncover and add 1/2 c. water if you wish to make gravy. Thicken with 1 T. flour or cornstarch. Good served with green vegetable or tomatoes. Serves 4.

If using onion soup, add half the soup with crumbled bacon. Add rest of soup at end, if desired, to make gravy.

Champion Liver Loaf   Jan and Laurel Harbour

1 lb. beef liver	1/2 t. Worcestershire
1/2 lb. pork sausage	1 t. salt
1 medium onion	Dash of pepper
1 c. dry bread crumbs	1 T. lemon juice
2 eggs, beaten	3 strips lean bacon, reserved
1/2 c. milk	to top loaf

Pour boiling water over liver and let stand 5 min. Drain. Grind onion with liver, using medium blade. Combine all ingredients very thoroughly, using hands to mix. Pack mixture firmly into a greased 5 x 9 in. bread pan. Top loaf with strips of bacon. Bake at 350F for 1 hr. Drain fat from pan after first 40 min. Loosen loaf with a knife 10 min. after taking from oven. Serve with sautéed onions and potatoes. Serves 6-8.

This is the recipe with which Jan and Laurel's 4-H team demonstration won a blue ribbon at the Iowa State Fair.

Fricadilla / Meat Balls   Christena Paulsen

1 lb. ground round steak	1/2 t. pepper
1/2 lb. lean fresh pork,	1/2 t. salt
ground fine	1 medium onion, minced
2 c. fine dried bread crumbs	1/8 t. allspice
3 T. butter	1 can beef broth *or* 1 bouillon
2 eggs	cube in 1 c. hot water
2 c. scalded milk	

In bowl beat eggs, add hot milk and crumbs. Let soak. Sauté onion in butter. Add onion, seasonings, and ground meat to bowl, mixing thoroughly with hands. Form into small balls, about 1-1/2 in. in diameter. Fry in butter (Crisco is also good) until a nice brown. Place in a casserole dish. Pour over broth or bouillon. Cover and simmer at 300F for about 30 min. Serves 8 or 9.

Grandma served these with boiled potatoes and carrots, a cabbage slaw, and homemade rye bread.

Italian Meat Balls

1 lb. chopped beef	1/2 t. pepper
1/2 lb. chopped pork	1 T. sage
or 1-1/2 lb. all beef	2 #1 cans tomato soup
1 c. bread crumbs	2 c. water
1/2 c. sharp cheese, diced	1 large onion, chopped
1 small onion, chopped	4 T. olive oil
2 eggs, beaten	2 T. brown sugar
1 T. salt	1 t. paprika

In large bowl, combine ground meat, bread crumbs, cheese, medium onion, eggs, salt, pepper, and sage. Mix well with hands. Form balls 1-1/2 in. in diameter and roll them in flour.

In heavy kettle, heat olive oil and sauté large onion. Combine and add soup, water, brown sugar, and paprika. Cook for 3 min. over medium heat. Add meat balls rolled in 3 T. flour, reduce heat, and cook 45 min.

♣ *If cooked foods have left unpleasant odors, put a pan of 1 c. water with 1/2 t. cloves and 1 t. cinnamon on medium low heat for 10 min. to produce a fragrant "baking cookies" aroma. This will also help to sell a house!*

Meat Loaf

Shirley Sisk

2 lb. hamburger	1/4 c. milk
1/2 c. green pepper, chopped	1/4 c. onion, chopped
2 T. horseradish	1 t. salt
1/2 c. cracker crumbs	1/4 c. ketchup
2 eggs	1 t. dry mustard

Combine all ingredients in large bowl. Mix well and shape for loaf. Bake at 350F for 1 hr. Pour sauce over loaf, and bake 30 min. longer. Let loaf stand 10 min. before cutting. Serves 8.

Sauce: Combine 1/2 c. ketchup, 1/2 c. brown sugar, 1 t. dry mustard, 1/2 c. cider vinegar, and 1 t. nutmeg. Blend well and pour over meat loaf two thirds through baking.

Bill Blass's Meat Loaf

2 lb. ground sirloin
1/2 lb. ground veal
1/2 lb. ground pork
2 T. butter
1 c. celery, chopped
1 c. onions, chopped
1/2 c. parsley, chopped
1/3 c. sour cream

1-1/2 c. soft bread crumbs
1 egg, beaten with
   1 T. Worcestershire sauce
Pinch of dried thyme
Pinch of marjoram
1 bottle Heinz chili sauce
Salt and pepper

Gently mix meats. Sauté onion and celery in butter for 10 min. Add all ingredients except chili sauce. Combine well. Place in 9 x 13 in. baking dish and top with chili sauce. Bake at 350F for 1 hr. Serves 6.

Ann Landers's Meat Loaf   Ann Landers

2 lb. ground round steak
2 eggs
1-1/2 c. bread crumbs
3/4 c. ketchup
1 t. Accent

1/2 c. warm water
1 pkg dried onion soup mix
2 strips of bacon (optional)
1 8-oz. can tomato sauce

Combine first seven ingredients. Mix thoroughly. Put into loaf pan. Cover with two strips of bacon if you like that flavor. Pour tomato sauce over all. Bake at 350F for 1 hr. Serves 6.

Ann Landers will be missed for her astute and good-humored advice to readers of her column throughout the country. Her coming from Sioux City, Iowa, may or may not have been the secret, but her meat loaf is delicious!

Basic Dough for Pizza

1 t. sugar
1 c. warm water
1 T. yeast

3 c. flour
1 t. salt
1/4 c. olive oil

Mix sugar and yeast with warm water; stir and set aside to rise. In a large bowl, blend flour and salt. Make a hole in the center, and pour in yeast mixture and olive oil. Mix until dough forms a ball. Turn onto board. Pour 1 T. olive oil into the bowl; grease sides. Gather pizza dough into a ball and turn it in bowl until it is coated with olive oil. Cover and let dough rise 1-1/2 hr. If you are unable to use dough at once, punch it down and let it rise again.

To shape dough into a 12-in. round crust, put a ball of dough on a lightly floured surface and dust top of dough lightly with flour. Using the heels of your hands, press the dough into a circle. Crimp dough up at edges to keep sauce from running off.

Italian Pizza Sauce

4 garlic cloves, minced
1 medium onion, chopped
1/4 c. olive oil
2 14-oz. cans Italian style
   whole tomatoes, chopped

2 t. sugar
2 t. salt
2 t. dried basil
1 bay leaf
1 t. pepper

In a large pan, sauté garlic and onion in oil until onion is soft and transparent. Add tomatoes with juice, sugar, salt, and seasonings. Bring the sauce to a boil. Turn down the heat to simmer for 1 hr. Stir frequently. Yield: sauce for two 12-in. pizzas. Store, covered, in refrigerator.

Porcupines
Aunt Alice Paulsen

1 lb. ground chuck steak
1/2 c. rice
1 medium onion, chopped fine
1-1/2 c. tomato juice

1 c. green pepper, chopped
1 medium onion, chopped
1 T. sugar
Salt and pepper

Combine ground chuck, uncooked rice, finely chopped onion, salt, and pepper. Mix well. Shape into 1-1/2-in. balls or rolls. Brown lightly. Place balls in casserole and cover with sauce.

Prepare sauce by combining tomato juice, green pepper, chopped onion, sugar, and salt and pepper to taste. Pour over meatballs. Bake at 350F for 1-1/2 hr. Baste meat with sauce every half hour. Serves 8.

Sausage Soufflé
JoAnn McElmuray

6 eggs
2 c. milk
6 slices white bread, cubed
1 t. salt

1 t. dry mustard
1 c. cheddar cheese, shredded
1 lb. bulk mild pork sausage *or*
   ham or cooked bacon

Brown sausage; drain. With electric mixer, beat eggs; add milk, salt, and dry mustard. Stir in bread, cheese, and drained sausage. Place mixture in 7 x 11-1/2 in. baking dish. Refrigerate overnight. Bake at 350F for 40 min. Remove from oven, let stand 15 min. before serving.

This is a good entrée for a special breakfast or a brunch buffet. It also makes a simple and delicious supper, served with green salad and rolls.

Shepherd's Pie

1 medium onion, chopped
1 lb. ground chuck steak
Salt and pepper
2 10-1/2-oz. cans condensed
   tomato soup

1 16-oz. pkg frozen mixed vegetables
6 medium potatoes
3/4 c. hot milk
1 egg, beaten

Brown onion with ground chuck; salt and pepper to taste. Add tomato soup and mixed vegetables; heat until bubbling. Pour into greased 9 x 12 in. pan or a deeper 9-in. square casserole. Top with mashed potatoes spooned in half-cup mounds around edge. Bake at 375F about 40 min.

To prepare mashed potatoes, peel and cook potatoes until tender. Drain, mash, and beat in hot milk, egg, and salt and pepper to taste. For special occasions pipe potatoes and brush with melted butter before baking.
Serves 6.

Variation: Chop large onion and brown with ground chuck; salt and pepper to taste. Add a spoonful or two of juices to 2 T. flour or cornstarch to make a paste. Mix into ground meat and add 1 c. hot water. Cook over medium heat, stirring constantly, until mixture thickens. Pour into 9-in. square baking dish, and top with mashed potatoes spread evenly over meat. Sprinkle with paprika. Bake at 375F about 40 min.

Shepherd's Pie originated in the British Isles and remains one of the most popular dishes in country pubs. The best ones are made by local farm wives, using locally grown, freshly dug potatoes.

Tricia's Tater Tot Casserole   Tricia Collier

1 lb. ground beef
Salt and pepper
1 2-lb. pkg Tater Tots

1 can cut green beans
1 can cream of chicken soup
1/2 c. chopped onion (optional)

Brown ground beef with salt and pepper to taste, including onion if desired. Drain off fat. Add green beans and chicken soup, and mix well. Pour into a greased 9 x 13 in. casserole. Spread Tater Tots in a single layer on top. Bake at 350F for 30 min. Serves 6.

Crab Maryland   Karen Pickett

3 T. butter or margarine
2 T. flour
3/4 c. milk
3/4 c. half and half
1/2 t. salt

Pinch of cayenne pepper
1 7-oz. can crabmeat
2 T. dry sherry or white wine
4 to 6 warm patty shells *or*
    toast rounds

Melt 2 T. butter in saucepan; stir in flour, and add milk slowly, stirring constantly. Add half and half, salt, and cayenne. Cook, stirring constantly, until smooth and thickened.

In small frying pan, sauté crabmeat in 1 T. butter until butter is absorbed. Add meat to sauce and stir in sherry. Taste for salt. Cook over low heat, stirring gently, about 3 min. Fill patty shells with crab mixture. Serves 4 to 6.

Fried Catfish

3/4 c. cornmeal
1/4 c. flour
2 t. salt
1/4 t. garlic powder

1 t. cayenne pepper
6 catfish fillets
Canola oil

Mix cornmeal, flour, salt, garlic powder, and cayenne in shallow dish. Roll fish in cornmeal mixture to cover evenly. In large cast-iron skillet, heat oil up to 1-1/2 in. (350F). Fry fish two or three at a time for 5 or 6 min. or until golden; drain on brown paper or paper towels. Serves 6.

Beer Battered Fish   Richard Olmstead

1 can beer
1 c. flour

Salt and pepper
12 catfish or other fresh catch
Vegetable oil

Blend beer and flour, beat well, and let stand at room temperature up to 3 hr. Roll cleaned fish in batter to cover evenly. Deep fry fish for 5 or 6 min. or until golden. Drain on brown paper, season with salt and pepper. Serves 12.

Richard used this batter to prepare delicious fish at a potluck picnic for Pierce School staff. When the batter is heated, the alcohol evaporates.

Cornmeal Fried Fish

1/2 c. canola or peanut oil	2 t. salt
1/2 c. flour	2-1/2 lb. fish fillets — catfish,
1/2 c. cornmeal	walleyes, or other catch
1 t. cayenne pepper	Tartar sauce
1/2 t. black pepper	Lemon slice

Combine flour, cornmeal, peppers, and salt in shallow dish. Roll fish in mixture to cover evenly. In large cast-iron skillet, heat oil over moderate heat. Fry fish until golden brown on both sides; drain on brown paper or paper towels. Serve with lemon and tartar sauce. Serves 6.

♣ *Fill lemon shells with tartar sauce to garnish fish and seafood dishes.*

Fried Whole Trout — Ozarks   Marvin Schrum

6 T. flour	Lake trout, cleaned, head removed
Salt and pepper	1 c. buttermilk

If using fry kettle or deep fryer with basket, heat vegetable oil to 375F. Mix flour and seasonings in shallow dish. Dip trout in buttermilk and then in seasoned flour. Lower into hot fat and cook 4-5 min, turning once. Serve with lemon wedges.

If using large cast-iron skillet, heat 1/2 c. oil over moderate heat. Fry fish 3 min. to a side, turning once.

Fisherman's Catch Fish Fry   Marvin Schrum

Cleaned and filleted fish —	1 c. milk
bass, croppies, etc.	1 c. cornmeal
2 eggs, beaten	Salt and pepper

Refrigerate filleted fish until ready to fry. Allow one fish (3/4 lb. dressed weight) per person.

Make egg-milk dip by whisking eggs and milk together well. Dip fillet in mixture, then roll in cornmeal. If using fry kettle, heat oil to 375F — almost smoking. Use a fry basket to avoid breaking cooked fish. Fry fish 3-5 min. or until golden brown. Remove to a hot platter; serve with tartar sauce. If using cast-iron skillet, fry fish 3 min. to a side, turning once.

White Clam Spaghetti

1/2 c. olive oil	1/4 t. ground thyme
1 small clove garlic, minced	1/4 t. salt
1/4 green pepper, minced *or*	1/4 t. pepper
1/4 c. pimiento	1/2 c. white wine
2 or 3 7-oz. cans clams, drained	1 lb. spaghetti or linguini
1/4 c. parsley, minced	Cornstarch

Heat olive oil in skillet. Sauté garlic and onion until soft and golden. Add green pepper; sauté 5 min. more. Mix 2 T. cornstarch with 1/2 c. water until smooth. Add to skillet with all other ingredients except spaghetti; simmer gently, stirring occasionally.

Cook spaghetti in 4 qt. rapidly boiling water with 1 t. salt. Cook to al dente stage. Drain well. Add 1 t. butter and toss. Add clam sauce and toss together. Serve with hot Italian bread and green salad. Serves 6.

Seafood Newburg

4 T. butter	Pieces of lobster, shrimp,
1 c. cream	scallops, oysters, and
2 egg yolks	cooked flaked fish
1/2 c. sherry	1-1/2 c. crushed saltines, divided
1/8 t. cayenne pepper	4 t. melted butter
Salt to taste	Paprika

Melt 4 T. butter in top of double boiler at low temperature over boiling water. Add cream and slowly add beaten egg yolks. Blend well, and stir over low heat for 10 min. Remove from heat and beat well. Add sherry, cayenne, and salt to taste.

In well-buttered casserole, combine pieces of seafood in layers with 1 c. crushed saltines. Pour the Newburg sauce over and top with 1/2 c. crushed saltines mixed with 4 t. melted butter. Sprinkle lightly with paprika. Bake at 350F about 20 min. Serve with green salad. Serves 6.

My Scalloped Oysters

1 pt. medium oysters	Pinch of salt
3 T. butter	Pepper generously
2 T. flour	2 c. buttered Ritz cracker crumbs
1-1/2 c. half and half	(1/2 sleeve of crackers)

Drain oysters and add enough water to the liquor to make 3/4 c. In a saucepan, melt butter. Blend in flour and seasonings. Gradually add half and half and oyster liquor, stirring until thick and smooth. In a greased 9-in. square baking dish arrange alternate layers of oysters, crumbs, and sauce, topping with crumbs. Bake in a hot oven (400F) for 15-20 min. until scallop is bubbling and crumbs are brown. Serves 5 or 6.

Variation: Add 2 c. frozen or 1 #202 can corn, drained, layering the corn alternately with oysters, crumbs, and sauce.

Paella

1/4 c. flour	1 clove garlic, crushed
1 t. salt	1/4 c. pimiento, diced
2-1/2 to 3 lb. chicken, cut up	1/2 t. salt
1/2 lb. ham, cut in 1-in. cubes	1/4 t. ground oregano
1/4 c. olive or salad oil	1/4 t. ground saffron
2 carrots, pared and sliced	2/3 c. uncooked long grain rice
2 medium onions, quartered	1 9-oz. pkg frozen artichoke hearts
1 celery stalk, chopped	3/4 lb. shelled raw shrimp
2 c. chicken broth	12 small clams in shells

Combine flour, salt, and dash of pepper in paper bag. Shake chicken to coat. In large heavy skillet, brown chicken in oil. Add ham, vegetables, broth, rice, and seasonings. Cover and simmer 30 min. Add shrimp, clams, and artichokes. Cover and simmer 15-20 min. longer. Serves 6 to 8.

In Spain, paella is served in the very large skillet in which it was cooked. Green salad and sangria go well with it.

Baked Perch Fillets

1 lb. fresh or frozen perch fillets	Juice of 1 lemon
2 T. soft butter	Cornmeal
Lemon slices	Salt and pepper

If fillets are frozen, thaw in refrigerator. Wipe fillets with paper towel. Roll in cornmeal. Place in a single layer in a well-buttered shallow baking pan. Dot with half the butter. Bake in preheated 350F oven for 10 min. Dot with rest of butter and pour lemon juice over fillets. Salt and pepper to taste. Turn heat to 350F and bake 15 min. longer. Transfer to warmed platter, sprinkle with paprika, and garnish with lemon slices. Serves 4.

Oven-Baked Fish Fillets
Anna M. Petersen

1 lb. perch or haddock fillets
1 T. butter
Salt and pepper

Paprika
Lemon wedges

If frozen, defrost fillets in refrigerator. Wipe off excess moisture with paper towels. Melt butter in a shallow baking dish. Place fillets in dish and brush with melted butter. Sprinkle with paprika. Bake in preheated oven at 350F for 20-25 min. or until fish flakes easily. Serve with lemon wedges or tartar sauce. Serves 4.

Fruits of the Sea Casserole

1 6-1/2-oz. can tuna
1 6-1/2 oz. can crabmeat
1 6-1/2 oz. can shrimp
1 c. celery, chopped fine
3/4 c. ripe olives, sliced
1/2 t. salt

1/8 t. pepper
1/4 c. lemon juice
1 c. mayonnaise
1/2 c. slivered almonds
3/4 c. cheese, grated
1-1/2 c. buttered cracker crumbs

Combine all ingredients except cheese and cracker crumbs. Blend well and pour into buttered 9 x 9 x 2 in. baking dish. Cover with a mixture of buttered cracker crumbs and grated cheese. Bake at 350F for 35-40 min. Serves 10.

♣ *Using Ritz crackers rather than saltines when buttered cracker crumbs are called for will give the dish a richer flavor.*

Salmon Croquettes I

1 can pink salmon, flaked
1-1/2 c. hot mashed potatoes
2 T. butter
1/4 t. salt

1 egg yolk
2 c. fine cracker crumbs
Pepper

Combine salmon, potatoes, butter, salt, and egg yolk. Beat well. Mold 1/2 c. at a time into a ball or roll. Roll croquette in cracker crumbs seasoned with salt and pepper. Fry in deep fat, or brown in butter. Serve with tartar sauce. Yield: 8 croquettes.

♣ *Pink salmon is the best choice for croquettes and loaves; the more expensive red salmon is good for salads.*

Salmon Croquettes II

1 can pink salmon, flaked	1 tube saltines, crushed
1 10-1/2-oz. can cream of	1 egg, beaten
mushroom soup	3 T. butter
1/2 t. salt	1 pkg frozen small peas

Mix flaked salmon, soup, salt, and beaten egg. Add all but 1/2 c. crushed saltines; mix very thoroughly. On an 8-in. piece of waxed paper, spread 1/2 c. crushed saltines. Divide salmon mixture into six parts. Drop each part onto crushed saltines, turn and press until covered. In large skillet, heat butter to very hot without burning. Put in croquettes and brown for 3 min., then turn and brown the other side. Place on absorbent toweling briefly, then in ring on serving platter. Fill center with buttered, cooked green peas. Serves 3-4.

Salmon or Tuna Croquettes

2 cans tuna in water *or*	2 hard-boiled eggs, shelled
1 large can salmon	1/4 c. onion, chopped
1 can mushroom soup, divided	1 egg, beaten
1 c. very fine bread or	3 t. lemon juice
cracker crumbs	2 T. butter or oil

Remove skin and bones from salmon. If using tuna, drain well. Combine fish, 1/2 can soup, onion, lightly beaten egg, and lemon juice. Form into croquettes, using a scant half cup for each. Roll in crumbs. Brown in melted butter or oil; turn once and brown the other side. Transfer to serving platter, surround with quartered hard-boiled eggs that have been lightly salted. Top with sauce. Serves 6 to 8.

Sauce: Combine remainder of mushroom soup in can with 1/2 c. milk, 3 T. mayonnaise, and 1 T. lemon juice. Heat but do not allow to boil. Pour over croquettes or serve in a sauce dish and pass.

Saucy Seafood

2 T. green pepper, chopped	1 can small shrimp
3 T. onion, chopped	1/2 t. salt
1 c. celery, sliced fine	1/4 t. pepper
1 c. mayonnaise	1 t. Worcestershire sauce
1 can crab meat	1-1/2 c. potato chips, crushed

Mix all ingredients except potato chips. Spread in well-buttered 8-in. pan. Sprinkle chips on top. Bake at 350F for 25-30 min. You may add a can of chunk tuna (in water, drained) to extend the amount. Serves 6.

Asparagus-Tuna Hot Dish

1 lb. fresh asparagus, cleaned, ends snapped off	1/4 c. butter
	1/2 t. salt
1 large can solid or chunk tuna, in water	1 T. sherry
	2 c. milk
1 4-oz. pkg slivered almonds	Nutmeg
1/4 c. flour	Paprika

Break asparagus into bite-sized pieces. Cook in boiling salted water 7 min. Drain. Arrange in a buttered 7 x 10 in. baking dish. Cover with tuna, drained and broken into pieces. Brown almonds in butter. Blend in flour, salt, and milk and cook until thickened. Stir in sherry. Pour sauce over tuna; sprinkle lightly with nutmeg and paprika. Bake at 350F for 25 min. Serves 4. A 15-oz.. can of asparagus may be substituted for fresh asparagus.

Favorite Tuna Casserole   **Sally Morris**

2 7-oz. cans tuna in water	Pimiento (optional)
1 can evaporated milk	1 small pkg Chinese noodles
1 can mushroom soup	1 4-oz. pkg cashews
1 4-oz. can mushrooms, drained	1 c. celery, chopped

Mix all ingredients. Bake in greased Pyrex casserole at 350F for 1 hr. Serves 8.

Tuna and Noodles

1 8-oz. pkg fine noodles	1/4 c. milk
1 T. onion, chopped	1 7-oz. can solid tuna in water
1 t. butter	3/4 c. crushed potato chips
1 can cream of mushroom soup	

Cook noodles in boiling water until al dente; drain. Sauté onion in butter until soft. Drain tuna and break into chunks. In large bowl, mix soup with milk, blending until smooth. Add noodles, onion, and tuna, mixing lightly. Place in buttered 1-1/2-qt. casserole. Top with crushed potato chips. Bake at 350F for 20-30 min. Serves 6.

Fettucine with Pesto Sauce

8 to 12 oz. fettucine	3 small cloves garlic
3 T. soft butter or 2 T. olive oil	1/4 t. salt
2 c. fresh basil, packed (no stems)	1/2 c. grated Parmesan cheese
1/2 c. good olive oil	1/4 c. pine nuts

Cook fettucine to al dente. Drain and toss with butter or olive oil. Keep hot. Place fresh basil, olive oil, garlic, and salt in blender and puree. Add pine nuts and Parmesan cheese and mix in. Toss pesto with hot pasta and serve. Serves 6 to 8.

♣ *Add a tablespoonful of oil to the water when boiling pasta to keep it from boiling over.*

Homemade Spaghetti Sauce

1 large onion, chopped	2 c. water
2 large cloves garlic, minced	1/4 c. parsley, chopped
3 T. olive oil	1/4 t. rosemary
1-1/2 lb. ground chuck steak	1/4 t. thyme
1 can tomato paste	1/4 t. basil
1 8-oz. can tomato sauce	1/4 t. oregano
1 16-oz. can tomatoes	1/2 t. salt
1 4-oz. can mushroom pieces	1/2 t. pepper
1 T. sugar	

Sauté onion and garlic in oil in an electric skillet. When limp, push to one side, and brown ground chuck. Skim off excess fat. Add tomato paste, sauce, and whole tomatoes; mushrooms with liquid; sugar, water, and parsley. Grind herbs together and sprinkle over all. Salt and pepper to taste. Stir well. Cover and simmer at 300F for 2 hr. Stir occasionally. Lower heat and add water if needed. Yield: 2-1/2 qt. Serves 8.

Denise's Pasta Sauce   Denise Catterall

1 lb. ground beef	1 #2 can chopped tomatoes
1 medium onion	Salt
1 T. olive oil	Pepper
1 clove garlic	

Chop onion. Peel garlic, and cut clove in half. In skillet, sauté onion and garlic in olive oil until soft. Remove garlic and discard. Add tomatoes, sugar, salt, and pepper to taste. Cover and simmer 20 min. In separate skillet, brown ground beef; drain it well, and add to tomato mixture. Simmer another 20 min. Serve over spaghetti, ziti, or other pasta. Top with freshly grated Parmesan cheese. This sauce keeps well refrigerated. Serves 4.

Macaroni and Cheese

1-1/2 c. macaroni
3 T. margarine
3 T. flour
2 c. milk
1 t. onion flakes

1/2 t. salt
1/8 t. pepper
2 c. cheddar cheese, cubed
    grated, or shredded
1 3-oz. pkg cream cheese

Cook macaroni to al dente stage. Drain and rinse with cold water. In saucepan, melt margarine. Stir in onion flakes, salt, and pepper. Blend, then add milk. Stir until thick. Add cheese and stir until melted. Stir macaroni into cheese sauce. Pour into 1-1/2-qt. casserole buttered or sprayed with Pam. Bake at 350F for 35 min. Serves 6.

Macaroni Loaf   Agnes Lester

2 c. cooked elbow macaroni
1 T. onion, chopped
1 T. pimiento, chopped
1 T. green pepper, diced
3 eggs, beaten

1 c. warm milk
1 c. bread crumbs
Salt and pepper
Parsley, minced
1 t. butter

Sauté onion, pimiento, and green pepper in butter. Mix macaroni, eggs, bread crumbs, milk, salt, and pepper in large bowl. Add sautéed vegetables and blend well. Pour into shallow baking dish. Bake at 350F for 50 min. Garnish with minced parsley. Serves 4.

Overnight Lasagna

1 lb. ground beef
1/2 lb. ground lean pork
1 t. salt
1 c. water
2 c. canned tomatoes with juice
2 small cans tomato paste
1 10-oz. pkg lasagna noodles
3 c. small curd cottage cheese
1/2 c. grated Parmesan cheese

3 T. parsley, chopped
1 T. dried basil
2 cloves garlic, minced
1/2 t. oregano
2 eggs, beaten
1 c. carrots, grated
1 lb. mozzarella cheese,
    sliced
Additional Parmesan cheese

Brown and drain beef and pork. In large bowl, mix water, canned tomatoes, tomato paste, salt, 1-1/2 T. parsley, basil, garlic, and oregano; add to meat. Simmer for 30 min.

In bowl, mix cottage cheese, 1-1/2 T. parsley, beaten eggs, Parmesan cheese, and grated carrots.

In greased 9 x 15 x 4 in. baking dish or aluminum pan, spread 2 c. meat mixture. Lay half the uncooked lasagna noodles on top. Next add a layer of half the remaining meat, and top it with half the cottage cheese mixture. Add another layer of noodles, a layer of meat, and the remaining cottage cheese. Cover lasagna with foil. Put baking dish into refrigerator overnight. Remove. Let it stand for an hour.

Place sliced mozzarella cheese to cover top. Grate additional Parmesan cheese over all. Bake at 375F about 45 min. or until dish is bubbling. Let stand to set for 20 min., then cut into squares to serve. Serves 10 to 12.

Italian Spaghetti I

2 lb. ground beef	1 c. olive or salad oil
1 lb. ground ham, raw	1 clove garlic, minced
1 #2-1/2 can tomatoes	2 c. onion, chopped
1 c. ripe olives, diced	1 green pepper, diced
Dash of oregano	2 T. Worcestershire sauce
Salt and pepper	Parmesan cheese
1/2 pkg long spaghetti	

In large skillet, brown meat, onion, green pepper, and garlic in oil. Add tomatoes and seasonings. Simmer slowly for 1 hr. or more, stirring occasionally. Add olives before serving.

Cook spaghetti to stage you prefer. Drain. Mound spaghetti on a large platter and pour sauce over; sprinkle with Parmesan cheese. Serves 6.

Italian Spaghetti II   Myrtle Hart

1/4 c. Mazola oil	1/2 t. basil
1 large onion, minced	1/2 t. Italian seasonings
1 clove garlic, minced	1/2 t. salt
1 lb. ground lean chuck steak	1/4 t. pepper
1 #2-1/2 can tomatoes	1 bay leaf
1 6-oz. can tomato paste	8 oz. thin spaghetti
1 8-oz. can tomato sauce	Parmesan cheese

In heavy frying pan, brown onion, garlic, and ground chuck in oil. Add all tomatoes and seasonings. Mix well and simmer 1 hr. or longer, adding 1/2 c. water if sauce gets too thick. Stir occasionally.

Cook spaghetti in boiling water to al dente stage; drain. Arrange spaghetti on dinner plates with generous topping of sauce. Pass freshly grated Parmesan cheese. Accompany with garlic bread and green salad. Serves 8.

Deviled Eggs for the Brunch Bunch

9 jumbo-sized eggs	1/8 t. white pepper
1 t. cider vinegar	1/2 t. Coleman's dry mustard
1 t. soft butter	2 T. Hellmann's mayonnaise
1/4 t. salt	9 ripe or stuffed green olives

Put eggs in a 2-qt. saucepan and cover with cold water. Heat to a brisk boil; remove from heat and let cool about 1 hr. Drain and cover with cold water. When cooled, remove shells carefully and rinse peeled eggs. Halve eggs lengthwise. Remove yolks to a quart mixing bowl and mash fine with pastry blender or fork.

Add to mashed yolks the vinegar, butter, seasonings, and mayonnaise. Mix thoroughly with a fork. If needed, add a little more soft butter. Fill egg white halves with a generous spoonful of yolk mixture. Top with half a black olive or stuffed olive. Arrange on platter of greens. Yield: 18 halves.

♣ *Eggs must be refrigerated to maintain their quality.*

Creamed Deviled Eggs

1 pkg frozen spinach	2 T. butter
8 deviled egg halves	1/4 t. salt
2 c. light cream sauce	1/2 c. buttered cracker crumbs

Cook spinach and drain well. Prepare deviled eggs (6 to 8 halves) and light cream sauce. Mix butter and salt with hot spinach and pour into a buttered shallow 8 x 8 in. baking dish. Arrange deviled egg halves on spinach. Pour cream sauce over eggs and spinach. Sprinkle with buttered cracker crumbs. Bake at 375F about 15 min. or until crumbs are brown. Serves 4.

This is a light, delicious supper dish.

Oven Omelet

June Anderson

8 eggs
1/4 t. salt
1 c. milk
Pepper to taste

1/2 c. crumbled bacon or diced ham
1 c. grated cheese
3 T. chopped onion

Beat eggs, salt, and milk until frothy. Add bacon, cheese, and onion. Pour into a greased 1-1/2-qt. baking dish. Bake uncovered at 325F for 40 min. until top is set.

Variation: Add 1 T. chopped green pepper and 1/2 c. sliced mushrooms and top with tomato slices if you would enjoy these flavors.

Super Brunch Omelet

Alice Wasson

1/2 stick margarine or butter
1/2 lb. Velveeta cheese, diced
1 c. half and half
1 t. prepared mustard
12 large eggs

1/2 t. salt
Dash of pepper
12 bacon curls, cooked and drained
12 cherry tomatoes, sliced

Butter a 9 x 12 in. Pyrex dish, or spray with Pam. Dot bottom with margarine. Distribute cheese evenly in dish. Combine half and half with mustard; mix well, and pour half over the cheese.

Beat eggs thoroughly; add salt and pepper. Pour eggs evenly into prepared dish. Pour remainder of half-and-half mixture over eggs. Cover dish tightly with Saran Wrap or foil and refrigerate overnight.

Preheat oven to 350F. Remove cover, and place dish in oven. Bake at 350F for 20 min. Then stir all outer edges of omelet toward center. Continue baking 10 min. Garnish with bacon curls and sliced cherry tomatoes. Serves 6 generously.

This is a fail-safe entrée for brunch.

Dutch Omelet

1 small onion, chopped
1/2 lb. ground pork sausage
2 c. raw shredded potatoes
3/4 t. salt, divided

6 eggs
1/4 c. milk
1/8 t. pepper
1 c. shredded cheese

Brown sausage and onion; drain. Salt potatoes lightly and spread in greased 8-in. square or round baking dish. Combine eggs, 1/2 t. salt, pepper, and milk; beat until frothy and pour over potatoes. Sprinkle sausage mix and cheese on top. Bake at 350F for 40 min. Serves 4.

Bachelor Breakfast   Jason Bledsoe

3 eggs
2 t. cold water
1/8 t. salt
Dash of pepper
1 T. butter

1/4 c. green pepper, diced
1/4 c. red pepper, diced
1/2 c. cheddar cheese, diced
1 t. onion, diced

Beat eggs, water, salt, and pepper with rotary beater until frothy. Heat butter in 6-in. skillet to sizzling hot. Pour egg mixture into hot skillet. Loosen edges to allow mixture to cook evenly. Pour peppers, onion, and cheese into egg mixture when it begins to set and stir as it cooks. Use a spatula to turn the mixture. Adjust heat to low, cover and let skillet remain on heat half a minute. Turn out onto warmed plate; serve with hot buttered toast and fresh fruit. Serves one.

Grandson Jason learned to cook plain egg omelets when he was six. An experienced "plain cook," he is a college senior preparing to become an elementary teacher.

Overnight Egg Casserole   Elizabeth Brandt

1 lb. bulk sausage
6 slices white bread
2 c. milk
4 eggs, beaten

1 t. dry mustard
1 t. salt
1/4 lb. grated American *or*
   sharp cheddar cheese

Dice, brown, and drain sausage. Remove crusts and cut bread into cubes. In large bowl, combine all ingredients, mixing well. Pour into greased 8 x 8 in. casserole. Cover with foil and refrigerate 12 hr. or overnight.

Bake covered at 325F for 1 hr. Remove foil for last 15 min. of baking time. Serves 8.

Egg-Sausage Casserole

10 slices bread
2 c. grated American or
   Cheddar cheese
1-1/2 lb. sausage
Salt and pepper

4 eggs
3 c. milk, divided
1/2 t. dry mustard
1 can cream of mushroom soup

Brown and drain sausage. Remove crusts from bread and cut into cubes. Place bread cubes in greased 9 x 13 in. pan. Sprinkle cheese over. Add sausage evenly over all. Combine eggs, 2-1/2 c. milk, and mustard, beating until frothy. Pour evenly over ingredients in pan. Refrigerate overnight. In the morning, combine soup and 1/2 c. milk, blending well, and spread over casserole. Bake at 300F for 1-1/2 hr. Serves 8.

Basic Quiche Crust

1-1/2 c. unsifted flour	6 T. chilled butter
1/2 t. salt	5 T. ice water
2 T. Crisco shortening	

Mix flour and salt in bowl. Cut in Crisco and butter with a pastry blender until crumbly. Add ice water slowly, mixing with a fork until blended. Place dough into plastic bag. Press dough together in a flat disk. Refrigerate 30-60 min.

On floured board, roll out dough disk to fit 10-in. round quiche pan 2 in. deep. Trim dough and turn under edge to form a rim. Flute edge. Put a layer of foil over dough and fill with pie weights or dry beans to keep crust from puffing up.

Bake crust at 450F for 15 min. Remove beans or weights and foil. Prick crust with fork several times and bake 10 min. more. The quiche crust is now ready for filling. Follow directions for preparing and baking your choice of filling.

Pickled Eggs

6 hard-cooked eggs	1/2 t. salt
1 jar beets	1/4 t. allspice
1/2 c. red wine	Pepper
3/4 c. vinegar	1 clove garlic, crushed

Peel eggs and put them in sterilized quart jar. Drain juice from beets, reserving beets for another purpose. Combine 3/4 c. beet juice with wine, vinegar, and seasonings in saucepan. Cook over medium heat, but do not boil. Pour hot beet juice mixture over eggs. Cool, cover, and refrigerate. Serves 6.

To hard cook eggs, start eggs in cold water, bring to a rolling boil, remove from heat, and let sit 15 min.

Barbecue Sauce I

1/4 c. onion, diced	1 c. ketchup
3/4 c. water	3 T. vinegar
2 T. Worcestershire sauce	1/2 t. salt
1 t. paprika	1 t. chili powder
1/2 t. pepper	

Combine all ingredients and mix well. Use to baste ribs that have been baked and the fat drained. Pour sauce over ribs, and bake 1/2 hr.

Barbecue Sauce II

1/2 c. onion, diced
1 t. Coleman's dry mustard
1/2 t. chili powder
1/4 t. cayenne
1 T. paprika
1 T. brown sugar
1 t. salt

1/2 t. black pepper
2 T. Worcestershire sauce
4 T. vinegar
1 c. tomato juice
1/2 c. ketchup
1/2 c. water

Combine all ingredients in saucepan. Bring to boil and simmer 15 min. Pour over ribs during last hour of baking. When ribs are done, remove to heated platter. Stir sauce, adding water if needed, and serve in gravy boat. Serve with rice or wild rice, a cooked green vegetable, and large green salad. Serves 6 to 8.

This sauce is also good with chicken. After browning chicken, place in large casserole and pour sauce over it. Bake at 350F for 1 hr. or until chicken is tender.

Barbecue Sauce III

1 large onion, diced
1 T. olive oil
3/4 c. chili sauce
3/4 c. Coca-Cola
1 T. Worcestershire sauce
1 T. brown sugar

1/2 t. salt
Dash of black pepper
1 T. Coleman's dry mustard
1/4 t. cayenne
1 T. paprika
2 T. white vinegar

Sauté onion in olive oil, cooking slowly until onion is caramel color. Stir in chili sauce, Coke, and seasonings. Bring to a boil. Cover, reduce heat, and simmer for 45 min. Stir occasionally. Makes 2 cups.

Cheese Sauce for Vegetables

6 T. butter
1-1/2 T. flour

2 c. milk
1 c. Velveeta cheese, diced

Melt butter and blend with flour. Stir in milk, and cook until mixture thickens. Add cheese. Stir over low heat until cheese melts. More milk may be added if sauce is too thick. Pour over cooked cauliflower, carrots, or asparagus.

Horseradish Sauce for Baked Ham I

1/2 c. mayonnaise	2 T. grated horseradish
1/2 c. yogurt or sour cream	1/4 t. salt
1 T. grated onion	Dash of hot sauce

Combine all ingredients and blend well. Serve in small bowl, and sprinkle with paprika. Makes 1 cup.

Horseradish Sauce for Baked Ham II

1/4 heavy cream	1/4 t. salt
3 T. grated horseradish	Pepper
1 T. vinegar	

Whip cream stiff. Add horseradish, vinegar, salt, and pepper to taste. Blend well and chill. Serve with baked ham.

Fresh Pesto Sauce

1 clove garlic, pressed	4 T. fresh basil, chopped fine *or*
1 c. good olive oil	1/4 c. dried basil
1 c. parsley, chopped fine	1/2 c. toasted pine nuts

Put garlic, olive oil, parsley, and basil into blender. Run on puree for 30 sec. Stir in pine nuts. Set aside. Leftover pesto sauce may be refrigerated in a covered pint jar.

Pasta: Prepared desired amount of fettucine or spaghetti according to package directions; drain. Add 2 T. butter and 2/3 c. grated Parmesan cheese. Toss with pesto mixture. Sprinkle with coarsely ground black pepper. Serves 8 to 12.

Tartar Sauce for Fish

1 c. mayonnaise	1 T. capers
1 t. onion juice	1 t. prepared mustard
1 T. sweet pickles, minced	

Mix all ingredients well and serve at once with any kind of fish.

Basic White Sauce

2 T. butter
2 T. flour
1 c. milk

1/2 t. salt
1/8 t. white or black pepper

Melt butter in a small saucepan. Add flour and stir with a wooden spoon until blended. Add milk gradually, stirring steadily until mixture begins to boil. Reduce heat and cook 3 min. longer. Add salt and pepper to taste, and blend. To make a thin white sauce, use 1-1/4 c. milk.

White sauce may be used for various sauces with the addition of cheese, condiments, or eggs. It also provides the base for creamed dishes on toast when combined with, for example, chopped hard-cooked eggs, shredded dried beef, tuna, chicken, or chopped cooked ham.

Vegetables

Cooked Side Dishes ♣
Casseroles ♣ *Scallops*
♣ *Soufflés*

Gardens and County Fair

The garden looked good after the rain. Nearly half an acre of vegetables — a third of it in the rows of sweet corn and another big plot in vining cucumbers, zucchini and squash — had been her 4-H garden project, and she hoped to exhibit some vegetables at the county fair in August. But right now the green beans were perfect for canning, so she hurried to the house to talk to her mother.

Her mother was scalding canning jars that had been cleaned with a bristle brush. The long counter, covered with oilcloth, held dozens of jars turned upside down on clean white cloths. The big iron pressure cooker was set on the stove's hot water reservoir ready for action. Mother and daughter nodded in agreement: early tomorrow morning, by seven at least, they would pick the beans, pull beets that were mature, and check on the sweet corn.

As she came downstairs the next morning, the girl was planning her work. She was eager to pick the beans before it got hot. She took baskets from the storage shed and soon was working on the first 50-foot row of green beans. She was pleased to find the plants heavy with clusters of uniform-sized beans and worked methodically along

251

the row. After she started on the second row, she saw her mother, sun hat askew, starting a third row. Soon when the first basket was full, she grabbed another. The two pickers finished four rows and had more than three bushels of beans. They carried the load to the house, and after a cooling drink, sat down for the task of snapping. After they had washed the beans, they stood at the counter and worked at cutting the beans into uniform pieces.

Mom started the next step, blanching the raw beans briefly before draining them and filling the scalded jars. The pressure cooker was lifted onto a burner of the kerosene stove in the lean-to. As fast as she filled jars, poured hot water in each and fitted scalded lids, Mom put the jars into the cooker rack. Then she put on the lid, screwed down the petcock, set a timer and jotted down the time the processing would be finished. The two continued their routine, stopping only to refill the pressure cooker. By the time the beans had all been processed, more than four dozen jars of beans stood on the counter. Mother and daughter exchanged proud glances. Four dozen meals with green beans on the menu! The two had worked four hours. It was a good job done.

A week later, the daughter was packing jars of beans for her canning exhibit. She had brought in an enormous perfect cabbage to enter and had a cluster of uniform-sized beets and four handsome ears of corn as well. Mom was putting an angel cake into a carrier when Dad and the boys appeared, freshly scrubbed and combed and looking very businesslike in new bib overalls. They had taken their 4-H lambs to the county fair yesterday. Today they would groom and feed their entries. The two boys wanted to see the competition and perhaps ride on the big ferris wheel.

Soon they were squeezed into the Ford and rolling over the new graveled road that led to the county seat. Everyone helped unload the exhibits. They agreed on the time to meet for lunch at the church food stand. Then each hurried to special interests: the lamb pens, the beef cattle division, the cakes competition, and the 4-H displays. The girl found that her entries looked good, and there was no other cabbage as big and green and perfect!

The family met for lunch at the big square Ladies Aid stand where diners could sit on plank seats out of the sun. It was easy to choose — either hot roast beef sandwiches or two pieces of fried chicken, each with mashed potatoes and gravy, for 75 cents. An ample side dish of coleslaw and a homemade bun completed the meal, along with coffee, tea or milk. The food was hot, delicious and filling. The family decided to forego dessert but stop for pie later.

They sauntered down the hard-packed walk and began a somewhat systematic visit to all the exhibits, beginning with livestock and 4-H entries. There were sleek, quiet black Angus and Hereford baby beeves munching on hay as their young owners continued grooming with brushes and combs. There were lambs of several breeds, the boys' black-faces looking solid and blocky — the type that would top the Eastern market for prime lamb. Farther on, the hog pens were noisy as pigs pushed one another away from feed. In a smaller building, poultry and rabbits claimed attention. Dad and the boys decided to look at the draft horses, powerful animals well built for pulling heavy loads. There were Percherons, Clydesdales and Belgians, brought by their owners as exhibits unusual in the area.

They lingered near the midway where a traveling carnival included a carousel, tilt-a-whirl and miniature bumper cars. A dozen stands urged fellows to throw balls, darts, beanbags, whatever, and win a prize! There were few takers. Nickels and dimes weren't plentiful in the 1930s, and even children knew that.

The family straggled back to the women's exhibit building next to the 4-H girls' section. Here were dozens of handiwork items: crocheted sets for chairs or dressers, embroidered pillowcases and dishtowels, hand-smocked boudoir pillows, and tables of articles made from beads, felt, old phonograph records, and other found materials. The practical blouses, skirts, bathrobes, baby clothes and quilts followed. Next was an area of shelves and counters with displays of baked products: breads and rolls, cookies, pies and cakes, Mom's angel food a standout among them. As they entered the 4-H section, Mom spotted her daughter's cabbage — easily the most splendid vegetable there!

The day passed quickly. Tomorrow judges would spend hours evaluating every division. They would examine and rate entries, giving verbal comments for the benefit of exhibitors and bystanders as they awarded ribbons. It would be an exciting day.

The family stopped for pie before they turned homeward. Somehow the trip seemed shorter. The boys were tired, but still reminisced about the fair. The girl was thinking about her big, perfect cabbage. Gardening was rewarding, but it was lots of hard work — dirt and sweat and achy muscles. But the rewards — hundreds of jars of vegetables on the cellar shelves for family meals, fresh vegetables any time one wished, and even the ribbons on the bulletin board in her room — made her feel grown up, doing her share toward her family's well-being.

Recipes

Sautéed Apple Rings

6 medium Jonathan apples	1/4 t. salt
2/3 c. milk	2 T. Crisco
1 egg	2 T. butter
1/2 c. sugar	Powdered sugar
2 T. flour	

Wash and slice across Jonathan apples to 1/2 in. thickness. Prepare a thin batter with milk, egg, sugar, flour, and salt, beating smooth with a rotary beater. In a 10-in. frying pan or electric skillet, heat butter and Crisco to 350F or until fat is bubbling. Dip apples in batter and place in a single layer in hot fat. Sauté about 10 min. or until a delicate brown. Turn slices with a spatula and cook 8-10 min. (You may need to reduce heat if the apples brown too much.)

Lift slices out and drain on brown paper. Sprinkle lightly with powdered sugar. Serve with browned link sausages or patties, two pieces to a serving.

Sautéed Apple Rings and link sausages were a weekend breakfast treat at the College Café in Wayne, Nebraska in the 1930's. The price for the treat was 35 cents. A great Sunday dish.

Jonathan apples are at their best in fall and early winter. They have a distinctive tangy taste that contrasts with pork.

Asparagus Bake

1/2 lb. fresh asparagus	2 T. butter
4 eggs, hard cooked and sliced	1 T. flour
2 pimientos, cut in strips	1/2 t. salt
1 c. grated American cheese	1 c. milk
1 c. soft bread crumbs	

Clean asparagus, snap off ends, and cut spears into 2-in. pieces. Cook 7 min.; drain. Put half the crumbs into a buttered baking dish. Make white sauce with butter, flour, salt, and milk. Layer eggs, pimiento, asparagus, and cheese. Pour sauce over all. Top with crumbs. Bake at 350F for 20 min. and crumbs are golden brown. Serves 4.

Asparagus Casserole

1 lb. fresh asparagus	1/3 t. pepper
1 c. soft bread crumbs	2 T. flour
1/2 c. dried buttered crumbs	1 t. salt
2 c. milk	3 T. butter
1/2 c. grated cheese	4 hard-cooked eggs, chopped

Clean asparagus, snap off ends, and cut into 1-in. lengths. Steam. Test with paring knife; when tender, drain. Make white sauce of butter, flour, milk, and seasonings. Stir in soft bread crumbs. Put a layer of asparagus in bottom of a buttered 1-qt. casserole. Add half the sauce and half the chopped eggs. Repeat layers. Sprinkle with buttered crumbs and grated cheese. Bake at 350F for 20 min. Serves 4.

Asparagus Ham Rolls

Roll a slice of boiled ham around 3 stalks (3-4 in. long) of cooked asparagus. Fasten with toothpicks and place in shallow, buttered baking dish. Cover with cheese sauce. Bake at 350F for 20 min. Sprinkle hot rolls with toasted, slivered almonds. Serve two rolls on toast or rusk.

Cheese sauce can be white sauce with shredded American or Velveeta cheese stirred in and melted. Or use Campbell's Cheddar Cheese soup, slightly diluted.

Lebanese Green Beans I   Maheaba Aossey

1 lb. lamb or beef steak	Salt to taste
1/4 t. allspice	1 large can tomato paste
1 c. onion, chopped	2 c. water, divided
1 lb. fresh green beans	2 T. butter

Cut steak into 1-in. cubes. Clean green beans, snap off ends, and cut in half. In 10-in. frying pan with cover, sauté onion in butter until soft. Add meat, pushing onion to one side. Add allspice and salt to taste, stirring until meat browns on all sides. Add water and cover. Cook for 1-1/2 hr. or until meat is tender. Drain meat, reserving juice. Add green beans to drained meat, and cook over low heat 20 min. Add tomato paste and reserved meat juice. Add 1 c. water; cover and cook until beans are tender. Serve over rice. Serves 8.

Lebanese Green Beans II

1/2 lb. ground chuck steak	1 lb. fresh green beans *or*
1 large onion, chopped	2 cans cut green beans, drained
4 c. tomato juice or sauce	Salt and pepper
1 T. butter	2 cloves garlic, cut fine

If using fresh beans, cut them into 2-in. lengths. In 10-in. skillet or electric frying pan, sauté onion and garlic in butter for 5 min. Push aside and brown ground chuck until it loses pink color. Break up meat into crumbled state. Salt and pepper to taste. Pour tomato juice or sauce over meat in skillet. Heat to boiling. Add beans to skillet. Reduce heat (300F), cover, and simmer for about 1 hr. Taste and add salt if needed. Stir from time to time. Serve with hot rice. Serves 6.

Green Beans with Pimiento

1-1/2 lb. fresh green beans
1 large onion, chopped
1 2-oz. jar pimiento
4 bacon slices
1/4 c. red wine vinegar

4 garlic cloves, chopped fine
1/2 t. salt
1/2 t. black pepper
1/2 t. cumin

Clean and snap ends of green beans. Cook in salted boiling water 4 min. Drain in colander; rinse with cold water to halt cooking. Set aside. In 10-in. skillet with cover, cook bacon until crisp; drain on paper towels or brown paper. Sauté onion and garlic in 2 T. bacon drippings until soft. Chop and add pimiento, vinegar, and seasoning; mix well. Stir in beans. Cover, reduce heat, and simmer 5 min. Place in serving dish and crumble bacon on top. Serves 6.

Bacon Top Baked Beans

1 large can pork and beans
   or 3 #2 cans
1 small onion
6 strips lean bacon

1/4 c. brown sugar
1 t. prepared mustard
1 t. liquid smoke
1/2 c. ketchup

Put beans, sugar, mustard, liquid smoke, and ketchup into 6 x 8 in. casserole and mix well. Peel onion and cut a crisscross an inch into top. Place onion into the middle of the beans. Cut uncooked bacon strips in half and arrange to cover beans. Bake in 350F oven about 45 min.

Lea's Stovetop Beans   Lea Christine Harbour

1 46-oz. can Van Camp or
   Bush's pork and beans
1 medium yellow onion
6 strips lean bacon

1 c. brown sugar
1 T. prepared mustard
1 t. liquid smoke

Combine beans, onion, brown sugar, and mustard in a heavy, oven-proof 4-qt. pan on stove top. Set heat at medium low. Stir ingredients to blend. Cover, stirring occasionally. When beans are simmering, turn heat to low. Cut bacon into 1-1/2 in. pieces, and cook in a sauté pan until lightly browned. Add bacon, 3 T. bacon drippings, and liquid smoke to beans and mix. At this point, beans may be served, or the pan can be covered and put in the oven at 325F for up to 1 hr. Serves 6 generously.

Five-Bean Bake

8 slices bacon
2 large onions, sliced and
   separated
1 c. brown sugar, packed
1 t. dry mustard
1/2 t. salt
1/2 c. vinegar

1/2 t. garlic powder
1 16-oz. can red kidney beans
1 16-oz. can butter beans
1 16-oz. can green beans
1 16-oz. can small green lima beans
1 16-oz. can baked beans

Cut bacon strips into 1-in. pieces, and fry until crisp. Drain on paper towels. Sauté onion rings in bacon grease until transparent. Combine brown sugar, mustard, salt, vinegar, and garlic powder; add to onions and simmer 20 min.

In a large bowl, combine five beans. Add onion mixture and mix gently. Pour into a 9 x 13 in. baking dish. Crumble bacon on top. Bake at 350F for 1 hr. Serves 12.

This casserole was served at Dickey's Prairie Home Restaurant Smorgasbord between Oskaloosa and Sigourney, Iowa, in the 1960's. It is perfect to carry to a big potluck or picnic.

My Lima Bean Casserole

2 c. dry lima beans (baby
   limas preferred)
6 c. cold water
2 to 3 large meaty bones
   from a baked ham
2 small pieces fat ham, cooked

1 medium onion, chopped fine
1 t. salt
1/2 t. pepper
1/2 t. dry mustard
1/2 c. brown sugar, packed
1 #2 can tomatoes and juice

Wash lima beans and put to soak covered with cold water in the evening. In the morning, drain and rinse beans and return them to kettle. Put in the ham bones. Add the pieces of cooked ham, salt, pepper, and enough cold water to cover the beans. Cover and cook on low heat (300F) for 1 hr. or until beans are tender. Add pepper, dry mustard, onion, brown sugar, and tomatoes. Pour this mixture into a deep 3-qt. casserole. Cover and bake at 300F for 1-1/2 to 2 hr., checking to be sure beans do not get dry. To serve, remove bones and ham pieces. Skim excess fat. Serves 6.

This casserole is delicious with cornbread. Dishes such as lima beans and ham were a good choice for busy washdays in the 1920's, when many loads had to be put through a wringer after a wash cycle and then two rinses, hung outdoors on the clothesline, and taken down when dry. This casserole provided hungry farm workers and family with a filling meal that did not require steady attention from the farm wife.

Lima Beans Creole

4 c. fresh lima beans	1 16-oz. can tomatoes with juice
6 slices bacon	1/2 t. salt
1/2 c. onion, chopped fine	1/4 t. pepper
1 T. green pepper, chopped	1/2 t. paprika

Cook beans in boiling salted water about 20-25 min., until tender; drain. Return to cooking pan, and set aside. Cook bacon until crisp, drain on paper towels or brown paper. Sauté onion and green pepper in 2 T. bacon drippings until tender.

Stir onion mixture, crumbled bacon, tomatoes, salt, pepper, and paprika into beans. Cover and simmer 15 min. Serve with cornbread and a green salad. Serves 6.

Buffet Bean Bake

1 can red kidney beans, drained	1 T. prepared mustard
1 can lima beans, drained	4 T. vinegar
1 large can pork and beans	2 c. chili sauce
1/2 lb. bacon	1/2 c. brown sugar, packed
2 large onions, diced	

Mix three beans in large casserole. In a 10-in skillet, partially cook bacon; remove from pan and drain on paper towels or brown paper. Add onion, mustard, vinegar, chili sauce, and brown sugar to bacon drippings. Simmer for 20 min. Pour onion mixture over beans and stir to mix. Top with bacon, cut into half strips. Bake uncovered at 350F for 1 hr. Serves 8 to 10.

Baby Beets Oven Roasted

2 lb. very small red or yellow beets	2 T. red wine vinegar
	Salt and pepper
3 T. olive or salad oil	

Scrub beets and trim tops, leaving 1 in. of top stems. Wrap 2 or 3 beets together in foil, placing packages of beets in shallow pan. Bake at 350F for about 1 hr., or until beets test tender. Cool. Slip skins off beets. Halve or quarter beets and place back in the pan. Whisk together oil and vinegar, with salt and pepper to taste; pour over beets. Roast at 350F for 20 min. Serve with fresh mint for garnish.

This is a fine way to use small beets when you thin them in the garden. Canned very small beets, drained, may be substituted.

Best Harvard Beets

1 can small quartered beets	1/4 c. cider vinegar
1/4 c. sugar	1 c. beet juice
1 T. cornstarch	2 t. butter

Drain beets, saving juice. In a saucepan, mix sugar, cornstarch, cider vinegar, and 1 c. beet juice. Simmer over low heat for 5 min. Adjust salt and pepper to taste. Add quartered beets; simmer 5 min. until hot. Add butter, mix, and serve. Serves 4.

You may substitute orange juice for the vinegar.

Oven Glazed Beets

1 bunch (4 to 6) medium beets	1/4 t. pepper
1/4 c. butter	1 cube chicken bouillon
1/4 c. brown sugar	1/4 c. pecan halves
1/4 t. nutmeg	Dash of salt

Clean beets and remove stems. Cook for 10 min.; drain. Cool, peel, and quarter beets. Cream butter, sugar, nutmeg, pepper, and crumbled bouillon cube. Scatter in a buttered 9 x 9 in. baking pan. Pour 1/4 c. water into pan. Distribute beets on top. Bake at 325F for 30 min. turning several times to glaze beets. Serves 4.

Oven Roasted Broccoli and Cauliflower

2 c. broccoli florets	1/2 t. salt
2 c. cauliflower florets	1/2 t. pepper
4 cloves garlic, chopped	Parmesan cheese
2 T. olive oil	

Combine broccoli, cauliflower, and garlic in 9 x 9 in. pan. Sprinkle olive oil over all. Bake at 450F for 25 min., turning occasionally. Turn into serving bowl and season with salt, pepper, and Parmesan cheese, tossing lightly. Serves 4.

♣ *For quick seasoning of vegetables and gravies, keep a large shaker containing 6 parts salt to 1 part pepper on the counter near the stove.*

Broccoli and Wild Rice Bake

3/4 c. wild rice
1 can cheddar cheese soup
1/2 c. water
Salt and pepper

1 lb. fresh chopped broccoli *or*
  1 pkg frozen
1 can mushroom soup

Mix soups and water in large bowl; blend well. Add raw wild rice and broccoli, and season to taste with salt and pepper. Turn into greased 1-1/2-qt. casserole. Bake uncovered at 350F for 1 hr. Stir before serving.

Brussels Sprouts with Onions

1-1/2 lb. Brussels sprouts
1 T. olive oil
1-1/2 T. Dijon mustard

1/4 c. water
2 T. butter
1 lb. red onions (ca. 2 medium)

Trim onions. Cut in half lengthwise. Turn and cut across in thin slices. In a heavy skillet, sauté onions in olive oil over medium heat until tender. Set aside. Trim outer leaves of Brussels sprouts. Cut off ends, and cut an X across them about 1/4 in. deep. In a large pan of boiling salted water, cook sprouts 8-10 min. until just tender. Drain in colander. Stir mustard and water together and add to sautéed onions in skillet. Add sprouts and butter. Cook over moderately high heat until heated through. Serves 6.

Stuffed Cabbage Rolls

1 large green cabbage
2 lb. ground chuck steak
2 eggs
1/2 c. onion, chopped
1 t. salt
Juice of 1 lemon
Tomato juice as needed

1 #2-1/2 can tomatoes, chopped *or*
  1 can stewed tomatoes
1/2 c. brown sugar, packed
1/2 c. fine dry bread crumbs
1/2 c. raisins
1 additional onion, chopped

Remove core of cabbage. Place cabbage upside down in kettle; pour boiling water over it to cover. Let boil about 10 min. or until leaves are loose. Remove cabbage, drain, and separate leaves.

In large bowl, combine ground chuck, eggs, chopped onion, salt, and pepper. Place about 2 T. meat mixture on center of each cabbage leaf and roll up, tucking ends in. Place rolls in a deep roaster or casserole, making as many layers as needed. Combine rest of ingredients and pour over cabbage rolls. Pour enough water or tomato juice over top to cover. Cover and bake at 350F for 1-1/2 hr. Serves 10.

Grandma's Sour-Sweet Cabbage   Christena Paulsen

3 pt. cabbage   Dash of pepper
1 c. sugar   Salt to taste
3/4 c. vinegar   Butter

Use a cabbage cutter over a washtub or large kettle to cut cabbage. Fill kettles with cut cabbage, adding enough water so cabbage will come to the top when boiling. Boil about 20 min. Drain off water.

In saucepan, combine sugar, vinegar, salt, and pepper to taste. Cook this mixture until sugar is melted. Pour over cabbage. Cook on slow fire 3 hr. Pack into sterilized jars while hot. Seal jars. When you open the jars for use, add 1 t. butter per pint when heating it, and add sugar if you desire it to be sweeter.

The amount of vinegar should be 1/2 to 3/4 c. per 1 c. sugar, depending on how sour you want it to be. This amount will take care of about 3 pt. cabbage after it has been cooked.

At my request, Grandma sent me this recipe on a penny post card postmarked Worthington, Minnesota, in 1942, and I have used it for 60 years. It is good hot or cold.

Danish Sweet-Sour Red Cabbage   Christena Paulsen

1 2-lb. firm head of new red   2/3 c. red wine vinegar
   cabbage, sliced very thin   1 T. caraway seeds
1/2 t. salt   1/2 c. butter
1 c. brown sugar, packed   1 medium onion, minced
1/4 t. white pepper   1 can cranberry sauce, jellied style
2 c. water

Discard any of the very thick or tough white core of cabbage. In a 3-qt. saucepan, cook cabbage with 2 c. water for 15 min. Drain, reserving 1 c. liquid. Add salt, sugar, pepper, vinegar, caraway seeds, and onion. Bring to a boil. Reduce heat to medium low and cook 1 hr., stirring occasionally. Add 1/2 c. reserved cooking liquid if it seems dry. Stir in cranberry sauce and butter; mix gently. Cook for 1 hr. Taste for seasoning. Cabbage should have a mild vinegar taste as well as sweet brown sugar flavor. Remove from heat. Let flavors blend. Serve hot as a vegetable dotted with a little butter. Chilled, it is a tasty relish with roasts. Refrigerated, it keeps for weeks. Yield: 8 cups.

Carrot Ring   Aunt Millie Manning

3 c. cooked, mashed carrots	3 T. melted butter
1/2 c. cream	5 eggs, separated
1/2 c. cracker crumbs	Salt and pepper

Cook and mash carrots to make 3 c. In large bowl, combine carrots, cream, cracker crumbs, melted butter, beaten egg yolks, and salt and pepper to taste. Beat egg whites until stiff and fold into the carrot mixture. Pour into a well-buttered 6-c. ring mold, setting pan in hot water to bake at 350F for 30-35 min. or until a silver knife inserted in carrots comes out clean. Turn mold out on serving plate and fill center with creamed peas or other green vegetable. Serves 6.

♣ *Add 1/2 t. sugar when cooking peas, corn, or carrots to help bring out flavor.*

Carrot Soufflé I   Piccadilly Restaurant

3/4 c. shortening	1/2 t. soda
1/2 c. brown sugar, packed	1/2 t. salt
1 egg	1 t. baking powder
2 c. grated carrots	1 t. nutmeg
4 T. orange juice	1 t. cinnamon
1 c. flour	1 t. cloves
1/4 t. pepper	1 c. pecans, chopped

Cream shortening and sugar. Add egg and beat well. Sift flour with soda, baking powder, salt, and spices, and add to creamed mixture. Stir in orange juice and grated carrots. Blend well. Add chopped pecans and mix. Spoon into a buttered 1-qt. casserole. *Refrigerate overnight.* Remove 30 min. before baking. Bake at 350F for 1 hr. Serve immediately. Serves 6 to 8.

Carrot Souffle II

1 c. light cream	1/2 t. nutmeg
1 c. sugar	1/2 t. cinnamon
2 eggs	1/2 t. cloves
1 t. vanilla	2 lb. carrots
1/2 t. salt	

Peel and slice carrots. Cook in salted water until tender; drain in colander. Combine all ingredients in blender or food processor; blend until smooth. Pour into buttered 2-qt. casserole. Bake at 400F for 30 min. Serve immediately. Serves 6.

Baked Corn Casserole   **Shirley Sisk**

1/2 c. celery, chopped	1 can celery soup
1/2 c. onion, chopped	1 c. sour cream
1/2 c. green pepper, chopped	1/2 c. grated cheddar cheese
1 can shoe peg corn, drained	1 stack Ritz crackers
Salt and pepper	1/2 c. melted margarine

In large bowl, combine corn, soup, and sour cream; blend well. Add chopped vegetables, grated cheese, and salt and pepper to taste. Mix well. Place in greased 9 x 9 in. casserole. Crush crackers and mix with melted margarine. Sprinkle atop corn mix. Bake at 350F for 40-45 min. Serves 6 to 8.

This is colorful and packed with good flavor!

♣ *If a recipe calls for cracker or cookie crumbs, place the crackers in a ziptop plastic bag, close it, and use a rolling pin or the heel of your hand to crush the crackers.*

Delicious Creamed Corn   **"Aunt Maude" Maddison**

1 pt. fresh corn, cut from cob	2 eggs
1/4 c. butter	Salt and pepper
1 c. light cream	1 c. cracker crumbs

Cut corn from the cob, pressing the creamy part from the ear with a knife. Beat eggs and blend with cream; mix well with butter and corn. Put in buttered 1-1/2-qt. baking dish. Cover with cracker crumbs. Bake at 350F for 30 min. Serves 6.

As every schoolchild needs to learn, corn is one of the many contributions of the Americas to the rest of the world. It was a staple for Native Americans, who introduced it to settlers. Without corn and beans, the Pilgrims probably would not have survived their first year in New England. Although corn is found throughout North and South America, Iowa is the state "where the tall corn grows," and Iowans have many recipes making use of it.

Corn and Oyster Scallop

2 c. whole kernel corn	Pinch of salt
1 pt. medium oysters	Dash of pepper
3 T. butter	1-1/2 c. milk
2 T. flour	1 c. buttered cracker crumbs

Heat corn. Drain oysters and add enough water to the liquor to make 3/4 c. In a saucepan, melt butter. Blend in flour and seasonings. Gradually add milk and oyster liquor, stirring until thick and smooth. In a greased 1-1/2-qt. baking dish, arrange alternate layers of corn, oysters, crumbs, and sauce, topping with crumbs. Bake in a hot oven (400F) for 15-20 min. until scallop is bubbling and crumbs are brown. Serves 5 or 6.

♣ *Oysters are seasonal. Look for them from September through April — "months with an R." Small size is perfect for a scallop or stew.*

Corn-Tomato Casserole with Garlic   Myrtle Hart

2 cans whole kernel corn, drained	1/2 t. pepper
1 #2 can whole tomatoes	2 cloves garlic, minced
1/2 t. salt	3 T. melted butter
1 t. sugar	2 c. crushed saltines

In a large bowl, combine salt, sugar, pepper, and garlic with tomatoes; break up tomatoes with spoon or spatula. In a greased 1-1/2-qt. casserole, layer first half the corn, then a third of the saltines, then half the tomatoes. Repeat layers, and end with saltines on top. Drizzle with melted butter. Bake at 400F for 30 min. Serves 6.

Corn Pudding

8-10 ears of yellow sweet corn	2 T. flour
3 eggs	4 T. melted butter
1/2 t. salt	1/2 c. half and half

Cut corn from cobs, scraping ears to get all the creamy part. Beat eggs well. Add salt, flour, melted butter, and half and half and blend until smooth. Add corn. Pour into a buttered 1-1/2-qt. baking dish set in a larger pan of hot water. Bake at 350F about 30 min. Stir mixture lightly. Continue baking until a silver knife comes out clean. Serves 4 or 5.

Savory Corn Bake

1/2 lb. thick sliced bacon *or* 1 c. diced ham	1 c. milk
3/4 c. flour	1 16-oz. can cream-style sweet corn
2 T. cornmeal	1/2 c. green pepper, chopped
1 t. salt	3 t. baking powder
1/8 t. pepper	2 eggs, divided

Fry bacon until crisp. Drain on paper towels. Crumble. In a large bowl, combine unbeaten egg yolks and milk; beat thoroughly. Sift together flour, cornmeal, salt, and pepper, and add to egg mixture; mix until smooth. Add corn, green pepper, and the crumbled bacon. Mix well.

Combine egg whites with baking powder. Beat until stiff. Fold into corn mixture. Turn into well-greased 2-qt. casserole. Bake at 350F about 1 hr. For extra light soufflé texture, set casserole in a pan of hot water during baking. Serves 6.

Spider Corn Pone

2 T. vegetable oil	1 T. sugar
2 c. yellow cornmeal	2 c. buttermilk
1/2 c. flour	2 eggs
1-1/2 t. baking powder	1/4 t. salt

Preheat oven to 450F. Heat oil in a cast-iron skillet for 5 min. Keep hot. Sift cornmeal, flour, baking powder, sugar, and salt into a mixing bowl. Make a well in the center. Beat eggs slightly and pour with buttermilk into dry ingredients. Stir briskly to moisten. Pour batter into the hot skillet. Reduce oven heat to 425F. Bake at 425F for 25 min. or until golden brown. Serve with honey butter.

Honey Butter: Blend 2/3 c. honey with 1 stick of soft butter or margarine or cholesterol-free low-fat spread. Keep refrigerated. Honey butter is wonderful on toast or pancakes too.

In the pioneer Midwest, corn pone was cooked in a spider set over the coals. A crusty, flavorful bread resulted — our cornbread.

Garlic Cheese Grits I   Hotel Iola

4 c. boiling water	1 roll garlic cheese
1 t. salt	2 eggs, beaten with
1 c. quick-cooking grits	1/4 c. water
1/2 c. butter or margarine	

Into boiling water, add salt and grits very slowly, stirring with wooden spoon over medium heat. When grits are quite thick, add cut-up butter and cheese. Stir well. Reduce heat to low and cover grits. Take 1 c. of grits mixture out and add it to the beaten eggs, beating well. Return to hot grits mixture slowly and blend. Pour grits into a buttered 1-1/2-qt. casserole. Bake uncovered at 350F about 1 hr. Spoon servings onto plates with ham, muffins, etc. Serves 6 to 8.

The Iola Hotel in Natchez, Mississippi, is an elegant antebellum hotel surrounded by mansions open to visitors during Pilgrimage weeks. Its meals represent Southern cooking at its finest.

Garlic Cheese Grits II

4 c. water
1/2 t. salt
1 c. quick-cooking grits
1/2 c. butter

2 large cloves garlic, slit
1/2 lb. Velveeta cheese, diced
1 T. Worcestershire sauce

Bring water with salt to a boil in a 2-qt. saucepan. Stir in grits gradually, add garlic, cover, and reduce heat to low. Stir occasionally. Cook about 5-6 min. until thick. Remove from heat. Remove garlic. Add butter, cheese, and Worcestershire sauce. Serve as cooked cereal if desired, about 1 c. per serving with whole milk.

Fried Grits: Pour grits into 3 x 5 in. bread pans that have been rinsed with cold water. Refrigerate. (If desired, you can stir in 1/4 c. chopped leftover ham.) Turn the chilled grits onto a flour-sprinkled square of waxed paper. Cut grits into thick slices. Dredge all sides in flour. Sauté in a well-oiled skillet until crisp and golden brown. Serve with syrup or butter.

These fried grits remind me of the wonderful scrapple Grandma served at butchering time on the farm!

Fried Okra

1 lb. fresh okra
2 c. buttermilk
1 c. flour
1 c. cornmeal
1 t. baking powder

1 t. salt
1/4 t. cayenne
8 slices bacon
Canola oil

Wash, trim off ends, and slice okra into 1/2-in. slices. Cover with buttermilk and refrigerate 1 hr. Sift flour, baking powder, salt, and cayenne and combine with cornmeal in shallow baking dish.

In large cast-iron skillet, fry bacon to desired doneness. Drain on paper towels in baking dish; place in slow oven to keep warm. Add oil to depth of 1-1/2 to 2 in. and heat to 375F.

Remove okra from buttermilk with slotted spoon. Dip as many slices in cornmeal mixture as needed to fill skillet. Fry okra until golden brown on both sides, 4-5 min. Drain on paper towels. Serve with bacon and scrambled eggs. Serves 4.

My Scalloped Onions

12 to 15 medium-sized
   mild onions
3 T. butter
3 T. flour

2 c. milk or half and half
2 c. crushed saltines
1/4 c. melted butter
Salt and pepper

Peel onions, trimming top and root lightly. Cook onions in salted water until tender but not soft. Drain and set aside.

Prepare white sauce in saucepan by melting butter over low heat, stirring in flour, and gradually adding milk. Heat, stirring constantly, until thickened. Season to taste with salt and pepper.

In buttered 9x12-in. baking dish, arrange onions. Combine crushed saltines with melted butter, and distribute 2/3 over onions. Pour white sauce over all. Top with remaining buttered cracker crumbs. Bake at 400F for 30 to 35 min. until bubbling and crumbs are brown. Serve 6 or 8.

Parsnip Bake

6 fresh parsnips
1/2 c. seasoned flour
Salt and pepper

1/4 c. butter, melted
1/2 c. half and half

Clean, peel, and cook parsnips in salted water until tender but not soft. Drain well. Cut parsnips into serving pieces about 4 in. long, halving large parsnips length-wise. Roll pieces in flour and melted butter. Place in shallow, buttered 8-in. square baking dish and spread remaining butter over them. Bake at 375F for 15 min. Pour the half and half over and bake 15 min. more. Serves 6.

Glazed Parsnips

6 fresh parsnips
2 c. water
1/2 c. flour

2 T. butter
2 T. orange juice
1 T. brown sugar

Wash and peel parsnips. Leave whole if small, or cut lengthwise in several slices if large. Boil in water until just tender. Do not overcook. Drain and cool. Roll pieces in flour before browning in hot butter (325F). Place in buttered 8-in. square baking dish. Top with brown sugar and orange juice. Bake at 325F for 20 min., turning in glaze once or twice. Serves 6.

Fresh Roasted Peppers

6 large firm red bell peppers	1 T. vinegar
1 clove garlic, minced	1/2 t. salt
1/4 c. olive oil	

Rinse and dry the peppers. Place on baking sheet and broil 4-5 min. on each side, 4-5 in. from heat. The entire surface of the pepper should be blistered and somewhat blackened. Cut each pepper lengthwise into 8 wedges or strips. While still hot, scrape off the skin with a sharp knife; scrape off the ribs and seeds.

In a shallow bowl, mix garlic, oil, vinegar, and salt. Add the peppers and turn to coat. Cover and refrigerate at least 4 hr. before serving.

This dish was served as hors d'oeuvre at a seaside restaurant in Lisbon, Portugal, along with plates of small fried fish. We found them as addictive as peanuts! It is also found throughout Italy and in many fine Italian restaurants elsewhere.

♣ *Cut washed, seeded bell peppers and red peppers and store in plastic freezer bags for quick use.*

My Stuffed Peppers with Creole Sauce

Shells & Stuffing:	*Creole Sauce:*
1-1/2 lb. ground chuck steak	1 large onion, minced
1 small onion, minced	1 T. green pepper, chopped
1/2 c. green pepper, chopped	1 T. red pepper, chopped
Shortening	1/2 t. garlic, minced
1 16-oz. can diced tomatoes	1 T. shortening
2 c. cooked rice	1/4 t. chili powder
1/2 t. salt	1 can beef broth
1/2 t. chili powder	2 large cans tomato sauce
1/2 t. paprika	1 can tomato paste
1/8 t. pepper	1 t. seasoned salt
3 medium green peppers	1/2 t. pepper
3 medium round red peppers	1 T. cornstarch

Shells: Wash peppers, cut in half horizontally, and remove seeds, white membrane, and stem. Cut a half-inch slice across one red and one green pepper and reserve for the sauce. In a saucepan, put six of the pepper halves into boiling water to cook 5 min. Remove and drain. Cook the remaining halves 5 min. and drain. Set aside.

Stuffing: In large skillet, sauté small chopped onion and chopped green pepper in 1 T. shortening for 5 min. Push to one side and brown meat, breaking it into very small bits as it cooks for about 8-10 min. or until it loses pinkness. Drain off fat. Put browned meat, onion, pepper, tomatoes with juice, rice, salt, chili powder, and pepper into large bowl. Mix thoroughly. Divide stuffing among the 12 pepper shells. Spoon about 1/2 c. of stuffing into each pepper shell, rounding tops. Set the stuffed peppers upright in one layer in a 9 x 13 in. baking pan. Sprinkle with paprika. Bake at 350F for 30 min. or until brown and pepper shell is tender. Remove from oven and spoon hot Creole sauce over each pepper. Alternate red and green peppers on serving platter, and surround them with additional sauce.

Creole Sauce: In 10-in. skillet, sauté large onion, chopped green and red pepper, and garlic in 1 T. shortening until tender. Sprinkle with chili powder and seasoned salt. Add beef broth and tomato sauce and paste; blend well and heat through. Combine a spoonful or two of cold water with cornstarch, make a paste, and stir into pan. Heat, stirring, until sauce thickens. Adjust salt and pepper to taste.

♣ *Save butter and margarine wrappers to grease sauté pan.*

Polenta

4-1/2 c. chicken broth	1 c. Parmesan cheese, grated
1 1/3 c. yellow cornmeal	1/2 t. salt
3/4 c. half and half	2 T. butter

In large saucepan, bring broth to a boil. Add cornmeal, very slowly, a tablespoonful at a time, stirring constantly. When all cornmeal has been added, reduce heat (300F) and simmer 20 min., stirring often. Stir in half and half, butter, and cheese. Add salt and pepper to taste.

Polenta may be used as the base when serving meat stews, in place of rice or noodles. Warm polenta may be poured into bread pans that have been rinsed with cold water. Chill. When set, unmold polenta and wrap in foil or Saran Wrap. Store in refrigerator or freezer. Cut in slices 1/2 in. thick, roll in flour, and fry in an oiled skillet until crisp. Serve with syrup or applesauce.

Scrapple: This delicious breakfast dish was made with a cornmeal mush base, with bits of cooked pork ("scraps") added before the mush was poured into molds. Whenever farmers butchered, every scrap was converted into tasty specialties. Today one can buy polenta in rolls in the refrigerated section of the supermarket.

Latkes / Potato Pancakes

2 large russet potatoes	1/2 t. baking powder
1 medium onion	1/2 c. flour
2 eggs, beaten	1/2 t. salt

Peel potatoes and grate through medium knife of grater with onion. Press and drain off juices. Combine potato-onion mixture with eggs, salt, baking powder, and flour. Mix well. Drop by heaping spoonfuls into a well-oiled electric skillet and fry slowly until golden brown. Turn and brown second side. Drain briefly on paper towels. Serve with warm applesauce. Yield: 6 latkes. Recipe may be doubled.

This traditional Hanukkah dish became a family favorite, especially delicious for weekend breakfasts.

Party Potatoes

8 large Idaho baking potatoes	1 t. garlic powder
1 8-oz. pkg Philadelphia	1/2 t. pepper
cream cheese	1 t. salt
1 8-oz. carton sour cream	3 T. butter

Peel and quarter potatoes, place in large saucepan, and cover with salted water. Boil 15 min. or until very tender. Drain. Using electric mixer, beat potatoes. Add chunks of cream cheese, sour cream, 2 T. butter, salt, pepper, and garlic powder. Beat on medium speed, mixing well, until mixture is very light.

Spoon potatoes into a baking/serving dish sprayed with Pam. Make a dent in the top and fill with 1 T. butter. If you plan to serve at once, bake at 325F for 30 min. If you are serving within 6 to 24 hr., cool potato mixture. Cover tightly with foil and place in refrigerator. Remove to room temperature 1 hr. before serving. After 20 min., place in 350F oven for 30-35 min. covered with foil. Uncover for the last 10 min. Serves 8.

This dish is a favorite with men. To make it healthier, use low-fat cream cheese, sour cream, and shortening. Cut costs by buying a 5- or 10-pound sack of potatoes (it costs less than a bag of potato chips!).

Twice-Baked Potatoes

6 large baking potatoes	8 T. fresh chives, chopped
Vegetable oil	1 pt. dairy sour cream
1/2 c. soft margarine	3/4 t. salt
6 strips lean bacon	1/2 t. pepper
2 T. onion, chopped fine	

Scrub potatoes and rub skins with oil. Prick skins with fork. Place on a shallow baking pan and bake at 400F until they can be pierced with a thin paring knife, about 1 hr. 10 min. Remove from oven. Cool to handle. Cut a thin slice across top of potatoes. With a tablespoon, remove potato pulp to a mixing bowl, leaving enough inside the potato skin to have a shell about 1/4 in. thick.

Cook bacon until crisp, drain on paper towels, and crumble. Combine removed potato pulp with margarine, onion, half the chives, sour cream, salt, and pepper. Mash and whip to consistency of mashed potatoes. Taste to correct salt. Stuff the shells with equal amounts of potato mixture and top with crumbled bacon, remaining half of chives, and paprika. Place in shallow baking pan, cover with foil pierced with several slits, and bake at 375F for 8-10 min. to heat through. Serves 6.

Baked Potatoes with Cheese Sauce

1/4 c. butter	1/2 t. dry mustard
1/4 c. flour	1/4 t. seasoned salt
2 c. hot milk	Pinch of pepper
1 c. grated mild cheddar cheese	Pinch of Accent
1/2 t. salt	Baking potatoes (1 per person)

Scrub baking potatoes and rub skins with oil. (For crisper skin, omit oil.) Prick skins with a fork. Place on shallow baking pan and bake at 400F for 1 hr. or until tender.

Cheese Sauce: In saucepan, melt butter. Add flour, stirring until smooth, and gradually add hot milk, stirring over low heat until thick. Add cheese, salt, and seasonings. Stir until cheese melts. Makes 2-1/2 cups, enough for 8-10 baked potatoes or a 2-qt. casserole of broccoli or cauliflower.

The potato is another contribution from the Americas to the world — first culti-vated in the Andes, the potato comes in hundreds of varieties. Many potato recipes can be found in many countries, but there are few so delicious as a simple baked potato with a little butter and salt and pepper. Should you wish for just a little something more, this cheese sauce is great!

Crunchy Baked Potatoes

4 or more large baking potatoes	1 T. melted butter
1/3 c. butter or oil	Salt and pepper
1 c. crushed cornflakes	Paprika

Peel and halve potatoes lengthwise. Parboil for 10 min.; drain. Melt butter in 9 x 13 in. baking pan. Place potatoes in pan and turn them twice to coat, flat side up to bake. Sprinkle lightly with salt and paprika. Mix crushed cornflakes with melted butter and sprinkle on top. Bake 30 min. at 350F until potatoes are tender. Serves 6.

Hash Brown Potato Bake   **Wally Harmon**

3/4 stick margarine
1 c. sour cream
1 can cream of chicken soup
1/4 c. chopped onion
1/2 t. salt
2 T. melted margarine

Dash of pepper
2 c. grated cheddar cheese
1 2-lb. bag of frozen hash brown
    potatoes, thawed
2 c. cornflakes

In 10-in. skillet, melt 3/4 stick of margarine over low heat. Mix with sour cream. Add soup, onion, salt and pepper, and cheese; mix well. Add hash browns, and mix lightly. Pour into buttered 9 x 12 in. Pyrex baking dish. Crush cornflakes and mix with 2 T. melted margarine. Sprinkle on hash brown mixture. Bake at 350F for 45-60 min. Serve with a crisp green salad and fresh fruit cup. Serves 12.

Sue's Hash Browns and Sauerkraut   **Sue Ahrens**

4 slices bacon
1/2 c. onion, chopped
1-1/2 lb. frozen hash
   brown potatoes, thawed
1 16-oz. can sauerkraut

1 T. instant chicken bouillon
1-1/2 c. boiling water
1/2 t. salt
Dash of pepper

In large skillet, brown bacon. Add onion and cook until tender. Separate potatoes and add. Drain and add sauerkraut; reserve juice. Mix bouillon with boiling water and pour over mixture. Add salt and pepper. Cover and cook in skillet or pour into a greased 2-qt. casserole and bake in oven at 350F for 1 hr. Serves 8.

Variation: Brown bacon in Dutch oven; remove bacon and drain on paper towels or brown paper. Add 1 or 2 T. butter to bacon fat. Dredge 8 pork chops in 1/4 c. flour, and brown both sides well. Add onion and bacon; cook until onion is tender. Combine 2 T. bouillon, 3 c. boiling water, and sauerkraut juice. If desired, add 1 t. caraway seed. Bake at 350F for 1-1/2 to 2 hr., turning mixture and pork chops gently with slotted spoon once or twice.

An unusual combination that gives potatoes and pork chops extra pizzazz.

Hot Potato Salad

6 large white potatoes,
   Maine or Russet
1/4 c. bacon, diced fine
1/4 c. onion, chopped
1 T. flour
1 t. salt

1/4 t. pepper
1 T. sugar
2/3 c. cider vinegar
1/3 c. water
1/2 t. celery seed
3 T. chopped parsley

Cook potatoes in jackets until tender. Cool, peel, and slice thinly into large bowl. Fry bacon crisp; remove from pan and drain on paper towels. Add onion to drippings and sauté 1 min. Blend in flour, salt, pepper, and sugar. Add vinegar and water. Cook, stirring well, 10 min. or until thickened. Pour over cooked potatoes, add crumbled bacon, and toss gently. Serve warm, sprinkled with celery seed and chopped parsley. Serves 6.

Laurel's New Potatoes   Laurel Harbour

1 lb. new potatoes   1/4 c. chives, chopped
1/2 green pepper   1/4 c. parsley, chopped
1/2 red or yellow pepper   2 or 3 T. olive oil or Italian dressing
1/4 c. green onions or shallots, Salt and pepper
    chopped

Clean new potatoes, slice in half, and cook in salted water until al dente; drain and place in large bowl. Chop and add peppers and other vegetables. Drizzle oil over all, grind pepper and salt to taste. Mix gently. Set aside 1 hr. to blend flavors. Serve warm or cold. Keeps well tightly covered in refrigerator. Serves 4.

Oven Roasted Potatoes Greek Style

8 medium yellow Yukon   Juice of 1 lemon
    potatoes   Crumbled oregano to taste
1 c. olive oil or melted margarine   Salt and pepper
1-1/2 c. water

Scrub potatoes and cut each into 6 or 8 wedges. Sprinkle oregano, salt, and pepper into a 9 x 12 in. baking pan. Add potatoes and turn to coat them well. Combine oil, water, and lemon juice and pour evenly over the potato slices. Bake at 350F for 1 hr., turning potatoes once. Increase heat to 375F and brown for 20 min. Serves 6.

Scalloped Potatoes

4 c. raw potatoes   1 t. salt
3 T. butter   Pepper
3 T. flour   1 c. Velveeta cheese, cubed
1-1/2 c. milk

Peel and slice 4 or 5 medium potatoes thin. Place in shallow, buttered baking dish.

In a saucepan, melt butter, blend in flour, then add milk slowly. Season with salt and pepper. Cook sauce until smooth and boiling. Reduce heat and add cheese.

Pour over sliced potatoes. Cover with foil. Bake at 350F for 2 hr. Remove foil for the last 20 min. Serves 6.

Scalloped Potatoes with Cream

6 medium potatoes   1 pt. half and half
1 small onion, chopped (optional)   Salt and pepper

Peel and slice potatoes into a buttered casserole, allowing one potato per person. If desired, layer chopped onion with potatoes. Salt and pepper generously. Pour half and half over to almost cover potatoes. Do not use flour. Bake, uncovered, at 375F for 30 min. Use a fork to mix potatoes lightly, and reduce heat to 350F. Bake until nicely browned. Serves 6.

Scalloped Potato Casserole

1 2-lb. sack frozen hash   1 can cream of celery soup
    brown potatoes, thawed   1 8-oz. carton sour cream
1 t. salt   2 c. cheddar cheese, grated
1/4 t. pepper   1/4 c. melted margarine
1/2 c. chopped onion   2 c. crushed cornflakes

In large bowl, blend soup and sour cream. Add seasonings and cheese; stir well. Gently fold in potatoes. Pour into a greased 2-qt. casserole. Pour margarine over all. Sprinkle cornflakes on top. Bake at 350F for 45 min. If you wish, bake in two 1-qt. casseroles; serve one immediately and freeze the other. Serves 8 to 10.

Ratatouille I

1 large onion, chopped   2 medium green peppers
2 cloves garlic, minced   6 ripe tomatoes
1/3 c. olive oil   1/2 c. pitted black olives
1 large eggplant   1/4 t. dried basil
1 large zucchini   1 t. salt
1/2 t. pepper   2 T. parsley, chopped

Peel and cube eggplant. Slice zucchini thin. Seed and dice green peppers. Cut tomatoes in 1/2-in. dice. Sauté onion and garlic in oil until tender. Add eggplant, salt, pepper, and basil. Cover and simmer 5 min. over medium heat. Stir in zucchini and green pepper; cook 5 min. covered. Add tomatoes and olives, and cook until thoroughly heated. Sprinkle with chopped parsley. Serve hot or cold. Serves 6 to 8.

Ratatouille is an excellent way to use the garden vegetables plentiful in August and September. A simple dish, the key to its flavor is very ripe, very fresh vegetables. If you do not have a garden, watch for farmers' markets with their abundance of fresh, locally grown produce. Some grocery stores also take care to stock ripe, local produce.

♣ *To draw off some of the water in eggplant, slice it and arrange on a wire rack in a roaster. Sprinkle the slices with salt, which will draw out water. After an hour or so, dry eggplant with paper towels, and proceed with recipe.*

Ratatouille II

1/2 c. olive oil
2 cloves garlic, crushed
1 large onion
1 large eggplant
2 medium green peppers

6 ripe tomatoes
2 medium zucchini
Salt
Pepper

Wash and slice onion, eggplant, peppers, tomatoes, and zucchini very thin. In heavy kettle, heat olive oil. Sauté garlic and onion for 5 min.; then add all other vegetables. Cook on medium high heat for 20 min., stirring from time to time with slotted spoon. Season with salt and freshly ground pepper to taste, and reduce heat. Simmer, stirring occasionally, until vegetables have lost color, 1 to 1-1/2 hr. Serve hot or cold. Serves 6 to 8.

Green Rice I   Stevenson's Apple Farm

3 c. cooked rice
1 c. parsley, chopped
1/3 c. green onion, chopped
1/4 c. green pepper, chopped
1/2 c. cheddar cheese, grated
1/2 t. seasoned salt
1/2 t. pepper

1 clove garlic, minced
1 14-1/2-oz. can evaporated milk
2 eggs, beaten
1/2 c. olive or vegetable oil
1 t. salt
1/4 t. Accent
Juice and grated rind of 1 lemon

In large bowl, combine all ingredients and mix with rice. Turn into 2-qt. casserole sprayed with Pam. Sprinkle with paprika. Bake at 350F about 45 min. or until it has the consistency of a soft custard. Serves 6 to 8.

Green Rice II

2 eggs, beaten	1/2 t. dry mustard
2 c. milk	1/2 c. Mazola oil
2 c. New York sharp	1/2 c. chopped parsley
cheddar cheese, grated	Salt and pepper
3 c. cold cooked rice	2 c. cooked ham, cubed (optional)

In large bowl, combine all ingredients. Season with salt and pepper to taste. Pour into greased 2-qt. casserole. Bake at 350F for 1 hr. Serves 6 to 8.

Green Chili Rice

2 4-oz. cans green chili, chopped	4 c. cooked white rice (not Minute)
2 c. dairy sour cream	1/2 t. salt
2 c. cheddar cheese, grated	Dash of pepper
2 c. mozzarella cheese, grated	

Drain chili, and combine with sour cream. Place half the rice in greased 1-1/2-qt. casserole, cover with half the sour cream mixture. Sprinkle half the grated cheeses atop. Then layer other half of rice, sour cream, and grated cheeses. Sprinkle with salt and pepper. Cover and bake at 350F for 25 min. Remove cover and bake until brown and bubbling, about 10-15 min. Serves 8.

Saffron Rice

2 T. butter	1 bay leaf
1/2 c. onion, chopped fine	1 c. dry rice
1/2 t. garlic, minced	1-1/2 c. chicken broth
1/2 t. thread (or powdered)	Salt and fresh pepper to taste
saffron	

Melt 1 T. butter in saucepan and sauté onion and garlic until onion is tender. Add saffron, bay leaf, and raw rice; stir to blend. Add broth, salt, and pepper; bring to boil. Cover and let simmer exactly 17 min. Discard bay leaf. Stir in the remaining 1 T. of butter. Serves 4.

When in Spain, I bought some packets of saffron, a rare seasoning collected from the blooms of autumn crocuses. I used it to prepare saffron rice. It tastes as good as it looks! Try turmeric as a substitute if saffron proves hard to find.

Special Rice Casserole

2 c. raw rice (not Instant)	1 4-oz. can mushrooms, drained
2 cans chicken broth	1/2 c. onion, chopped fine
1/2 c. butter	1 can sliced water chestnuts
1 c. celery, cut fine	Salt and pepper

In heavy skillet, melt butter over low heat. Add rice and stir until it begins to brown. Remove from heat. Put rice in greased 2-qt. casserole. Bring broth to boil and pour over rice. Cook, covered, at 350F for 30 min. Then add vegetables and season with salt and pepper to taste. Stir with rice, cover, and bake about 30 min. more. Fluff rice. Garnish with chopped parsley. Serve as a side dish or as the base for chicken or meat.

Spinach Soufflé

2 10-oz. pkg frozen chopped spinach	1 c. Parmesan cheese, grated
	1 T. flour
1 T. onion, diced fine	3 T. soft butter
3 eggs, beaten	Dash of nutmeg
1 c. dairy sour cream	Salt and pepper

Cook spinach in 1 c. water according to package directions. Drain. Add remaining ingredients to cooked spinach and mix well. Season with nutmeg, salt, and pepper to taste. Pour into a greased 1-1/2-qt. casserole. Bake at 350F for 30-35 min. or until set when tested with a silver knife. Serve at once. Serves 6 to 8.

Baked Acorn Squash

Cut squash in half, removing seeds. Place cut side down in shallow baking pan. Add 1/4 in. water. Bake at 400F for 25 min. Turn squash up. Fill with 1 t. butter and 1 T. brown sugar or maple syrup. Bake at 325F until squash is tender. Serves 6.

Squash is another contribution of the Americas to the world. It comes in many varieties, but the acorn squash can be found in stores throughout the country labeled "Iowa squash," perhaps because it grows so well there.

Stuffed Acorn Squash

3 small acorn squash	1/4 t. cloves
2 tart apples	1/4 t. salt
3 T. brown sugar	3 T. melted margarine
1/4 t. cinnamon	6 brown-and-serve link sausages

Cut each acorn squash in half. Discard seeds and pith. Place squash, cut side down, in a 9 x 13 in. pan. Pour 1 c. hot water around them. Bake at 375F for 20 min. Remove from oven and set aside.

Peel, core, and chop apples. In a small bowl, combine with brown sugar, spices, salt, and margarine. Place 1 link of sausage in each acorn half. Divide the apple mixture evenly among acorn halves. Return to baking pan and bake at 375F for 40 min. or until squash is tender. Serves 6.

Butternut Squash Soufflé

3 c. baked butternut squash, mashed	1/2 c. butter
1 c. milk	3 eggs
1 c. sugar	1/4 t. salt
1/2 t. nutmeg	Dash of pepper

Mix all ingredients, beat well, and put in 1-qt. baking dish. Top with 1 t. butter. Bake at 350F for 40 min.

Squash are plentiful in our markets all fall and winter. Bright yellow vegetables are very nutritious.

Baked Summer Squash / Zucchini

2 lb. summer squash *and /or* zucchini	1 can cream of chicken soup
1/4 c. onion, chopped	1 c. dairy sour cream
1 c. carrot, shredded	8 oz. herb seasoned stuffing mix
	1/2 c. butter, melted

Slice squash thin and cook with chopped onion in salted water until tender; drain. In large bowl, combine soup and sour cream; blend well. Fold in squash and onion. In separate bowl, pour melted butter over stuffing mix. Spread half stuffing in bottom of greased 1-1/2-qt. casserole. Spoon squash mixture on top. Sprinkle rest of stuffing on top. Bake, uncovered, at 350F for 25-30 min. Serves 6.

Candied Sweet Potatoes

6 medium sweet potatoes or yams	3 T. butter
1 t. salt	24 large marshmallows
2/3 c. brown sugar	Pepper

Scrub potatoes and put them in a large saucepan; cover with water. Cook on medium heat (350F) for 20 min. or until potatoes can be pierced with a paring knife. Drain and cool potatoes and remove skin. Cut crosswise into slices 1/2 in. thick. Place one layer in a well-greased 9 x 13 in. baking pan. Salt and pepper. Sprinkle half the brown sugar, dot with half the butter, and place 12 marshmallows on top. Add a second layer of potatoes and each ingredient, with marshmallows on top. Bake at 375F for 20-25 min. Serves 8 or 9.

Coconut Topped Sweet Potatoes

3 c. mashed sweet potatoes
2 T. sugar
1/4 c. half and half
3 T. melted margarine
2 eggs, beaten
1/2 t. vanilla

Topping:
3/4 c. brown sugar, packed
2 T. flour
1 c. flaked coconut
1 c. pecans, chopped
3 T. melted margarine

In large bowl, combine mashed sweet potatoes, sugar, half and half, 3 T. margarine, eggs, and vanilla. Beat well and pour into a buttered 1-1/2-qt. casserole. In small bowl, combine topping ingredients and mix well. Sprinkle over mashed sweet potatoes. Bake at 350F for 30 min. until golden brown. Serves 6 to 8.

Southern Sweets Casserole

1 #2 can apricot halves
1 #2 can pineapple chunks
6 large yams
1 c. pecan halves

2 c. miniature marshmallows
1/2 c. brown sugar
1 stick butter
1 T. cornstarch

Scrub yams, put them in large saucepan, and cover with water. Cook over medium heat (350F) for 20 min. or until potatoes can be pierced with a paring knife. Drain, cool, and remove skins. Drain apricots and pineapple chunks, saving juices. Spray a 9 x 13 in. baking dish with Pam. Slice the yams and layer in order with apricots, pineapple, and pecans to make two layers of each. Top with marshmallows.

In saucepan, mix fruit juices with brown sugar, butter, and cornstarch. Cook until syrup thickens. Pour over casserole. Bake at 350F for 30 min. Serves 12.

Sweet Potato Delight

6 sweet potatoes	1 c. apricot juice
1-1/4 c. brown sugar	2 T. butter
1-1/2 T. cornstarch	1/2 c. nuts, chopped
1 t. grated orange rind	1 c. crushed cornflakes
1 c. apricot halves, drained	

Cook sweet potatoes, peel, and slice. Butter a 9 x 13 in. baking dish. Stagger sweet potato slices in layers. In a saucepan, combine cornstarch, orange rind, and apricot juice; heat, stirring steadily, until sauce thickens. Pour over potatoes. Top dish with apricot halves, nuts, and cornflakes. Dot with butter. Bake at 350F for 30 min. or until bubbling.

Roasted Sweet Potatoes

6 medium sweet potatoes	1 t. garlic powder
3 medium onions	1/2 t. salt
2 T. olive oil	

Scrub and peel sweet potatoes. Slice each into 2-in. pieces. Peel onions and slice into 1-in. pieces. Spray a 9 x 13 in. baking pan with Pam. Mix sweet potato and onion pieces in pan. Drizzle with olive oil, and sprinkle with garlic powder and salt. Toss to mix. Bake at 425F for 35 min. or until vegetables are tender, stirring occasionally. Serves 8 to 10.

Fried Green Tomatoes

1/2 c. flour	1/2 t. pepper
1/4 c. cornmeal	6 large green tomatoes
1/2 t. salt	1/4 c. Mazola oil
1 T. sugar	3 T. butter

Wash and slice tomatoes about 1/3 in. thick, discarding the end pieces. Combine flour, cornmeal, and salt in shallow dish. Cover each tomato slice with cornmeal mixture and lay on waxed paper near the stove.

In large skillet, heat oil and butter on medium high heat. Fry tomato slices in hot oil, using a spatula to turn when brown. Place on a heated platter in warm oven until all tomatoes have been fried. Sprinkle with sugar and pepper and serve. Serves 4 to 6.

Green tomatoes are not often for sale, but very pale firm tomatoes fry as well.

Broiled Stuffed Tomatoes

Karen Pickett

6 firm, ripe tomatoes
Salt and pepper
3 T. fresh parsley, minced
2 cloves garlic, mashed
3 T. green onions, minced

1/8 t. thyme
1/4 t. salt
1 T. basil
1/4 c. olive oil
1/2 c. bread crumbs

Remove stems and cut tomatoes in half crosswise. Gently press out juice and seeds. Sprinkle halves lightly with salt and pepper. Blend remaining ingredients. Fill each tomato half with mixture. Sprinkle with a few drops of olive oil and arrange on roasting pan. Bake at 400F for 10-15 min. or until tops are browned. Serves 12.

♣ *To peel a tomato easily, set it stem end down in dish drainer over sink. Pour boiling water over it about 10 sec. The skin will slip off.*

Tomatoes with Pesto

2 T. red wine vinegar
1/4 c. fresh basil leaves
1 clove garlic, minced
1/4 t. salt
1/4 t. sugar

1/3 c. olive oil
1/4 c. Parmesan cheese, grated
6 or 8 ripe medium tomatoes
Pepper
3 T. pine nuts (optional)

Combine vinegar, 1/4 c. loosely packed fresh basil, garlic, salt, sugar, cheese, and oil in blender. Blend until smooth. Let stand 2 hr. to blend flavors. Whisk well before using.

Wash, core, and slice tomatoes 1/2 in. thick. Arrange on serving dish, or on lettuce if desired. Grind fresh black pepper over tomatoes. Drizzle with pesto sauce. Sprinkle with toasted pine nuts if desired.

Turnip Puff

4 c. cooked, mashed white
    turnips
2 c. soft bread crumbs
1/2 c. butter, melted

2 T. sugar
1 t. salt
1/4 t. pepper
4 eggs, slightly beaten

In a large bowl, mix all ingredients together thoroughly. Spoon into a greased 1-1/2-qt. casserole. Brush with a little melted butter. Bake at 375F for 1 hr. Goes well with Thanksgiving menu. Serves 8.

Turnip Casserole

1-1/2 lb. turnips, peeled
  and sliced thin
2 T. butter
1 onion, diced
2/3 c. green pepper, chopped

2 T. flour
1 c. milk
1/2 c. grated sharp cheddar cheese
Salt and pepper
3 T. buttered crumbs

Cook turnips in boiling salted water until tender; drain. In large skillet, sauté onion and green pepper in butter. Sprinkle with flour and cook 1 min. Add milk, stirring until thickened. Stir in cheese, salt, and pepper. Combine lightly with turnips. Place in buttered baking dish and top with crumbs. Brown under the broiler. Very good with roast meat or fowl. Serves 4.

Turnip Soufflé

3 lb. medium turnips
2 small onions, diced
2 c. whole milk
1/2 c. cream
2 T. flour
3 T. butter

1/2 t. dried thyme, crumbled
1/4 t. salt
White pepper
1/4 t. cloves
1/2 t. nutmeg

Peel and quarter turnips. Boil in salted water until tender. Drain well. Sauté onions in 1 T. butter until tender. In saucepan, make white sauce with 2 T. butter, flour, and milk. Add seasonings, with pepper to taste. With electric mixer, beat turnips until fluffy. Add turnips and sautéed onions to white sauce and cook mixture over low heat, stirring occasionally, until hot. Top with parsley or chopped chives. Serves 6.

Baked Vegetables, Greek Style

1/2 c. olive oil
1 Knorr's bouillon cube
  (beef or chicken)
2 summer squash
2 medium zucchini
2 medium Yukon potatoes

3 onions
2 green peppers
9 baby carrots
3 medium tomatoes
Salt
Paprika

Pour olive oil into a 9 x 12 in. baking dish. Crumble bouillon cube evenly over oil. Wash and cut vegetables into 1/2-in. slices. Arrange slices in baking dish. Sprinkle with salt and paprika. Cover with foil. Bake at 350F for 1 hr.

Vegetable Medley

2 pkg frozen chopped broccoli	1 c. grated cheese
1 can sliced carrots, drained	1 T. minced onion
1 can baby limas, drained	Dash of pepper
1 can sliced water chestnuts,	1 t. salt
drained	1 t. dry mustard
1 8-oz. can mushroom pieces	1 4-oz. pkg sliced almonds
2 cans mushroom soup	

Cook broccoli until just tender, and drain well. Combine all drained vegetables and spread in a buttered 9 x 13 in. baking dish. Mix soup, onion, salt, dash of pepper, and mustard well; pour over vegetables. Sprinkle with cheese and almonds. Bake at 350F for 35-40 min. or until bubbling. Serves 6 to 8.

Vegetables Tempura

2 medium zucchini	3/4 c. cornstarch
2 medium summer squash	1/2 c. water
1 medium onion	1 egg, lightly beaten
4 small yellow marigolds,	Mazola oil
if desired	Salt and pepper
1/2 c. cornmeal	Soy sauce

Wash vegetables and slice 1/4 in. thick. Discard ends. Wash marigolds and cut off stem, retaining just enough green so that flower holds together. Combine cornmeal and cornstarch; pepper to taste. Stir in water and egg.

In a heavy skillet, add oil to 1/2 in. Heat to 375F. Dip vegetables and marigolds into cornmeal batter and fry 4 min. or until golden. Place items on paper towels to drain, and continue until all vegetables have been fried. Serve on a heated platter, with small bowls of salt and soy sauce for dipping. Serves 4.

Dutch Mixed Vegetables   Marge Helsell

2 10-oz. pkg frozen mixed	3 c. Edam or Gouda cheese,
vegetables in butter sauce	shredded
1 10-3/4-oz. can condensed	Salt and pepper
cream of mushroom soup	1 15-oz. can sliced mushrooms
1 can sliced water chestnuts	2 c. bread crumbs
3 T. dry white wine	1 T. melted butter
1 t. nutmeg	

Cook frozen vegetables 4 min. Drain and set aside. Mix soup, wine, cheese, salt, pepper, and nutmeg. Drain mushrooms and water chestnuts; stir them and drained vegetables into soup mixture. Pour into greased 2-qt. casserole. Top with bread crumbs whisked with butter. Decorate with cheese slices if desired. Bake uncovered at 350F for 40 min. Serves 8.

Marinated Vegetables

2 16-oz. cans red kidney beans	1 c. Mazola oil
2 16-oz. cans whole baby carrots	1 c. cider vinegar
	3 T. sugar
3 10-oz. pkg frozen broccoli spears	4 t. salt
	1 t. pepper
1/2 c. onion, chopped fine	Parsley

Cook and drain broccoli. Drain beans and carrots, and arrange in a buttered 9 x 13 in. baking dish. Sprinkle with onion. Spread broccoli evenly over all. In small bowl, whisk together oil, vinegar, sugar, salt, and pepper. Pour over vegetables. Cover; refrigerate 24-48 hr., stirring gently occasionally. To serve, drain, and arrange on platter. Garnish with sprigs of parsley. Serves 12.

Wild Rice Pilaf

1-1/2 c. wild rice	1/2 t. dried thyme
5 c. chicken broth (about 3 cans)	1/2 t. dried marjoram
	1/4 t. pepper
8 slices bacon	1 t. salt
1 large onion, chopped	2 carrots, diced
1/2 lb. mushrooms, sliced	

Rinse wild rice and combine with chicken broth in 2-qt. saucepan. Bring to a boil, cover, and simmer until just tender (35-40 min.). Do not drain. Cut bacon into 1-in. strips and cook until crisp; drain. Sauté onion in 2 T. bacon drippings 3-4 min. until tender. Stir in mushrooms, ground thyme and marjoram, and pepper; sauté 2 min. longer. Combine rice mixture, mushroom mixture, carrots, and bacon in buttered 2-1/2-qt. casserole. Bake, covered, at 350F for 35-40 min. or bubbling. Let stand 5-10 min. before serving. Serves 6 to 8.

Wild rice has been gathered from lakes and rivers by Native Americans for centuries. Today natural stands of wild rice are harvested in Minnesota in the same way: two people use a canoe, a long pole for pushing the boat, and a set of flails for knocking ripe grains of rice into the canoe.

Wild rice is not really rice, but seed from a wild grass. It is the only grain native to the North American continent.

Wild Rice Casserole

1 c. wild rice	1 4-1/2-oz. can mushroom pieces
1 c. chopped tomatoes (canned)	1 t. salt
2 c. longhorn cheese, shredded	Pepper
1 c. ripe olives, chopped	1-1/2 c. boiling water
1/2 c. olive oil	

Rinse rice and soak for 2 hr. in cold water, changing water often. Drain thoroughly. Combine with tomatoes and juice, cheese, olives, olive oil, drained mushrooms, and salt. Add pepper to taste. Place in greased 1-1/2-qt. casserole and pour boiling water over all. Bake at 325F for 1-1/2 to 2 hr. or until rice is tender. Add water if it appears dry. Serves 6.

Wild Rice Bake

1-1/2 c. wild rice	2 10-oz. cans condensed
1-1/2 t. salt	chicken broth
1-1/2 c. water	1 4-1/2-oz. jar whole mushrooms
1/4 c. onion, chopped	2 or 3 T. sliced almonds (optional)
1/4 c. butter or margarine, melted	Pepper

Rinse rice and place in an ungreased 2-qt. casserole with water, onion, melted butter, chicken broth, and mushrooms with juice. Stir in salt and pepper to taste. Cover and bake at 350F for 1 to 1-1/2 hr., stirring occasionally, until rice is tender and liquid is absorbed. Garnish with almonds. Serves 8.

Best Wild Rice Casserole

1-1/2 lb. cubed veal	2 c. celery, sliced
1-1/2 lb. cubed lean pork	2 T. soy sauce
2 T. shortening	2 cans cream of mushroom soup
1 large onion, chopped	1 4-1/2-oz. can mushroom pieces
3/4 c. wild rice	4-1/2 c. water
3/4 c. white rice (not Instant)	Salt and pepper

Rinse wild rice. In a large skillet, brown veal, pork, and onion in shortening. Add wild and white rice and the rest of the ingredients. Adjust salt and pepper to taste. Stir, then pour mixture into a buttered 2-qt. casserole. Cover and bake at 350F for 2 hr., stirring occasionally. Add more water if needed. Uncover the last half hour. Serves 8.

Wild Rice Almondine

1-1/2 c. wild rice	1/2 c. onion, chopped fine
1 T. butter	4 c. water
2 cubes Knorr's chicken bouillon	Salt to taste
1/2 c. slivered almonds	

Rinse rice thoroughly. Place in heavy 2-qt. saucepan with water and bouillon cubes. Bring to a boil; reduce heat, cover, and simmer 45 min. until rice is tender but not mushy. Uncover; fluff with a fork.

In small skillet, sauté onion in butter until tender. When rice is done, add onion to hot rice, cover and let stand for 5-8 min. to absorb liquid. Serve topped with almonds. Serves 6.

Zucchini-Corn Casserole

3 or 4 small zucchini	1 15-1/2-oz. can whole kernel corn
1 T. butter	1 t. salt
1 T. olive oil	2 T. fresh basil, chopped
2 cloves garlic, minced	1/2 c. mozzarella cheese, shredded
1 2-oz. jar pimiento, diced	Pepper

Wash and cut zucchini into quarters lengthwise; thinly slice each quarter, discarding ends. In large cast-iron skillet, heat butter and oil. Sauté zucchini and garlic 4 min. Drain and add corn and pimiento; add salt and freshly ground pepper to taste. Continue to sauté until zucchini is tender. Turn into baking dish and sprinkle with cheese and basil. Broil about 6 in. from heat for 3-5 min., until cheese melts. Serves 6 to 8.

Italian Zucchini Pie   Connie Woods

4 c. thinly sliced, unpeeled zucchini	1/4 t. garlic powder
	1/4 t. basil
1 c. onion, chopped coarsely	1/4 t. oregano
1/2 c. butter	2 eggs, well beaten
1/2 t. salt	2 c. mozzarella cheese, shredded
1/2 c. parsley, chopped *or* 2 T. parsley flakes	1 8-oz. can refrigerated crescent rolls
1/2 t. pepper	2 t. prepared mustard

Sauté zucchini and onion in butter until tender, about 10-15 min. Stir in seasonings. In separate bowl, blend eggs, cheese, and mustard. Stir in vegetable mixture. In ungreased baking dish, press rolls to form a crust on bottom and sides. Pour in vegetable-cheese mixture. Bake at 375F for 25 min. until knife comes out clean. Cover lightly with foil if crust becomes too brown during last 10 min. Let stand 10 min. before serving. Serves 6.

Zucchini Casserole

6 c. sliced, unpeeled zucchini
3 T. butter
1/4 c. onion, chopped
1 c. carrots, grated
1 c. sour cream

1 can cream of chicken soup
Salt and pepper
2 c. herb seasoned stuffing mix
1/2 c. melted butter

In a large skillet, sauté zucchini and onion in 3 T. butter. Combine sour cream and soup, and stir into zucchini. Add carrots and salt and pepper to taste. Pour melted butter over stuffing mixture, and stir. Place half stuffing in a buttered 1-1/2-qt. casserole, add zucchini-carrot mix, and top with the rest of the stuffing. Bake at 350F for 30-35 min. Serves 6.

Yummy Zucchini

2 medium zucchini
1-1/2 lb. lean ground beef
2 T. onion, minced fine
1 small can tomato sauce

1 can cream of celery soup
4 oz. American cheese, shredded
1 c. herb seasoned croutons
Salt and pepper

Wash and peel zucchini and slice thin over the bottom of a buttered 9 x 13 in. baking dish. In a large skillet, brown ground beef and onion; drain. Stir in tomato sauce, and salt and pepper to taste. Pour meat mixture over zucchini slices. Spread celery soup evenly over the top, and sprinkle with cheese. Arrange croutons over the top. Bake at 350F for 30-40 min. or until zucchini is tender. Serves 10 to 12.

Salads

Fruit ♣ *Poultry, Meat, Seafood*
♣ *Vegetable* ♣ *Pickles* ♣ *Dressings*

<u>Moving Day</u>

Every area has its traditions etched in stone after years of repetition, honored without much question because they seem eminently sensible and no sound objections have been raised. In the Midwest, such a tradition is Moving Day, when farmers — the renters, farm buyers and others working the land — pack up their worldly goods and move to their new location on March first. On that day, a domino effect ripples through the community. Those moving out are assisted by their friends, just as those moving in begin to arrive with their possessions and helpers. At the end of the day, most of the participants are settling into their quarters and stay settled until next year's Moving Day — and with luck, for many years to come.

Early on, the month and day probably were chosen because that date precedes sowing spring crops and usually occurs after the earliest lambs, pigs, calves and foals arrive and before the spring's later arrivals. The worst winter storms may have subsided. Country dirt roads are still frozen solid enough to support teams with loaded wagons. Since the fields are untillable and the harvest completed, farmers have some time for moving, a huge undertaking that takes careful planning. Whatever the original reasons, land owners and tenant farmers still sign leases that make March 1st the official date when most leases begin; hence, Moving Day.

In 1894 a couple, immigrants and new settlers in a community of relatives and friends, rented a small farm and began saving toward their dream, a home on their own land. They made good strides toward becoming independent, acquiring equipment (used, but in good repair), livestock and household essentials. They had started a family and studied to become naturalized citizens. Finally, they had been frugal, setting aside enough savings for a down payment on land. Their neighborhood did not have any land for sale, so the settlers looked toward the hill country farther west and located a farm 14 miles away they bought for $40 per acre — $9,600. Awed by their good fortune and by the debt they had assumed, they began preparing for the big move.

Thus, long before dawn on March 1st, a caravan of farm wagons and hayracks was loaded with machinery, livestock, hay, straw and household goods by volunteers — loyal family and neighbors who were helping the Danish-American family move to the farm they had bought. The caravan was an odd sight, much like others that would be on the roads that day. The hay and straw stacks had been loaded onto racks, some moved earlier to the new place in anticipation of the needs of livestock before forage would be available.

The household wagons bristled with bedsteads, cupboards, stoves, tables, kitchen chairs, homemade cradles, washtubs, steamer trunks and boxes of provisions — everything needed to make a home livable. Other wagons held homemade crates full of hens and a couple of aggressive cocks, two pairs of geese huddling close together, various farm partitions, pails, milkstools, hoes, forks, scoops, and sacks holding corn and oats for the fowl. A noisy group of several sows and half-grown pigs squealed and grunted, frustrated with being crowded; a nearby wagon held several young calves. Three sedate cows tethered to this wagon would walk behind the calves. It was a noisy parade waiting to move.

The homemaker had organized the household wagon so that heavy blankets covered a deep layer of straw at the front end. The children lay there in a cozy nest of pillows and blankets. At the back, baskets of food were stowed beside the carefully stoppered two-gallon coffeepots. These would provide meals for the day. Everyone was dressed warmly, and the wagon's sides offered protection from the light wind.

When the farmer gave the signal, the caravan rolled out at a steady pace onto the lowland road. Here they could see the low, dark huddle of farm buildings set back from the road and surrounded by fields. At five o'clock there was already a faint glow from some windows. Farmers carrying kerosene lanterns and milk pails were moving toward barns. By the time the sun rose at nine, the caravan had reached the place where they would turn left on the steep roads westward. There the leaders decided to stop for coffee. Two men watched the teams, while the others climbed down, stretching arms and legs, and walked back to the wagon where the farmwife had uncovered a basket of sandwiches and was handing coffee cups to the men. They munched on thick slices of rye bread filled with creamy homemade cheese or liver paté as they sipped steaming, strong coffee. They spoke cheerfully of the morning's progress, scanned the skies for nonexistent clouds, and moved quickly back to the wagons. Within minutes they were creaking into the turn west.

As they began long, steep hill climbs, the men walked beside the wagons to lighten the loads. The downhill slopes were a different challenge; the drivers held the brakes to keep the wagons from racing downhill. Gradually, men and teams became accustomed to the changes and made good time. When the sun was high overhead, the group stopped where a lane joined the road, making a wider place for the caravan. There was a hot pot of soup to sip from cups, buttered rye bread with meat, sweet raisin bread spicy with cinnamon, and prune coffeecake — all accompanied by fragrant hot coffee.

After their midday stop, the long steep hills and deep wooded valleys became a changing landscape. Smaller rolling hills climbed higher and there were no steep descents. Copses of scrub oaks and junipers dotted the hillsides. There were few rocks and no broad bands of trees, but many plum thickets bordered the road, and grapevines climbed the isolated trees. Rabbits and birds scattered as the wagons passed. The whirring rush of pheasants rising from thickets woke the older children, who watched for animals and birds along the roadside.

Dusk was falling as they made a turn into a narrow track up a steep hill. They reached a large clearing, a square bordered on three sides by buildings. Straight ahead on the south was a long barn. To the left, there were several buildings for fowl and grain storage, and to the right, facing the barn, was a house. The farmer had moved the house on rollers to its location during the winter, and with several workers' help, dug a cellar and laid a sturdy foundation.

The drivers of the wagons waited in the great central square until directed to the spot where they would unload. There they unhitched their teams, led the horses to a tank at the south side of the barn for water, and tied them to a hitching post after putting feedbags over their heads. The men then turned to unloading livestock. The cows and their calves followed docilely into the barn, where the new owner had built a partition to make a snug loafing shed. The sows were unloaded and enticed with ears of corn to one of the sheds, and the young hogs scrambled after feed. The hens and geese, drowsy and reluctant to be disturbed, were hoisted out of the crates and onto fresh straw to spend the night.

The jobs were done quickly, and these men then joined those unloading the household wagon. By the light of kerosene lanterns, the men had set up the ample cookstove; with the stovepipes fit into the chimney, a fire was warming the kitchen and a fresh pot of coffee was already started. The table had been covered with oilcloth, and the farmwife had brought out more food. Sandwiches, sweet raisin bread, slices of meat, a jar of pickles and prune pastry were welcomed by the tired men. Some sat on kitchen chairs, others squatted on the floor. The farmwife thanked them graciously for all their help.

The neighbors had agreed to make the return trip at once if the weather remained clear, so except for the farmer's brother, who stayed to help settle in, the men hitched their teams to start back home. Although it was dark at six o'clock, the moon shone on the shrunken caravan marked by kerosene lanterns hung from cross-pieces at wagon fronts. With lightened rigs, the teams moved fast and soon the caravan moved out of sight.

While the men checked their horses and all the stock for the night, the farmwife tucked her children into bed and crib. She washed dishes, put food away, and checked the coffeepot. When the brothers came in, the new farm owner looked about with pride. He knew his wife had done her job well, providing good food and cheer for the helpers on the long, bumpy trip. Their children had behaved well, not fussing about discomfort or confinement. It had been a good Moving Day. He was proud of everyone. He looked around the room crowded with possessions but cozy with the warm stove and lamplight, and he made a dignified old-world bow toward his wife. Their eyes met, and she smiled and thought: The dream is real. In America we have a home on land that is our own!

Recipes

Apricot Nectar Salad

1 pkg (4 oz.) orange Jell-O
1 pkg lemon Jell-O
2 c. boiling water
1 #2-1/2 can crushed pineapple
1 # 2-1/2 can apricots
1-1/2 c. miniature marshmallows
1 c. shredded medium sharp
    cheddar cheese

1 c. chopped pecans
1 egg, beaten
1/2 c. sugar
1 T. flour
1 T. butter
2 c. whipped cream or
    Cool Whip

Mix orange and lemon Jell-O with boiling water. Drain crushed pineapple, saving juice. Drain apricots, saving 1 c. juice separately and adding remainder to pineapple juice; add water to make 2 c. liquid. Add to Jell-O.

Cut apricots in quarters. Add to Jell-O with crushed pineapple and pecans. Pour into 9 x 13 in. pan. Cover with miniature marshmallows. Refrigerate until set.

Mix the 1 c. apricot juice, beaten egg, sugar, flour, and butter in a saucepan. Cook and stir until thick. Cool. Add 2 c. whipped cream and mix lightly. Spread on chilled gelatin mixture. Sprinkle with shredded cheese. Refrigerate and serve. Serves 12 to 15.

May's ABC Citrus Avocado Salad

May Marshall

Head of iceberg lettuce
1 large (1 lb.) grapefruit
1 avocado
Lemon juice
1/2 c. olive oil

1/4 t. salt
2 T. sugar
1 T. balsamic vinegar
2 T. lemon juice
1/2 c. crumbled blue cheese

Crisp a head of iceberg lettuce by cutting out core and washing with cold water. Drain. Put to chill in a large freezer bag. Peel and section a large grapefruit, removing all white membrane. Put the sections to chill. Select an avocado that yields to a slight pressure. Peel it and cut lengthwise into 8 or 12 sections. Sprinkle with lemon juice and put in the bowl with grapefruit to chill.

Make a vinaigrette with olive oil, salt, sugar, balsamic vinegar, and 2 T. lemon juice. Add blue cheese.

To serve, place three or four large torn lettuce leaves in glass bowl. Arrange grapefruit sections on lettuce with avocado sections over the grapefruit. Spoon blue cheese dressing on top. Serves 4.

Very refreshing as first course.

♣ *Select grapefruit by lifting to determine weight. Compare several. A juicy fruit will be very heavy. It will probably also have a smooth skin.*

Florida Avocado Citrus Salad

3 T. cider vinegar
2 T. olive oil
1 T. sugar
1/4 t. salt
8 c. torn romaine lettuce
1 grapefruit, peeled and sectioned

2 oranges, peeled and sectioned
2 ripe avocados, peeled and sliced
1 c. seedless green grapes, halved
2 T. chopped almonds, toasted
   (optional)

Whisk together oil, vinegar, sugar, and salt. Place greens in a large bowl. Add orange and grapefruit sections, avocado, and grapes. Drizzle with dressing, tossing gently to coat. Sprinkle with almonds, if desired. Serve immediately. Serves 6.

♣ *Ripen avocados, melons, and pears at room temperature; then refrigerate.*

Blue Cheese Salad

6 c. mixed salad greens
4 oz. blue cheese, crumbled
2 oranges, peeled and sliced

1 pt. strawberries, quartered
Vinaigrette

Toss greens with vinaigrette and crumbled blue cheese. Place on six salad plates. Arrange orange slices over greens; sprinkle with strawberries. Serves 6.

Vinaigrette

1/2 c. red wine vinegar
2 T. Dijon mustard
3 T. honey
2 garlic cloves, minced

1 small onion, minced
1/4 t. salt
1/2 c. olive oil

Whisk seasonings into vinegar until blended. Gradually whisk in olive oil. Makes 1 cup.

"Holiday Fair" Blueberry Salad   St. Paul's, Cedar Rapids

2 pkg black raspberry Jell-O
2 c. boiling water
1 t. lemon juice

1 #2 can blueberries
1 #2 can crushed pineapple
1 c. finely chopped celery

Combine Jell-O and boiling water. Stir to dissolve. Let cool to lukewarm, then add remaining ingredients, using blueberry juice and pineapple juice as it comes from the can. Pour into a 9 x 13 in. pan. Refrigerate. Serve with a dollop of mayonnaise if desired. Serves 12 to 15.

This colorful salad is a traditional favorite at St Paul's United Methodist Church fair, Cedar Rapids, Iowa.

"Holiday Fair" Cherry Salad   St. Paul's, Cedar Rapids

1 pkg cherry Jell-O
1 c. boiling water
1 can Wilderness cherry pie filling

1 #303 can crushed pineapple, drained

Combine Jell-O and boiling water. Stir until dissolved. Add cherry pie filling and crushed pineapple. Pour into a 9 x 9 or 8 x 10 in. pan. Chill to set. Top with a teaspoonful of whipped cream. Serves 9 to 10.

♣ *If a recipe calls for drained fruit, chill the juice in a covered glass container and use it in a fruit drink or gelatin dessert.*

Cheese Pineapple Salad

3/4 c. sugar
1 small can crushed pineapple
1/2 c. pineapple juice
1 c. whipped cream

1 env. Knox gelatin
1/4 c. cold water
1 c. grated American or
    mild cheddar cheese

Drain juice from pineapple. Dissolve sugar into 1/2 c. pineapple juice over low heat Add gelatin that has been softened in cold water. Chill until partially set. Add 1 c. drained, crushed pineapple and grated cheese. Fold in whipped cream. Pour into 9 x 12 in. pan. Chill until firm. Serves 8 to 10.

♣ *Fresh pineapple does not ripen further after being picked. Test for ripeness by pulling a top leaf spear. It will pull out easily if ripe. Use within 3-5 days.*

Cherry Coke Salad   Corinne Tucker

2 #2 cans black cherries
1 #2 can crushed pineapple
1 small bottle Coca-Cola

1/2 c. chopped pecans
1 pkg cherry Jell-O

Heat cherries and juice to boiling. Add Jell-O and stir until dissolved. Add other ingredients. Place in 8-c. mold and chill. Serves 6 to 8.

A winning combination for a ladies' luncheon!

♣ *Grease molds for congealed salads with mayonnaise.*

Cinnamon Apple Salad

Opal Grier

6-8 medium large tart apples, such as Jonathans
2 c. sugar
2 c. water
1/4 c. cinnamon "red hots"

1/2 c. chopped nuts
1/2 c. chopped celery
1/2 c. mayonnaise
Lettuce

Peel and core apples. In a 2-qt. saucepan, cook sugar, water, and cinnamon red hots for 3 min. Carefully place apples in syrup, reduce heat to simmer, and cook until tender. Remove from heat and cool in syrup.

Lift out apples and chill, or chill in syrup, turning to absorb red color. Make a stuffing of nuts, celery, and mayonnaise. Place apples on lettuce and fill centers.

Cream cheese, nuts, and celery are also a good combination for filling. A very good salad with roast chicken.

My Cranberry Sauce

1 12-oz. pkg Ocean Spray cranberries

2/3 c. sugar
2/3 c. water

Wash and drain cranberries; put into a 2-qt. saucepan. Add sugar and water. Cover. Turn heat to medium high. When cranberries begin to pop, turn heat down to medium low. Tilt the lid and stir to avoid boiling over. After 10 min., most berries will have popped. Stir berries. Remove from heat and pour sauce into a 1-qt. refrigerator container. Chill. Stir before serving. Yield: 3 cups.

The cranberry is native to North America. Harvested from bogs in Massachusetts and Wisconsin in the autumn, cranberries are a bright and nutritious dish that goes especially well with roast fowl.

♣ *Cranberries freeze perfectly in the plastic bags in which they are bought.*

Cranberry Holiday Fluff

1 pkg (12 oz.) cranberries
1/2 lb. miniature marshmallows
1-1/2 c. chopped nuts
1 c. whipping cream

1 small can crushed pineapple
    and juice
1/4 c. sugar

Grind raw, washed cranberries. Add marshmallows, nuts, crushed pineapple and juice, and sugar. Mix well. Whip 1 c. cream and blend with cranberry mixture. Refrigerate several hours. Stir lightly. May be frozen.

Very good served with roast fowl. Can be made ahead because it keeps well several days. The rose-pink color brightens holiday tables.

Cranberry Orange Relish

1 lb. (4 c.) cranberries
2 oranges

2 c. sugar

Put cranberries and peeled oranges through food chopper. Add sugar. Chill well a few hours before serving. Yield: 5 cups.

Delicious with chicken, fish, or meats. Keep chilled or freeze.

Quota Brunch Fruit Compote   Waterloo Quota Club

5 3-oz. pkg lemon Jell-O (or 2
    large & 1 small pkg)
5 c. boiling water
No. 10 can pineapple tidbits

No. 10 can mandarin oranges
5 small (or 2 large) cans frozen
    orange juice
25 bananas, diced

Dissolve Jell-O in boiling water. Add frozen orange juice and mix thoroughly. Add fruits, together with juices. (May wait until day of serving to add bananas.) Refrigerate overnight in covered containers. Serve cold with whole strawberry or cherry on top. Serves 75 to 100 4-oz. cups.

This colorful, refreshing fruit cup, served at annual brunches, is good served with a casserole or sandwiches for brunch. One-fifth amount serves 15.

Char's Grape Salad

Char Petersen

2 pkg Concord grape Jell-O
3 c. hot water (including
    pineapple juice)
Chopped nuts

1 can blueberry pie filling
1 #303 can crushed pineapple
Cool Whip

Combine ingredients. Pour into 9 x 13 in. pan. Cool and set overnight. Top with Cool Whip and chopped nuts.

Ginger Ale Peach Salad

2 T. Knox gelatin
1/4 c. cold water
1/3 c. hot water
2 c. ginger ale

1 T. lemon juice
2 T. sugar
6 spiced peach halves
Sprinkle of salt

Dissolve gelatin in hot water; add cold water with ginger ale, lemon juice, sugar, and salt. Put peach halves into rinsed individual molds and pour ginger ale mixture over peaches. Chill. Unmold on crisp greens. Serves 6.

Mandarin Orange Salad

Marianne MacCurdy

1/4 head iceberg lettuce
1/4 bunch romaine lettuce
    or spinach
2 green onions, sliced
11-oz. can mandarin oranges,
    drained

1/4 c. salad oil
1 T. sugar
2 T. vinegar
1 t. salt
Dash dry mustard (optional)
1/2 c. celery, chopped (optional)

Combine salad ingredients. Prepare dressing and pour over lettuce-orange mixture. Toss and chill.

Laurel's Standby Super Salad

Laurel Harbour

Large head romaine lettuce
1 large red onion
5 or 6 stalks celery
1 c. black olives
1 c. pecans or walnuts, toasted
1 11-oz. can mandarin oranges

1/2 c. red wine vinegar
1 c. olive oil
1/2 t. salt
Dash of Italian seasoning
1 T. sugar

Wash, dry, and shred lettuce. Chop onion fine. Chop celery into bite-size pieces. Chop olives and nuts. Drain oranges. Combine all ingredients, cover, and chill thoroughly. When ready to serve, combine vinegar, oil, and seasonings; shake and pour over greens. Toss. Serves 8 to 10.

This is the No. 1 salad at the Harbours, served (along with others) for every occasion.

Grandma's Overnight White Salad   **Christena Paulsen**

4 egg yolks
Juice of 1 lemon
1/2 c. milk
1 lb. marshmallows, quartered
1 #2-1/2 can pineapple
    tidbits, drained

1 lb. white grapes or
    Queen Anne cherries, halved
1 c. sliced blanched almonds
1 c. whipping cream
Maraschino cherries
Lettuce

Beat egg yolks, lemon juice, and milk together and cook in top of double boiler. Add marshmallows. Cool. Add grapes or cherries, drained pineapple, and almonds. Let stand in refrigerator overnight.

The next morning, whip 1 c. cream, mix with overnight ingredients, and chill several hours. Serve on lettuce. Decorate with maraschino cherries if desired. Serves 12 to 15.

Grandma served this for Christmas 75 years ago. It remains a favorite of today's hostesses and their guests.

Crunchy Peanut-Apple Salad

3 c. diced unpeeled tart apples
1 c. chopped celery
1 t. lemon juice
1 t. sugar
2 T. mayonnaise

1/3 c. plain yogurt
1/2 c. coarsely chopped
    peanuts
Lettuce

Combine apples, celery, and lemon juice. Toss well. Combine sugar, mayonnaise, and yogurt, mix well and fold into apple mixture. Chill.
Add peanuts, toss lightly. Serve on crisp lettuce. Serves 4.

Raspberry Frost Salad

2 pkg raspberry Jell-O
3 c. boiling water
1 c. smooth applesauce
2 pkg frozen raspberries

2 t. lemon juice
16 marshmallows, quartered
1/2 pt. sour cream

Mix Jell-O *into* boiling water until dissolved. Add applesauce and thawed raspberries (including juice). Pour into a 9 x 13 in. pan and chill. Mix cut marshmallows and sour cream; refrigerate overnight. The next day, spread sour cream mixture on top of salad in pan. Return to refrigerator to set before serving. Serves 10 to 12.

Strawberry Frost

1 15-1/2-oz. can crushed
    pineapple, with juice
3 bananas, mashed fine
2 pkg strawberry Jell-O

1 c. boiling water
1/2 pt. dairy sour cream
1 large or 2 small pkg frozen
    strawberries, thawed

Dissolve Jell-O in boiling water. Add thawed berries, pineapple and juice, and bananas. Spread half of this mixture in 9 x 13 in. baking dish. Chill until firm. Keep other half at room temperature. Spread the sour cream on congealed layer. Cover with remaining Jell-O mixture and chill. Serve with crisp crackers. Serves 10 to 12.

Summer Fruit with Rieke's Dressing   Barbara Weirick

1 c. salad oil
3/4 c. sugar
1 t. Coleman's dry mustard
1 t. salt
1 T. finely grated sweet onion
2/3 c. white vinegar
1 T. celery or poppy seed

1 pt. fresh blueberries
1 #2 can pineapple chunks, drained
3 fresh oranges, in medium chunks
2 c. green grapes
1 c. cantaloupe, cut in chunks
1 c. honeydew melon, cut in chunks

Beat together dressing ingredients with electric mixture (makes 1-1/2 c.). Chill. Pour over fruit, and allow to marinate and chill for 1 hr.

This dressing from Rieke's Restaurant in New York is superb with summer fruits!

Sunshine Salad

2 pkg lemon Jell-O
2 c. boiling water
1 #303 can crushed pineapple
2/3 c. cold water
1/4 t. salt

1 T. vinegar
1-1/2 c. grated carrots
1/2 c. mayonnaise
1 c. whipped cream
1 c. cheddar cheese, grated

Dissolve Jell-O in boiling water. Drain pineapple; save the juice and add with 2/3 c. cold water to Jell-O. Stir in salt and vinegar. Chill. When mixture begins to thicken, add crushed pineapple and grated carrots. Pour into a 9 x 13 in. pan and chill until congealed. Top each serving with mayonnaise mixed with whipped cream. Sprinkle with grated cheese. Serves 10 to 12.

Watergate Salad

Charlotte Koenigsdorf

1 pkg pistachio pudding mix
1 16-oz. can crushed pineapple
1/2 c. chopped pecans

9 oz. Cool Whip
1 c. miniature marshmallows

Stir pudding mix into pineapple and juice. Fold in Cool Whip, marshmallows, and pecans. Chill. Serves 8.

Slush Fruit Cup

1/2 c. sugar
6 c. water
4 ripe medium size bananas
1 large can pineapple juice

1 12-oz. can frozen orange
    juice concentrate
1 6-oz. can frozen lemonade
1 liter lemon-lime soda

Mash bananas in blender. Add all other ingredients except lemon-lime soda. Freeze the mixture. Before serving, remove from freezer for 1 hr. Break up frozen mixture with a potato masher. Add soda to make slush. Yield: about 24 servings.

Florence Jean's Frozen Salad

Florence Jean Dearborn

2 c. commercial sour cream
2 T. lemon juice
1/2 c. sugar
1/8 t. salt
1 banana, diced
1/4 c. chopped pecans

1-lb. can pitted bing cherries,
    drained
1 8-oz. can crushed pineapple,
    drained
4 drops red food coloring
Salad greens

Combine sour cream, lemon juice, sugar, salt, pineapple, and red coloring. Fold in nuts and bing cherries. Spoon into fluted paper muffin cups (large size) fitted into 3-in. muffin cup tins. Freeze. Cover with plastic wrap and store in freezer.

Remove from freezer about 15 min. before serving. Peel off paper cups and place on greens. Makes enough for 12 large muffin cups.

Fran's Frozen Cranberry Salad   Fran Church

1 large pkg strawberry Jell-O
2 c. boiling water
1 #2 can crushed pineapple,
    including juice

2 cans whole cranberry sauce,
    broken in small pieces
1 c. chopped nuts
8 oz. Cool Whip

Dissolve Jell-O in boiling water. Stir pineapple and cranberry sauce into Jell-O. Let partly congeal. Add nuts. Fold in Cool Whip. Freeze in paper cups or a 9 x 12 in. pan. Serves 12.

This is especially good with chicken dishes.

Frozen Party Salad   Mary Davis Schrum

1 c. Miracle Whip salad dressing
1 8-oz. pkg Philadelphia cream
    cheese, softened
1 8-1/4 oz. can pineapple
    chunks, drained
1/2 c. maraschino cherries
    chopped

1 16-oz. can apricot halves,
    drained and quartered
2 T. powdered sugar
Red food coloring
2 c. marshmallows, halved
1 c. whipped cream
Lettuce

Combine salad dressing and softened cream cheese. Stir in fruit, sugar, and a few drops of food coloring; fold in marshmallows and whipped cream. Pour into 9 x 5 in. loaf pan; freeze. Unmold; surround with lettuce. 10 to 12 servings.

Variation: Substitute a 16-oz. can peach slices, drained, for apricots.

This recipe dates from 1934. The original has inspired many variations over the years.

Pink Champagne Salad

1 8-oz. pkg cream cheese,
  softened
3/4 c. sugar
1 10-oz. pkg frozen strawberries

1 #2 can crushed pineapple
2 bananas, sliced
9 oz. Cool Whip

Mix together cheese and sugar, then add other ingredients. Place in a 9 x 13 in. pan and freeze. To serve, cut in 3-in. squares. Serves 12.

Strawberry Fruit Freeze

1-1/2 c. sugar
1 c. water
2 pkg frozen strawberries
Commercial sour cream

1 #2-1/2 can apricots, cut up
1 #2 can pineapple tidbits
6 bananas, diced

Combine sugar and water in a saucepan. Bring to a boil and boil for 1 min. Pour over combined fruit. Freeze in muffin tins with paper liners. Unmold and garnish with sour cream.

My Aloha Chicken Salad

4 c. chopped cooked chicken
  breast meat
2 c. diced celery
1 20-oz. can pineapple chunks,
  drained
1 lb. seedless green grapes,
  halved

2 11-oz. cans mandarin oranges,
  drained
1 c. chopped pecans
1 c. mayonnaise or salad
  dressing—thinned with
  1 to 2 T. half and half
Lettuce leaves

Combine all ingredients except lettuce leaves. Toss until well coated. Chill. Serve on lettuce. 8 main-dish servings.

♣ *A 3-1/2-pound chicken will yield 3 c. diced cooked chicken. Six half chicken breasts equal 2 2/3 c. diced cooked chicken.*

Hot Chicken Salad

3 c. cooked chicken or turkey,
  cubed
2 c. chopped celery
1 c. mayonnaise
1/2 c. toasted almonds

1 can sliced water chestnuts,
  drained
2 T. lemon juice
2 t. grated onion
1/2 t. salt

Mix together all ingredients; place in a casserole dish. Top with 1/2 c. grated
cheddar cheese and 1 c. crushed potato chips. Bake in 450F oven 20 min.

Oriental Chicken Salad

2 c. diced cooked chicken
  or turkey
1 c. diced celery
2 T. minced onion
2 hard-boiled eggs, sliced
1/4 c. sweet pickle relish
1 c. LaChoy chow
  mein noodles

1/2 c. chopped cashews or
  slivered almonds
1/2 c. mayonnaise
2 T. lemon juice
1 T. Worcestershire sauce
1 t. salt
Pepper to taste
1 can sliced water chestnuts

Put all ingredients except nuts into a large bowl and chill 2 or 3 hr. Before serving,
toss the salad. Serve on crisp greens or individual salad plates. Sprinkle with
cashew or almonds. Serves 6.

Chicken Wild Rice Salad

2/3 c. mayonnaise
1/3 c. milk
2 T. lemon juice
1/4 t. dried tarragon
3 c. cooked cubed chicken
3 c. cooked wild rice
1/3 c. finely sliced
  green onion

1 8-oz. can sliced water
  chestnuts, drained
1/2 t. salt
1/8 t. pepper
1/2 lb. seedless green grapes,
  (1 c.), halved
1 c. salted cashews
Grape clusters

Blend mayonnaise, milk, lemon juice, and tarragon; set aside. In large bowl,
combine chicken, wild rice, green onion, water chestnuts, salt, and pepper. Stir in
mayonnaise mixture until blended. Refrigerate covered for 2 to 3 hr. Just before
serving, fold in grapes and cashews. Garnish with grape clusters. Serves 8.

Curry Turkey Salad

2 c. coarsely shredded turkey
1 c. diced (1/4 in.) celery
1 c. seedless red grapes,
   halved crosswise

1-1/2 c. flaked coconut, divided
1 large head iceberg lettuce
1 c. curry mayonnaise

When shredding turkey, combine white and dark meat to add moisture. Combine turkey, celery, grapes, and coconut in bowl. Toss with curry mayonnaise. Set aside. Arrange lettuce leaf cups on plates. Fill with equal amounts of turkey salad. Garnish with coconut. Serves 6.

Curry Mayonnaise: Combine 1 c. mayonnaise, 1/2 t. sugar, and 1/2 t. curry powder.

Hot Turkey Salad

2 c. roast turkey, cubed
2 c. celery, chopped
1/2 c. blanched almonds, chopped
1/3 c. green pepper, chopped
2 T. onion, chopped
1 t. salt

2 T. lemon juice
1/2 c. mayonnaise
1/2 stick melted butter
1 c. fine cracker crumbs
4 slices Swiss cheese

Combine cracker crumbs and melted butter. Set aside with Swiss cheese. Combine all other ingredients lightly. Put into a greased casserole dish; top with cheese. Sprinkle with buttered cracker crumb mixture. Bake in preheated 350F oven about 25 min. or until bubbly and crumbs are brown. Serves 6.

This is a fresh way to serve leftover turkey or roast chicken.

My Spicy Ham Loaf Salad

1 pkg lemon Jell-O
1 3/4 c. boiling water
2 t. vinegar
1/4 t. mustard
2 T. mayonnaise
1 pimiento, diced
2 T. Worcestershire sauce

Dash of pepper
Dash of cloves
Dash of nutmeg
2 c. cooked ham, diced
1 T. horseradish
1/2 t. onion pulp

Dissolve Jell-O in boiling water. Add vinegar, Worcestershire sauce, and mustard. When slightly thickened, add other ingredients. Mix well, and pour into 9 x 13 in. pan. Chill until set. Cut into squares, place on lettuce. Serves 12.

Ham Soufflé Salad   Anna M. Petersen

1 pkg. lemon Jell-O	1/4 t. pepper
1/4 t. salt	1 c. finely diced cooked ham
1 c. boiling water	1/2 c. chopped celery
1/3 c. cold water	2 T. chopped sweet pickle
1 T. vinegar	Lettuce
1/3 c. mayonnaise	

Dissolve Jell-O and salt in boiling water. Stir to mix. Add cold water, vinegar, mayonnaise, and pepper. Beat well with beater. Put in refrigerator and chill until partially set. Remove from refrigerator and beat until fluffy. Fold in ham, celery, and pickle. Pour into 4- to 5-c. mold. Chill until firm. Unmold on crisp green lettuce. Serves 6.

Crabmeat Salad

1-1/2 env. Knox gelatin	1 medium onion, chopped
1/2 c. cold water	1-1/2 c. chopped celery
1 can Campbell's tomato soup	1 c. Miracle Whip
3 oz. Philadelphia cream cheese	2 cans crabmeat or tuna, drained
1 small green pepper, chopped	Lettuce
Cucumber and tomato slices	

Soak gelatin in cold water for 5 min. Heat tomato soup and cream cheese; mix well, add gelatin mixture, and cool. Add chopped vegetables, Miracle Whip, and crabmeat. Pour into 9 x 13 in. Pyrex pan. Chill. Serve on lettuce with garnish of cucumber and tomato slices. Serves 12 to 14.

Crab Caribbean

2 (6 oz. or 8 oz.) pkg. Crab Delights, flake style	1 T. freshly squeezed lime juice
1/4 c. mayonnaise	Lettuce leaves
Cayenne pepper	2 oranges, peeled and sectioned
2 T. chopped cilantro	or 1 16-oz. can mandarin oranges, drained

In bowl, combine Crab Delights, mayonnaise, cilantro, lime juice, and cayenne pepper to taste, mixing thoroughly. Arrange 1/4 of orange sections over lettuce leaves on four individual salad plates. Top with crab mixture. Serves 4.

Crab Luncheon Salad

1/3 c. olive oil	1 medium onion, diced
1/2 c. water	3 tomatoes, sliced
1/4 c. cider vinegar	Lettuce leaves
1/2 t. salt	3 hard-cooked eggs, quartered
1/2 t. pepper	12 ripe olives
1/4 t. Worcestershire sauce	12 pimiento-stuffed olives
2 cans crabmeat	

Whisk together oil, water, vinegar, salt, pepper, and Worcestershire sauce. Add crabmeat and onion, tossing gently to coat. Cover and chill 3 hr. Drain. Arrange tomato slices on lettuce-lined plates; top with crabmeat mixture. Garnish with egg quarters and olives. Serves 4.

Crab Tostados

1 head iceberg lettuce	1-1/2 c. cheddar cheese, shredded
1 avocado	2 cans crabmeat
2 T. lemon or lime juice	3/4 c. ripe pitted olives
Garlic salt	2 c. taco sauce
2 medium very ripe tomatoes,	Tortilla chips, heated at 300F
diced into 1/2-in. cubes	for 10 min.
1 can refried beans	

Shred lettuce and mound on six salad plates. Peel and seed avocado; sprinkle with lemon or lime juice and garlic salt and mash with a fork.

Heat beans for 3-5 min. Spoon equally over lettuce. Sprinkle cheese over beans, and cover with a layer of crab. Spoon avocado equally over crab. Surround salad with diced tomatoes, ripe olives, and warm tortilla chips. Spoon 1 T. taco sauce on each salad, and pass the remainder. Serves 6.

Salmon Summer Salad

1 16-oz. can salmon, chilled	1 small can peas
1-1/2 c. creamed cottage cheese	1/2 t. salt
1/2 c. green pepper,	1/8 t. white pepper
finely chopped	2 T. lemon juice
1/4 c. sweet pickle relish	3/4 c. mayonnaise
Black olives	

Drain, bone, and flake salmon in a medium bowl. Add cottage cheese, green pepper, pickle relish, peas, salt, and pepper. Mix lightly. Scatter a few black olive slices atop salad before serving. If desired, pass mayonnaise mixed with lemon juice.

Shrimp Remoulade   New Orleans

6 T. olive oil	1/4 c. finely minced celery hearts
2 T. vinegar	1/4 c. finely minced white onion
4 t. Creole mustard	1 t. finely minced parsley
1/2 t. horseradish	2 lb. shrimp
1/2 t. pepper	Lettuce
Salt to taste	

Combine ingredients for remoulade; chill. Clean, boil, and peel shrimp; chill 2 hr. or more. Place the shrimp on shredded chilled lettuce and top with remoulade sauce. Serves 8.

Fiesta Shrimp Salad

2 cans large shrimp	2 large pink grapefruit,
3 large oranges, peeled	peeled and sectioned
and sectioned	2 medium avocados,
6 c. mixed salad greens	peeled and sliced

Arrange salad greens on individual plates; top with shrimp, fruit, and avocado. Serve with sour cream horseradish dressing. Serves 4 to 6.

Sour Cream Horseradish Dressing: Stir together 8 oz. commercial sour cream, 1/4 c. orange juice, 1 T. Dijon mustard, 2 t. prepared horseradish, and 4 diced green onions until well blended. Chill. Makes 1 1/3 cup.

Shirley's Shrimp Salad   Shirley Haskins

1 pkg lemon Jell-O
1 c. hot water
1/2 t. salt
1 T. grated onion
1/2 c. cream, whipped

1/2 c. Miracle Whip
3 hard-boiled eggs, chopped
1 T. green pepper, chopped
1-1/2 c. celery, chopped
1 can small shrimp

Dissolve Jell-O in hot water; stir in salt and onion. Let set until syrupy, then whip. Fold in whipped cream, Miracle Whip, eggs, green pepper, celery, and shrimp. Pour into 9 x 9 in. pan; chill. Double recipe for 9 x 13 in. pan. You can also add 1/2 c. chopped walnuts.

Pippin's Shrimp Salad

Iceberg lettuce
Romaine lettuce
1/2 c. finely cut celery
1 c. small cooked shrimp

2 medium tomatoes, sectioned
Ripe olives
2 hard-cooked eggs, quartered

Core and chill iceberg lettuce and romaine. Line large salad bowl with large lettuce leaves. Tear lettuces into bite-sized pieces to make 2 c. Toss with 1/4 c. Louis dressing. Add celery and drained shrimp. Toss lightly and place in lettuce nest. Garnish with tomato sections, ripe olives, and egg quarters. Pass extra Louis dressing. Serves 4.

Louis Dressing

1 c. mayonnaise
1/2 c. chili sauce
1 T. minced parsley
1 t. lemon juice

1 t. prepared horseradish
1/2 t. grated onion
1/8 t. salt
1/8 t. pepper

Stir together all ingredients. Cover and chill. Yield: 1-1/2 cups.

Shrimp Supper Salad   Eunice Wilson

1 can small shrimp, drained
    and rinsed
1 can tiny peas, well drained
1 c. finely chopped celery
1 T. minced sweet pickle

1 head iceberg lettuce, chilled
    and torn into bite-size pieces
1/2 c. Hellmann's mayonnaise
Pinch of salt

Put all ingredients into mixing bowl. Toss lightly until dressing has coated all ingredients. Chill until serving. Spoon about one cup on salad plates, with potato chips and a sweet pickle on the side. Serves 4.

Tuna Mousse   Bernice Peterson

2 env. unflavored gelatin
1/2 c. cold water
1 c. mayonnaise
2 c. (2 cans) tuna, drained
    and flaked
1/2 c. diced celery

1/4 c. stuffed green olives, sliced
2 T. lemon juice
1-1/2 t. horseradish
1/4 t. salt
1/4 t. paprika
1 c. heavy cream, whipped

Soften gelatin in cold water. Dissolve over boiling water. Stir gelatin into mayonnaise. Add tuna, celery, olives, lemon juice, horseradish, salt, and paprika. Mix
well. Fold in whipped cream. Chill until firm in 10 x 6 x 1-1/2 in. pan. Cut in
squares and serve on greens. Serves 8 to 10.

Tuna Summer Salad

2 c. diced American cheese
2 c. celery, sliced fine
2 cans solid tuna (in water),
    drained
6 hard-cooked eggs, chopped

Dash of salt and pepper
1/2 c. stuffed green olives, sliced
Mayonnaise to moisten,
    thinned with 1 T. lemon juice
1 4-oz. can shoestring potatoes

Combine ingredients except potatoes; mix gently. Just before serving, add
shoestring potatoes and toss. Serves 6.

Asparagus Molded Salad

2 lb. fresh asparagus
1-1/2 c. water
Dash of salt
1 T. Knox gelatin
1/4 c. cold water
1 c. boiling water

1/2 c. mayonnaise
1/2 t. salt
2 T. lemon juice
1/2 c. cream, whipped
1 small jar pimento, chopped

Wash and snap ends of asparagus; break into 1-1/2 in. pieces. Put into
2-qt. saucepan with 1-1/2 c. salted water. Cover. Steam 7 min. Remove from heat
and quickly run cold water over asparagus, draining well. Set aside. Dissolve
gelatin in 1/4 c. cold water; add 1 c. boiling water. Chill. Add mayonnaise, 1/2 t.
salt, lemon juice, and whipped cream. Add asparagus and pimento. Pour into mold
and chill. Serves 6.

Asparagus-Bacon Salad

1 lb. fresh asparagus	5 strips bacon, fried crisp
1/2 t. salt	and crumbled
1/2 head lettuce, torn and chilled	1 4-1/4-oz. can chopped
Cucumber dressing	ripe olives

Wash and snap tough ends off asparagus; steam in 1 in. salted water. Drain and chill. Place 3 to 5 asparagus spears on bed of lettuce on 6 salad plates. Top with cucumber dressing, crumbled bacon, and olives. Serve cold. Serves 6.

Cucumber Dressing: Blend 1-1/4 c. mayonnaise, 1 c. chopped drained salad cucumber, and 1 t. dill seed.

Sweet and Sour Beet Salad   Aunt Elta Petersen

2 c. diced canned beets, drained	1/2 c. chopped celery
1 pkg lemon Jell-O	2 T. vinegar
1/2 c. beet liquid	1 T. prepared horseradish
2 T. lemon juice	1-1/2 t. onion salt
Cottage cheese	Mayonnaise

Dissolve lemon Jell-O in 1-1/2 c. boiling water. Add beet liquid, lemon juice, and vinegar. Chill until slightly thickened. Add beets, horseradish, salt, and celery. Chill in an 8 x 8 in. mold. To serve, cut in squares and put a heaping spoonful of cottage cheese on top. Pass mayonnaise.

Flavors blend after salad chills. Very pretty salad.

BLT Salad

8 oz. commercial sour cream	1 large head iceberg lettuce,
1 c. mayonnaise	torn (about 6 c.)
1 T. lemon juice	12 thick bacon strips,
1 t. dried basil	cooked crisp and crumbled
1/2 t. salt	4 medium tomatoes, sliced thin
1/2 t. pepper	2 c. croutons
1/4 t. garlic powder	

Stir together sour cream, mayonnaise, and seasonings until well blended. Layer lettuce, bacon, and tomato in a 9 x 13 in. glass dish. Spread mayonnaise mixture evenly over tomato, sealing to edge of dish. Cover and chill salad at least 2 hr. Sprinkle with croutons, and serve immediately. Serves 8.

312

Broccoli Overnight Salad

1 bunch fresh broccoli	4 hard-cooked eggs, chopped
1 6-oz. can ripe olives, sliced	1/4 c. sweet pickle relish
1 5-oz. jar stuffed green	2/3 c. mayonnaise
olives, sliced	1 t. lemon juice
1 small onion, chopped	

Cut broccoli into small florets. Mix with olives, onion, and eggs. Add relish, mayonnaise, and lemon juice; mix all well. Put into covered bowl and refrigerate overnight. Stir well and serve. Yield: 4 to 6 servings.

Broccoli-Raisin Salad

1 lb. frozen broccoli (do	1 c. mayonnaise
not cook)	2 T. lemon juice
1 c. raisins	2 T. sugar
1 c. dry roasted peanuts	

Cut broccoli into bite-size pieces. Combine ingredients the night before serving. Refrigerate overnight. Toss before serving.

Super! An interesting way to present fresh-tasting broccoli.

Broccoli-Cauliflower for a Dozen

1 small bunch broccoli	1-1/2 c. cheddar cheese
1 head cauliflower	1 c. mayonnaise
1/2 large red onion	1/2 c. sugar
3/4 c. raisins	2 T. vinegar
1 lb. bacon	

Cook bacon crisp and crumble. Shred cheese. Finely chop broccoli, cauliflower, and red onion and place in large bowl. Add bacon and cheese; toss. Combine mayonnaise, sugar, and vinegar. Pour over salad and toss. Cover, chill 3-4 hr. or overnight, and serve. Serves 12.

Broccoli-Cauliflower Salad

1/2 head fresh cauliflower	1 8-oz. can sliced water chestnuts
1 small bunch fresh broccoli	1/2 c. green onions, chopped

Separate cauliflower into florets. Cut broccoli fine. Combine in bowl with drained water chestnuts and onions. Pour dressing over vegetables and toss; chill overnight. Serves 6.

313

Dressing: 1/2 c. Hellmann's mayonnaise, 1/4 c. sugar, 2 T. salad oil, 1/4 c. wine vinegar; blend.

Hot Bacon–Cabbage Slaw

1 medium cabbage	6 bacon slices
3 T. minced onion	1/3 c. sugar
1/2 t. salt	1/3 c. water
1/4 t. pepper	1/4 c. vinegar

Shred cabbage; combine with onion, salt, and pepper. Cook bacon until crisp; drain, break into pieces, and reserve drippings in skillet. Stir sugar, water, and vinegar into reserved drippings. Bring to boil, and remove from heat. Stir in bacon; drizzle over cabbage mixture, and toss. Serve immediately. Serves 6.

Caesar Salad

1 garlic clove, halved	1/4 c. red wine vinegar
2 heads romaine lettuce, torn	2 garlic cloves, minced
1 6-oz. pkg seasoned croutons	1 T. Worcestershire sauce
1/2 c. olive oil	1/2 c. grated Parmesan cheese
1 2-oz. can anchovies (optional)	

Rub wooden salad bowl with garlic halves. Add lettuce and croutons, tossing well. Drain and add anchovies, if desired. Mix olive oil and remaining ingredients in blender until smooth. Pour over lettuce mixture; toss well. Serves 6 to 8.

Cobb Salad

1 large head iceberg lettuce	2 c. julienne strips cooked chicken
2 large tomatoes, peeled and diced	1 3-oz. pkg Roquefort cheese
3 hard-cooked eggs, chopped	2/3 c. French dressing
1/2 lb. bacon, cooked crisp	Romaine lettuce leaves
and crumbled	1/2 c. black olives
2 medium avocados, peeled,	3 radishes, sliced
pitted, and diced	1 T. chopped chives

Shred lettuce. Crumble cheese. Combine with bacon, eggs, avocados, tomatoes, and chicken. Toss with dressing. Arrange on lettuce leaves. Garnish with olives, radishes, and chives.

My Zesty Calico Slaw

1 1-lb. pkg. finely cut slaw (cabbage and carrot)	1/4 c. red wine vinegar
1/2 c. green onions	1/4 c. sugar
1 large green pepper	1 T. lemon juice
1 large red pepper	1/2 t. Worcestershire sauce
2 stalks celery	1/2 t. salt
1 large carrot	1 t. Italian herbs
	1/4 c. salad oil

Slice green onions fine. Wash, seed, and dice green and red peppers into 1/2-in. cubes. Chop stalks of celery fine. Place all vegetables in a 2-qt. refrigerator container with tight lid. Combine all marinade ingredients and beat 2 min. with rotary or electric mixer. Pour marinade over vegetables; toss well. Cover and chill 8 hr. or overnight. When ready to serve, toss again to marinate. Yield: about 8 cups.

This slaw improves every day — just toss it and serve.

♣ *To give any cabbage slaw a delightfully crisp snap, add 1/4 to 1/2 c. hulled sunflower seeds.*

Corn and Cabbage Slaw

4 c. shredded cabbage	1/2 c. diced sharp cheese
1/2 c. chopped onion	2 T. sliced black olives
1 to 1-1/2 c. cooked corn (fresh or canned), drained	1/3 c. mayonnaise
2 T. chopped parsley	2 t. prepared mustard
	1/4 t. celery salt

Combine vegetables, cheese, and olives. Whisk together mayonnaise, mustard, and celery salt; pour over slaw, and chill. Toss and serve.

A real salute to the fall garden.

♣ *To keep fresh parsley, wash it thoroughly, spin dry, and place in covered glass jar in refrigerator. If you do not have a salad spinner, remove extra moisture by placing it between folds of a clean tea towel.*

Creamy Coleslaw

1 medium fresh green cabbage	1 T. sugar
1 c. carrots, shredded	1 T. vinegar
1/2 c. sweet onion, finely diced	1 t. salt
1 c. celery, sliced thin	1/2 t. Coleman's dry mustard
1/2 c. mayonnaise	1/4 t. black pepper
1/2 c. sour cream	1 T. lemon juice

Slice cabbage thin; combine with carrots, onion, and celery. Mix all dressing ingredients and pour over vegetables. Toss well. Chill before serving. Serves 8 to 10.

Tart Coleslaw

1 head cabbage	1/4 t. celery salt
1/4 c. vegetable oil	2 T. mayonnaise
2 T. vinegar, lime juice,	Salt
or lemon juice	Pepper
1/2 t. prepared mustard	Paprika

Shred cabbage. Mix oil and vinegar; add mayonnaise, mustard, celery salt, and seasonings to taste. Pour over cabbage and toss.

Cheese Relish Salad

1 pkg lemon Jell-O	1 c. grated cheddar cheese
1 pkg lime Jell-O	1/4 c. stuffed olives, sliced
3-1/2 c. boiling water	1/4 c. sweet pickles, chopped fine
1/2 c. whipping cream	1/4 c. nuts, chopped
1 c. crushed pineapple, drained	

Prepare Jell-O with boiling water; chill. When almost set, whip cream; blend into Jell-O. Then add other ingredients. Pour into a 9 x 12 in. dish, chill, and cut into squares. Serves 8 to 12.

Copper Pennies — Carrot Salad

2 bunches carrots (16 carrots)	1 c. sugar
1 medium onion, diced	3/4 c. cider vinegar
1 green pepper	1 t. dry mustard
1 c. tomato sauce	1 t. Worcestershire sauce
1/2 c. salad oil	

Scrape carrots and slice circles 1/4 in. thick. Cook until just tender in salted water. Drain. Cool. Seed and cut green pepper in large dice. Combine carrots, onion, and pepper in container with tight cover. Set aside. Combine other ingredients for marinating sauce, mix well, and pour over vegetables. Refrigerate 4 hr. or longer. Scoop vegetables out of marinade to serving bowl with slotted spoon; serve as a side salad. Serves 4 to 6.

This keeps well in the marinade, chilled.

Garden Cukes and Onions

3 or 4 fresh 6-in. cucumbers	1/2 c. cider vinegar
1/2 t. salt	1 T. sugar
2 or 3 fresh white Bermuda onions	1 c. cold water

Peel and cut cucumbers in 1/8-in. slices. Remove skin of onions and slice very thin. Combine cucumber and onion slices. Cover with mixture of vinegar, sugar, and water; sprinkle with salt and pepper. Stir to blend.

German Cucumber Salad

3 cucumbers	1 T. lemon juice
1/2 c. sour cream	1 t. dry dill seed or
1/4 t. salt	finely cut chives or parsley
1/4 t. white pepper	

Score cucumbers with a fork and slice thin. Add a little salt and set aside. Combine remaining ingredients. Drain cucumbers and mix lightly with dressing. Chill well before serving.

You may substitute 1/2 c. yogurt for the sour cream.

Cucumber Soufflé

1 3-oz. pkg lime Jell-O	1 t. onion juice
1/2 c. boiling water	1 c. chopped unpeeled
1/4 c. lemon juice	drained cucumber
1 c. sour cream	

Dissolve Jell-O in boiling water. Add lemon and onion juice. Chill. When partially set, fold in sour cream and cucumber. Turn into oiled individual molds. Chill. Unmold onto a leaf of lettuce; serve with mayonnaise and tomato wedges. Serves 4.

Homesteaders' Dandelion Salad   Christena Paulsen

4 to 5 c. young dandelions,
   chopped
3 or 4 strips of bacon
3 hard-boiled eggs
1 medium onion, chopped

1 t. salt
1 T. sugar
1/4 c. vinegar
1-1/2 c. whole milk
1-1/2 T. flour

Gather a basket of young dandelion tops before they flower. Sort and wash them thoroughly, discarding any that are ragged or blemished. Chop the leaves. Measure about 4 to 5 c. and put in cold water to keep crisp. Cut 3 or 4 strips of bacon (side meat) into 1-in. pieces and fry crisp; drain on brown paper. Cook 3 eggs to hard boiled; cool, shell, and chop. In the bacon drippings, brown the onion. Then add the flour, salt, sugar, vinegar, and, gradually, milk; stir over medium heat to make a smooth sauce. Let it cool slightly. Then pour over most of the chopped eggs and prepared dandelions, well drained; toss. Sprinkle salad with chopped egg and crisp bacon.

Settlers in the Midwest had been accustomed to tending kitchen gardens in their homelands. They planted gardens in their new home, but long before lettuce, radishes, and onions were ready to pick, nocturnal visitors — such as raccoons and deer—might visit and harvest. Longing for greens after the bitter Midwestern winter, the settlers welcomed the sight of the plentiful dandelions for a salad that tasted fresh and green. At the Amanas in central Iowa, the tradition of this salad is still a rite of spring. And on the rolling hills of western Iowa in the 1920s, Grandma and I walked along the roadside in April collecting dandelion greens for a supper salad my Danish grandfather relished.

Those dandelions had another use that continues as a profitable enterprise today: making dandelion wine.

Dutch Lettuce with Sour Cream

8 c. washed and dried leaf
   lettuce, torn and chilled
1 c. sour cream
2 T. sugar
1/2 t. salt
Pepper

1 t. dry mustard
2 T. chopped spring onion
1/4 c. cider vinegar
4 hard-boiled eggs, chopped
8 strips bacon, fried crisp & crumbled
3 T. bacon grease

In tightly covered contained, mix all ingredients except lettuce, eggs, and bacon. Refrigerate overnight. Just before serving, place lettuce, eggs, and crisp bacon bits in large bowl; add dressing and toss.

Dutch Lettuce   Zylstra's Restaurant, Sully, Iowa

Iceberg lettuce   Bacon, fried crisp, drained
Radishes   2 c. salad dressing
Green or red peppers   3 T. prepared yellow mustard
Green onions   1/2 c. sugar
Hard-cooked eggs,   Pepper
    chilled and sliced   1 t. celery salt

Combine all dressing ingredients and warm in top of double boiler. This makes enough dressing for 8 to 10 individual salads. Dressing may be refrigerated and heated as needed.

Place washed, dried, and torn lettuce in salad bowl. Slice radishes, green or red pepper, and green onions (quantities to taste) and toss with lettuce. Spread some Dutch lettuce dressing over top. Arrange egg slices and bacon bits on top of lettuce. Serve untossed and pass dressing.

Fire and Ice

6 large, firm, ripe tomatoes   1-1/2 t. celery seed
2 large red onions   1 t. mustard seed
1 green pepper   1/2 t. salt
3/4 c. cider vinegar   2 T. sugar
1/4 c. water   1/2 t. coarse grind pepper

Peel and slice tomatoes in 1/4-in slices. Cut onions into 1/4-in. slices. Seed and cut green pepper in 1/2-in. dice. Alternate tomato and onion slices in dish, sprinkling with green pepper. Put the other ingredients in a small saucepan and bring to a boil for only 1 min. Pour over vegetables and chill several hours.

Fresh Garden Relish   Faye Hoelker, Diane Rosteck

2 large, peeled, diced tomatoes   1/3 c. vinegar
1 peeled, diced cucumber   1 t. salt
1/2 c. diced green pepper   1/2 t. celery seed
    or green chili   1/2 t. black pepper
1/3 c. onion, chopped fine   2 T. brown sugar, packed

Combine ingredients and chill.

Gazpacho

1-1/2 c. tomato or V-8 juice
1 beef bouillon cube, crushed
2 T. red wine vinegar
1 T. salad oil
1/2 t. Worcestershire sauce
1/4 t. salt
3 drops Tabasco sauce

1 large ripe tomato, chopped
1/4 c. cucumber, peeled & diced
2 T. green pepper, diced
2 T. onion, diced
4 to 6 crushed ice cubes
1 avocado, peeled & diced

Heat tomato juice. Stir in beef bouillon cube until dissolved; then stir in rest of seasoning. Chill several hours. Prepare vegetables and crush ice. Add to chilled mixture. Serve in soup plates or mugs. Serves 4.

Greek Salad

4 firm ripe tomatoes
1 medium cucumber
1 medium onion
1 green pepper
1/2 c. Greek olives

4 oz. feta cheese
1 T. capers
1/2 c. olive oil
1/4 t. oregano
Salt

Wash the tomatoes, cut in eighths and halve again. Peel and slice cucumber. Slice onion and separate into rings. Seed green pepper and cut in rings. Place vegetables in salad bowl; add olives, oregano, salt, and capers and mix lightly. Break or slice the feta cheese into bite-sized pieces and sprinkle on top of salad. Pour olive oil over salad.

Guacamole

2 large ripe avocados
2 to 3 T. lime juice
1 garlic clove, minced
Salt to taste

2 t. chopped parsley
4 mild jalapeno peppers, minced
1 small tomato

Cut avocados in half. Remove seeds and scoop out pulp with a spoon or peel. Mash pulp coarsely with fork while blending in lime juice. Add the remaining ingredients. Makes about 2 c. guacamole.

Use guacamole as a dip for tortilla chips or fresh vegetables, or serve it as a salad on a bed of lettuce.

Majestic Layered Salad

1 qt. torn spinach	1 c. mayonnaise
2 c. mushroom slices	1/2 t. sugar
1-1/2 c. red onion rings	1/2 t. curry powder
2 c. frozen peas,	2 bacon strips, crisply
cooked & drained	fried & crumbled

In a large salad bowl or casserole, layer spinach, mushrooms, onions, and peas. Combine mayonnaise, sugar, and curry powder. Spread over salad to seal. Cover and refrigerate overnight. Top with bacon before serving. Serves 8.

Seven-Layer Vegetable Salad

6 c. iceberg lettuce,	11/2 c. mayonnaise
torn and chilled	8 strips bacon, fried crisp
1 c. celery, chopped	and crumbled
1/2 large red onion, sliced thin	1-1/2 c. grated sharp
1 10-oz. pkg frozen peas,	cheddar cheese
unthawed	

In a 9 x 13 in. glass dish, layer the listed vegetables in order given, beginning with half the lettuce and ending after the peas with the other half of the lettuce. Spread the mayonnaise evenly, sealing to the edge of the pan (you may need a little more). Sprinkle the grated cheese evenly over the mayonnaise, and sprinkle the crumbled bacon over all.

Cover the dish tightly with Saran Wrap. Chill overnight until ready to serve. Yield: 12 servings.

Everyone enjoys this salad. It provides color, good nutrition, and an interesting combination of textures and taste. For variety, substitute fresh spinach, sliced green onions, and cherry tomatoes for the lettuce, red onion, and peas and omit cheese. Substitute prepared or homemade Ranch dressing for mayonnaise for a wholly different look and taste.

Spinach Layered Salad

1 lb. fresh spinach, torn	1 8-oz. can sliced water chestnuts,
Salt, pepper, sugar to taste	1 10-oz. pkg tiny frozen peas, thawed
8 strips bacon, cooked crisp	1 medium onion, diced
6 hard-cooked eggs, chopped	2 stalks celery, chopped
1/2 c. mayonnaise	1/2 c. grated cheddar cheese
1/2 c. Italian dressing	

Put spinach in a 3-qt. serving dish. Sprinkle with salt, pepper, sugar, and crumbled bacon. Layer chopped eggs. Salt and pepper. Then layer drained water chestnuts, peas, onion, and celery. Combine mayonnaise and Italian dressing and spread over top, sealing to edge of bowl. Sprinkle with cheese. Cover. Chill overnight. Toss lightly to serve. Serves 10 to 12.

Marge's Bibb Lettuce Mimosa

Marge Van Doornevelt

Bibb lettuce—1/2 head per person
Olive oil
Wine vinegar
1 t. Dijon mustard
Salt and pepper

Fresh parsley, chopped
Green onions or shallots,
  chopped (optional)
2 hard-boiled eggs, finely chopped

Wash, dry, and chill lettuce. Tear into pieces. Add any extras you like—vegetables, slivered meats, etc. Prepare dressing with 3 parts olive oil to 1 part wine vinegar, adding mustard (adjust to amount of lettuce), salt and pepper to taste; shake well in jar or use blender. Add chopped parsley and onion before pouring over salad. Sprinkle with chopped eggs.

Bishops' Lettuce Supreme

Medium head iceberg lettuce
Hellmann's mayonnaise

Blue cheese
Paprika

Wash and drain lettuce. Remove the core. Chill. Cut head crosswise in slices 1 in. thick. Place rings on 7-8-in. chilled salad plates. Spread 1 T. mayonnaise to cover each slice. Crumble blue cheese generously atop, and sprinkle with paprika. Keep salad chilled in refrigerator until serving time.

This very refreshing salad was a specialty of Bishops' Buffets.

Wilted Lettuce

2 large bunches fresh
  leaf lettuce
2 green onions, sliced
4 bacon slices, chopped

1/4 c. cider or white vinegar
2 T. water
2 t. sugar
Salt and pepper to taste

Shred lettuce and place in salad bowl. Season with salt and pepper, and sprinkle with green onions. Fry bacon until crisp. Remove bacon with slotted spoon, leaving drippings. Stir vinegar, water, and sugar into drippings; heat until boiling, stirring to combine. Sprinkle crisp bacon over lettuce. Pour hot dressing over all, and toss until lettuce wilts.

Macaroni Salad

2 c. elbow macaroni, uncooked
1/3 c. minced onion
2 c. celery, sliced fine
1/2 c. chopped pimento
1 t. salt

1/2 c. chopped sweet pickle
2 hard-boiled eggs, chopped
3/4 c. salad dressing
1/3 c. sour cream
1 t. chopped fresh dill

Cook macaroni in salted water until tender. Drain, rinse, and chill. Mix salad dressing, sour cream, and dill. Pour it over the macaroni combined with all other ingredients. Mix together lightly. Pour into salad bowl and sprinkle with paprika. Chill well. Serves 8.

Macaroni Tuna Salad

1 12-1/2 oz. can solid
    albacore tuna
3 c. cooked elbow macaroni,
    drained
1 c. celery
1 green pepper

3 green onions
1/4 c. black olives, sliced
1/4 t. salt
2 T. tarragon wine vinegar
1 c. salad dressing
Lettuce

Slice celery and green onions. Seed and chop green pepper. Combine these with tuna, macaroni, and olives; mix well. Add salt and vinegar to dressing and blend. Pour dressing over tuna mixture and toss to coat. Chill several hours. Serve in bowl lined with crisp lettuce leaves. Serves 8 to 10.

Salad Nicoise

2 heads Bibb lettuce
2 6-oz. cans white tuna, drained
1/2 lb. cold, cooked green beans
8 new potatoes, cooked,
    skinned, and sliced

1 2-oz. can anchovy fillets
2 T. capers
1 large ripe tomato, quartered
1/2 c. sliced black olives
2 hard-boiled eggs, quartered

Tear lettuce and divide among six individual salad bowls. Divide rest of ingredients among the bowls, arranging to make a colorful bowl. Refrigerate. To serve, drizzle with homemade or commercial vinaigrette dressing. Alternatively, pass both vinaigrette and garlic mayonnaise. Serves 6.

Jan's Pea Salad

Jan Harbour

2 16-oz. cans peas, drained
1/2 large red onion
Greens from 4 or 5 spring onions
3 stalks celery

4 large hard-boiled eggs
4 heaping T. pickle relish
1 2-oz. jar pimientos
Miracle Whip dressing

Slice red onion, and separate slices. Chop tops of green onions fine. Chop celery into small pieces. Peel and slice eggs crosswise. Drain and slice pimientos. Combine all ingredients in large mixing bowl, and mix gently. Add dressing to desired consistency. Cover and refrigerate 2 hr. or until flavors blend. Serve on lettuce. Serves 6 to 8.

Black-Eyed Pea Salad

3-1/2 c. black-eyed peas,
   cooked and drained
1 red pepper
1 green pepper
3 green onions
1 large tomato

1/2 c. celery
3/4 c. parsley
Salt and pepper
5 T. white vinegar
3/4 c. olive oil
2 t. grated orange peel

Chop red and green peppers, onions, celery, and parsley. Seed and dice tomato. Combine with black-eyed peas in large bowl. Whisk together vinegar, oil, and orange peel. Pour on salad and toss gently. Salt and pepper to taste. Cover and chill. Remove from refrigerator 30 min. before serving. Serves 6.

Perfection Salad

Clara Shedd

2 T. Knox gelatin
1/2 c. cold water
1/2 c. vinegar
Juice of 1 lemon
2 c. boiling water
1/2 c. sugar

1 c. cabbage, finely shredded
1/2 c. pimiento, diced
1/2 c. celery, finely cut
1/2 c. green pepper, diced
1 t. salt
Lettuce

Soak gelatin in cold water; add boiling water and stir until gelatin is dissolved. Add vinegar, lemon juice, sugar, and salt. Cool. When it is the consistency of egg white, add the chopped vegetables. Stir to distribute evenly. Pour into individual half-cup molds or into a 9 x 9 in. pan. Chill 4 hr. Serve on lettuce with salad dressing. Serves 9.

This colorful congealed salad is a tangy contrast served with a beef or chicken entrée. It is as fresh as when it was introduced in the 1920s.

324

German Potato Salad

4 lb. potatoes, preferably new
1/2 c. olive oil
1/2 c. vinegar
1 t. onion, finely sliced

1/2 c. warm bouillon or water
Salt to taste
1/4 t. coarsely ground pepper

Boil potatoes in jackets; peel and slice. While potatoes are still warm, add bouillon and vinegar, then the oil, onion, and seasonings. Mix gently without breaking potatoes. Refrigerate at least 1 hr., adding seasoning if necessary at serving time. Serves 6.

This is the potato salad typically found in New York delicatessens.

Mother's Deluxe Potato Salad   Anna M. Petersen

6 medium potatoes
1 t. salt
1-1/4 t. curry powder, divided
3 T. French dressing
2 T. lemon juice
1 t. garlic salt
1/2 t. salt

1/4 t. Accent
1/8 t. pepper
3 hard-cooked eggs, diced
1/2 c. green pepper, diced
1/2 c. green onions, diced
1 c. celery, chopped
1/2 c. or more mayonnaise

Wash, pare, and dice potatoes. Cook in boiling water with 1/2 t. salt and 1 t. curry powder until tender. Drain. Put in mixing bowl with French dressing, lemon juice, garlic salt, 1/2 t. salt, Accent, 1/4 t. curry, and pepper. Toss lightly. Refrigerate to marinate 1-2 hr. Prepare eggs, green pepper, onions, and celery. Add with mayonnaise to potato mixture; toss lightly. Refrigerate to chill. Serves 6.

My Picnic Potato Salad

3 lb. white potatoes (10 medium)
2 T. cider vinegar
1 t. sugar
1 T. salt
1/4 c. salad oil
1/2 c. green onions, minced
2 c. mayonnaise
Green pepper, sliced in rings

1 c. sour cream
1 T. prepared horseradish
2 c. celery, chopped
6 hard-cooked eggs, diced
4 T. minced parsley
2 jars chopped pimiento
1/2 c. sweet pickle relish
Black olives, sliced

Boil potatoes in skins until tender. Drain. While warm, peel, cube, and marinate potatoes in vinegar, salt, sugar, salad oil, and onions. Chill thoroughly. Then add celery, eggs, parsley, pimientos, and pickle relish. Mix. Chill to blend flavors.

Mix mayonnaise, sour cream, and horseradish. Pour over potato mixture. Toss lightly. Use a little pickle juice if needed to moisten salad. Chill several hours. Serve in a large salad bowl; garnish with rings of green pepper and black olive slices. Refrigerate leftovers after serving. 12-14 servings.

My Potluck Potato Salad

8-10 new red potatoes,
   medium sized
2 t. prepared mustard
1/2 c. chopped green onion
1 t. salt
1/2 c. salad oil

1 c. celery
1/4 c. sweet pickles
3 hard-cooked eggs
1 c. Hellmann's mayonnaise
1 c. dairy sour cream

Cook potatoes, drain, peel, and cut into cubes. Mix mustard, onions, salt, and salad oil; pour over warm potatoes and, as they cool, stir occasionally so that marinade moistens potatoes. Chop celery, sweet pickles, and eggs. Add to potatoes. Mix mayonnaise and sour cream, and pour over potatoes. Fold lightly. Taste to correct seasoning. Cover and refrigerate several hours. Mix very lightly before serving. Attractive with greens tucked around bowl and garnished with sliced olives or pickles or egg slices. Refrigerate leftovers promptly. Serves 8.

Rotini Salad

2 8-oz. pkg rotini, cooked
2 c. mayonnaise
1/4 c. vinegar
1/2 c. sugar
1 large green pepper, diced

1 large onion, chopped fine
3 large carrots, grated
1 can Eagle brand sweetened,
    condensed milk

Cook rotini to al dente; for extra color, use rainbow rotini. Mix all ingredients in a large refrigerator container with lid. Chill. You may omit onions. Serves 10-12.

Sauerkraut Salad I

1 #2-1/2 can sauerkraut, drained
1-1/2 c. sugar
1-1/2 T. cider vinegar
1/2 t. celery seed

1 small jar pimiento, diced
1 large green pepper
2/3 c. sweet onion

Seed, remove membrane, and chop green pepper. Chop onion fine. Combine all ingredients and mix well. Chill in refrigerator several hours or overnight. Stir well before serving. Keeps several days in refrigerator.

Sauerkraut Salad II

1 large can sauerkraut, drained	1/2 c. carrot
1/2 c. sugar	1 2-oz. jar pimiento, drained
1/2 c. onion	and diced
1/2 c. celery	1/4 c. Mazola oil
1/2 c. green pepper	

Mix sugar into drained sauerkraut. Set aside to blend half an hour. Chop onion, celery, and green pepper. Grate carrot. Add all ingredients to sauerkraut; mix well. Cover and chill overnight. Stir before serving. Serves 6.

Wally's Spiced Salad   Wally Harmon

3 c. water	2 pkg lemon Jell-O
1 c. sugar	1 c. sweet pickles
2 t. whole cloves	1 small jar pimiento
2 t. vinegar	1 c. pecans
Lettuce	Mayonnaise

Boil water, sugar, cloves, and vinegar for 5 min.; strain and add Jell-O while hot, stirring until dissolved. Chop pickles (or use pickle relish), pimiento, and pecans. Blend with warm Jell-O and pour into a 9 x 12 in. Pyrex dish. Chill 4 hr. Cut into squares and serve on a lettuce leaf with half a teaspoonful of mayonnaise.

Salad Superb   Sue Arthaud

1 head romaine lettuce	Red and green peppers, sliced
1 head Bibb lettuce	2 oz. blue cheese, crumbled
1 small head iceberg lettuce	1 c. salad oil
1/2 c. Parmesan cheese, grated	1/4 c. vinegar
2 or 3 avocados	1 t. salt
1 large cucumber, peeled	1/2 t. white pepper
and diced	1/2 t. celery salt
6 slices bacon, fried crisp	1/4 t. cayenne
and crumbled	1/4 t. dry mustard
1/2 c. ripe olives, sliced	1 clove garlic, minced
1-1/2 c. cherry tomatoes, halved	Dash tobasco sauce

Combine oil with other dressing ingredients in a jar; cover, shake, and chill. Tear salad greens into bite-sized pieces; combined in large bowl. Sprinkle cheese over the greens. Slice avocados and arrange with cukes, tomato, pepper, bacon, and olives on top of greens. Chill 2-3 hours. Pour dressing over salad; toss. Serves 10 to 12.

Rose's Tabbouleh   Rosemary Keese

1 c. bulgar wheat
4 c. boiling water
6 or 8 green onions
1 bunch parsley
6 or 8 sprigs fresh mint

4 ripe large tomatoes
Juice of 3 lemons (1/2 c.)
1/2 c. fresh olive oil
Salt and pepper to taste

Pour boiling water over bulgar wheat in large bowl; let soak 1/2 hr., then drain in colander until dry. Chop onions fine, including some green tops. Chop parsley and mint fine. Dice tomatoes. Combine all ingredients in large bowl, mix well. Adjust salt. Chill. Serve on lettuce or as a side dish. Serves 6 to 8.

This Middle Eastern salad keeps very well, covered and refrigerated. Bulgar wheat can be obtained in a Lebanese grocery or health food store.

Three Bean Salad

1 can cut green beans
1 can cut yellow wax beans
1 can kidney beans
1 large onion
1 green pepper

1/2 c. sugar
1/2 c. white vinegar
1/2 c. salad oil
1/2 t. salt
Pepper

Drain cans of vegetables. Chop onion and green pepper and add. Combine dressing ingredients, blend well, and pour over vegetables. Mix gently. Refrigerate 3-4 hr. before serving. Keeps several days under refrigeration.

Tomato Aspic   Marianne MacCurdy

4 c. V-8 juice
1 large pkg lemon Jell-O
1/4 c. stuffed olives

1 c. mayonnaise
1/2 c. cucumber, peeled,
    seeded, and minced

Heat V-8 juice and pour over Jell-O; stir until dissolved and chill until partially thickened. Fold in olives. Pour into 9 x 9 in. dish or salad mold. Chill until set. Serve with cucumber dressing: blend minced cucumber into mayonnaise.

Tomato Cucumber Salad

3 tomatoes
1 medium cucumber
Fresh basil

1/2 c. prepared French dressing
Salt

Wash tomatoes and cut into 1/4-in. slices. Peel cucumber, slice, and place on shallow serving platter alternating with tomato slices. Sprinkle with fresh chopped basil and salt. Drizzle French dressing over salad. Chill 2 hr. and serve.

This salad should be served when fresh home-grown tomatoes, cucumbers, and basil are at their peak.

♣ *Sprinkle dried or crushed thyme, oregano, or basil on tomatoes or greens for extra flavor with no extra calories.*

Italian Flag Salad (Tomato-Avocado)   Il Portico, London

6 large fully ripe tomatoes
4 ripe avocados
1 lb. fresh mozzarella cheese
Lettuce

Italian oil dressing or
    fresh olive oil
Lemon juice

Peel and slice tomatoes into 1/2-in slices; do not use ends. Peel and cut avocados into 1/2-in. wedges; sprinkle with lemon juice. Slice fresh (not cured) mozzarella into 1/4-in. slices. Arrange tomato, mozzarella, and avocado alternately on lettuce-lined plates. Repeat, making six stripes. Drizzle lightly with Italian oil dressing or olive oil. Sprinkle with pepper. Yield: 8 servings.

This very attractive salad shows the colors of Italy's flag. Il Portico in High Street Kensington features this and many other superb Italian dishes.

Ishmael's Turkish Salad   Ishmael Yiyit

1 large head romaine lettuce
4 large ripe tomatoes
1/2 large sweet onion
1/2 c. black olives,
    halved

2/3 c. olive oil
Juice of 1 large lemon
1 T. brown sugar
1/2 t. salt
1/4 t. pepper

Wash lettuce and blot until completely dry; chill. Tear into bite-sized pieces. Peel tomatoes. Squeeze slightly to remove seeds. Cut pulp into bite-sized pieces. Chop sweet onion (such as Vidalia or Bermuda), to make about 3/4 c. In large salad bowl, combine olive oil, lemon juice, brown sugar, salt, and pepper to make vinaigrette; beat well. Add lettuce, tomatoes, onion, and black olives to the vinaigrette and toss lightly. Chill at least 2 hr. Toss again before serving. Serves 6.

Ishmael is an exchange student studying in New York. A native of Turkey, he made this salad for our family while a Christmas guest. The lemon and brown sugar give it a tangy, unusual flair.

Diane's Marinated Vegetables   Diane Santee

2 cans French-cut green beans	2 cans lima beans
2 cans small peas	1 small can mushrooms
2 cans fingerling carrots	1 small jar pimiento, chopped
2 cans whole kernel corn	1 medium onion, chopped
1 medium green pepper, chopped	

Drain all vegetables, mix together, and add marinade. Mix and pour into sterilized jars. Chill. Keeps for weeks in refrigerator. Yield: 3 to 3-1/2 qt.

Marinade: Mix 1/2 c. salad oil (Wesson), 1 c. sugar, 1 c. white vinegar (Speas), 1-1/2 t. celery salt, 1-1/2 t. salt, 1-1/2 t. paprika. Heat to boiling; pour over vegetables in sterilized jars. Cover tightly and chill.

Faye's Vegetable Relish   Faye Hoelker

1 10-oz. can French-cut green beans	1 t. salt
1 can whole kernel corn	1/4 t. pepper
1/2 c. carrot, diced	1 T. water
1 c. celery, diced	1 c. sugar
1 c. onion, diced	1/2 c. salad oil
1 2-oz. jar pimiento, chopped	3/4 c. vinegar

Drain canned vegetables and combine with prepared fresh ones in a large bowl. In a saucepan, combine seasonings with water, oil, and vinegar and bring to a boil. Pour over vegetables and mix to coat. Store in jars in refrigerator.

Vegetable Salad   Donna Lunsford

1 head cauliflower	1 10-oz. pkg frozen peas
1 bunch broccoli	1 c. mayonnaise
2 small onions	1 c. sour cream
1 can water chestnuts drained and sliced	1 pkg Hidden Valley salad dressing mix

Break cauliflower and broccoli into small pieces. Slice onions and separate into rings. Combine with water chestnuts and peas. Mix mayonnaise, sour cream, and salad dressing mix; pour over vegetables and toss. Chill 3-4 hr. Serves 12.

Favorite flavors give a boost to good health. This salad also helps to cheer a long winter.

Congealed Vegetable Salad

4 oz. pecans, chopped
3 c. carrots, grated
3 c. celery, chopped fine
1 5-oz. jar stuffed green
    olives, halved
2 17-oz. cans baby peas
    and onions, drained

2 6-oz. pkg lemon Jell-O
Juice of 1 lime
1 c. sour cream
2 T. chopped chives
1/2 t. garlic powder
1 T. horseradish
Salt and pepper to taste

Sprinkle pecans over bottom of a 9 x 13 in. pan. Layer vegetables over these. Prepare Jell-O according to package directions; stir in lime juice. Pour cooled mixture carefully over vegetables just to cover. (Some gelatin may be left over.) Do not stir. Chill until firm. Mix sour cream with seasonings, and spread evenly over gelatin. Serves 12 to 15.

Wild Rice Salad   Anne Harbour

1 c. wild rice
4 c. water
1 t. salt
4 T. olive oil
1/2 c. green onion
Salt and pepper

1/2 c. green pepper
1/2 c. red pepper
1/2 c. yellow pepper
1/2 c. parsley
1/2 c. cherry tomatoes,
    quartered (optional)

Rinse wild rice; drain. Bring rice, water, and salt to boil in heavy pan. Reduce heat and simmer, covered, until kernels open and are tender but not mushy (45-50 min.). Drain. Conserve water for soup if desired. Sprinkle olive oil on hot rice 1 T. at a time, turning gently with wooden spoon. Cool. When rice is lukewarm, chop vegetables and add to rice; mix well. Salt and pepper to taste. Refrigerate. If desire,d add tomatoes just before serving. Serves 6-8.

This dish keeps well without tomatoes, but small firm ones can be included when the dish will be consumed immediately.

Zucchini-Apple Slaw

1/2 c. low-fat vanilla yogurt
1/2 to 1 t. grated orange peel
2 small zucchini

2 tart Jonathan apples
1/4 c. raisins
2 T. unsalted shelled sunflower seeds

In small bowl, combine yogurt and orange peel; blend well. Shred zucchini. Chop apples. Combine in large bowl with raisins and sunflower seeds. Pour dressing over salad; toss well until coated. Serves 4 to 6.

Candied Sweet Dill Pickles

1 jar dill spears
3 c. sugar
2/3 c. cider vinegar

2 T. mixed pickling spice
1/8 t. red pepper

Drain and rinse pickles. Discard brine. Put pickles in two sterilized pint jars. Combine sugar, vinegar, and spices in a heavy saucepan and bring to a boil. Boil until sugar is dissolved and syrup clear, stirring constantly. Strain syrup and pour over pickles, leaving a 3/4-in. headspace while covering pickles. Put on lids and store in refrigerator 1 week before serving.

Corn Relish

2 #2 cans yellow whole
   kernel corn, drained
2 #2 cans tomatoes, drained
1 large cucumber, unpeeled
   and chopped
1-1/2 c. onion, chopped
1 c. green pepper, chopped

3/4 c. sugar
2/3 c. cider vinegar
1 t. mustard seed
1 t. celery seed
1 t. salt
1 small jar pimiento, diced *or*
   1/2 c. chopped red pepper

Mix all ingredients in 4-qt. kettle. Boil for 10 min., stirring often. Seal in hot sterilized half-pint jars. Makes about 10 half pints.

Cranberry Chutney

1 c. Granny Smith apples, chopped	1 12-oz. bag cranberries
1 c. raisins	1-1/2 t. curry powder
1 c. chopped onion	1 t. nutmeg
1 c. sugar	1 t. cinnamon
1 c. white vinegar	1-1/2 t. ground ginger
	1/4 t. ground cloves

Combine all ingredients in a large saucepan. Bring to a boil, reduce heat. Simmer uncovered for 30 min., or until slightly thickened, stirring occasionally. Cover and refrigerate. Yield: 4 cups.

Serve with roast turkey or chicken, roast pork, or ham. Can be stored in refrigerator for weeks.

My Sweet Onion and Apple Chutney

3-1/4 lb. sweet onions	2 lemons
3-1/4 lb. cooking apples	3 3/4 c. brown sugar
3 c. golden raisins	2-1/2 c. cider vinegar

Chop onions. Peel, core, and dice apples. Grate lemon peel; then squeeze both lemons. Combine lemon peel and juice with all other ingredients in kettle and heat gently until the sugar has dissolved, stirring constantly. Bring to boil and allow to simmer 30-40 min. or until thickened and all liquid is absorbed. Pour chutney mixture into hot, sterilized half-pint or pint jars and seal. Keeps about a year. Makes 4 pints.

Chutney is traditionally served with curry. It is also good with cheese or turkey sandwiches or as a side dish with meat casseroles.

Spiced Peaches

1/2 c. vinegar	1 t. whole cloves
3/4 c. brown sugar	1 29-oz. can cling peach halves
Cinnamon stick	

Drain peaches and reserve juice. Boil vinegar, brown sugar, cinnamon, and cloves 5 min. Add peaches and peach juice; and simmer 5 min. Cool and place in quart jar to store in refrigerator.

These make a beautiful garnish for baked ham or a tasty salad stuffed with cream cheese.

333

Watermelon Pickles

Madge Thompson Petersen

3 lb. watermelon rind
1 pt. white vinegar
5 c. sugar

Whole cloves
Cinnamon stick
2 or 3 bottles maraschino cherries

Cut watermelon rind into 1-1/2 in. pieces and soak overnight in salt water. Pour off in the morning, put on fresh water and boil until tender. Make a syrup of white vinegar and sugar, adding a few cloves and the cinnamon stick. Boil 30 min. and then pour over hot, drained rinds. Let stand in syrup overnight. Stir occasionally. Next morning, add maraschino cherries, with juice. Bring to a good boil and seal in hot, sterilized pint jars.

These are a colorful, tasty treat on Christmas tables.

Blender Mayonnaise

3 egg yolks
1/4 t. dry mustard
1/2 t. salt
1/2 t. lemon juice

1/2 t. vinegar
Up to 2 c. very fresh
    Wesson or Mazola oil

Beat egg yolks 1-1/2 min. Add mustard, salt, lemon juice, and vinegar; beat 1 min. Add up to 2 c. oil, beating constantly. May add lemon juice to taste. Pour into glass jar, cover. Keeps well refrigerated. Use for mixed salads, potato salad, or fish salad.

Blue Cheese Dressing

2 T. wine vinegar
1/2 c. olive or Mazola oil
1/4 t. dry mustard

4 oz. Roquefort or Newton
    blue cheese, crumbled

In a covered bottle or half-pint jar, combine all ingredients. Shake hard. Chill and shake before serving. Pour over citrus fruits and avocado on lettuce.

Chunky Blue Cheese Dressing

1/2 c. (2 oz.) blue cheese,
   crumbled
1/2 c. light mayonnaise

1/2 c. light sour cream
1 T. Worcestershire sauce

Stir all ingredients together. Chill. Serve 2 T. over chilled wedges of iceberg lettuce. Leftover dressing keeps up to 1 week if covered and refrigerated. Yield: 1-1/2 cups.

Cooked Salad Dressing

4 eggs
1 T. flour
1/2 t. salt
1 t. Coleman's dry mustard

1 scant c. sugar
2 T. soft or melted butter
2/3 c. cider vinegar
1-1/2 c. water

Beat eggs with rotary bleater. Mix flour, salt, and mustard; add to beaten eggs, blending well. Add sugar and butter; beat. Lastly, add vinegar and water. Beat. Cook in double boiler over slow heat (300F), stirring constantly, until thick. Thin with cream to use. Store, covered, in the refrigerator. Excellent for potato salad and coleslaw. Yield: 3 cups.

French Salad Dressing   Margaret Hunter

1 can tomato soup
1 c. salad oil
3/4 c. sugar
3/4 c. vinegar

1/2 t. salt
1 T. Worcestershire sauce
1 t. celery salt
2 T. grated onion

Mix at high speed with rotary beater or electric mixer. Store in covered glass jar for weeks. Yield: 2-1/2 cups.

Mrs Hunter headed the school lunch program in Correctionville, Iowa, for many years, pleasing students and teachers alike with inventive and delicious home-cooked meals — all produced strictly within budget.

Spicy Garlic Vinaigrette

3 T. red wine vinegar
1/2 t. salt
1/2 t. oregano

1 clove garlic, crushed
1/8 t. cayenne pepper
1/2 c. olive oil

Mix vinegar and seasonings. Gradually whisk in oil until well combined. Yield: 3/4 cup.

Green Goddess Dressing I

1 t. chopped parsley	1 clove garlic, crushed
2 t. chopped chives	2 anchovies, mashed
1 t. tarragon vinegar	2 c. Hellmann's mayonnaise

Combine seasonings. Add mayonnaise and blend well. Chill. Use with mixed greens for a tossed salad. Yield: 2 cups.

Green Goddess Dressing II

1 clove garlic	1 T. lemon juice
3 T. chopped anchovies	1 T. tarragon vinegar
3 T. finely chopped chives	1/2 c. sour cream
1/2 c. finely chopped parsley	1 c. mayonnaise
Salt	White pepper

Crush garlic. Combine with other ingredients. Beat with electric mixer for 3 min. Add salt and white pepper to taste. Refrigerate overnight. Serve on salad greens. Will keep several days in refrigerator.

Honey-Mustard Dressing

4 T. honey	1-1/2 c. mayonnaise
2 T. onion, minced fine	1-1/2 t. Dijon mustard
2 T. fresh lemon juice	

Beat all ingredients with rotary beater until creamy (or use blender). Chill to blend flavors. Serve over chef's salad or a chunk of chilled iceberg lettuce. Yield: 1 3/4 cup.

Italian Dressing

1/2 t. fresh garlic, minced	1 t. oregano
1/4 c. fresh lemon juice	1/4 t. salt
1/2 c. olive oil	1/4 t. pepper

Shake all ingredients well in tightly covered bottle. Pour over fresh salad greens, tomatoes, rings of red onion, or sliced fresh mushrooms. Yield: 3/4 cup.

Louis Dressing

1 c. mayonnaise
1/2 c. chili sauce
1 T. parsley, minced
1 t. lemon juice

1 t. prepared horseradish
1/2 t. onion, grated
1/8 t. salt
1/8 t. pepper

Stir together all ingredients. Cover and chill. Serve with chunks of crabmeat or cooked shrimp, tomato slices, and sliced hard-cooked egg. Yield: 1-1/2 cups.

Remoulade Sauce   New Orleans

2 T. horseradish
2 T. ketchup
1 T. mustard
1 t. paprika
1/4 t. cayenne pepper

1/2 t. salt
1 clove garlic, pounded
2/3 c. olive oil
1/3 c. green onion, minced
1/3 c. celery, cut fine

Mix horseradish, ketchup, mustard, paprika, cayenne, salt, and garlic. Add olive oil, using mixer or blender to blend. Stir in onions and celery. Serve with boiled shrimp, well chilled, as an appetizer.

Rieke's Poppy Seed Dressing   Rieke's Restaurant

1 c. salad oil
3/4 c. sugar
1 t. Coleman's dry mustard
1 t. salt

1 T. finely grated onion
2/3 c. white vinegar
1 T. celery salt
1 T. poppy seed

Beat ingredients together with electric mixer. Store in a covered jar in refrigerator for weeks.

This dressing is especially delicious as a marinade for a combination fruit salad. It is also very good with citrus fruits. It was original to Rieke's Restaurant in New York.

Roquefort Cheese Dressing

2/3 c. Mazola oil
1/4 c. vinegar
1/2 t. dry mustard
1 T. sugar

1 t. finely scraped sweet onion
1 clove garlic, mashed
1/4 t. salt
1/2 c. finely crumbled blue cheese

Mix all ingredients and shake in pint jar. Cover and keep in refrigerator.

Russian Dressing

Dodie Barnett

1 c. sugar
1 c. vinegar
1 t. salt
4 t. celery seed

4 t. paprika
1 large onion, minced
1 c. Mazola oil
Juice of 2 lemons

Purée all ingredients in blender. Yield: 3 cups.

Seafood Cocktail Sauce

1/4 c. chili sauce
3/4 c. ketchup
2 T. horseradish

2 T. lemon juice
1 T. Worcestershire sauce
Dash of hot sauce

Mix all ingredients and chill. Serve with boiled or fried shrimp, fried clams, or oysters.

Sour Cream Salad Dressing

3 eggs
1/2 c. vinegar

1/2 c. sugar
1 c. dairy sour cream

Beat eggs until light. Add other ingredients. Cook in double boiler until thick. Mix with cream to use. This is very good for potato salad.

Sugarless Salad Dressing

2/3 c. water
1/3 c. Mazola oil
1/4 c. vinegar
1/4 t. Coleman's dry mustard

1/3 t. celery seed
Dash of salt
1 T. artificial sweetener

Mix all ingredients well. Refrigerate. Shake or stir before using.

Thousand Island Dressing

1-1/2 c. mayonnaise
1 c. Heinz ketchup or chili sauce
2 hard-cooked eggs,
  chopped fine

1 t. Worcestershire sauce
1/2 t. A-1 sauce
1 t. finely scraped onion

Mix all together with rotary beater. Refrigerate leftover dressing. Will keep for 2 days or more. Yield: 2-1/2 cups.

Soups and Sandwiches

Soups ♣ *Stews* ♣ *Chili*
♣ *Chowders* ♣ *Hot and*
Cold Sandwiches

Country School Program and Box Social

The little one-room school sat on a level acre bordered by half a dozen box elder trees, sturdy natives that had started as saplings along the four-foot wire fence that enclosed the schoolyard on three sides. Several branches were low enough to support a rope swing with a smooth board seat. A well-trod path circled the building where eager pupils had run, shouting as they pursued the opposite side in the game they called "Andee Over!" When they tired of that game, they changed to "Last Couple Out" or "Simon Says." They were a lively, imaginative group, 12 in all, eager to play and eager to learn. So they trooped into the classroom when their teacher rang a brass handbell, ready to sit and catch their breath and ready to tackle assignments.

Their teacher had given much thought to the assignment she intended to propose: that the school prepare a program, an evening affair for parents and friends, and that afterward there would be a box social when the box suppers folks brought would be auctioned as a benefit for buying books to add to the school's small collection. Usually such events were held in the fall after harvest, but an outbreak of measles had curtailed those plans. Now, late in March, there would be ample time to prepare the program for an evening in May. She explained the idea to her pupils. They were so excited that they cheered and clapped their approval. Thus, it was decided to hold a program and box social on Friday of the first week of May.

When the children were quiet, they talked about what they could do for the program. Songs, recitations, skits, a play — these suggestions were listed. One of the older boys suggested that they bring toy instruments they might have and perform as a band. Another had heard tunes played on a comb covered with tissue paper. This would give everyone a part in the band. The ideas came quickly, and soon the list covered the page. The teacher listed the kinds of help she would need, and the pupils agreed to ask if their parents might help.

Planning the program and doing the work tested everyone's commitment. The teacher looked at copies of *The Instructor* and *Grade Teacher* to find new recitations, skits, and ideas for schoolroom decorations. The pupils hunted for instruments at home and began to practice the tunes they would play. Those who lacked an instrument found that the comb played with tissue paper made a sound like a horn or flute. They memorized pieces and skits and practiced during recess or lunchtime. They prepared their assignments promptly to have extra practices.

Some of the teacher's high school friends offered help. Two of the young men came after school and put up wires that stretched across the room. These would support sheets to serve as curtains for the program's stage. A mother offered to lend sheets. Two other mothers offered to help with makeup and costumes. The school had no lighting, but a parent volunteered to bring Coleman lanterns, which radiated a clear, bright light, and others promised to bring tin kerosene lanterns.

Finally, the first Friday evening in May arrived. As dusk fell, the glow from tin lanterns hung at the school's entrance welcomed the guests. Inside, the adult-sized desks were offered to parents holding small children. Several rows of planks placed on blocks of wood and the medium-sized school desks provided seating for everyone else. Very small desks were near the front. Coleman lanterns cast light over the scene. Two small boys peeked through the white curtain sheets, then withdrew quickly. Helpers took brightly decorated boxes from women who had prepared them for the auction and set them on a table.

Promptly at eight o'clock, a pink-cheeked girl stepped in front of the curtain to recite a poem welcoming the audience. When the curtain was drawn open, four of the youngest children sang and held up letters to spell "W E L C O M E," to hearty applause. The curtain closed, then opened for a skit. Entertaining songs, recitations, and a tap dance followed rapidly.

Finally, eyes sparkling and faces beaming, all twelve pupils were on stage with the instrumental band. Trumpeters; banjo, triangle, and xylophone players; a drummer; and five comb blowers performed with great gusto, jingling, tootling, and blowing "Dixie," "Yankee Doodle," "You're a Grand Old Flag" and "America" to loud applause, a standing ovation, and calls for an encore. They obliged with "Good-Night, Ladies" as the curtain closed.

The teacher appeared and thanked the audience, clapping for the students as they found seats, and then introduced the auctioneer, who was ready to begin. The helpers prepared to hand him boxes as he began his singsong chant and held up the first box, "Here's a beauty! And it's heavy! Now what am I bid? Fifty cents? Now I gotta fifty, wanna one? Got one, now fifty! One-fifty, do I hear two? Wanna two, got two, wanna three, two-fifty, do I hear three? Two-fifty, going, going, gone! Now here's a purty one — what am I bid?"

The bidding continued; then several young fellows competed for a box that might belong to a young lady, and when a box decorated like a schoolhouse was offered, they entered a bidding battle that a determined bidder took to nine dollars. It was the last box. The auctioneer bowed and stepped aside.

Now the buyers found the names of the ladies who had brought the boxes and sought their partners for supper. The tempting foods were laid out on napkins: fried chicken, every variety of filled sandwich, dill and sweet pickles, deviled eggs, ham salad, slices of apple pie, rhubarb, raisin and cherry pies, and slices of chocolate cake or spice cake, all accompanied by steaming, fragrant coffee. The food was a fitting conclusion to a congenial, entertaining evening. When the auctioneer announced that the auction had raised over one hundred dollars for the school library, the audience cheered — a few even stomped their feet. The teacher thanked everyone, and the program was over.

As the parents gathered their sleepy children for the ride home, willing helpers dismantled and folded the sheet curtains. Men removed the plank seats and restored desks to the usual places while others took down the curtain wires. Within an hour, the room was back in order amidst cheerful joking and good humor. Lanterns, except one, were extinguished, and the helpers moved to leave.

As she locked the door, the young teacher glowed with excitement and pride in her pupils' performance and the success of the evening. They had all worked hard, and she knew their parents were pleased to see them do well. What fun they would have on Monday as they recalled all the happenings of their program and the box social's success!

1921 – At age four, I walked 1/2 mile to Kedron No. 1 school for K-1st grades. The older boys only attended school a few winter months.

1925 – Kedron No. 1 was known as the "Smallest School in Iowa," with only six pupils from two families. Yet they gave a complete program for the school's box social. The teacher taught all subjects daily to the two students in kindergarten, the two in first grade, and the two in fourth grade.

1927 – Miller No. 9, a rural school. There were 26 students in grades K-8, with the oldest student 18 years old. There was only one teacher, and no electricity, water or furnace.

1927 – Miller No. 1. This building was newer and well kept, and served eight families, grades K-7. The teacher had a college degree and taught all subjects, as well as art, music, and physical training.

1928 – Miller No. 1. Note the baseball mitt – this group played ball every recess, and sometimes played "Andee Over."

The children, ages 3 and 1-1/2, ride Topsy and Florrie. White Florrie was retired from fieldwork, but still pulled a light drag to smooth the barnyard.

Two years later, the children ride Old Buck, a retired racehorse.

1928 – The children wash the family car, one of their weekly chores. Florrie is hitched to the drag.

Camping and cooking at the Iowa State Fair in 1956 – our two-day summer vacation with good friends.

1942 – Friends bring food for a picnic at the park.

1951 – Al fresco lunch was sometimes cooked over a small bonfire, always a favorite treat, with hot dogs, homemade buns, beans, fruit, salad, and toasted marshmallows.

<u>Recipes</u>

Famous U.S. Senate Bean Soup

1 pkg. (2 c.) Hallmark Precooked Beans	1 medium onion, diced fine
6 c. boiling water	1/2 t. celery salt
1 ham hock	2 drops Tabasco sauce
1 c. smoked fully cooked ham, diced	2 t. salt 1/2 t. sugar

Combine all ingredients in 4-qt. kettle and bring to a rolling boil. Reduce temperature and simmer 30 min. If thin soup is desired, use 8 c. water. Yield: 6 one-cup servings.

Two versions of this soup are served in the Senate, neither precisely following the recipe. In the Senate dining room, the chef adds garlic; in the Senate cafeteria, the chef adds carrots, celery, and chicken stock. All are justly famous — and all are delicious.

Senate Bean Soup

2 lb. small navy beans	4 qt. hot water
1-1/2 lb. smoked ham hocks	2 T. butter
1 medium onion	Salt and pepper

Wash beans and run through hot water until white. Drain. Add hot water, ham hocks, and 1/2 t. salt. Simmer covered 3 hr. Remove ham hocks and cool. Pull meat from bones and return to pot. Chop onion and sauté in butter until slightly brown. Add to soup. Season with salt and pepper to taste. Serves 8.

Calico Bean Soup

1 pkg mixed soup beans	1 large can tomatoes
1 T. salt	1 large carrot, grated
1 qt. water	1 large potato, diced
2 ham hocks	Salt
1 large onion, chopped	Pepper

Wash beans and place in 8-qt. kettle. Cover with water, add salt, and soak overnight. Drain and rinse. Add 1 qt. water and ham hocks, bring to a boil, and simmer 2-1/2 to 3 hr. Add vegetables, salt and pepper, and water if needed. Simmer 1 hr. Serves 6.

Broccoli-Cheese Soup

4 T. butter or margarine, melted
1/4 c. flour
2 c. whole milk
2-1/2 c. cubed sharp
    cheddar cheese
2 large white potatoes,
    peeled and cubed
3 c. water

1/2 c. sliced celery
1 c. sliced baby carrots
1/4 c. diced onion
1/2 t. salt
1/4 t. pepper
3 c. fresh broccoli,
    broken into bite-size pieces

Combine water, vegetables, and salt in a 4-qt. kettle. Bring to boiling. Reduce heat and cover. Cook 10-12 min. until vegetables are tender.

Cheese Sauce: Melt butter in a heavy 2-qt. saucepan. Add flour and stir smooth, cooking 1 min. Add milk gradually, stirring constantly until mixture is creamy and bubbling. Lower heat and stir in cheese, stirring until cheese is melted. Remove from heat.

Stir cheese sauce into hot vegetable soup, stirring constantly. Add pepper. Serve steaming hot. Serves 8.

Budget Stretcher Soup

1/2 lb. ground beef or chuck
5 large carrots, sliced or chunked
3 large potatoes,
    peeled and cubed

1 large onion, chopped
1/2 t. salt
4 c. water
1 c. elbow macaroni or Minute Rice

Combine vegetables, salt, and water on medium heat. Crumble the beef on top. Cover and simmer 10 min. Add macaroni or rice. Cook 8-10 min. Lower heat. Let stand 5 min. Skim excess fat. Serve with crackers and celery sticks. Serves 4.

Variation: Substitute 3 chicken leg-and-thigh joints for ground beef. Combine chicken, salt, and water; cook on medium high heat 45 min. Add vegetables and pasta or rice. Cook 8-10 min. Lower heat. Let stand 5 min. Skim excess fat. Remove chicken, take meat off bones, and cut into bite-sized pieces; add to soup or serve on separate plate.

♣ *Buy beef or fresh chicken when it is on special; ask the butcher to freezer wrap it for you. Label the packages, and keep a supply in the freezer for budget days! A sack of frozen soup vegetables could be used instead of fresh vegetables to make this a no-work recipe.*

Carrot Purée

2 T. onion, finely chopped	4 c. homemade chicken broth *or*
1/4 c. celery, finely chopped	2 cans broth plus 1 chicken
6 medium carrots, sliced	bouillon cube
1 T. flour	Salt
2 T. soft butter	White pepper
2 T. cornstarch, mixed with	1/2 c. whipping cream
2 T. water	3 t. chopped chives
1 c. half and half	

Sauté onion, celery, and carrot slices in butter. Add chicken broth and cook until carrots are tender. Transfer half the mixture to blender; purée for 2 min. and pour into 2-qt. saucepan. Repeat with the rest of the mixture. Add half and half. Combine cornstarch and water until blended; add 1/2 c. soup purée and whisk smooth. Stir this into purée and increase heat to 325F. Stir steadily until purée thickens. Salt and pepper to taste. When soup is piping hot, ladle about 1 c. into each of six soup plates. Use pastry bag technique to pipe three concentric circles of whipping cream on soup. With a knife, draw six spokes (like cutting pie) from center out to make design. Sprinkle each serving with 1/2 t. chopped chives. Serves 6.

Carrot Swirl Soup

3 c. carrots, chopped	1 t. sugar
1 small onion, chopped	1/2 t. nutmeg
1 bay leaf	Salt and pepper
2 T. butter	1-1/2 T. parsley, chopped
4 c. chicken broth	1/2 c. cream

Combine carrots, onion, bay leaf, butter, and 1/2 c. chicken broth in saucepan. Cover and cook over low heat until carrots are tender, about 8 min. Cool slightly. Remove bay leaf. Pour carrots into blender. Add 1 c. broth. Blend 10 sec. on low, then 30 sec. on high. Return to saucepan. Add remainder of broth, sugar, salt and pepper to taste. Reheat; do not boil.

To serve, pour a generous cup of soup into each of six soup plates. Drizzle 2/3 T. cream in three concentric circles on soup. Quickly draw a silver knife through circles, as if cutting sixths. Sprinkle with 1/2 t. parsley. Yield 6 servings.

Chicken Broth

2 lb. chicken leg-thigh	2 medium carrots, cut in thirds
joints (watch for sales)	Salt
2 or 3 ribs of celery	Pepper
1 small onion	

Wash chicken joints thoroughly. Blot dry. Put all ingredients into deep kettle and cover with water. Bring to a boil. Skim any fat. Reduce heat, cover, and simmer 2 hr. Remove meat and vegetables and serve, if desired. Strain broth into a freezer container. Refrigerate. Skim off fat. Freeze broth up to 4 weeks. Yield: about 1 qt.

My Clam and Corn Chowder   Ruth Harbour

2 6.5-oz. cans minced clams
1/2 c. chopped onion
1/2 c. celery, finely chopped
3 medium red potatoes,
   peeled and cubed
3 T. soft butter, divided
4 c. fresh corn (about 10 ears) *or*
   1 pkg frozen whole-kernel corn

2-1/2 c. whole milk
2 T. flour
2 Knorr's chicken bouillon cubes,
   dissolved in 2 c. hot water, *or*
   1 can chicken broth
1/2 t. salt
Pepper to taste
3-4 t. chopped chives (optional)

Sauté chopped onions and celery in 1 T. butter in a large kettle. Add corn, diced potatoes, and bouillon. Cover and cook until potatoes are tender, about 12 min. Add minced clams, undrained. With wire whisk, combine whole milk and flour. Add salt and pepper. Stir into corn-clam mixture. Cook on medium heat until chowder is steaming hot but not boiling. Reduce heat to 250F. Add 2 T. butter and stir. Cover and let flavors blend 3-5 min. Serve 3/4 cup in soup plates. Garnish with chopped chives or float a few oyster crackers atop. 8 servings.

Corn Chowder   Anne Harbour

1/2 c. salt pork, washed
   and chopped
1/4 c. onion
1/2 c. celery
1/4 c. green pepper
1 large potato (1 c.)
2 c. fresh corn (about 5 ears)

2 c. water
1/2 t. salt
1/4 t. paprika
Bay leaf
3 T. flour
2 c. milk, divided
2 T. butter

Slowly sauté salt pork until light brown. Chop and add onion, celery, and green pepper. Peel and dice potato. Add potato, water, and seasonings to mixture. Simmer until potatoes are tender. In separate saucepan, scald 1-1/2 c. milk. Slice corn off the cob (or use whole-kernel canned or frozen corn) and add to scalded milk. In small bowl, add a little hot soup liquid to flour; gradually stir in 1/2 c. milk. Gradually stir into soup mixture. Then add milk and corn to soup. Heat thoroughly, but do not boil. Remove from heat, add butter and adjust seasonings. Serve in bowls with oyster crackers or saltines. Yield: 6 cups.

Chili (Crockpot)

1 #2 can chili beans
1 #2 can red kidney beans
1 lb. browned hamburger
1 T. chili powder (more
   to taste)

1/2 pkg dry onion soup mix
1 12-oz. can tomato paste
1 #2-1/2 can whole tomatoes
1 46-oz. can tomato juice

Put browned, drained hamburger and remaining ingredients in Crockpot. Add enough tomato juice to fill to within 2 in. from top. Cook on low heat 7-8 hr. Stir contents several times. Makes about 5 qt.

Cowboy Chili

2 lb. coarsely ground beef chuck
1 medium onion, chopped fine
2 #2-1/2 cans tomatoes, chopped
2 #2 cans red kidney beans

1 T. chili powder *or*
  1 pkg Williams chili mix
1/2 t. salt
1/4 t. pepper

Brown ground beef and onion in a Dutch oven or electric frying pan. Add tomatoes and kidney beans with juice and seasonings. Bring to a boil. Simmer about 2 hr. at 300F, stirring occasionally. If using a Dutch oven, you may put it into the oven to cook at 300F for 2 hr., stirring once. Serves 6 to 8.

This makes a hearty meal for 6 to 8. It may be extended by adding 2 c. tomato juice. Excellent the second day!

Iowa Chili   Ruth Harbour

1 large green pepper, chopped
2 large yellow onions, chopped
1-1/2 T. salad oil
2 cloves garlic, chopped fine
1/4 c. chopped parsley
2 lb. ground beef chuck
1/2 lb. lean pork sausage

1/4 c. butter
2 cans pinto beans, drained
2 #2-1/2 cans tomatoes with juice
3 T. chili powder
3/4 t. pepper
1-1/2 T. salt
1 t. ground cumin

Sauté green pepper and onion in salad oil until soft. Add garlic and parsley, reduce heat. Set aside. In a large skillet, brown beef and pork sausage in butter until it is no longer pink. Add onion mixture, tomatoes, and pinto beans to meat. Mix well. Stir in chili powder, salt, pepper, and cumin seed; cook, covered, in 325F oven for 1 hr. or longer. Uncover, stir, and add 1/2 c. water if needed. Skim off fat and serve with saltines. Makes about 3 qt. (10 servings).

This is very good reheated. It may be extended by adding tomato sauce or juice and then simmering until hot.

L.B.J.'s Chili   President Lyndon B. Johnson

4 lb. beef chuck, ground coarsely
1 large onion, chopped
2 cloves garlic, crushed
2 T. chili powder
2 t. salt

1/2 t. ground oregano
1 t. ground cumin
2 16-oz. cans tomatoes, mashed
2 c. (or more) hot water

In a large Dutch oven, cook meat, onion, and garlic together until meat loses pink color. Add rest of ingredients and mix well. Simmer, covered, about 1 hr. You may put the covered Dutch oven into the oven at 300F for 1-1/2 hr. Skim fat and add 1 c. hot water as needed. 8 servings.

This is good served in soup bowls that are deep enough to hold a generous cupful. Pass celery sticks, dill pickle spears, and crackers. This reheats well.

Texas Chili

1/4 c. salad oil
3 lb. beef chuck or round,
    cut into 1-in. cubes
3 cloves garlic, crushed
4 to 6 T. chili powder
2 t. salt

2 t. ground oregano
2 t. ground cumin
2 t. Tabasco sauce
6 c. water
1/3 c. white cornmeal

Brown beef in oil in large frying pan or Dutch oven. Add garlic, seasonings, and water; stir to mix well. Bring to boil, cover, and reduce heat. Simmer 2 hr., stirring occasionally. If using Dutch oven, cover and bake at 350F for 2 hr. Add cornmeal and mix well, Simmer uncovered for an additional 30 min. or until meat is tender. Garnish with chopped parsley if desired. Serve with rice and crackers. Serves 6 to 8.

Danish Fruit Soup   Christena Paulsen

1/2 lb. prunes
1 c. golden raisins
1/4 lb. dried apricots
1/4 lb. dried apples
1/4 lb. dried cherries
1 c. orange juice

1 lemon
1 orange
1-1/2 c. sugar
1 stick cinnamon
1/4 c. Minute Tapioca

Simmer all dried fruits and cinnamon in about 3 c. water until fruits are tender but not mushy. Peel and slice lemon and orange, removing seeds. Mix lemon, orange, orange juice, and tapioca; cook on low heat until tapioca is cooked and fruit juices are clear. Combine dried fruits and tapioca mixture and pour into large serving bowl. 12 servings.

Fruit soup may be served hot or cold. A great favorite of the Paulsen family, especially in winter.

Gazpacho (Cold Spanish Soup)

4 fully ripe, medium tomatoes	1/2 t. salt
1 cucumber	1/4 t. cayenne pepper or paprika
1 large clove garlic	2 c. V-8 juice
1 small onion	1 avocado
1 green pepper	1 ripe tomato
1/4 c. olive oil	Lemon juice
1/4 c. red wine vinegar	

Peel the tomatoes, peel and slice cucumber, cut garlic clove in two, chop onion, and seed and chop green pepper. Purée these and transfer to large bowl. Add all ingredients except avocado and lemon juice, and mix well. Chill several hours. Stir well and serve in soup bowls. Peel and cut avocado fine; sprinkle with lemon juice. Peel and finely dice tomato. Sprinkle avocado and tomato on each serving as garnish. Serves 6.

This refreshing soup is easy to prepare for lunch or a light supper. It is particularly welcome in hot weather when appetites are flagging but vegetables are at their peak.

Goulash Soup

2 T. vegetable oil	1-1/2 t. caraway seeds
1-1/2 lb. beef chuck, cubed	1 28-oz. can tomato paste
4 oz. salt pork, rinsed, diced	6 c. beef broth
2 c. coarsely diced onion	1 lb. sauerkraut, drained
1 c. celery, chopped	3 c. potatoes, peeled and diced
2 large cloves garlic, minced	1 lb. Polish-style Kielbasa, cut
3 T. paprika	into 1/4-in. slices
2 T. brown sugar	Yogurt
1 t. dried thyme	Fresh chopped parsley

Heat oil in deep, large soup pot and brown beef quickly on all sides. Remove beef and set aside. Sauté salt pork in same oil until softened and pale golden brown. Add onion, celery, and garlic and sauté until vegetables are softened. Return beef to mixture. Add paprika, brown sugar, thyme, and caraway; toss to mix thoroughly (2-3 min.). Add tomato paste, beef broth, and sauerkraut. Cook over medium heat until mixture comes to a simmer; reduce heat, partly cover pot, and cook 2 hr. Add potatoes to soup and cook another 30 min., partly covered. Add Kielbasa and heat 15 min., uncovered. Serve piping hot in deep, large soup bowls. Top with spoonful of yogurt and sprinkle with chopped parsley. Serves 6 to 8.

This goulash soup was served in Hungary with big chunks of fresh homemade bread. For best flavor, allow cooked soup to sit several hours or overnight in refrigerator. If you cannot obtain Kielbasa, substitute Polish sausage.

Onion Soup

1/2 c. unsalted butter
5 large onions, chopped
3 leeks (white part only), well washed and chopped
6 shallots, minced
3 garlic cloves, minced
4 c. chicken broth
3 c. beef broth

2 c. whipping cream
Salt to taste
Ground red pepper to taste
2-3 T. cornstarch
3-4 T. cold water
1/2 c. chives, chopped
3 green onions, chopped

Melt butter in large saucepan over low heat. Add onions, leeks, shallots, and garlic. Cover with circle of waxed paper, and cook slowly for about 20 min. Remove paper, stir in broths, and bring to boil. Reduce heat and simmer uncovered until reduced by 1 or 2 c., about 45 min. Transfer mixture to blender, and purée until smooth. Return to saucepan. Stir in cream. Heat through, but do not boil. Season with salt and red pepper. Dissolve cornstarch in cold water and add to soup, stirring until thickened. Garnish each serving with chives and green onions. Serves 6.

Tender green tops of leeks not needed in this recipe can be chopped fine and used in potato soup or in beef stew.

My Oyster Stew   Ruth Harbour

1 pt. medium oysters
1 pt. whole milk
Salt and pepper

1 pt. half and half
2 T. butter

Heat oysters and juice until bubbling and edges start to curl. Simultaneously, in separate pan, combine and scald milk with half and half; do not allow to boil. Combine oysters in juice with scalded milk. Season with salt and pepper to taste, and add butter. Let stand 5 min. to meld flavors. Serve with oyster crackers.

My family made a special request that I include my clam and corn chowder, Iowa chili and oyster stew. I make those when each one visits me in Kansas City, now in my Shawnee home. We all enjoy simple side dishes — celery stalks, bread-and-butter pickles, or beets, just like the years on the farm.

Peasant Soup

1 to 1-1/2 lb. meaty beef soup bone	1/3 lb. peeled baby carrots (about 20)
6 c. cold water	3 turnips, peeled and cubed
1/2 t. salt	2 large potatoes, peeled and cubed
1 small head cabbage (ca. 2 lb.)	1/2 c. green onion, chopped
2 cubes Knorr's beef bouillon	

Cover soup bone with cold water in 2-1/2-qt. soup pot. Add salt and bouillon cubes. Bring to a boil, then reduce heat to medium and simmer 1-1/2 hr. Remove soup bone; skim broth. Add potatoes and turnips; cook 10 min. Add carrots. Cut cabbage into 8 wedges, discarding woody core. Add to pot. Cover and cook 15 min. more. Cut meat from soup bone and add to soup. Serve with toasted French bread; sprinkle green onion on each serving. Serves 6-8.

A delicious supper on a cold night!

Plaza III Steak Soup   Plaza III, Kansas City

1 stick margarine	1 pkg frozen mixed vegetables
1 c. flour	1 T. Accent
5 c. cold water	1/2 t. salt
1 c. carrots	1 cube Knorr's beef bouillon
1 c. onion	1/2 t. black pepper
1 c. celery	1 #2-1/2 can tomatoes, diced style
1 lb. browned ground beef	1-1/2 t. Kitchen Bouquet

Chop carrots, onion, and celery; cook 8-10 min. in water. Melt margarine, stir in flour, adding hot liquid from vegetables slowly, stirring constantly. When thickened, gradually stir into vegetables and rest of cooking liquid. Add remaining ingredients. Simmer for 45 min. Serve when steaming hot. Serves 10 to 12.

This signature soup from the Plaza III Restaurant is a favorite throughout the Kansas City area. "Home Style" is thicker, with simpler seasoning.

Plaza III Steak Soup — Adapted Home Style

1 lb. ground beef	1 can diced tomatoes
1 onion	2 beef bouillon cubes
3 c. hot water	Salt
1-1/2 c. carrots, thinly sliced	Black pepper
1 lb. bag mixed vegetables	Flour
4 T. water	

Brown hamburger and onion; drain. Add hot water, crumbled bouillon cubes, all vegetables, salt and pepper to taste. Simmer until vegetables are tender. Mix 2 T. flour with 4 T. water until smooth. Add 1/2 c. of the hot soup broth, blend, and then stir into the soup. Cook, stirring, about 5 min. Serve with crackers. Serves 6 to 8.

Tip-Top Potato Soup

4 c. cubed potatoes
2 medium onions, chopped
1 c. water
1 t. salt
1/2 t. garlic salt

1 can cream of celery soup
1/4 t. pepper
4 c. whole milk
3 T. butter

Combine potatoes, onions, water, salt, and garlic salt in 2-1/2-qt. saucepan. Cover, bring to a boil, and simmer until potatoes are tender. Mash potatoes slightly. Add celery soup, pepper, and milk, and heat thoroughly. Stir occasionally. Do not let soup boil. Add butter. Serve with saltines or oyster crackers. Yield: 10 cups.

Variation: Chopped leeks can be substituted for onions. This is a good way to use tender green tops when white part of leeks has been used elsewhere.

Cheesy-Potato Soup

6 medium potatoes
6-8 slices bacon or ham
1 medium onion
1 T. salt
1 t. Worcestershire sauce

1/2 t. nutmeg
1/4 t. dry mustard
3 c. whole milk
1 c. Swiss cheese, shredded
Chopped parsley (optional)

Peel and quarter potatoes; cook until tender. Meanwhile, cut up bacon, chop onion, and cook together until brown and tender. Drain. Add seasonings. Whip potatoes; blend in half and half. Stir in bacon mixture. Add cheese, and cook over slow heat until cheese melts. Serve hot garnished with parsley.

This hearty soup can be served as a main dish with green salad and bread.

Old-Fashioned Tomato Soup

1 medium onion, chopped
1 #2-1/2 can whole tomatoes,
    chopped
1 t. baking soda

1 qt. whole milk
1 T. butter
Salt
Pepper

In a 2-1/2-qt. saucepan, cook onion 5 min. in 1/2 c. water. When tender, add tomatoes. Bring to a boil and add soda. Stir until it stops foaming. Add milk, butter, salt and pepper to taste. Reduce heat. Heat but **do not boil,** because it may cause the soup to curdle. Serve with oyster crackers or saltines. Celery sticks add nice crunch as a side dish. Yield: 6 cups.

Variation: Substitute 3 c. tomato juice for whole tomatoes.

The whole family enjoyed this soup when made with a quart of home-canned tomatoes from the garden.

Day-After Turkey Soup   Laurel Harbour

Turkey carcass, gravy, and skin	1/8 t. salt
2 bay leaves	1 c. carrots, cut fine or grated
1 c. celery, chopped fine	2 sticks celery, minced
1/8 t. paprika	1 T. onion, minced
1/8 t. white pepper	1 c. small peas
	1/4 c. sherry (optional)

As you put away the leftovers from Thanksgiving or Christmas dinner, put bones from the turkey or other fowl, scraps of skin, slivers of meat, bits of giblet gravy, and other leftovers into a large plastic-covered container, and refrigerate. When ready to make the day-after soup, put these leftovers into a 2-1/2-qt. pot with water to cover. Add seasonings. Simmer for 30 min. or until meat has left the bones. Strain broth into the plastic-covered container and refrigerate until fat rises; skim the fat.

Pick over the bones and save all pieces of meat. Add meat to broth. Add carrots, celery, and onion; simmer 20 min. Add peas. Test and adjust salt. Add sherry. Serve piping hot with croutons browned in butter. Yield: 4 servings.

Dieter's Vegetable Soup

48 oz. tomato juice	2 c. chopped cabbage
2 c. water	6 or 8 baby carrots, chopped
4 beef bouillon cubes	1/2 onion, diced
2/3 c. chopped celery	1/4 t. salt

Combine all ingredients in large pan. Bring to a boil, then reduce heat and simmer for 2 hr. One large cup has 30 calories.

He-Man Vegetable Soup

1/2 lb. bacon
1 lb. hamburger
1/3 c. rice
1 can condensed tomato soup
2 c. water

1 medium onion, chopped
1/2 c. celery, chopped
2 c. carrots, chopped
2 c. potatoes, diced

Chop bacon into 1-in. pieces and brown. Remove from pan and brown hamburger in drippings. Drain excess fat. Add remaining ingredients, including bacon. Simmer 2-3 hr.

This thick soup makes a good main dish on a cold day, with plenty of homemade bread and crisp relishes.

Vegetable Beef Soup I

2 lb. stewing beef
4 c. water
4 c. tomato juice
1/2 c. onion, chopped
1 T. salt
1 T. sugar

2 t. Worcestershire sauce
1/2 t. chili powder
1/4 t. pepper
2 c. carrots, chopped
2 c. potatoes, chopped
2 c. cabbage, chopped

Brown meat in 1 T. fat. Add water, tomato juice, onion, and seasonings and bring to boil; then reduce heat and simmer for 2 hr. Add vegetables and simmer 2 hr. Serves 6.

Vegetable Beef Soup II

2 lb. soup bone (1/2 meat)
2 T. fat
2 qt. water
1-1/2 T. salt
1/4 t. pepper
2 bay leaves
2 T. minced parsley
1/4 c. barley
1 c. carrots, diced

1/4 c. onion, chopped
1/2 c. celery, chopped
1 c. tomatoes, chopped
1/2 c. peas
1 c. potatoes, diced
1 c. cabbage, chopped
1/2 c. string beans
1 t. sugar

Remove meat from bone, cut into cubes, and brown lightly in hot fat. Place meat, soup bone, and seasonings in soup kettle. Cover tightly, simmer 1 hr. Add barley, simmer 1 hr. more. Cool and skim off fat. Remove soup bone. Add vegetables except peas; simmer 45 min. Add peas; simmer 15 min. Serve hot with crackers.

Barley makes this a favorite vegetable beef soup recipe. It can be prepared in a crockpot by simmering the soup bone with seasonings overnight and adding vegetables in the morning.

Vegetable Beef Soup III

1 lb. hamburger	1 t. salt
4 c. water	2 cubes Knorr's beef bouillon
1 c. carrots, sliced	1/2 t. pepper
1 c. celery, chopped	1 bay leaf
1 c. onions, chopped	1 #2 can crushed or diced tomatoes
1 large potato, peeled and diced	1 t. oregano

Brown hamburger lightly; drain fat. Put all ingredients into a 2-1/2-qt. kettle or stewpot. If tomatoes are whole, cut through each with heavy knife several times. Heat to boiling, reduce heat, and simmer until vegetables are tender. Yield: 12 cups.

Vichyssoise

2 c. raw potatoes, cubed	3/4 c. milk
1 c. onion or leeks, chopped	1/4 t. pepper
2 c. water	2 T. parsley clusters
3 cubes Knorr's chicken bouillon	2 T. chives or onion greens, chopped
2 T. butter	1/2 c. heavy cream

Combine potatoes, onions or leeks, water, and bouillon cubes in saucepan. Cook until just tender, about 15 min. Do not drain. Pour into blender. Add remaining ingredients except cream. Blend on high for 30 sec. Pour into bowls and add a teaspoon of cream. Serve hot or chilled. Sprinkle with a few chopped chives or onion tops. Serves 6.

Classic Vichyssoise

2 T. butter or margarine	1 t. salt
2 c. leeks (white part only), well washed and sliced	1/4 t. pepper
	1 c. shredded cucumber, drained and chilled
2 T. flour	2/3 c. half and half
4 c. water	Chopped parsley
3 medium potatoes, peeled and diced	

Melt butter in saucepan. Add leeks and cook over medium heat 5 min. Blend in flour, cook and stir 2 min. Gradually stir in water, potatoes, and seasonings. Bring to boil; reduce heat and simmer 30 min. Cool slightly; purée in blender until smooth. Chill. Stir in cucumber and half and half just before serving. Garnish each serving with parsley. Serves 6 to 8.

My Best Chicken Sandwiches

2 chicken thighs	1/4 c. sweet pickle, finely minced
3 split chicken breasts	1/2 t. onion, finely minced
2/3 c. Hellmann's mayonnaise	Loaf of sandwich bread
1/2 c. celery, finely minced	Softened butter or spread
Salt	

Wash chicken pieces. In a 2-qt. saucepan, cover chicken with water and bring to a boil. Reduce heat to simmer. Cook until chicken is very tender. Lift it out of broth with a tongs or pierced tablespoon, and let it cool in a bowl. Remove skin and bone. Put chicken meat and skin of one breast through fine knife of food grinder. Mix ground chicken, salt, celery, onion, and sweet pickle well. Add mayonnaise a tablespoonful at a time to moist and spreadable consistency — 2/3 c. should be enough for a consistency neither dry nor runny.

Using fresh or day-old sandwich bread, pair two slices in open book style. Spread soft butter or a low-fat spread all the way to the edges. Use 1-1/2 T. or more chicken and spread to edges of bread. Top with second slice. Stack three sandwiches, wrap snugly, and chill several hours before serving.

To serve: If for a tea, trim crusts. Cut sandwich diagonally to produce four small triangles. Place on serving plate and keep covered with wrap. Yield: 20-24 quarters.

Our four daughters always asked that these chicken sandwiches be featured at birthday or graduation parties. Along with ribbon and open-faced cucumber sandwiches, the serving platters were colorful and delicious. (Plan on one of each kind, and then double it. Double or triple the recipes, and keep the fillings and sandwiches refrigerated.)

Our grandson chose larger sandwiches with this filling. The guys also like the sandwiches filled with minced ham or braunschweiger ball (see under Appetizers). Also, a less formal party might feature taverns or sloppy joes, or tuna salad in a bun wrapped and heated.

Planning with the guests of honor so they make their choices is a way to let young folks know we feel their preferences are important. They like to help prepare the food too. Just don't worry if the sandwiches aren't perfect. It takes practice to develop a steady hand.

Cashew Chicken Sandwiches

3/4 c. canned chicken, shredded
1/4 to 1/2 c. roasted salted
    cashews, finely chopped
1 T. green onions, finely chopped
3 T. mayonnaise

Salt
Pepper
6 very thin square slices white or
    whole wheat bread
1 T. softened butter

Combine chicken, cashews, onions, mayonnaise, salt and pepper to taste, stirring until smooth. Take three pairs of two slices of bread, open like a book so facing sides will match. Spread lightly with butter. Divide chicken mixture evenly and spread on one slice of each pair. Top with matching slice, press down gently, and trim off crusts with serrated bread knife. Cut each sandwich into four triangles to serve. Serves 12.

Cucumber Tea Sandwiches   Anne Harbour

2 or 3 large cucumbers
Mayonnaise
Pitted black olives

Loaf of thin-sliced square
    white bread

Cucumbers should be 1-1/2 to 2 in. in diameter. Peel them and slice thin (1/8 in.). With 2-in. cookie cutter, cut two or three rounds out of each slice of bread. Spread lightly with mayonnaise and top with slice of cucumber. Garnish with a centered slice of black olive. Cover with Saran Wrap or tea towel until served.

Alternatively, take two slices of bread at a time, open like a book, and spread both lightly with mayonnaise. Arrange cucumber to cover one slice, place second slice on top, and cut into four triangles. Crusts can be trimmed or not, as preferred.

♣ *The kind of tea sandwiches to make will depend on the occasion. Open-faced sandwiches in shapes are a nice touch at an elegant ladies' tea or afternoon reception. A mixed group of men, women, and children like a selection of filled sandwiches.*

Cheese Tea Sandwiches   Anne Harbour

1/4 lb. sharp cheddar cheese
Mayonnaise

Loaf of thin-sliced square white
    or whole wheat bread

Grate cheese coarsely. Take two slices of bread at a time, open like a book, and spread both lightly with mayonnaise. Sprinkle layer of cheese to cover one slice, place second slice on top, and cut into four triangles. Crusts can be trimmed or not, as preferred.

Deviled Ham Sandwich Filling

1 2-1/2-oz. can deviled ham
1 3-oz. pkg cream cheese
4 T. mayonnaise
2 T. chopped pimiento

1/2 t. finely scraped onion
1/4 t. Worcestershire sauce
1/2 t. paprika

Combine all ingredients. Mix until well blended. May chill and use for two days. May be used as one of the fillings in Ribbon Sandwiches. Yield: about 1 2/3 cups.

Deviled Ham Tea Sandwiches

1 2-1/2-oz. can deviled ham
Mayonnaise
Green olives with pimiento
Pitted black olives

Loaf of thin-sliced square
    white bread
Softened butter

Mix deviled ham with just enough mayonnaise to spread. With 2-in. cookie cutter, cut two or three rounds out of each slice of bread. Spread lightly with butter, then with deviled ham mixture. Slice olives, discarding end pieces. Top half the rounds with slice of green olive with pimiento, the other half with slice of black olive. You can also cut half the sandwiches into triangles or other shapes for variety.

Egg Salad Tea Sandwiches

4 hard-boiled eggs, peeled
1 t. minced onion
1/4 c. salad dressing
1 T. cider vinegar

1 t. prepared mustard
Salt
Pepper
Softened butter

Use pastry blender to chop eggs fine. Add onion, mustard, cider vinegar, and salt and pepper to taste. Mix in 2 T. salad dressing, then add more to obtain spreading consistency. Pair slices of white or wheat bread, open like a book, and butter both slices sparingly but out to the crusts. Allow 1 T. or more filling evenly spread on one slice; top with the other slice, and cut into four triangles. Cover in Saran Wrap and keep chilled until serving. Makes about 32 quarter sandwiches.

♣ *Use the bread wrapper to keep sandwiches fresh, securing it with the tie.*

Ginger Orange Sandwiches

8 oz. cream cheese, softened
1/4 c. mayonnaise
3 T. grated orange rind
2 t. orange juice

1/2 t. ground ginger
Raisin, pumpkin, or Boston brown
   bread
Softened butter

Combine cream cheese, mayonnaise, orange rind and juice, and ginger; beat until fluffy. Spread 1 T. filling between lightly buttered bread slices; cut into triangles. Makes 60 quarter sandwiches.

Hawaiian Sandwiches

2 T. milk
3 T. mayonnaise
8 oz. cream cheese
Softened butter

1/2 c. crushed pineapple, drained
3 T. finely chopped pecans
2 loaves raisin bread

Blend softened cream cheese with milk and mayonnaise. Add pineapple and pecans. Mix well. Pair slices of raisin bread, open like a book, and lightly butter both slices. Spread 1 T. filling on one slice, top with the other. Cut into four triangles. Wrap in waxed paper and chill. Yield: 60 sandwiches.

Hot Dog Special

2 c. chopped wieners
1/2 c. grated cheese
2 hard-boiled eggs, chopped

1/4 c. chili sauce
2 T. sweet pickle relish
1/2 t. prepared mustard

Combine ingredients thoroughly. Spread on 8 hot dog buns and wrap each in foil. Bake at 375F for 10-12 minutes. Yield: 8 sandwiches.

Olive Sandwich Spread

8 oz. cream cheese
1/4 c. walnuts, roasted in oven
   for 8-10 min. and chopped

1/4 c. chopped stuffed green olives
1/4 c. chopped pitted black olives

Starting with cream cheese at room temperature, use electric mixer to beat it until creamy. Stir in remaining ingredients. Store in covered container and refrigerate. Yield: 1 3/4 cups.

Reuben Sandwiches

4 slices corned beef
4 slices Swiss cheese
4 heaping T. sauerkraut,
   well drained

Dijon mustard
4 T. Thousand Island dressing
8 slices rye bread

Take two slices of bread at a time, open like a book, and spread lightly with Dijon mustard. On one slice of bread, place a slice of corned beef, then a slice of Swiss cheese, then a heaping tablespoon of sauerkraut spread out with a fork to cover. Drizzle each with 1 T. Thousand Island dressing, and top with matching slice of bread. Broil or sauté sandwich long enough to heat it. Serve with dill or sour pickle slices. You may prefer to wrap the sandwiches in foil and heat in hot oven (400F) for 15 min. Yield: 4 sandwiches.

Ribbon Sandwiches

Trim crusts from 6 slices of day-old bread. Spread softened butter thinly on one side of each slice. Make two stacks of 3 slices each. On first slice of stack, spread deviled ham filling. Top with second bread slice, buttered side up. On second slice, spread egg salad or pimento cheese filling. Place third slice of bread on top, buttered side down. Repeat with second stack. Wrap stacks in Saran Wrap and chill until you plan to serve. Then put one stack of 3 filled slices on cutting board. With a sharp serrated knife, cut down and through stack to make four "ribbons." Repeat if desired. Remove to serving platter, and cut second stack. You will have 8 filled sandwiches about 1 in. wide, 3 in. long, and 2 in. high. Arrange with additional fancy sandwiches.

School Lunch Ham Spread   Margaret Hunter

1 lb. minced ham
4 large sweet pickles
3 hard-boiled eggs
3/4 c. salad dressing

1 t. onion, grated fine
2 t. pickle juice
Dash of salt
1/8 t. Worcestershire sauce

Grind minced ham and sweet pickles medium fine. Chop hard-boiled eggs fine. Combine ham mixture and eggs with salad dressing, onion, salt, Worcestershire sauce, and mix well. Add enough pickle juice to moisten but not make too juicy. Pair two slices of bread, and open like a book. Spread with softened butter or margarine to edges. Allow generous 2 T. of filling spread almost to edges, top with second slice. Stack sandwiches in threes, cut cornerwise in half. Wrap snugly with plastic wrap. Store in large covered plastic container, refrigerated, until needed. Serve two halves, with potato chips if desired. Meat mix will keep for 1-1/2 days when refrigerated. (Run one slice of bread through grinder to clear it. Discard bread).

*These were served for school hot lunch at an elementary school in Iowa. The
students ate every bite and asked for a third sandwich. The bread should be fresh,
either white or whole wheat. Men like them for afternoon lunch break in the field,
on either bread or buns.*

Sloppy Joes I   Gertrude Davis

1-1/2 lb. hamburger	2 T. brown sugar
1 T. shortening	1 t. salt
1 medium onion, chopped	2 T. flour
1-1/2 c. tomato juice	1 T. Worcestershire sauce

Brown hamburger and onion in shortening until hamburger is no longer pink.
Drain all grease. Sprinkle flour, sugar, and salt over meat. Stir well. Add tomato
juice, and stir until it is simmering. Add Worcestershire sauce. Reduce heat and
simmer 20 min. Serve on warmed hamburger buns with dill pickle slices.

Variation: Cook hot dogs, place in hot dog buns, and top with 1 T. or more of the
Sloppy Joe mix.

*Both versions of this sandwich are excellent for groups. The meat mix will keep 2
days if refrigerated.*

Sloppy Joes II

1-1/2 lb. ground beef	Salt and pepper
1/4 c. chopped onion	2 T. ketchup
1 can chicken gumbo	2 T. prepared mustard
soup (undiluted)	2 T. brown sugar

Brown beef with onion, salt, and pepper in 2 T. lard or oil. Drain off grease. Add
rest of ingredients and simmer 1 hr. Use 2 T. meat and dill slices to make sandwiches on hamburger buns. Yield: 10-12 sandwiches.

Spam Sandwich Filling

1 12-oz. can Spam or	1/4 lb. sharp cheddar
luncheon meat	2 T. melted margarine
1 medium onion	2 T. ketchsup
6 sweet pickles	2 T. salad dressing

Run meat, onion, pickles, and cheese through meat grinder. Add margarine,
catsup, and salad dressing. Mix well. Spread on 12 unbuttered buns, and wrap
individually in foil. To serve, heat at 375F for 20 min. Yield: 12 buns.

These filled buns freeze well. Although Spam became famous for its contribution to the war effort during World War II, thrifty farm wives have continued to serve it in a variety of recipes ever since.

Taverns I

Florence Dreeszen

2 lb. hamburger
Salt and pepper
1 small onion, diced fine
1 T. canola or other
    vegetable oil

3/4 c. Heinz ketchup
1-1/2 t. chili powder
1 t. dry mustard
1 c. hot water

Brown hamburger slowly in 1 T. oil in large skillet until it is no longer pink. Push meat to one side, and sauté onion about 5 min. but do not brown. Skim all grease, pressing down on meat. Add chili powder, mustard, salt, and pepper; stir well. Add ketchup and hot water, and mix thoroughly. Reduce heat to low, about 275F, and cook slowly, stirring often. Add water by tablespoonfuls to make a juicy filling that holds its shape. Cook up to 30 min. on top of stove or in 325F oven for 40 min.

When ready to serve, skim off any fat. Use 1/4 c. mix on small-size bun or 1/3 c. on large-size bun. Wrap buns in fold of waxed paper restaurant style. Refrigerate meat mix to store. Yield: 16-24 sandwiches, depending on size.

Variation: Add 1 T. of your favorite barbeque sauce (Gates, Masterpiece, and Bryants are well-known Kansas City varieties) and 1/2 t. liquid smoke after all other ingredients have been added. Garnish sandwich with two dill pickle slices.

Taverns II

2 lb. ground beef
1 can condensed tomato soup
1 small onion, diced
1 T. chili powder
Salt and pepper

1/2 c. ketchup
1 t. prepared mustard
1/2 c. water
1 T. Worcestershire sauce

In large skillet, sauté onion in 1 T. oil. Brown beef, cooking about 15 min. Drain off grease. Combine meat and onion with soup, chili powder, salt and pepper, mustard, and ketchup and simmer (300F) until meat is tender and flavors melded. Serve about 1/4 c. on a heated bun. This mixture may also be used to top wieners in a weiner bun, using a scant tablespoonful per bun. Yield: 20-25 sandwiches.

Hot Tuna Sandwiches

1 can tuna fish, minced
3 hard-boiled eggs, chopped
1/4 c. Velveeta cheese, diced

1 T. minced onion
1 T. sweet pickle relish
1/2 c. salad dressing

Mix ingredients well. Put about 1/3 c. on the bottom half of a buttered bun. Wrap each filled bun in foil. When ready to serve, heat at 350F for 15 min. Serve with potato chips and pickles.   Yield: 6 filled buns.

Vegetarian Sandwich

2 slices of bread (rye, whole
    wheat, or a firm artisan bread)
2 lettuce leaves
2 slices ripe tomato
Alfalfa sprouts or watercress

2 slices avocado
2 slices cucumber
Soft butter or spread
1 t. mayonnaise

Lightly butter bread. Spread one slice with mayonnaise. Layer lettuce, tomato, cucumber, and avocado on top of mayonnaise. Top with 1 T. or more sprouts and second slice of bread. Press firmly and cut across sandwich to make two servings. Serve with a cup of soup or, if preferred, with slaw or lettuce salad. Serves 2.

Sandwich Fillings

Chicken Salad: 1/2 c. cooked or canned chicken, finely minced, with 1/2 c. finely chopped celery, 1 t. minced onion, 2-3 T. mayonnaise, salt and pepper.

Egg Salad: 1 hard-boiled egg, finely chopped with fork or pastry blender, 1 T. mayonnaise, 1 t. prepared mustard, pinch of salt.

Creamy Pecan: 1 3-oz. pkg softened cream cheese, 3 t. light cream, 1/2 c. chopped pecans.

Pimiento-Cheese: Blend 3 oz. softened cream cheese and 1 T. mayonnaise. Mince and add 1 piece of canned pimiento, diced fine. Mix well.

Olive-Cheese: Blend 3 oz. softened cream cheese and 1 T. olive juice. Add 2 T. minced stuffed olives and blend.

American Cheese: Mash 1/4 lb. American cheese with 1 T. salad dressing, 1 t. finely grated onion.

Tuna: Select Solid grade (Albacore) tuna for salads when it will be left in chunks and less expensive grades for sandwiches. Choose water-packed tuna to reduce calories. Always drain tuna.

Beverages and Appetizers

Beverages
♣ *Appetizers* ♣
Snacks ♣ *Hors d'oeuvre*

Church Potluck Dinner

On a sunny Sunday in September, three cousins and their wives sat visiting on a shady porch after dinner. The three men had settled in Iowa in the 1890s, the oldest sponsoring his younger relatives. They were farmers in an area six miles south of the town where the oldest couple had moved the year before. Today the couple had invited their relatives to attend church and stay for dinner. Now they were having a jovial visit and catching up on family news.

They began to discuss the topic that was on their minds. Soon after settling on their farms, the families had found others who missed having religious services. Although rural areas did not often have church buildings, the settlers met in homes or sometimes in the one-room school. Itinerant preachers met with groups who were willing to have joint services. They banded together with the nearby towns and shared part-time preachers. The town preacher was then "in charge of" the rural "charge" as well as ministering to the town. The cousins had become active in such a charge, and the oldest was active in the church in town. The traveling preacher who served the four charges and town had called for a quarterly meeting to be held the second Sunday in October. The town church would host the meeting.

As a member of the town church also responsible for planning and organizing, the oldest cousin spoke first. Since the itinerant preacher had suggested the second Sunday in October for the meeting and would spend the afternoon discussing each charge's concerns, Was the day agreeable? The others glanced at each other and nodded that it was. Could the three cousins be responsible for communicating with the charges, get volunteers to help with the agenda, and get members to turn out for a good representation? Again, they nodded.

One cousin's wife asked if it wouldn't be practical and friendly to have a potluck dinner after the morning service. Her husband suggested having coffee ready when the more distant members arrived. Everyone agreed. The ladies excused themselves and adjourned to the kitchen to plan and wash dishes. As suggestions were made, one kept notes. They would serve coffee for the early arrivals at ten, and the potluck dinner at 12:30. Town ladies and they themselves would bring hot dishes, and those who came greater distances could bring desserts and cold foods. They would ask for volunteers as dining hostesses, and everyone would help to clear up afterward. And each decided to accompany her husband when he visited the charge leaders. They all wanted the day to be a success and would encourage others to be part of it.

Since the two visiting couples had come together, they continued planning on the ride back to their farms. The bay team stepped out at a smart pace. The men each chose charges to visit and agreed to start at once to encourage a large attendance in October. The potluck dinner was a fine idea, because good food and friendly visiting always brought folks together. The women were thankful all the cousins had subscribed to telephones when the rural exchange put in lines. That would save time, and this was a busy season putting the pullets into the laying house, as well as finishing canning before the frost. By the time the couple who had ridden along were dropped off, they all felt ready for the task.

370

There were many farm activities to tend, but all the cousins made their contacts and received promises from volunteers who would spread word of the potluck and meeting. "Nothing like a good dinner to get folks out on a Sunday!" one lady commented.

The second Sunday in October had seemed far off, but now it was Saturday, the day before. Ladies had cut all their best dahlias, zinnias, and early button mums and decorated the meeting rooms. The committee had dusted the long pine pews and distributed the hymnals and gospel songbooks. The organist had practiced hymns on the old pump organ. Some ladies had washed the oilcloth that covered the serving tables in the basement hall, while others cleaned silver and serving spoons and set out plates and coffee cups. It was all covered with clean towels. The church was ready, hushed in the pre-Sabbath evening.

A large family who lived in the farthest charge arrived first on Sunday morning. The father held the reins while two teenage boys leaped out, helped their mother and sisters down from the buggy, and carried huge covered baskets downstairs to the hall. Their mother pointed out the table reserved for desserts before donning an immaculate full-length white apron over her navy polka-dotted dress. The boys dashed upstairs with baseball and bats they had brought to play ball with friends.

Soon other women arrived carrying desserts, breads, salads, and jars of pickles and jam. As the foods arrived they were placed on tables, covered with netting, and the baskets stowed beneath the tables. A large area had been reserved for hot dishes, and a smaller table with stacks of cups was ready for beverages.

Just before ten o'clock the word spread that the preacher had arrived and services would begin. Most of the ladies went up to join their families; two or three remained downstairs in charge of the food. Soon they heard the wheezing old organ and the buoyant baritone voice of the preacher singing the Doxology, "Sweet Hour of Prayer," "Faith of Our Fathers," and "Old Rugged Cross." A lull meant prayers, and the food ladies bowed their heads. Next the men's quartet sang, "What a Friend." Shuffling feet marked the passing of the collection plates, and after a pause, a wailing baby was presented for baptism. That over, the young mother brought the baby downstairs, where he went back to sleep. The congregation settled down for a long sermon — the silence broken occasionally by the rising cadence of the preacher's voice. Then, led by the organist, members asked for favorite gospel songs — "Shall We Gather at the River," "When the Roll Is Called Up Yonder," and finally, "In the Garden" sung in parts, to sustained applause.

During the gospel singing, a steady stream of ladies carrying casseroles, platters, and covered dishes descended to the church basement. The service was ending, and the blessing would be given. Now food wrappings were removed, serving spoons and forks placed next to dishes. Pies and cakes had been cut, bread buttered, and the big three-gallon coffee pots put in place, filling the air with fragrance.

A sedate group came down the stairs, led by the preacher escorted by the church minister, the hosts, charge leaders, the elderly and disabled, women and girls, teenage boys, and children permitted to be on their own.

What a sight greeted them! Enough baking dishes and platters to stock a china shop! Such a variety of delicately browned, tastefully garnished hot dishes that making one's selection was nearly impossible. The fall gardens had provided golden brown corn puddings and scalloped corn, heaping yellow mounds of baked or mashed squash, green beans with glistening bits of bacon, navy beans baked with molasses, scalloped potatoes, creamed onions, glazed carrots, and mashed turnips. There were platters of sliced pink ham, roast pork trimmed with baked apples, roast chicken, chicken and dumplings, chicken and noodles, and sausage with kraut. The cold table was loaded with rye breads, sweet breads, and rolls; cabbage slaw, pickled beets and cucumbers, deviled eggs, and many kinds of salad. Toward the end of the serving line, a dozen kinds of pie, cake, cookies, and doughnuts offered tempting sweets to go with the steaming Real Egg Coffee or cold milk.

As the diners moved along the tables, hostesses urged them to "have just a bit" of everything. Their hospitality was so genuine and the food so tempting that few could resist. More than one plate "needed sideboards," as one of the teenagers teased another. Somehow everyone squeezed into seats and benches, with the youngest sitting on the steps. People went back for seconds, amid compliments, coaxing, laughter, and joking.

As the time for the afternoon meetings neared, the men moved upstairs. The ladies began the task of picking up their pie pans, casserole dishes, platters, and serving spoons and returning these to their baskets. There were requests for recipes and compliments on food. As they visited, they were busily wiping the oilcloth on the tables, sweeping up crumbs, folding the varnished wood-slatted chairs, washing and wiping church dishes and silver. As with every presentation of a superbly satisfying meal, there was the action behind the scenes: the planning and cooking had been done; the tables loaded with food; now any evidence of disarray was being removed. It was very well organized. They agreed that having the potluck meal was a splendid idea. All the families got better acquainted and made new friends. It was fun to share food and recipes. It would be a good idea to do this regularly.

The meetings continued until four o'clock. Decisions were made. One charge would definitely begin to build a church next spring. Two others decided to combine groups and search for a building they could move to a site agreeable to both. They would need a part-time preacher. With enthusiasm, all sang "God be with you till we meet again!" and made their goodbyes.

Already those who had come a long way had their minds turned toward livestock moving restlessly around feed bunks, and cows ambling along familiar paths toward milking barns, but their conversation returned to the day. Sharing plans was good. Coming together to share a potluck meal with friends gives everyone the feeling of belonging to a real community. Already the church existed in spirit; the building would follow in good time.

Recipes

Real Egg Coffee

1 c. regular grind coffee   Cold water
1 egg

In bowl, mix coffee with egg, slightly beaten, the crushed eggshell, and a cup of cold water. Bring 2 qt. cold water to a rolling boil in a 2-gal. coffee pot. Add the prepared coffee with eggshell and stir well. Let boil up again. Simmer for 10 min. Remove from heat and slowly pour 2 c. very cold water into spout of pot. Let stand 5 min. for grounds to settle. Pour slowly into an electric coffee pot to maintain heat. Yield: 12 cups.

This coffee is very clear and very flavorful. The eggshell helps the grounds to settle.

In the twenties there were many evening social occasions involving couples: card parties where folding tables were set up in every available space, house and barn dances (held in lofts reached by stairs), fraternal and lodge meetings, box suppers, church potlucks — any opportunity to get together and have fun. Certain women had the role of coffee maker and prepared as many big coffee pots full of fragrant, satisfying coffee as needed. Farm wives were rated on their coffee and pie.

Cold Morning Cocoa

3 T. cocoa   1/2 c. water
3 t. sugar   3 c. whole or 2% milk
1/4 t. salt   1/2 t. vanilla

In a medium saucepan, mix cocoa, sugar, salt, and water. Cook on slow heat, stirring until mixture boils for 1 min. Add milk. Blend. Let heat almost to boiling. Remove from heat, add vanilla, and beat with wire whisk until frothy. Serves 3.

We children liked to make cocoa when we came in on a cold day after doing farm chores. Great with toast or a cookie!

Cooler for Children

Save juice when a recipe calls for drained fruits. Combine the fruit juices, add a package of Kool-Aid or a can of frozen lemonade and 1 T. sugar. Stir well and serve over ice.

My mother noted that children love fruit coolers and never miss soda pop when a pitcher of iced cooler is ready to pour on a hot day.

Cranberry Cider

1-1/2 qt. cranberry juice
   (not cocktail)
2 qt. apple juice or cider
3 or 4 cinnamon sticks

2 t. whole cloves
1/3 c. brown sugar
1/2 t. salt

Put cranberry and apple juices in bottom of a 30-cup percolator. Place cinnamon sticks, cloves, sugar, and salt in the basket. Perk 10 min. Yield: 24 servings.

*Eggnog

2 eggs, well beaten
1 14-oz. can sweetened
   condensed milk
1 t. vanilla
1/4 t. salt

1 qt. homogenized milk
1 c. whipping cream,
   whipped
Nutmeg
3/4 c. bourbon (optional)

Combine eggs, condensed milk, salt, and milk. If desired, stir in bourbon. Fold in whipped cream. Sprinkle each serving with nutmeg. Yield: 10 to 12 servings.

Health experts warn that consuming uncooked eggs may be dangerous.

French Café au Lait

3 c. boiling water
1/2 c. freshly ground coffee

3 c. very hot milk

Using a drip coffee maker, pour vigorously boiling water over freshly ground coffee. For café au lait, use equal parts of very hot milk and boiling hot coffee.

Grape Cooler

1 46-oz. can pineapple juice
1 qt. ginger ale
2 6-oz. cans frozen lemonade

2 6-oz. cans frozen white
   grape juice
1 pt. small fresh strawberries

Combine and chill pineapple juice, frozen lemonade, and white grape juice. Chill ginger ale. When ready to serve, add ginger ale, pour over crushed ice, and serve in wine glasses with a strawberry garnish. Serves 20.

This is an elegant punch for high school graduation and other parties including young people. Older people like it, too!

(= adult beverages)*

Instant Hot Chocolate Mix

1 8-qt. box of instant dry milk
2 lb. box Nestle Quik

8 to 11 oz. jar nondairy creamer
1 lb. powdered sugar

Mix all ingredients thoroughly. Use 3/4 c. with 1 qt. hot water to make hot chocolate. Top with a marshmallow. Store in covered container.

The P.T.A. supplied ingredients to make this mix so that school crossing guards had a cup of hot chocolate after their chilly 10 minutes on duty. Store in covered containers and refrigerate.

Lime Punch

2 qt. ginger ale
1 46-oz. can pineapple juice

1 qt. lime sherbet

Combine chilled liquids. Stir in softened sherbet. Yield 20 one-cup servings.

Old-Time Lemonade

6 juicy lemons
1-1/2 c. sugar

2 qt. water

Have lemons at room temperature. Roll them firmly on counter top to maximize juice. Cut each in half crosswise and squeeze juice. Discard seeds. Mix lemon juice, sugar, and water. Stir to dissolve sugar. To serve, pour lemonade over ice cubes in each glass. Garnish with lemon slice. Yield: 8-10 glasses.

*Mimosa

1 qt. orange juice, chilled

1 fifth champagne

Just before serving, mix orange juice and champagne in large chilled pitcher. (They may also be mixed individually.) Serve over ice. Yield: 2 qt.

This adult brunch beverage was a specialty at the Cedar Rapids Sheraton's Sunday brunch.

Mocha-Coffee Frostee

1 c. double-strength coffee
2 c. milk

1/2 tray ice cubes
1 pt. chocolate ice cream

Blend coffee, ice cubes, and milk 2 min. Add ice cream, blend 1 min. more. Serves 6.

Orange-Banana Frostee

12 ice cubes
1 6-oz. can frozen orange
   juice concentrate, thawed
1 c. milk

1 pt. vanilla ice cream
3 ripe bananas (light brown
   spots), quartered; reserve
   six slices of banana for garnish

In a blender, partly crush ice cubes. Add orange juice, milk, and banana quarters, blending 30 sec. Add ice cream by large spoonfuls. Blend until smooth. Top with banana slice. Serves 6.

Orange Flip

12 ice cubes
1 c. milk
1/4 c. sugar

6 oz. frozen orange juice
1 c. water
1/2 t. vanilla

Partially crush ice cubes in blender. Add all ingredients and blend until frothy and ice cubes are blended. Yield: 4 one-cup servings.

My Party Punch   Ruth Harbour

1 48-oz. can pineapple juice
1 12-oz. frozen orange juice
1 12-oz. can frozen lemonade

4 16-oz. bottles ginger ale
3 c. water
3 qt. ice cubes or very large ice block

Combine juices and water; chill. When ready to serve, pour juices over ice and add ginger ale slowly from side to maintain fizz. Garnish with orange slice and maraschino cherry. Yield: about 50 half-cup portions.

♣ *An empty frozen orange juice container may be filled with water and frozen to chill a pitcher or punch bowl of cold drinks. Or fill the container with the beverage to freeze so the drinks will not be diluted. Cut the bottom and push the ice out.*

*Peach Fizz

Sue Arthaud

4 fresh peaches
6 oz. frozen lemonade
6 oz. frozen limeade

8 or 10 ice cubes
1 c. vodka

Peel and slice peaches. Partially crush ice cubes in blender. Add other ingredients and blend until frothy and ice cubes are broken up.

Canned or frozen peaches may be substituted for fresh ones. Strawberries may be used for Strawberry Fizz.

Russian Tea / Spiced Tea Mix

1/2 c. instant tea powder
2 c. Tang orange drink powder
2 c. dry lemonade mix
1 c. sugar

1 t. ground cinnamon
1 t. ground cloves
Boiling water

Mix all dry ingredients together and store in covered container. To make Russian or spiced tea, use 1 heaping teaspoonful to a cup of boiling water. Stir well. Serve in glass mug with slice of lemon.

*Sangria I

1 c. unsweetened pineapple juice
1 c. orange juice
1/4 c. lemon juice
2 T. lime juice

6 T. sugar
1 qt. dry white wine or Chianti
1 large bottle 7-Up

Mix all ingredients except 7-Up and chill 4 hr. Add the 7-Up just before serving. Pour over ice cubes. Thread a pineapple chunk and orange slice on a toothpick as garnish. Serves 6.

*Sangria II

Anne Harbour

3 oranges
3 lemons
3 limes
1/2 c. sugar

1/2 c. brandy
4 bottles red wine
2 trays ice cubes

Wash fruit and cut crosswise into 1/4-in. slices, discarding seeds. Put into large punch bowl. Sprinkle sugar and brandy over fruit. Add ice cubes. Pour wine over all.

*Singapore Sling   Raffles Hotel

30 ml. Seagram's gin
15 ml. Peter Heering
Dash of Triple Sec
Dash of Benedictine Dom

7.5 ml. lime juice
120 ml. pineapple juice
10 ml. grenadine syrup
1 drop Angostura bitters

This recipe for the famous drink invented in Singapore was provided by the bartender in the Writers' Bar.

Strawberry Frostee

1 6-oz. can frozen pink
    lemonade concentrate
1 c. milk
1 pt. vanilla ice cream

1 c. frozen strawberries
    in syrup, thawed *or* 1 pt. fresh
    strawberries, washed and hulled

Partially thaw lemonade. Place all ingredients into blender in the order given. Blend until smooth. Pour into glasses. Yield: 4-6 servings.

Tangy Tomato Juice

2 qt. tomato juice
1 t. celery salt
1/4 t. Tabasco sauce
1/2 t. Worcestershire sauce

1 t. onion salt
1/4 t. garlic, pressed
3 T. sugar
2 c. club soda

Combine all ingredients. Serve over crushed ice with a celery stick stirrer. Yield: 12 servings.

Wassail

2 c. water
1 qt. apple cider or juice
1 pt. cranberry juice
1 c. orange juice
1/2 c. lemon juice

1/2 c. sugar
1 t. whole cloves
1 t. whole allspice
3 cinnamon sticks

Combine water and juices in automatic percolator. Place sugar and spices in percolator basket. Allow to perk through cycle. Serve hot. May be reheated. Yield: 10-12 servings.

Wassail Punch

1/2 gal. apple cider or juice
2 c. orange juice
1 c. lemon juice
2 c. water

1/4 c. sugar
2 cinnamon sticks
4 or 5 whole cloves
1 T. butter

Combine all ingredients in electric coffee urn and bring to a boil. Simmer 1 hr. Yield: 12-14 servings.

You may add 1 qt. cranberry juice cocktail if desired.

*T*empting bites to stave off hunger until the main course appears, appetizers have come a long way since frontier days. When families exchanged Sunday dinners in the thirties, guests politely visited about crops, the weather, and prices of live-stock, while inhaling wonderful fragrances from the kitchen. Children who were restive were cautioned, "We mustn't spoil our appetite!" or "It won't be long now!" — which only prolonged their misery.

Then the celery, olives, and carrots left the dining room and became crudités that sat on the coffee table to appease nibblers. The English offered cheese straws and biscuits. The Danish and Norwegians laid out cheese cubes and pickled herring. The spread of tart, spicy, savory items grew with the arrival of cheese balls, dips, and ethnic snacks. The half hour we spend sampling is such a sociable, informal occasion that it becomes another meal.

Appetizers become a healthful prelude to the main event if we plan to balance choices by including fresh, crisp vegetables and fruits and yogurt or vinaigrettes for dipping. The recipes here include the tempting baked Chiles Rellenos dip Gail served on her patio overlooking the Rockies, and a dill dip Connie served in a Rye Bread bowl for a holiday coffee. They remind me of many happy times as we nibble and nosh with friends.
Bon appetít!

Gail's Artichoke-Chili Dip
Gail Bahnson Matheson

2 cans artichoke hearts,
  chopped (not marinated)
2 cans mild green chiles

1 c. freshly grated Parmesan cheese
1 c. mayonnaise

Combine ingredients, stir, and bake at 300F for 25 min. Serve with tortilla chips.

Bacon-Pineapple Broil

1 #2 can pineapple chunks   Soy sauce (optional)
1/2 lb. lean bacon strips

Drain pineapple chunks, reserving juice for other use. Cut bacon strips in half crosswise. Wrap a chunk of pineapple in 1/2 strip bacon and secure it with cocktail toothpick. Arrange chunks on foil that covers the broiling rack. Broil about 5 in. from heat, moving pan so the pieces broil evenly. Broil until bacon crisps and begins to curl. Remove from broiler, place on serving platter, and prepare for applause. If you wish, sprinkle soy sauce over pineapple chunks.

Boursin Cheese Spread

1/4 c. butter or margarine   1/8 t. oregano
1 8-oz. pkg cream cheese   1/8 t. dill seed
1/4 t. garlic powder   1/8 t. dried basil, crushed
1-1/2 T. milk   1/8 t. black pepper
1/4 t. ground savory

Let butter and cream cheese soften. Combine all ingredients in small electric mixer bowl until well blended. Cover and store in an airtight container overnight to allow flavors to blend. Serve at room temperature on crackers or party rye bread. Keeps well chilled. Yield: 1 1/3 cups.

My Braunschweiger Ball   Ruth Harbour

1 lb. braunschweiger   1/4 c. chutney or chili sauce
1 8-oz. pkg cream cheese   1/2 t. Worcestershire sauce
3 T. very finely chopped   1/4 t. Tabasco sauce
     mild onion

Blend all ingredients at low speed in small mixer bowl. Add a small amount of mayonnaise if needed for smooth consistency. Form mixture into two 3-1/2-in. balls. Place each on waxed paper and chill for 2 hr.

Topping: Combine 1 8-oz. pkg cream cheese, 1 T. prepared yellow mustard, 1 T. half and half in small mixer bowl and blend until smooth. Using a small spatula, spread a generous layer of topping to cover chilled balls. Use a wide spatula to center each ball on a 7- or 8-in. plate. Decorate balls with halved ripe or stuffed olives. Surround balls with Ry Krisp or buttery crackers. Provide plastic knives for spreading. Yield: 24 to 30 servings.

This also makes an excellent sandwich spread. It may be frozen up to 3 weeks.

Celery Swirls

1 bunch celery
1 8-oz. pkg cream cheese
1/2 c. grated mild cheddar
1 T. milk

1 T. minced onion
1 clove garlic, minced
1 T. green pepper, finely minced
Salt and pepper

Wash, trim, and separate celery into spears about 4 in. long. Combine softened cheeses and blend until smooth. Add onion, garlic, green pepper, milk, and salt and pepper to taste. Spread mixture in center of each spear. Press three spears together with cheese facing the center and celery surrounding it. You may add another layer. Fasten bundle with rubber bands. Chill several hours. Remove bands and use sharp knife to slice across to make 1/2-in. thick cheese-stuffed swirls. Serves 12-15.

Cheese Puffs

Gladys Casford

1 loaf firm, unsliced white bread
1 3-oz. pkg cream cheese
1/4 lb. sharp cheddar cheese

2 egg whites
1 stick butter or margarine

Trim crusts from bread; cut bread into 1-in. cubes. Melt cheese and butter in top of double boiler over hot water until of rarebit consistency. Remove from heat; fold in stiffly beaten egg whites. Dip bread cubes into cheese mixture until well coated. Place on cookie sheets. Refrigerate overnight. Bake in hot oven (400F) for 12-15 min. or until puffy and golden brown. Yield: about 4 dozen.

Cheese Straws

Fiona Wilkinson

3/4 c. butter, softened
1 lb. extra sharp cheddar
   cheese, grated

2 c. flour
1 t. salt
1/2 t. red pepper

Mix butter with grated cheese. Add flour, salt, and red pepper; blend well. Put dough into cookie press. Press onto ungreased cookie sheet using star-shaped disc. Bake at 350F for 10-12 min. Yield: 4 dozen.

Fiona served these zesty appetizers with tomato juice before dinner in her home near Bristol, England.

Cheese Wafers I

2-1/2 c. flour
1/2 t. salt
1/2 t. garlic salt
1/4 t. red pepper

1 stick butter (1/4 lb.)
1 lb. sharp cheddar cheese,
   grated

Sift dry ingredients together. Cut in butter with pastry blender. Add cheese and mix well. Shape dough into rolls 1 in. in diameter. Wrap in waxed paper. Chill overnight. Cut into thin slices. Bake at 350F for 20 min., until light brown. Yield: 4 dozen.

Cheese Wafers II   Gladys Casford

1 stick butter or oleo
1 c. sharp cheddar cheese,
   grated

1 c. flour
1/4 t. red pepper
1 c. Rice Krispies

Melt butter; add grated cheese and melt until grainy. Add flour and pepper. Mix well. Add Rice Krispies. Stir just enough to mix well. Shape into small balls. Place on lightly greased cookie sheet. Mash down balls with fork. Bake at 350F until golden brown. Leave in pan until cooled. Yield: 25-30 wafers. Do not try to double recipe.

Chiles Rellenos Casserole   Gail Bahnson Matheson

1-1/2 lb. Monterey Jack cheese
2 7-oz. cans green chiles

7 large eggs
1 pt. sour cream

Grease 2- to 3-qt. casserole (8 x 13 dish). Grate cheese. Slice green chiles length-wise. Alternate layers of chiles and cheese. Beat eggs until blended. Add sour cream to eggs; mix until smooth. Pour over top of chiles and cheese layers. Bake at 350F uncovered for 60 min. Let stand 10 min. before serving. Yield: 10 servings.

Dill Dip in a Rye Bowl   Connie Woods

1 6-in. round pumpernickel
   rye loaf of bread, unsliced
1 pt. dairy sour cream
1 c. mayonnaise

1 t. Accent
3 T. minced sweet onion
2 T. parsley flakes
1 T. dried dill or dill seed

Buy or bake bread. Using a sharp knife, cut a circle an inch in from the outer edge of the loaf, cutting through to within an inch of the bottom of the loaf, and hollow the loaf as if you were making a jack-o'-lantern. Try to keep the part you remove as intact as possible. Then cut or tear this inner part into 1-inch cubes. Cover the cubes with Cling Wrap and set aside.

Dip Filling: Combine sour cream, mayonnaise, and seasonings, and mix well. Chill in a covered container overnight to blend flavors.

When ready to serve, place rye bowl on a 10-in. round plate or platter. Pile rye cubes around it. Set out another server with fresh vegetable strips: peppers, cucumber, carrot, and celery. Stir the prepared dip and pour it into the hollowed rye bowl. Delicious. Yield: 3 cups.

Dilly Dip

Pam Handke

2/3 c. mayonnaise
2/3 c. sour cream
1 T. Beau Monde

1 T. parsley flakes
1 T. onion flakes
1 T. dill seed

Mix all ingredients. Refrigerate 3-5 hr.

Excellent dip with fresh vegetables: cucumbers, cauliflower, zucchini, etc.

Dried Beef in Cheese Ball

1/4 lb. dried beef, finely
  shredded
8 oz. cream cheese
1 t. milk

2 t. horseradish
2 t. minced onion
Chopped walnuts

Combine beef, softened cream cheese, and seasonings. Mix thoroughly, adding a teaspoonful of milk to make into a ball. Roll in chopped nuts and chill. Ball is best if it ripens 8-12 hr. Serve with crackers or party rye bread. Serves 6-8.

Guacamole Dip

2 large ripe avocados
2 or 3 T. lime juice
1 large garlic clove

1/4 t. salt
2 t. parsley, finely chopped
2 t. Hellmann's mayonnaise

Peel avocados and remove seeds, putting pulp in a 4-c. bowl. Mash coarsely with a fork while blending in lime juice. Mince a good-sized garlic clove, and blend with avocado. Add salt and parsley, mixing well. You may wish to mix in a little Hellmann's mayonnaise to add creamy texture. Yield: 2 cups.

May be used as a dip with hot tortilla chips, or as a salad atop crisp shredded lettuce.

Greek Garbanzo Dip (Hummus)

1 16-oz. can garbanzos
3 T. liquid from garbanzos
1/4 c. sesame sauce (tahini)
1/2 c. fresh lemon juice

2 T. olive oil
1 large clove garlic, crushed
1/2 t. salt

Drain garbanzos, reserving 3 T. liquid; heat garbanzos and reserved liquid in saucepan. In blender put sesame sauce, lemon juice, and olive oil. Blend on high speed for 10 sec. Gradually add hot garbanzos with 3 T. liquid. Blend to a smooth paste. Add crushed garlic and salt; blend briefly. Chill in a covered container until ready to serve. Serve with carrot and celery sticks, triangles of pita bread, or cocktail crackers. Serves 8-10.

Hummus

2 16-oz cans garbanzos
3 cloves garlic, crushed
2 T. lemon juice
6 T. sesame sauce (tahini)

1/4 t. ground cumin
Salt to taste
Finely chopped parsley

Drain first can of garbanzos and reserve liquid for another use. Put drained garbanzos into blender. Add second can garbanzos and all its liquid, lemon juice, and tahini. Blend to a smooth paste. Add crushed garlic, cumin, salt and more lemon juice to taste; blend briefly. Chill several hours in tightly covered container. Serve in bowl garnished with parsley on a plate surrounded by fresh vegetables in bite-sized pieces.

Cheese with Jezebel Sauce   Corinne Tucker

1 18-oz. jar apple jelly
1 18-oz. pineapple or pineapple-
   apricot preserves

1 5-oz. jar horseradish
1 T. dry mustard
1 8-oz. pkg cream cheese

Combine all ingredients except cream cheese; mix well. Refrigerate. To serve, arrange cream cheese on a serving plate. Spoon about 1 c. of Jezebel Sauce atop. Serve with buttery crackers. Serves 8-10.

A real crowd pleaser. Easy and tasty. Jezebel Sauce keeps for weeks when refrigerated.

Mexi-Dip

1/2 lb. ground beef
1 15-1/2-oz. can mashed
  refried beans
8 oz. tomato sauce
1 pkg taco seasoning mix
1 small onion

1/2 medium-sized green pepper
1/2 t. dry mustard
1/2 t. chili powder
Sour cream topping
Cheddar cheese, shredded
Lettuce, finely shredded

Brown ground beef, and drain fat. Chop onion and green pepper fine and stir into ground beef. Add refried beans, tomato sauce, and seasonings; mix well. Heat to boiling, stirring constantly. Spread mixture into ungreased 9-in. pie pan. Cover with layer of sour cream topping. Sprinkle with shredded lettuce and cheese. Serve with tortilla chips.

Sour Cream Topping: Combine 1 c. dairy sour cream, 2 T. grated American cheese, and 1/4 t. chili powder.

Mexican Hot Dip

2 cans bean dip
1 lb. ground beef chuck, browned
1 can mild green chiles, chopped
1 c. picante sauce

1 c. shredded cheddar cheese
2 ripe medium tomatoes, diced
Tortilla chips

Layer bean dip, browned meat, chiles, and picante sauce in 3-qt. casserole. Top with shredded cheese. Heat in 375F oven to melt cheese. Scatter tomatoes atop and serve with tortilla chips. Serves 8-10.

Mexican Hot Taco Dip

Middie Mae Morf

1 lb. ground beef
1 lb. Velveeta cheese
4 or 5 green onions

1/2 green pepper
1/4 jalapeño pepper
1 small can tomato sauce

Brown and drain ground beef. Melt cheese in top of double boiler. Chop onions and peppers fine. Add beef, vegetables, and tomato sauce to melted cheese. Heat thoroughly. Serve with taco chips or corn chips.

Mexican Topper Tortilla Dip
Sue Arthaud

2 small cans jalapeño bean dip	1 pkg taco seasoning
3 ripe avocados	1 large bunch green onions,
2 T. lemon juice	chopped fine with part of tops
1 t. salt	3 ripe medium tomatoes, chopped
1/4 t. pepper	1 4-oz. can chopped ripe olives
1 c. sour cream	8 oz. cheddar cheese, shredded
1/2 c. mayonnaise	Tortilla chips

First layer: Spread bean dip on a 10-in. serving platter.

Second layer: Peel and seed avocados; blend with lemon juice, salt, and pepper. Spread on top of bean dip.

Third layer: Blend softened sour cream, mayonnaise, and taco seasoning. Spread this on avocado layer. Sprinkle with chopped onions.

Fourth layer: Sprinkle on tomatoes, then olives, then cheese. Chill. Yield: 1 qt. Serves 6-8.

Serve this with warm tortilla chips. It also goes well with celery spears.

Olive Cheese Ball
Kris Larson

1 8-oz. pkg cream cheese	1/2 c. chopped black olives
1 stick margarine	1/4 c. chopped green olives
1/2 t. garlic salt	

Cream softened cream cheese and margarine with garlic salt. Add chopped olives. Shape into ball and chill on waxed paper. Serve on a plate surrounded by assorted crackers.

Pickled Eggs

1 can sliced beets	1 stick cinnamon
1 c. cider vinegar	6 whole cloves
1/3 c. brown sugar, packed	12 to 18 medium-sized eggs

Cook as many eggs as you wish to serve. They should be 3 or 4 days old (very fresh eggs will not peel well). In a large saucepan of cold water, put the eggs on medium heat to cook. When the eggs begin to boil, remove pan from heat. Cool for 30 min. in the hot water. Then drain eggs, run cold water to cool them, peel, and rinse. Put eggs in a sterilized quart jar.

Drain beet juice into a saucepan; set beets aside for another use. Add vinegar, brown sugar, and spices. Boil 10 min, strain, and pour over eggs. Tightly cover jar and chill.

Shrimp Dip

1 8-oz. pkg cream cheese
1 T. catsup
Dash of salt

1/2 medium onion
1 can small shrimp
Mayonnaise

Chop onion fine. Combine with softened cream cheese, catsup, and salt. Drain and rinse shrimp; cut into small pieces, and add to mixture. Blend well, adding mayonnaise if necessary for desired consistency. Chill overnight. Serve with crackers.

Spinach Appetizers

2 boxes frozen chopped spinach,
    cooked and well drained
2 c. Pepperidge Farm herb
    stuffing mix
2 small onions, chopped fine
4 eggs, beaten

4 T. butter, melted
1/2 c. Parmesan cheese
1 T. garlic salt
1/2 t. thyme
1 t. monosodium glutamate

Mix ingredients. Make balls, using a teaspoonful for each. Bake on lightly greased baking sheet at 350F for 20 min. May freeze before baking or after. Serve hot. Yield: 4 dozen.

Tapenade / Olive Spread

1 6-oz. jar pitted kalamata olives
1 T. drained capers
1 T. white wine vinegar
1 t. lemon juice

1 small garlic clove
1/4 t. freshly ground pepper
3 T. olive oil

Pulse first six ingredients in blender 3 or 4 times. Add olive oil. Pulse 3 or 4 times until mixture forms a chunky paste. Serve with thin toasted French baguette slices and fresh raw vegetables.

Tortilla Pinwheels   Nancy Savely

1-1/2 8-oz. pkg cream cheese   1/2 pkg taco seasoning
1 8-oz. carton sour cream   1/4 t. garlic powder
4 T. picante sauce   1/2 t. seasoning salt
1/2 c. green onions, chopped fine   6 10-in. flour tortillas
1/2 c. black olives, chopped fine

Mix ingredients together. Spread over tortillas. Roll up, wrap in Saran Wrap, and
chill overnight. To serve, cut into 1-in. pieces. Serve with salsa. Yield: 2 dozen.

Blue Cheese Vegetable Dip

1 pt. sour cream   1/2 pkg. Hidden Valley dry
1 pt. Hellmann's mayonnaise   dressing mix
1 4-oz. pkg Bleu Cheese, crumbled

Mix all ingredients well. Chill. Use for dip with raw broccoli, cauliflower, celery,
carrots, cucumber, and other fresh vegetables.

Vegetable Dip I

1 c. mayonnaise   1 t. vinegar
2 T. chopped onion   1 t. ginger
1 t. milk   2 t. soy sauce

Combine all ingredients and mix well. Refrigerate at least 24 hr. for best flavor.
Use as a dip for carrot sticks, celery, cucumber spears, pepper rings, and cauliflower florets. Yield: 1 cup.

Vegetable Dip II

1 c. Hellmann's mayonnaise   Dash of salt and pepper
1 t. Worcestershire sauce   1/4 t. garlic powder
2 T. Heinz chili sauce   1 t. onion juice
2 t. curry powder

Mix all ingredients and refrigerate 4-6 hr. Yield: 1 cup.

Vegetable Dip III

1 pt. Hellmann's mayonnaise
2/3 c. sour cream
1/2 c. fresh spinach, finely
    chopped
4 T. green onions, finely chopped

2 t. parsley, chopped
1/8 t. pepper
1/4 t. Accent
Dash of Worcestershire sauce
Dash of Tabasco sauce

Mix all ingredients well and refrigerate overnight. Excellent as dip for raw vegetables or potato chips. Yield: 3 cups.

ABOUT THE AUTHOR

Ruth Petersen Harbour was the first granddaughter born in her family. She grew up having a close personal relationship with each grandparent and loved hearing stories about "the old country" — Denmark and Schleswig-Holstein in northern Germany. Passage in steerage to America sounded very difficult, but it ended safely with Grandpa or Grandma.

Two younger brothers arrived, and Ruth went to visit the country school a half-mile distant. The visit stretched into six years, for she was an eager pupil. Her brothers and she learned to ride bareback on the family's gentle old horse. They visited their grandparents and their forty-two young cousins. In winter, Dad guided the team pulling a sled as they visited the town three miles away. A third brother completed the family. It was a good life.

Highlights of Ruth's education in Anthon High School were cooking in home economics and creative writing in English class. Talented teachers made each day challenging. When Ruth graduated at 15, she entered college to prepare for a career in teaching.

After two years' study and five years of elementary teaching, Ruth married Ray Harbour. He had graduated from Iowa State College in forestry and supervised the Iowa Geodetic Survey's remap of Shelby County before the couple began 18 years of farming. Their experiences included soil conservation, raising quality flocks of sheep and cattle feeding. Ruth was busy with gardening, canning, family food preparation and meals for harvesters and other seasonal workers. This expanded her large collections of recipes grandmas, mother and 12 aunts had passed on to her.

Four daughters arrived to bless the Harbour family. They did the drill: 4-H club, gardening, poultry, along with church and community affairs. Two were in college by 1963, when the family left the farm and moved to Cedar Rapids, Iowa. Ruth had commuted to complete her B.A. at Morningside College and M.A. at the University of South Dakota. She resumed teaching in Cedar Rapids.

The M.A. in English helped her enter a new phase in her profession. She was selected to open the new Taft Junior High School's

I.M.C. in 1965 with an emphasis on the I.M.C. as hub of curriculum enhancement, and she completed study toward the M.S. in library science. After eight fulfilling years, Ruth transferred to Pierce Elementary School as principal and leader of staff development. The next nine years were the greatest challenge in her 35 years as an Iowa teacher, and the most rewarding.

When she retired in 1982, Ruth Harbour moved to the Kansas-Missouri area, where her three grandchildren are students. Daughters Laurel and Lea follow their professions in Kansas City, Janet is a compliance officer at Tinker Air Force Base in Oklahoma, and Anne continues her career in marketing in Minneapolis.

Ruth is always ready to assemble the Thanksgiving feast or help with a family potluck or a meal, and she will pack a travel bag at a moment's notice. She enjoys friendships with members of several women's organizations.

This book is a selection of recipes from family and friends and "faraway places" she has visited. Can you catch the aroma of *Real Egg Coffee?*

INDEX

BREADS

My White Bread 9
No-Knead White Bread 9
Dorothy's Oatmeal Bread 10
Raisin Bread 10
Rye Bread 11
Charlotte's Rye Bread 11
Grandma's Rye Bread 11
Norwegian Rye Bread 12
Rye Cardamom Bread 12
Raisin Rye Bread 13
Brown Wheat Bread 13
Whole Wheat Bread 14
Batter Bread 14
Dilly Bread 15
Butter Flake Brioche 15
Butterhorns 16
Butterscotch Pecan Rolls 17
Gerry's Rohliky-Crescent Rolls 17
Danish Rolls 18
Dinner Rolls 18
Dutch Buns 19
Hot Cross Buns 19
Czech Town Kolaches 20
Sharon's Kolaches 20
Light Rolls — Bake and Brown 21
No-Knead Refrigerator Rolls 21
4-H Basic Sweet Rolls 22
Bernice's Rolls 23
Cinnamon Rolls 23
Sweet French Buns 23
Sally Lunn 24
Steamed Boston Brown Bread, 1920s 24
Banana Nut Bread 25
Edna's Cranberry Orange Bread 25
Nut Bread 26
Betty's Nut Bread 26
Brazil Nut Apricot Loaf 26
Date Nut Bread 27
Date Nut Whole Wheat Bread 27
Best Gingerbread 27
Laura's Gingerbread 28
Mother's Gingerbread 28
Irish Soda Bread 29
Orange-Date Loaf 29
Pecan Breakfast Loaf 29
Kim's Pumpkin Bread 30
Pumpkin Bread 30
Zucchini Bread 30
Raisin Pecan Coffee Bread 31

Blueberry Coffee Cake 31
Marie's Heath Brickle Coffee Cake 31
My Quick Streusel Coffee Cake 32
Aunt Luella's Filled Coffee Cake 32
Spicy Breakfast Puffs 33
Peanut Bubble Ring 33
Blueberry Muffins 33
Kansas Blueberry Muffins 34
Blueberry Streusel Muffins 34
Bran Muffins 34
Alexis's Bran Muffins 35
Bran Flakes Muffins 35
Cranberry Muffins 35
Early Riser Muffins 36
Minute Muffins 36
Morning Glory Muffins 37
Aunt Amy's Surprise Muffins 37
Baking Powder Biscuits 37
Aunt Millie's Corn Bread 38
Southern Spoon Bread 38
Dumplings 38
Tama Fried Bread 38
Scones 39
Festive Scones 39
Grandma's Plain Griddle Cakes 40
Griddle Cakes and Variations 40
Swedish Pancakes 41
Blueberry Topping for Pancakes 41
Honey Butter 41
Norwegian Pancakes (Lefse) 41
Belgian Waffles 42
Jean's Waffles 42
Wesson Waffles 42
Herb Bread 43
Bread-Making Suggestions 43-45

COOKIES

Apricot Bars 51
Bohemian Cherry Bars 51
Best Brownies 52
Blond Brownies 52
Fudge Brownies 52
Helen's Brownies 53
Rocky Road Fudge Brownies 53
F.J.'s Brownies 53
Southern Brownies 54
May's Chocolate Tops 54
Orange Coconut Bars 54
Date Bars 55
Date and Apricot Bars 55

Chewy Date Bars 56
Crispy Date Bars 56
Dream Bars 56
Seven Layer Bars 57
Lemon Love Notes 57
Salted Peanut Bars 57
Pecan Pie Bars 58
Pecan Tassies 58
My Prayer Bars 59
Pumpkin Bars 59
Frosted Raisin Squares 60
Ammonia Cookies — White 60
Ammonia Cookies — Yellow 60
Sugar Cookies 61
My Crisp Sugar Cookies 61
Aunt Luella's Sugar Cookies 62
Meta's Rolled Sugar Cookies 62
Tea Cookies 62
White Butter Cookies 63
Butterscotch Cookies 63
My Butterscotch Refrigerator Wafers 63
Delicious Chocolate Chip Cookies 64
Iced Chocolate Cookies 64
Chocolate Top Hats 64
Cherry Coconut Cookies 65
Coconut Crispies 65
Coconut-Oatmeal Crispy Cookies 65
Chocolate Macaroons 66
Date Cookies 66
My Filled Date or Raisin Cookies 66
Date-Orange Softies 67
Ginger Cookies (Pecan Top) 67
Crackly Ginger Snaps 67
Soft Ginger Cookies 68
Rolled Ginger Cookies 68
M & M Cookies 69
Mexican Wedding Cakes 69
My Mincemeat Surprise Cookies 69
Molasses Cookies 70
Scottish Oat Cakes 70
Spicy Oatmeal Cookies 70
Unusual Oatmeal Raisin Cookies 71
Peanut Butter Cookies 71
Peanut Blossoms 71
Salted Peanut Nuggets 72
Peter Pan Cookies 72
Pecan Ice Box Cookies 72
Pefferneuse/Peppernuts 73
Potato Chip Cookies 73
Raisin Apple Drop Cookies 74
Ranger Cookies 74
Snickerdoodles 74
Walnut Rolled Cookies 75

St. Nicholas Koekjes 75
Festive Christmas Thins 75
Thumbprint Cookies 76
Dutch Letters 76
Scottish Shortbread/Petticoat Tails I 77
Scottish Shortbread/Petticoat Tails II 77
Spritz Cookies 77
Cake Doughnuts 78
Favorite Doughnuts 78
Unbaked Butterscotch Cookies 79
Unbaked Chocolate Cookies 79
Unbaked Date Cookies 79
No-Bake Peanut Butter Cookies 79
Unbaked Ritz Cookies 80

CAKES
Angel Food Cake 84
Chocolate Angel Food 84
Gold Angel Cake 85
Apple Harvest Cake 85
Nancy's Apple Cake 86
Apple Pie Cake 86
Applesauce Cake 86
Banana Cake 87
Aunt Anna's Banana Nut Cake 87
Burnt Sugar Cake 88
Butternut Cake 88
14-Carat Gold Cake 89
Carrot Cake 89
Maraschino Cherry Cake 90
Lemon Chiffon Cake 90
Orange Chiffon Cake 91
Golden Chiffon Cake 91
Best Red Chocolate Cake 91
Chocolate Joy Cake 92
Chocolate Cake 92
Sunbeam Chocolate Cake 93
Abby's Fabulous Chocolate Cake 93
Cocoa Fudge Cake 94
Prize Chocolate Cake 94
Creole Chocolate Cake 95
German Sweet Chocolate Cake 95
Brazil Nut Sensation/Fruit Cake 95
Crystal Fruit Cake 96
Dark Sweet Fruit Cake 96
Deluxe Fruit Cake 97
Holiday Fruit Cake 97
Lee Corn's Fruit Cake 98
White Fruit Cake 98
Gold Cake 99
Hummingbird Cake 99
Jiffy One-Egg Cupcakes 100
Lady Baltimore Cake 100

Lazy Daisy Oatmeal Cake 101
Lemon Bundt Cake 101
Citrus Dream Cake 101
Mocha Cake 102
Delicate Nut Cake 102
Lisa's Orange Cake 103
Orange Glaze Cake 103
Orange-Raisin Cake 104
Orange Surprise Cake 104
Paprika Cake 104
Petits Fours 105
Poppy Seed Bundt Cake 106
Poppy Seed Cake I 106
Poppy Seed Cake II 107
Pound Cake I 107
Pound Cake II 107
Chocolate Pound Cake 108
Mrs. Kringel's Prune Cake 108
Raisin Layer Cake 108
Raisin Nuggets Cupcakes 109
Southern Favorite Cake 109
Spice Cake 110
Strawberry Cake 110
Sunshine Cake 110
Tea Cupcakes 111
Texas Sheet Cake 111
White Layer Cake 112
Wine Cake 112
Brown Velvet Frosting 85
Butter Frosting 112
Chocolate Icing 112
Chocolate Frosting 113
Caramel Frosting 113
Lady Baltimore Cake Filling 100
Lemon Butter Cream 113
Lemon Filling for White Cake 113
Lemon Sauce 114
Mocha Frosting 114
Nutmeg Sauce 114
Orange-Cream Cheese Frosting 114
Orange Fluff Topping 115
My Peanut Butter Icing 115
Penuche 115
Pineapple Filling or Topping
    for White Cake 115
Sea Foam 116
Seven-Minute Frosting I 116
Seven-Minute Icing II 116

CANDIES
Anise Candy 117
Bourbon Balls 117
Buckeyes 117

Cream Butterscotch Candy 117
Rice Krispies Treat/Children's Candy ... 118
Children's Candy 118
Choice Candy 118
Christmas Wreaths 119
Coconut Mink 119
Lea's Cornflake Candy 119
Divine Divinity 120
Mother's Cream Fondant 120
No-Cook Fondant 121
Remarkable Fudge 121
Velvet Fudge 122
Jan's Fudge 122
My Peanut Butter Fudge 122
Pecan Fudge 122
White Fudge 123
Candied Grapefruit Peel 123
Party Mints 123
Party Patties 124
Oriental Fruit Balls 124
Peanut Brittle 124
Jack's Peanut Brittle 124
Peanut Butter Bonbons 125
Peanut Clusters 125
Penuche 125
New Orleans Pralines 125
Creamy Texas Pralines 126
Coconut Strawberries 126
English Toffee 126
Toffee Treats 127
Truffles 127
Caramel Corn 127
Chow Mein Haystacks 128
Holiday Nibbler Mix 128
Nut Clusters 128
Sugared Pecans I 128
Sugar-Coated Pecans II 129
Sugared Walnuts 129

DESSERTS
Ambrosia 135
Angel Supreme Dessert 135
Apple Crisp 136
Bavarian Cream 136
Strawberry Bavarian Parfait 136
Blackberry Cobbler 137
Blueberry Dessert 137
Bread Pudding 138
Caramel Pan Dumplings 138
Dixie Cheesecake 139
Golden Glow Cheesecake 139
Pineapple Cheesecake 140
Cherries Jubilee 140

George Washington Cherry Pudding 141
Pauline's Chocolate Sauce 141
Rio Chocolate Sauce 141
Hot Fudge Sauce 141
Hot Fudge Ice Cream Topping 142
Hot Fudge Topping 142
Cream Puffs 142
Basic Crepes and Fillings 143
Curried Fruit 144
Baked Custard 144
Custard with Caramel Glaze/Flan 144
Grandma's Danish Christmas Cake 145
Danish Puff 145
Date Pudding 146
Devil's Float 146
Dump Cake 147
Dutch Apple Cake with Lemon Sauce ... 147
Fruit Cocktail Dessert 147
Hot Fruit Compote 148
Indian Pudding 148
Linda's Luscious Creamy Dessert 148
Jelly Roll Cake 149
Pavlova 149
Peanut Buster Bars 150
Fruit Pizza 150
Prune Compote 151
Chocolate Pudding Cake 151
Aunt Myrtle's Lemon Cake Pudding 151
Mrs. Truman's Ozark Pudding 152
Martha Washington Pudding 152
Alexis's Pumpkin Pudding 152
Summer Pudding 153
Rhubarb Cake Dessert 153
Glorified Rice 154
Rice Pudding 154
Aunt Myrtle's Suet Pudding 154
Strawberry Shortcake (Biscuit) 154
My Shortcake for Berries 155
Orange Cream Tarts 155
Apple Torte 156
Mocha Chocolate Torte 156
Lemon Meringue Torte 157
Aunt Alice's Forgotten Torte 158
Trifle — American Style 158
Pineapple Upside Down Cake 159

Pies

American Apple Pie 159
English Apple Pie 160
Lazy Day Banana Pie 160
Very Berry Pie 161
Blueberry Cream Pie 162
Blueberry Mystery Pie 162
Fresh Blueberry Pie 162

Butterscotch Cream Pie 163
My Cherry-Ripe Pie 163
Tiptop Cherry Pie 164
Chocolate Pie 164
Choco-Chip Pie 165
Bishop's Chocolate Marshmallow Pie ... 165
Fantastic Fudge Pie 165
Coconut Meringue Pie 166
Coconut Supreme Pie 166
Custard Pie 167
Lemon Pie 167
Irene's Lemon Pie 167
Stone's "Mile High" Lemon Pie 168
Lemon Chess Pie 168
Key Lime Pie 169
Fresh Peach Pie 169
Waid's Peanut Butter Pie 169
Lady Bird's Pecan Pie 170
Pineapple Pie 170
Libby's Famous Pumpkin Pie 171
Mamie's Pumpkin Chiffon Pie 171
Pumpkin Chiffon Pie 172
Sour Cream Raisin Pie 172
Red Raspberry Pie 172
Creamy Rhubarb Pie 173
Rhubarb Custard Pie 173
Shoo-Fly Pie 174
Jean's Fresh Strawberry Pie 174
Fresh Strawberry Pie 174
Strawberry Glaze Pie 175
Strawberry-Rhubarb Pie 175
Sweet Potato Pie 175
Toll Crest Pie 176
White Christmas Pie 176

Pastry and Meringue

Pastry for A Double-Crust 9-in. Pie 177
Pie Crust I 177
Basic Pie Crust II 178
Pie Crust with Egg and Vinegar 178
Graham Cracker Crust 178
Meringue — Tried and True 179

MAIN DISHES

Beef

Beef Burgundy 191
Beef Burgundy/Crockpot 191
Burgundy Beef Casserole 191
Beef Burney 192
Marinated London Broil 192
Baked Brisket 193
Spicy Brisket 193
Savory Beef Loaf 194
Snappy Beef Short Ribs (Crockpot) 194

Beef Stew (Crockpot) 194
Sr. Pat's Casserole 195
Corned Beef Casserole I 195
Corned Beef Casserole II 195
Cheesy Beef Casserole 195
Grillade and Grits 196
Amana Hamburgers 197
Malayan Beef 197
Minute Steak Espanol 197
Grandpa Ben's Pot Roast 198
Pot Roast (Crockpot) 199
Grandpa's Sauerbraten 199
Chicken Fried Steak 200
Pepper Steak 200
Spanish Steak 201
Swiss Steak 201
Beef Stroganoff 202
Veal Birds 202
Veal Marsala 202

Fowl and Dressing

Chicken a la King 203
Baked Favorite Chicken 203
Barbecued Chicken 204
Chicken with Biscuits 204
Buffalo Wings 205
Chicken Cacciatore 205
Chicken Chow Mein 206
Corn Crisp Oven Chicken 206
Curried Chicken 206
My Chicken Divan 207
Original Farm Bureau Chicken 207
Glazed Cornish Hens 207
Honey Comb Chicken 208
Mrs. Nixon's Hot Chicken Salad 208
My Pheasant Fricassee 208
Pheasant Breasts with Mushrooms 209
Chicken Paprika 210
Baked Parmesan Chicken 210
Pepper Chicken 211
Chicken Tarragon 211
Chicken or Turkey Tetrazzini 212
Chicken Tetrazzini 212
Chicken Tortilla Casserole 213
Chicken-Wild Rice Casserole 213
Turkey Casserole 214
Mrs. Reagan's Cornbread Dressing 214
Dressing for Fowl 214
Dressing for Turkey or Chicken 215
Fruit Dressing 215
Oyster Stuffing 216
Pecan Stuffing for Turkey 216
Sage Dressing 216

Kabobs

Beef Kabobs I 217
Beef Kabobs II 217
Kabobs III 217
Chicken Kabobs 218
Skewered Pork 218
Satay 219
Shish Kabob Marinade 219
Skewered Lamb/Souvliakia 219

Lamb

Leg of Lamb 220
Lamb Ragout 220
Braised Lamb Shanks 221
Olga's Lamb Stew 221
Lamb Shanks Stew 222

Pork

McGonigle's Glazed Ham Loaf 222
Ham Loaf 223
Ham and Broccoli Bake 223
Creole Ham 223
Ham and Asparagus Casserole 224
Iowa Pork Chops with Stuffing .... 224.
Pork Chops Hawaiian 224
Laurel's Pork Chops 225
Pork Chops Supreme 225
Slow Cooker Roast Pork 225

Meat Hot Dishes

Broccoli, Chicken and Rice Bake 226
Cabbage Roll-Ups 226
Chow Mein Casserole 227
Cornish Pasties 227
Iowa Goulash 228
Danish Baked Liver Sausage 228
Beef Liver and Onions 228
Champion Liver Loaf 229
Fricadilla/Meat Balls 229
Italian Meat Balls 230
Meat Loaf 230
Bill Blass's Meat Loaf 231
Ann Landers's Meat Loaf 231
Basic Dough for Pizza 231
Italian Pizza Sauce 232
Porcupines 232
Sausage Souffle 232
Shepherd's Pie 233
Tricia's Tater Tot Casserole 233

Seafood

Crab Maryland 234
Fried Catfish 234
Beer Battered Fish 234
Cornmeal Fried Fish 235
Fried Whole Trout — Ozarks 235
Fisherman's Catch Fish Fry 235

White Clam Spaghetti 236
Seafood Newburg 236
My Scalloped Oysters 236
Paella 237
Baked Perch Fillets 237
Oven-Baked Fish Fillets 238
Fruits of the Sea Casserole 238
Salmon Croquettes I 238
Salmon Croquettes II 239
Salmon or Tuna Croquettes 239
Saucy Seafood 239
Asparagus-Tuna Hot Dish 240
Favorite Tuna Casserole 240
Tuna and Noodles 240

Pasta

Fettucine with Pesto Sauce 241
Homemade Spaghetti Sauce 241
Denise's Pasta Sauce 241
Macaroni and Cheese 242
Macaroni Loaf 242
Overnight Lasagna 242
Italian Spaghetti I 243
Italian Spaghetti II 243

Eggs

Deviled Eggs for the Brunch Bunch 244
Creamed Deviled Eggs 244
Oven Omelet 245
Super Brunch Omelet 245
Dutch Omelet 245
Bachelor Breakfast 246
Overnight Egg Casserole 246
Egg-Sausage Casserole 246
Basic Quiche Crust 247
Pickled Eggs 247

Sauces

Barbecue Sauce I 247
Barbecue Sauce II 248
Barbecue Sauce III 248
Cheese Sauce for Vegetables 248
Horseradish Sauce for Baked Ham I 249
Horseradish Sauce for Baked Ham II 249
Fresh Pesto Sauce 249
Tartar Sauce for Fish 249
Basic White Sauce 250

VEGETABLES

Sautéed Apple Rings 255
Asparagus Bake 255
Asparagus Casserole 256
Asparagus Ham Rolls 256
Lebanese Green Beans I 256
Lebanese Green Beans II 256
Green Beans with Pimiento 257

Bacon Top Baked Beans 257
Lea's Stovetop Beans 257
Five-Bean Bake 258
My Lima Bean Casserole 258
Lima Beans Creole 259
Buffet Bean Bake 259
Baby Beets Oven Roasted 259
Best Harvard Beets 260
Oven Glazed Beets 260
Oven Roasted Broccoli and Cauliflower . 260
Broccoli and Wild Rice Bake 261
Brussels Sprouts with Onions 261
Stuffed Cabbage Rolls 261
Grandma's Sour-Sweet Cabbage 262
Danish Sweet-Sour Red Cabbage 262
Carrot Ring 263
Carrot Soufflé I 263
Carrot Soufflé II 263
Baked Corn Casserole 264
Delicious Creamed Corn 264
Corn and Oyster Scallop 264
Corn-Tomato Casserole with Garlic 265
Corn Pudding 265
Savory Corn Bake 265
Spider Corn Pone 266
Garlic Cheese Grits I 266
Garlic Cheese Grits II 267
Fried Okra 267
My Scalloped Onions 268
Parsnip Bake 268
Glazed Parsnips 268
Fresh Roasted Peppers 269
My Stuffed Peppers with Creole Sauce . 269
Polenta 270
Latkes 270
Party Potatoes 271
Twice-Baked Potatoes 271
Baked Potatoes with Cheese Sauce 272
Crunchy Baked Potatoes 272
Hash Brown Potato Bake 273
Sue's Hash Browns and Sauerkraut 273
Hot Potato Salad 273
Laurel's New Potatoes 274
Oven Roasted Potatoes Greek Style 274
Scalloped Potatoes 274
Scalloped Potatoes with Cream 275
Scalloped Potato Casserole 275
Ratatouille I 275
Ratatouille II 276
Green Rice I 277
Green Rice II 277
Green Chili Rice 277
Saffron Rice 277

Special Rice Casserole 278
Spinach Souffle 278
Baked Acorn Squash 278
Stuffed Acorn Squash 278
Butternut Squash Soufflé 279
Baked Summer Squash/Zucchini 279
Candied Sweet Potatoes 279
Coconut Topped Sweet Potatoes 280
Southern Sweets Casserole 280
Sweet Potato Delight 281
Roasted Sweet Potatoes 281
Fried Green Tomatoes 281
Broiled Stuffed Tomatoes 282
Tomatoes with Pesto 282
Turnip Puff 282
Turnip Casserole 283
Turnip Soufflé 283
Baked Vegetables, Greek Style 283
Vegetable Medley 284
Vegetables Tempura 284
Dutch Mixed Vegetables 285
Marinated Vegetables 285
Wild Rice Pilaf 285
Wild Rice Casserole 286
Wild Rice Bake 286
Best Wild Rice Casserole 286
Wild Rice Almondine 287
Zucchini-Corn Casserole 287
Italian Zucchini Pie 287
Zucchini Casserole 288
Yummy Zucchini 288

SALADS
Fruit Salads
Apricot Nectar 294
May's ABC Citrus Avocado 294
Florida Avocado Citrus 295
Blue Cheese Salad 295
"Holiday Fair" Blueberry 295
"Holiday Fair" Cherry 296
Cheese Pineapple 296
Cherry Coke 296
Cinnamon Apple 297
My Cranberry Sauce 297
Cranberry Holiday Fluff 298
Cranberry Orange Relish 298
Quota Brunch Fruit Compote 298
Char's Grape Salad 299
Ginger Ale Fruit 299
Mandarin Orange 299
Laurel's Standby Super Salad 299
Grandma's Overnight Salad 300
Crunchy Peanut -Apple 300

Raspberry Frost 301
Strawberry Frost 301
Summer Fruit 302
Sunshine Salad 302
Watergate Salad 302
Slush Fruit Cup 302
Florence Jean's Frozen 302
Fran's Frozen Cranberry 303
Frozen Party 303
Pink Champagne 304
Strawberry Fruit Freeze 304
Meat and Seafood Salads
My Aloha Chicken 304
Hot Chicken Salad 305
Oriental Chicken 305
Chicken Wild Rice 305
Curry Turkey 306
Hot Turkey 306
My Spicy Ham Loaf Salad 306
Ham Soufflé 307
Crabmeat 307
Crab Caribbean 307
Crab Luncheon 308
Crab Tostados 308
Salmon Summer 309
Shrimp Remoulade 309
Fiesta Shrimp 309
Shirley's Shrimp 310
Pippin's Shrimp 310
Shrimp Supper 310
Tuna Mousse 311
Tuna Summer 311
Vegetable Salads
Asparagus Molded 311
Asparagus-Bacon 312
Sweet and Sour Beet 312
BLT Salad 312
Broccoli Overnight 313
Broccoli-Raisin 313
Broccoli for a Dozen 313
Broccoli-Cauliflower 313
Hot Bacon-Cabbage Slaw 314
Caesar Salad 314
Cobb Salad 314
My Zesty Calico Slaw 315
Corn and Cabbage Slaw 315
Creamy Coleslaw 316
Tart Coleslaw 316
Cheese Relish Salad 316
Copper Pennies — Carrot 316
Garden Cukes and Onions 317
German Cucumber Salad 317
Cucumber Soufflé 317

399

Homesteaders' Dandelion 318
Dutch Lettuce with Sour Cream 318
Dutch Lettuce 319
Fire and Ice 319
Fresh Garden Relish 319
Gazpacho 320
Greek Salad 320
Guacamole 320
Majestic Layered 321
Seven-Layer Vegetable 321
Spinach Layered 321
Marge's Bibb Lettuce Mimosa 322
Bishops' Lettuce Supreme 322
Wilted Lettuce 322
Macaroni Salad 323
Macaroni Tuna 323
Salad Nicoise 323
Jan's Pea Salad 324
Black-Eyed Pea 324
Perfection... 324
German Potato Salad 325
Mother's Deluxe Potato 325
My Picnic Potato 325
My Potluck Potato 326
Rotini 326
Sauerkraut I 326
Sauerkraut II 327
Wally's Spiced 327
Salad Superb 327
Rose's Tabbouleh 328
Three Bean 328
Tomato Aspic 328
Tomato Cucumber 329
Italian Flag (Tomato-Avocado) 329
Ishmael's Turkish Salad 329
Diane's Marinated Vegetables 330
Faye's Vegetable Relish 330
Vegetable Salad 330
Congealed Vegetable 331
Wild Rice Salad 331
Zucchini-Apple Slaw 332

Pickles

Candied Sweet Dills 332
Corn Relish 332
Cranberry Chutney 333
My Sweet Onion and Apple Chutney 333
Spiced Peaches 333
Watermelon Pickles 334

Dressings and Sauces

Blender Mayonnaise 334
Blue Cheese 334
Chunky Blue Cheese 335
Cooked Salad Dressing.......................... 335

French 335
Spicy Garlic Vinaigrette 335
Green Goddess I 336
Green Goddess II 336
Honey-Mustard 336
Italian 336
Louis 337
Remoulade Sauce 337
Rieke's Poppy Seed 337
Roquefort Cheese 337
Russian 338
Seafood Cocktail Sauce 338
Sour Cream Salad 338
Sugarless Salad 338
Thousand Island 338

SOUPS AND SANDWICHES
Soups

Famous U.S. Senate Bean Soup 347
Senate Bean Soup 347
Calico Bean Soup 347
Broccoli-Cheese Soup 348
Budget Stretcher Soup 348
Carrot Purée 349
Carrot Swirl Soup 349
Chicken Broth 349
My Clam and Corn Chowder 350
Corn Chowder 350
Chili (Crockpot) 351
Cowboy Chili 351
Iowa Chili 351
L.B.J.'s Chili 352
Texas Chili 352
Danish Fruit Soup 352
Gazpacho 353
Goulash Soup 353
Onion Soup 354
My Oyster Stew 354
Peasant Soup.. 355
Plaza III Steak Soup 355
Plaza III Steak Soup — Home Style 355
Tip-Top Potato Soup 356
Cheesy-Potato Soup 356
Old-Fashioned Tomato Soup 356
Day-After Turkey Soup 357
Dieter's Vegetable Soup 357
He-Man Vegetable Soup 358
Vegetable Beef Soup I 358
Vegetable Beef Soup II 358
Vegetable Beef Soup III........................ 358
Vichyssoise 359
Classic Vichyssoise 359

Sandwiches

My Best Chicken Sandwiches 360
Cashew Chicken Sandwiches 361
Cucumber Tea Sandwiches 361
Cheese Tea Sandwiches 361
Deviled Ham Sandwich Filling 362
Deviled Ham Tea Sandwiches 362
Egg Salad Tea Sandwiches 362
Ginger Orange Sandwiches 363
Hawaiian Sandwiches 363
Hot Dog Special 363
Olive Sandwich Spread 363
Reuben Sandwiches 364
ribbon Sandwiches 364
School Lunch Ham Spread 364
Sloppy Joes I 365
Sloppy Joes II 365
Spam Sandwich Filling 365
Taverns I 366
Taverns II 366
Hot Tuna Sandwiches 367
Vegetarian Sandwich 367
Sandwich Fillings 367

BEVERAGES, APPETIZERS
Beverages

REAL EGG COFFEE 374
Cold Morning Cocoa 374
Cooler for Children 374
Cranberry Cider 375
Eggnog 375
French Café au Lait 375
Grape Cooler 375
Instant Hot Chocolate Mix 376
Lime Punch 376
Old-Time Lemonade 376
Mimosa 376
Mocha-Coffee Frostee 377
Orange-Banana Frostee 377
Orange Flip 377
My Party Punch 377

Peach Fizz 378
Russian Tea/Spiced Tea Mix 378
Sangria I 378
Sangria II 378
Singapore Sling 379
Strawberry Frostee 379
Tangy Tomato Juice 379
Wassail 379
Wassail Punch 380

Appetizers

Gail's Artichoke-Chile Dip 380
Bacon-Pineapple Broil 381
Boursin Cheese Spread 381
My Braunschweiger Ball 381
Celery Swirls 382
Cheese Puffs 382
Cheese Straws 382
Cheese Wafers I 383
Cheese Wafers II 383
Chiles Rellenos Casserole 383
Dill Dip in a Rye Bowl 383
Dilly Dip 384
Dried Beef in Cheese Ball 384
Guacamole Dip 384
Greek Garbanzo Dip (Hummus) 385
Hummus 385
Cheese with Jezebel Sauce 385
Mexi-Dip 386
Mexican Hot Dip 386
Mexican Hot Taco Dip 386
Mexican Topper Tortilla Dip 387
Olive Cheese Ball 387
Pickled Eggs 387
Shrimp Dip 388
Spinach Appetizers 388
Tapenade/Olive Spread 388
Tortilla Pinwheels 389
Blue Cheese Vegetable Dip 389
Vegetable Dip I 389
Vegetable Dip II 389
Vegetable Dip III 389